Labour Revolt in Britain 1910–14

'A fascinating book that reminds us, with passion and vigour, of the years of political and trade union organisation of the English workers' movement on the eve of the Great War. Unmissable.'

—Raquel Varela, labour historian, professor at FCSH-Universidade Nova de Lisboa and author of *A People's History of Europe: From World War I to Today*

'Drawing on modern historical research, Darlington depicts a broad working-class revolt in which radical activists played an important catalysing role. In discussing both the successes and the failures of the movement, he demonstrates its continued contemporary relevance.'

—Richard Hyman, Emeritus Professor of Industrial Relations, London School of Economics, and Founding Editor, *European Journal of Industrial Relations*, Fellow of the British Academy

'Based on meticulous historical research, this important study refutes once again the myth of working-class "quiescence". Addressing the remarkable eruption and trajectory of the great Labour Revolt in the years before World War I, Ralph Darlington reconstructs the many forms of autonomous worker resistance and its entanglement with trade union officialdom, as well as close links to radical socialist politics. His book provides a highly significant new contribution to the analysis of the limits and potential of industrial militancy and its relationship to political action and organisation.'

—Marcel van der Linden, International Institute of Social History, Amsterdam

'In the first book-length study of the 1910–14 Labour Revolt, Ralph Darlington convincingly conveys the breadth, depth, and limitations of its many strike movements. Within ten years, British politics, trade unionism and industrial relations would be transformed.'

—Dr Dave Lyddon, Keele University, founding editor of *Historical Studies in Industrial Relations*

'A timely warning from history. Rising poverty and strike action. Collective bargaining, a tool for managing workers' discontent. Westminster failing workers. An active rank and file holding unions accountable. All vital lessons we must apply during this current period of unrest.'

—Henry Fowler and Robert Poole, Co-Founders, Strike Map

'Ralph Darlington's book is a major and thorough study of the powerful strike wave of 1910–14. It was, as he notes, "a fulfilment of the promise of New Unionism of 1888–90". It is an excellent and a timely study given the huge industrial unrest of late 2022.'

—Chris Wrigley, Emeritus Professor of History, Nottingham University

Labour Revolt in Britain 1910–14

Ralph Darlington

First published 2023 by Pluto Press
New Wing, Somerset House, Strand, London WC2R 1LA
and Pluto Press Inc.
1930 Village Center Circle, 3-834, Las Vegas, NV 89134

www.plutobooks.com

British Library Cataloguing in Publication Data
A catalogue record for this book is available from the British Library

ISBN 978 0 7453 3903 0 Paperback
ISBN 978 0 7453 4806 3 PDF
ISBN 978 0 7453 4807 0 EPUB

Typeset by Stanford DTP Services, Northampton, England

Simultaneously printed in the United Kingdom and United States of America

Contents

Figures

Tables

Acknowledgements

I would like to express my gratitude to all the archivists and librarians who helped me access material at the National Archives, Kew; Churchill Archives Centre, Cambridge; Modern Records Centre, University of Warwick; Working Class Movement Library, Salford; Labour History Archive and Study Centre, People's History Museum, Manchester; University of Manchester Library, University of Salford Library, and Manchester Central Library. I am also indebted to the enormously expanded online material now available on the British Newspaper Archive website.

Thanks to David Howell, Dave Lyddon and Chris Wrigley for providing constructive feedback and advice on my initial book proposal, and to many others who raised probing questions when I presented conference and seminar presentations on different aspects of the research at the International Association of Strikes and Social Conflicts, Australian Society for the Study of Labour History, British Universities' Industrial Relations Association, Working Class Movement Library, North East Labour History Society, 1911 Llanelli Railway Strike Festival Historians' Forum, and United Voices of the World 'Union Talks' event.

I owe a special debt of gratitude to John Dobson, Silvia Holden, Hamish Mathieson, Ken Mulkearn, Stephen Mustchin, Jack Robertson, Harry Taylor and Martin Upchurch who generously read drafts of individual chapters and/or the entire book manuscript and offered valuable suggestions for improvement, including copyediting amendments. In particular, John Dobson's contribution went beyond the call of comradely duty for which I'm so grateful.

Thanks to Pluto Press, particularly David Castle, for backing and overseeing publication.

The book is dedicated to my partner for many years, Carol McFarlane, and daughter Saskia Darlington, for their love, support and encouragement.

Note: Some of the material in the book was published, albeit in a much shorter and differently structured form, in my article 'Strikers versus Scabs: Violence in the 1910–1914 British Labour Revolt' in *Labor History* (63: 3) in 2022.

Abbreviations

ASD: Amalgamated Society of Dyers
ASE: Amalgamated Society of Engineers
ASLEF: Associated Society of Locomotive Engineers and Firemen
ASRS: Amalgamated Society of Railway Servants
ASWL&B: Amalgamated Society of Watermen, Lightermen and Bargemen
BAIU: British Advocates of Industrial Unionism
BSP: British Socialist Party
BWIU: Building Workers' Industrial Union
CGT: Confédération Générale du Travail
CLC: Central Labour College
CPGB: Communist Party of Great Britain
DDJFWU: Dundee and District Jute and Flax Workers' Union
DMA: Durham Miners' Association
DWRGWU: Dock, Wharf, Riverside and General Workers Union
ELF: East London Federation
ELFS: East London Federation of the Suffragettes
GRWU: General Railway Workers' Union
IDL: Industrial Democracy League
ILP: Independent Labour Party
IRA: Irish Republican Army
IRB: Irish Republican Brotherhood
IRSP: Irish Socialist Republican Party
ISEL: Industrial Syndicalist Education League
ITGWU: Irish Transport and General Workers' Union
ITUC: Irish Trades Unions Congress
IWGB: Industrial Workers of Great Britain
IWW: Industrial Workers of the World
IWWU: Irish Women Workers' Union
LRC: Labour Representation Committee
MFGB: Miners' Federation of Great Britain
MP: Member of Parliament
NFWW: National Federation of Women Workers
NSFU: National Sailors' and Firemen's Union
NTWF: National Transport Workers' Federation
NUBSO: National Union of Boot and Shoe Operatives

NUDL: National Union of Dock Labourers
NUGGL: National Union of Gas and General Workers
NUR: National Union of Railwaymen
NUWSS: National Union of Women's Suffrage Societies
PLA: Port of London Authority
SDF: Social Democratic Federation
SDP: Social Democratic Party
SLP: Socialist Labour Party
SUDL: Scottish Union of Dock Labourers
SWMF: South Wales Miners' Federation
TUC: Trades Union Congress
UPSS: United Pointsmen's and Signalmen's Society
URC: Unofficial Reform Committee
WSPU: Women's Social and Political Union
WU: Workers' Union

Introduction

The so-called 'Labour Unrest' – or what more accurately should be termed 'Labour Revolt' – that swept Britain in the years leading up to the outbreak of the First World War between 1910 and 1914 was one of the most sustained, dramatic and violent explosions of industrial militancy and social conflict the country has ever experienced. After some 20 years of relative quiescence in strike activity, there was a sudden and unanticipated eruption that spread rapidly on a scale well in excess of the 'New Unionism' upsurge of 1889–91. By the time Robert Tressell's celebrated classic novel of working-class life and politics, *The Ragged Trousered Philanthropists*, had been published in 1914, three years after the author's death, its representation of the apparent weakness and 'apathy' of exploited workers had been superseded by the actuality of an explosion of self-confidence, organisation and militancy by a working class that had 'thrust itself into the centre of Britain's social and political life'.[1]

The strike wave involved a number of large-scale disputes in strategically important sections of the economy. A protracted strike in the South Wales coalfields in 1910–11 was followed in the summer of 1911 by national seamen's, dockers' and railway workers' strikes, as well as a Liverpool general transport strike. There were national miners' and London transport workers' strikes in 1912, a series of Midlands metal workers' strikes and Dublin transport workers' lockout in 1913, and a London building workers' lockout in 1914. A significant minority of the industrial workforce were involved in 4,600 other strikes for higher wages, better working conditions and trade union organisation. Women workers played an active and prominent role within a number of strikes; and what the Fabian couple Sidney and Beatrice Webb described as the 'spirit of revolt in the Labour world'[2] even spread to school students' strikes in September 1911.

It was not only the scale and diverse range, but also the character of strike action that seemed extraordinary. It was a revolt dominated by unskilled and semi-skilled workers, encompassing both members of established and recognised trade unions, and also workers hitherto unorganised and/or unrecognised who became engaged in a fight to build collective organisation and for union recognition against the hostility of many employers. Action

1. Cronin (1979: 1).
2. Webb and Webb (1920: 528).

largely took place independently and unofficially of national trade union leaderships whose unresponsiveness to workers' discontents, endeavours to channel grievances through established channels of collective bargaining and conciliation machinery, and advocacy of compromise and moderation was often rejected by workers in favour of militant organisation and strike action from below. Alarmed by the way in which the initiative often came unofficially from rank-and-file union members, or non-unionised workers, the Webbs referred to 'insurrectionary strikes' that were:

> … designed, we might almost say, to supersede collective bargaining – to repudiate any making of long-term agreements, to spring demand after demand upon employers, to compel every workman to join the Union, avowedly with the view of building up the Trade Union as a dominant force. This spasm of industrial 'insurrectionism' was [only] abruptly stopped by the outbreak of the war.[3]

George Askwith, the Board of Trade's Chief Industrial Commissioner and Liberal government's leading adviser on industrial relations, warned that the older generation of conciliatory 'official leaders could not maintain their authority. Often there was more difference between the men and their leaders than between the latter and the employers.'[4] Yet while the unofficial and apparent impulsive dynamic of strike militancy took the majority of labour movement leaders by surprise, some national trade union officials (not only left-wing figures like Ben Tillett of the transport workers but also moderate figures like James Sexton of the dockers' union) found themselves obliged to support strikes and articulate their members' demands, rather than lose all influence over the latter's actions. This official backing in turn then opened up possibilities for the rank-and-file to escalate militancy even further.

An important factor in the development of this assertion of independent working-class power was the role assumed by young workers (both men and women) who were largely free from the defensive mentality associated with earlier forms of official trade unionism conditioned since the defeat of 'New Unionism', and who eagerly sought new forms of militant organisation that would allow a direct struggle against the employers and the state.[5]

'Direct action' became the gospel of the day – the notion that no one could help the workers unless they helped themselves, by taking into their own hands the task of organising against employers. Belligerent working-class

---

3. Ibid.: 667, 665.
4. Askwith ([1920] 1974: 177).
5. Woodhouse (1995: 18).

self-confidence, and the vigorous and emancipatory nature of much strike activity with its underlying demand for dignity, self-respect and control over working lives, was a feature of this 'effervescence of youth'.[6] The spirit of revolt was captured by the Irish Transport and General Workers' Union strike leader, Jim Larkin, when he observed: 'Labour has lost its old humility and its respectful finger touching its cap.'[7]

The realisation that militant strike action could win major concessions from employers had a 'demonstration effect' that encouraged strikes as a key weapon across many industries and led, despite a dramatic reversal of fortune in some individual battles, to a spectacular growth in the total power of organised labour:

> ... unions became the beneficiaries of a virtuous circle of effectiveness and membership. As the scale of strike activity increased, so did the win rate, and as the win rate increased, bargaining coverage rose, more workers perceived unions to be effective and joined them, which in turn enabled more strikes to be called ... and so on.[8]

Previously unorganised workers flocked into unions, with the general unions catering for less skilled workers growing much faster than the movement as a whole. In the process, trade union organisation in Britain was completely transformed, surpassing (in absolute if not relative terms) the 'New Unionism' strike wave achievements of 1888–89, with a 62 per cent increase in union membership from 2.5 million in 1910 to 4.1 million by 1914 and an accompanying increase in union density (the proportion of workers in the labour force who were union members) from 14.6 per cent to 23.0 per cent.

In fact, the strike wave saw the fulfilment of the promise of 'New Unionism' in terms of a sustained huge advance in membership. a promise largely unfulfilled owing to an employers' counter-offensive in the early 1890s involving a series of major lockouts and defeats for cotton, engineering and other workers. Moreover, what sharply differentiated this strike wave and accompanying union growth from its late nineteenth-century predecessor was both its generalised nature and its substantial basis in manufacturing factory-based industries that had only been marginally affected by the earlier upsurge, including an extension of union organisation among women workers by 54 per cent, thereby creating a credible foundation for the spread of female trade unionism beyond its previous textile industry enclave.

---

6. Kenefick (2012); Askwith ([1920] 1974: 353); Dangerfield ([1935] 1997: 313).
7. Larkin (1968: 85).
8. Kelly (1988: 101).

An important novel characteristic was the willingness of significant sections of workers to take sympathetic action for others in dispute, both within and between different industries, and then often taking the opportunity to advance demands on their own employers, with strikers from separate but simultaneous disputes pledging not to go back to work until the demands of all had been satisfactorily settled. Such widespread solidarity broadened day-to-day struggles against individual employers into a struggle against employers in general and was accompanied by the widespread appeal of industrial unionism as the means to overcome the inherent fragmentation and sectionalism of existing trade unionism. This led to breakthroughs and innovations in union organisation straddling a multiplicity of occupational and industrial boundaries.

Thus, in 1910 there was the establishment of the National Transport Workers' Federation that brought together numerous unions organising in ports across the country, in 1913 the amalgamation of three existing organisations into the National Union of Railwaymen (a 'triumph of industrial unionism'),[9] and in 1913–14 a formal attempt to link the action of 1.5 million miners, transport workers and railway workers' unions into a 'Triple Alliance' that raised the potential for coordinated strike action between its three powerful affiliates.

Liberal government ministers became increasingly alarmed at the threat posed by nationwide strikes perceived as being severely disruptive to the functioning of the economy, as well as a threat to social order. The waterside and transport strikes held up perishable goods and considerably disrupted food supplies, the miners' strike threw up to a million other workers out of work, and the railway strike paralysed the movement of goods and passengers. The Cabinet responded with a series of initiatives. While these included the spread of Conciliation and Arbitration Boards, the utilisation of the indefatigable Board of Trade's industrial trouble-shooter George Askwith in rushing from one dispute to another to assist parties in negotiating settlements, and various social and industrial legislative reforms (including the 1911 National Insurance Act and 1912 Miners' Minimum Wage Act), it also involved encouraging hard-line police action against mass picketing, and supporting or authorising the deployment of large detachments of troops in numerous industrial disputes.

In July 1911 Home Secretary Winston Churchill acknowledged in a Cabinet memorandum that the government needed to use the police and military because the leaders of the unions were unable to control their members and there was the widespread adoption of the sympathetic strike:

9. Knowles (1952: 177).

> There is grave unrest in the country. Port after port is called out. The police and military are asked for at place after place. Fresh outbreaks continuously occur and will go on. The railways are not sound. Transport workers everywhere are getting to know their strength … and those conversant of labour matters *in practice* anticipate grave upheaval … and now specially a new force has arisen in trade unionism, whereby the power of the old leaders has proved quite ineffective, and the sympathetic strike on a wide scale is prominent. Shipping, coal, railways, dockers, etc. etc. are all uniting and breaking out at once. The 'general strike' policy is a factor which must be dealt with.[10]

Throughout 1910–14 employers attempted to break strikes by encouraging 'blackleg' labour (*sic*)[11] which, combined with the unequivocally partisan intervention of police and troops, led to repeated outbursts of dramatic violent confrontation (including sometimes even street rioting) in numerous places across the country (including Liverpool, Tonypandy and Llanelli), and resulted in numerous casualties and on occasion fatalities.

The aggressive challenge to the legitimacy of public order and state power mounted by strikers produced deep levels of social polarisation between local communities in which strikebound workplaces were located, on the one hand, and the employers and representatives of civil, police, military and government authorities, on the other. It spurred a culture of community solidarity and self-defence that encompassed both the relatives and friends of those directly involved in strikes, as well as local trade unionists and other supporters, in the picketing and direct action. This collective willingness to flout, challenge and defy the established authorities encouraged a serious questioning of traditional patterns of respect for 'law and order' and constitutional behaviour and allegiance.[12] Once again there was an important difference with the earlier 'New Unionism' strike wave, with the widespread aggressive and often violent militancy during the 'mass rebellion' of the later explosion contrasting with the largely more peaceful action previously.[13]

---

10. 'Notes concerning the widespread industrial unrest', CHAR 12/12/10-11; Churchill (1969: 1263–4).
11. The term 'blackleg', although utilised colloquially without any direct racist overtones by strike participants, has been placed in inverted commas to highlight it is not the author's term of choice. Both terms 'scab' and 'blackleg' are used interchangeably as they were by strike participants.
12. Holton (1973a: 218–19).
13. Hobsbawm (1968: 51); Holton (1976: 73–4). Even though the level of industrial militancy during the pre-First World War 'Labour Revolt' was overtaken in magnitude by the subsequent post-war period of 1919–21, there was not as high a level of violence.

There was also widespread questioning of the political system. While the journalist George Dangerfield went so far as to suggest 'the workers ... contrived to project a movement which took a revolutionary course and might have reached a revolutionary conclusion',[14] many historians such as Henry Pelling[15] have insisted that the struggles were only really significant in terms of securing limited immediate improvements in wages and conditions and the right to union organisation, demonstrating only 'trade union consciousness' with no significant section being politicised. Arguably, while the former viewpoint was an exaggerated portrayal of the potential rather than more sober reality, the interpretation of strike militancy as merely the pragmatic pursuit of demands on wages and conditions completely ignored the inherent radicalised sentiment and behaviour expressed amongst at least a sizeable layer of workers.

In pursuing their immediate goals of increased wages, better working conditions and trade union organisation and recognition, workers were confronted not only with intransigent employers and hesitant union leaders, but also hostile government officials and magistrates, and persistent attacks by police and troops. Many workers also became disaffected with parliamentary politics caused by the functioning of the newly formed Labour Party in the House of Commons which acted as a mere adjunct of the post-1906 Liberal Party government and frowned on militant industrial struggle. Consequently, the established 'rules of the game' – piecemeal social reform by means of institutionalised collective bargaining, on the one hand, and parliamentary action, on the other – were widely questioned and put under considerable strain, reinforcing the appeal of combative industrial struggle as the weapon to advance labour movement interests.[16]

Even the government's own leading industrial relations adviser viewed the unrest as motivated by a 'general spirit of revolt, not only against the employers of all kinds, but also against leaders and majorities, and Parliamentary or any kind of constitutional and orderly action'.[17] It encouraged a process of radicalisation, a counter-politics which stood for the celebration of class solidarity, aggressive strike action and mass picketing that had the effect of shifting the balance of class forces in society towards the working class. This workers' rebellion took place within the broader context of a battle for Irish independence from British imperialism and threat of civil war in Ireland arising from a Home Rule Bill, alongside an escalating militant civil disobe-

14. Dangerfield ([1935] 1997: 179).
15. Pelling (1968).
16. Kirk (1994: 108); Darlington (2013b: 45).
17. Askwith ([1920] 1974: 347).

dience 'Deeds not Words' campaign mounted by the suffragettes to force the Liberal government to give women the vote, that fed the wider challenge to the political system in Edwardian Britain.

Within this process of political radicalisation, the role of a significant number of combative leaders and activists, including militant trade unionists, socialists, Marxists and syndicalists, was significant. Invariably strike action derived from factors directly related to economic grievances, work intensification, erosion of job control, and either lack of union recognition or the constraints of existing union organisation, as well as certain contingent circumstances that gave workers the self-confidence to take collective action. But workers' readiness to engage in militant strike action also often critically depended upon the encouragement they received from the minority of uncompromising propagandists and agitators within their own ranks. And the radical left's anti-capitalist objectives proved to be of appeal to a large minority of workers (much wider than mere formal political party membership figures would indicate) because they expressed workers' rising level of organisation, confidence and class-consciousness during what was an exceptional period of industrial and political militancy.

It follows that the prevalent term 'Labour Unrest' used by many contemporary observers and historians alike is inadequate because it implies the strike wave was a relatively unproblematic and temporary challenge to a normally peaceful and stable society. By contrast, with its overall characteristic features of unofficial rank-and-file insurgency, solidarity action, defiance of trade union and Labour Party leaders, violent social confrontations, and challenge to the Edwardian economic and political system, the strike wave deserves to be termed a 'Labour *Revolt*'.

However, the forward momentum of this working-class revolt, let alone any revolutionary outcome, was to be seriously undermined by numerous underlying limitations and weaknesses. Amongst these was some serious strike setbacks and even disastrous defeats, combined with the way in which national trade union officials were often ultimately able to reassert their authority and control over embryonic rank-and-file networks and organisations with detrimental consequences. The Liberal government was able to accommodate the simultaneous three 'rebellions' (labour strikes, threat of civil war in Ireland and campaign for women's suffrage) because they were essentially discrete struggles only bound together tangentially in a diffuse and uncoordinated fashion.[18] The political, organisational, strategic and tactical shortcomings of the radical left, notably the separation made between indus-

18. Phelps Brown (1959); Pelling (1968); Read (1982); Powell (1996); Phillips (1971); Meacham (1972); Darlington (2020).

trial and political struggles, also hampered developments. And of course, the strike wave was to suddenly shudder to a halt, stopped in its tracks by the onset of the First World War in August 1914.

RESEARCH APPROACH

It is remarkable that unlike the 1926 general strike and 1984–85 miners' strike, both of which led to workers' defeats, only three full-length detailed books specifically focused on the 1910–14 strike wave, a period of overall workers' victories, have been published. These are George Askwith's *Industrial Problems and Disputes* (1920), George Dangerfield's *The Strange Death of Liberal England 1910–1914* (1935) and Bob Holton's *British Syndicalism 1900–1914* (1976).

Nonetheless, there also exists a substantial volume of related literature, with many book-length broader labour movement and political histories of the Edwardian period in which the 'Labour Unrest' has often prominently featured,[19] numerous briefer studies contained within journal articles and book chapters that touch on some aspects within wider social and political considerations, and more focused studies on particular individuals, groups of workers, unions or strikes.[20] Special issues of the journals *Historical Studies in Industrial Relations* and *Labour History Review* in 2012 and 2014, respectively, provided additional contributions from a number of different commentators to celebrate the one hundredth anniversary of the period.

Much of this existing body of literature has provided an invaluable resource which has extensively been drawn upon within my own study. But much previous work has been constrained by its fragmentary and partial nature, failing to adequately outline the full scale and range of militant union activity during the period, and in some cases ignoring, only briefly touching upon, or downplaying crucial features of the development and trajectory of the strike wave, such as the rank-and-file/union official dynamic and the relationship between the industrial militancy and its broader political context. Sometimes it has overstated the elemental 'spontaneous' nature of the revolt while insufficiently highlighting the role of organisation and leadership in the mobilisation of collective discontent. In addition, much of the 'Labourist'-politically informed analysis and interpretation of existing literature has

---

19. For example, Halévy (1961); Clegg (1985); Cole (1946; 1948a); Cronin (1979); Powell (1996); Heffer (2017); Burgess (1980); Phelps Brown (1959; 1983); Wrigley (1979; 1985); Laybourn (1997a; 1997b); Hyman (1971; 1985); Price (1986); White (1982); Weinberger (1991).

20. For example, Bagwell (1963), Brown (1974; 1975), Howell (1999), Lovell (1969); Taplin (1986).

tended to underestimate both the level of political radicalisation inside the working-class movement generally and the significance of radical left influence specifically.

As such, the main objective of this book's distinct revolutionary Marxist assessment of what was one of the most important periods in British trade union history has been to provide a multidimensional portrayal of the context, origins, causes, actors, processes, outcomes, meanings and significance of the Labour Revolt. Such an analytical vantage point means it is unequivocally sympathetic to the class struggle aspirations of militant workers and the radical left. It involves recognition of the highly contradictory nature of trade unionism – which both *expresses* and *contains* working-class resistance to capitalism – and its reflection in the underlying antagonism of interests between full-time union officials (notwithstanding some political differences between left and right officials) and rank-and-file workers. It follows that the book's emphasis is on the self-activity of the working class, on socialism *from below*, rather than the socialism *from above* of both trade union and Labour Party leaders, and on the role of the radical left and the relationship between *industrial* struggles and *political* ideas, organisation and leadership.

In re-examining the historical record, it deploys some new archival findings to reveal fresh factual insights, alongside previously utilised evidence to foreground hitherto neglected aspects, into a comprehensive narrative account and analytical assessment. Sources of primary evidence have included Home Office and Cabinet papers; Board of Trade's annual *Report on Strikes and Lockouts*; House of Commons' debates; police reports; TUC and trade union conference reports; national and provincial newspapers; left-wing press and publications; and personal reflections by a range of participants.

STRUCTURE

The book is structured into four parts. Part I (Chapters 1–2) outlines the general economic, political and social contexts and underlying causes of the Labour Revolt, and the influence of the left. Part II (Chapters 3–7) surveys the scope, variation and outcomes of strike activity, followed by a broadly chronological structured account of some important and/or characteristic individual strike movements, including the 1913–14 Dublin lockout in Ireland.[21] There follows in Part III (Chapters 8–12) a thematic and analytical assessment of some of the most distinctive features of the strike wave, and

21. Although Ireland was part of the 'United Kingdom of Great Britain and Ireland' and therefore formally cannot be subsumed within 'Britain', for the purposes of shortened exposition the book refers differentially to Ireland and Britain.

finally in Part IV (Chapter 13) the denouement, sequel and political legacy of the revolt with respect to the radical left, which still has relevance for today, is briefly explored. The endmatter include a list of biographical profiles of leading individuals and a series of tables with figures on strike activity and trade union and political party membership.

The bibliography is structured into archival sources; newspapers and periodicals; conference reports; other contemporary material; autobiographies; biographies; theses and dissertations; and books: articles and other material.

PART I

BACKCLOTH

1
Contexts and Causes

In order to understand the immediate and underlying roots of the 1910–14 Labour Revolt this chapter outlines a multifaceted set of contextual and causal factors that contributed to the nationwide upsurge. These include the economic, industrial and social backcloth; industrial relations and trade union framework; political context; bargaining capacity; leadership and mobilisation resources; and broader *zeitgeist* of defiance. Each of these influencing variables are discussed in turn (with an additional overview of the influence of left-wing groups in Chapter 2), although attention is also drawn to the way workers were motivated by the interaction between different features.

ECONOMIC, INDUSTRIAL AND SOCIAL BACKCLOTH

In the early 1900s Britain's economic supremacy as the 'workshop of the world' had become severely threatened as her two emerging rival competitors, the United States and Germany, developed more rapidly and began to outstrip its industrial production, resulting in a huge reduction in Britain's share of the world's industrial market.[1] An over-reliance on old staple industries, failure to play a leading role in new and rapidly expanding industries, and lack of investment and modernisation of domestic industries generally, compared with an increase in foreign investment in other countries, squeezed profit margins and spurred many employers to attempt to reduce labour costs, a process that manifested itself in a variety of ways.[2]

Business amalgamation created larger units of production with concentrated ownership and control and led to just a few giant companies dominating an industry in some sectors. The growing number of employers' associations (such as the Engineering Employers' Association and Shipping Federation) also strengthened capitalist industrial power and unity. Both developments undermined the prevailing local or sectional nature of much of the established trade union movement (with 1,174 separate unions in 1910)[3] although

1. Aikin (1972: 10).
2. Moss (1983: 54); Pollard (1963: 19); Challinor (1977: 57).
3. Board of Trade (1913b: 197).

in turn it encouraged the successful campaign towards industry-wide forms of union organisation with the capacity to match the powerful combinations on the employers' side.[4] Technological innovation and rationalisation of productive techniques was also important in some industries (notably engineering) as a means of lowering labour costs and increasing efficiency, usually resulting in the displacement or downgrading of craft skills to semi-skilled status. While this led to strike activity by craft workers who resented the loss of job control, it also encouraged a growing assertiveness among the new mass ranks of semi-skilled and unskilled workers.

Meanwhile, there were relentless cross-industry attempts to drive workers 'at a faster pace'[5] via the speed-up of production and intensified exploitative working conditions, along with imperatives towards a greater assertion of managerial authority through tighter discipline and supervision. And in many industries and workplaces employers adopted a belligerent stance towards workers' claims for pay increases, even imposing pay cuts in some sectors. Although wages rose between 1895 and 1910, they failed to keep pace with the rise in the cost of living, with the consequence that between 1909 and 1911 workers received in real terms only 90 per cent of what they had ten years before, such that five out of every eight adult male manual workers earned less than the minimum living wage of 25 shillings a week.[6]

Even though the majority of strikes were channelled towards the issue of pay, many also included demands for better working conditions and job control. And while those in relatively well-organised industries, such as cotton, textile, coal mining and engineering industries, had grievances about the constraints imposed by collective bargaining agreements reached between union officials and employers, there were also numerous strikes over the closed shop (which insisted that all workers employed in the establishment had to be a member of an appropriate trade union) and the refusal to work with non-unionists.[7] Those in weak or non-organised industries demanded not just improved pay and working conditions but also trade union recognition and bargaining rights.

For example, seamen were employed casually, worked long hours for low pay, with often poor conditions on board ships, subject to strict discipline with a system of fines for minor infringements, and able to secure work only if they were granted a Shipping Federation ticket which was denied to union members. Dockers were exploited under the system of day labouring, where

4. Holton (1985: 275; 1976: 29).
5. Crowley (1952: 140).
6. Halévy (1961: 441); Pollard (1963: 25).
7. White (1982: 83–4); Board of Trade (1914: xvii).

they were at the mercy of employers who hired and paid them on a daily casual basis with no job security or guaranteed wage and could instantly dismiss them if they were found to be union members. Railway workers suffered from long hours, low pay, quasi-military discipline, failure of conciliation machinery and lack of union recognition. It was years of pent-up frustration and collective sense of injustice at their appalling pay and conditions and lack of control or effective union representation that helps to explain the intensity and explosive character of workers' strike activity.

Concerns over employment conditions were accompanied by growing resentment at the contrast between many workers' impoverished social conditions and the unequal share in the distribution of wealth they produced. The scale of deprivation had been documented in social surveys of London and York by, respectively, Charles Booth (1903) and Seebohm Rowntree (1901), revealing nearly a third of the population lived in poverty and with high rates of infant and maternal mortality. Subsequent pre-war social investigations of other towns in England revealed that, notwithstanding differences between individual towns and between sections of the working class (skilled and unskilled), overall levels of poverty may well have been higher.[8] They were noticeably much worse in places like the port city Liverpool with its predominantly unskilled and casually employed workforce, as Jack and Bessie Braddock recalled:

> It's difficult to describe how poor the people were without making it seem incredible ... A kid with shoes was an event. The children had tuberculosis, rickets and ringworm and thousands were stunted from lack of food, like ragged shrubs in the Arctic.[9]

The problem of poverty had been highlighted in graphic relief when unemployment rocketed in the short recession of 1907–09, leading to hunger marches across the country and riots in Glasgow and the East End of London. What the Social Democratic Federation leader H.M. Hyndman in *The Times* (25 August 1911) described as the 'intolerable conditions of labour' and 'neglect of the misery and squalor in our great cities' was officially emphasised in a 1917 government-appointed *Commission of Enquiry into Industrial Unrest* which referring back to the pre-war causes of militancy concluded:

> The conviction that Capital and Labour are necessarily hostile, a conviction engendered by conflict on industrial matters, has been accentuated by

8. Chinn (2006: 24–30).
9. Braddock and Braddock (1963: 9).

> the fact that the social [and living] conditions of the working classes are of an unsatisfactory nature ... The influence of social factors on the creation of industrial unrest is great ... [and] ... undeniable.[10]

At the same time as workers experienced growing impoverishment, they also saw other sections of society becoming richer, with an extraordinary concentration of wealth in Edwardian Britain. In 1910 just 10 per cent of the population owned 92 per cent of total wealth, making Britain perhaps more unequal than ever before (or since) and more unequal than most European countries.[11] The ostentatious display of the wealth and luxury consumption and lifestyles of the upper and middle classes, such as dining out, motoring, holidays, and other forms of conspicuous expenditure, were widely reported on by the popular press and cinema and exacerbated workers' resentment. In the midst of the summer 1911 transport strikes, the Board of Trade's George Askwith submitted a memorandum to the Cabinet considering the reasons for the growing industrial unrest. While noting the issue of wages, he also explicitly drew attention to the flamboyant lifestyle of wealthy Edwardians, and attributed the contrast between this and the precarious existence of working-class families as one of the causes of discontent.[12] In turn, such social factors contributed to the desire for fundamental social change amongst many workers.[13]

Of course, poverty was nothing new in Britain, but according to the author of a 1911 study of the Labour Revolt, 'it speaks volumes for the patience of the British people that they have not long ago risen in revolt against these scandalous conditions of life which have been imposed on them'.[14] The mass expansion of compulsory elementary school education, increased literacy, rise of adult education and radical independent working-class education classes organised by the Plebs League and other left-wing political groups, and expansion of mass national communication (via more widely read newspapers and journals) were probably influential in sharpening critical faculties and encouraging a rising standard of expectation as to workers' position – only for this to be dashed.

---

10. *Commission of Enquiry into Industrial Unrest*, No. 7 Division (1917) Report of the Commissioners for Wales, including Monmouthshire, London: HMSO, 1917 (Cd 8668), p. 23.
11. Edgerton (2018: 119).
12. Askwith, Memorandum to Cabinet, 'The Present Unrest in the Labour World', 25 June 1911, TNA/CAB 37/107/70.
13. Knowles (1952: 212–13).
14. Ellis Barker (1911: 446).

As the Dean of Manchester, Bishop Welldon, explained: 'Men are breaking loose from the social and intellectual restraints of the past; they are indulging in new flights of hope and fancy and aspiration.'[15] The old social order in which 'conflicts of interest between social classes had been contained in a structure of hierarchy and deference' in which workers 'knew their place' was breaking down.[16]

Added to the mix was the way more socially segregated patterns of residence in urban areas had created distinct working-class residential environments in which there was the development of communities of mutual support, which often became the centres of trade union and political organising during the Labour Revolt. In sum, Askwith recalled the way strikes were an expression of 'a spirit and a desire ... to achieve a greater amount of economic equality' in which there were 'demands for shorter working-hours, more pay and more power, both over industry and in the government of the country'.[17]

INDUSTRIAL RELATIONS AND TRADE UNION FRAMEWORK

The industrial relations and trade union framework is also crucial to an understanding of the underlying causes of the Labour Revolt. Following the 'New Unionism' strike wave many of the new 'general unions' had enrolled large numbers of unskilled workers, but this growth faltered in the economic downturn and employers' counter-attack that followed, with many of the gains made undermined. For example, the newly formed Shipping Federation launched an offensive against the dockers' and seamen's unions by supplying ships laden with non-unionised 'free labour' to companies involved in disputes, successfully breaking strikes at individual ports across the country for the next 20 years.[18] On the London docks membership of the new dockers' union fell from 56,000 in 1890 to below 14,000 by 1900.[19]

Likewise, employers' lockouts in the cotton, coal and engineering industries seriously impacted the predominant longer-established craft unions that organised skilled workers. And there were a series of adverse civil court decisions against the unions – culminating in 1901, when the Taff Vale Railway Company established its right to sue the Amalgamated Society of Railway Servants for damages following a hard-fought strike in South Wales over lack of union recognition and low wages. This judgement effectively meant

15. Skidelsky (2014: 142–3).
16. Hebert (1975: 32).
17. Askwith ([1920] 1974: 348, 353).
18. Saville (1967: 323–4; 1996: 13).
19. Burgess (1980: 85).

that any trade union which organised a strike risked being sued for all of the economic costs imposed on the employer, thereby acting as a deterrent to strike action that could place union funds in jeopardy.

However, many employers stopped short of an all-out attempt to destroy trade unionism. The early years of the twentieth century up to 1910 saw a period of exceptional industrial peace not merely because of the proceeding setbacks, or a result of Taff Vale. In the latter case, union activity was legalised by the Liberal government's 1906 Trade Dispute Act which granted unions widespread legal immunities from prosecution, albeit not legal rights. The low level of strike activity was more a symptom of the stalemate reached in many industries in which employers supported the development of sophisticated collective bargaining and disputes arrangements and conciliation and arbitration procedures that acknowledged the legitimacy of trade unions and enshrined their role in channelling disputes between workers and employers.

By no means did the majority of employers embrace union recognition and collective bargaining; shipping, railway and many manufacturing companies remained highly resistant. Yet the period also witnessed a significant shift away from reliance on overt confrontation with the trade union movement towards more subtler methods of containment[20] as it became increasingly apparent to some employers that unions were double-edged. While they might challenge employers' prerogatives, the spread of formal collective bargaining machinery over wages and hours of work (usually on a district-wide basis incorporating a minimum wage) alongside industry-wide procedure agreements (which outlined the stages of bargaining and often required conciliation or arbitration before a strike could take place) had some distinct advantages.

Although these institutions created opportunities for trade unions (for example, in the building, coal mining, iron and steel, engineering, cotton and railway industries) to stabilise their membership and to make some gains on behalf of their members, they also allowed employers to work with 'responsible' national union officials who were willing to help enforce a systematic framework of dispute resolution, limiting strikes and effectively reducing wage competition among employers. Certainly such arrangements helped to ensure the number of disputes, although increasingly following the removal of the Taff Vale judgement remained at low levels, until this was overturned by the rank-and-file revolt from 1910 (Table 1).[21]

At the same time, the growth of state intervention shaped a new industrial relations system with an extensive 'voluntary' regulatory code governing

20. Davidson (1985: 264).
21. Hinton (1982: 58, 32; 1983: 64–9).

the relations between employers and workers.[22] The 1896 Conciliation Act created a new Labour Department attached to the Board of Trade, to prevent disputes through mediation and conciliation. The number of Conciliation and Arbitration Boards increased from 105 in 1896 to 325 by 1913, handling an enormous 7,810 disputes (not necessarily involving strikes) between 1908 and 1911.[23] From 1907 onwards the Board of Trade actively sponsored trade union recognition, collective bargaining, disputes procedures, and conciliation and arbitration as a permanent means of channelling workers' grievances into negotiation, avoiding industrial conflict and encouraging both employers and union officials to regulate agreements and maintain order.[24] The highly interventionist role played by the Board of Trade was manifested in the way George Askwith and other officials intervened in over 85 per cent of major industrial disputes between 1906 and 1914, resolving 75 per cent of them. By 1911 the Labour Department was, on average, involved in almost two strikes per week.[25]

But paradoxically, it was precisely such processes designed to contain industrial unrest that contributed to the rank-and-file revolt during 1910–14. Although by 1910 *national* agreements laying out a national disputes procedure to be followed following a failure to agree had been signed by unions and employers' federations in engineering, shipbuilding, cotton weaving and spinning, printing, building and footwear industries, collective bargaining until as late as 1914 was overwhelmingly *local*, or at best *regional*. Sometimes, as in cotton spinning, there was only limited bargaining over the substantive issue of pay, and in many industries any negotiated wage rises were below the rate of inflation. Conciliation schemes proved slow and unable to resolve workplace grievances, which generated considerable rank-and-file discontent.[26]

Crucially this development of institutionalised collective bargaining and conciliation machinery required an increase in professional full-time union officials to staff the newly formed mediating bodies at national, regional and local level.[27] While union membership grew steadily, if unspectacularly, from 2 million in 1905 (11.9 per cent) to 2.5 million (14.6 per cent) by 1910,[28] the number of full-time union officials expanded proportionally at an even faster

22. Howell (2005: 67).
23. Great Britain, Parliament, *Parliamentary Papers* (Commons), 1915, Cd 7733; Board of Trade (1915: 193–4); Cole (1973: 316).
24. Burgess (1975: 229–34); Weinberger (1991: 121).
25. Davidson (1978: 576; 1974: xi).
26. Clegg (1985: 65).
27. Darlington (2008: 108–12; 2014a: 10–13).
28. Hyman (1985: 257).

rate in many of the most important industries. The evolving relationship between the unions and the state was further expanded and institutionalised with the movement of union officials into full- or part-time posts in government departments to administer the embryonic social welfare services introduced by the Liberal government; by 1912 some 374 posts had been provided for union officials in the factory inspectorate, Home Office, Board of Trade and National Insurance administration.[29] One observer complained that such measures had 'sterilised the Socialist and Labour Movement, by enlisting it in the ranks of the bureaucracy and seriously attaching it to the governing classes'.[30]

Impatience with the ineffectiveness of bargaining arrangements and conciliation machinery became linked with frustration at the inadequacy of growing trade union officialdom to represent workers' discontent over the decline in real wages and impact of deteriorating working conditions. Officials were often reluctant to call strike action, or even support disputes involving their members, on the basis that this might jeopardise bargaining procedures and relations with employers, with the goal of ensuring union recognition and maintaining negotiating rights becoming an end in itself. Concern with unions' financial stability provided an additional incentive to impose central authority over the pursuit of local demands that might result in conflict and strike pay and other dispute costs. As a result, full-time union officials were often viewed with growing distrust by many rank-and-file union members. They appeared remote and unresponsive to their members' discontent, losing any sense of militancy the deeper they became embroiled in bargaining and conciliation responsibilities. As the syndicalist newspaper *Solidarity* explained:

> The attitude of a large number of prominent officials more resembles that of a manager of a limited liability company than an elected official of a working-class organisation. It happens far too often that the unionist has to fight not only the tyranny of the boss, but also the bureaucracy of his own union officials.[31]

Thus, during the Labour Revolt much of the strike action that took place was unofficial and hostile to the existing official leadership. Indeed, what most disturbed employers and government was the failure of union officials to channel industrial grievances through the increasingly acceptable insti-

29. Halévy (1961: 446–7).
30. Orage (1914: 217–18).
31. *Solidarity*, September 1913.

tutions of collective bargaining and conciliation. As Austen Chamberlain, Conservative Party MP and ex-Chancellor of the Exchequer, told the House of Commons on 16 August 1911 when industrial turmoil was at its height: 'I think the most prominent feature of the present unrest is the extent to which agreements made under the arbitration of the Board of Trade have failed to obtain acceptance by the men after their leaders have signed them.'[32]

Shortcomings in formal collective bargaining could not be held entirely responsible for all of the industrial militancy among unskilled workers given that many of them were not covered by such agreements. Of the five main industries affected by strikes during the Labour Revolt, the mines, railways, shipping, docks and building, only two, mining and building, had established collective bargaining procedures and employers' recognition of unions. In 1910 the vast majority of workers did not belong to trade unions and were outside the collective bargaining system, and so did not have access to any established procedures that could handle their grievances.[33] This meant that a significant proportion of workers who participated in the Labour Revolt had never experienced the (double-edged) benefits of collective bargaining, and were striking *for* rather than *against* trade union regulation – both for union recognition and bargaining rights.

Nonetheless, underlying employment conditions for workers in unorganised workplaces and industries were indirectly affected by the broader context of official union accommodation that took place within bargaining channels in those industries where it existed. In some industries (including the railways), where union officials were ineffective in representing and/or resolving workers' grievances over pay and working conditions through existing conciliation and arbitration procedures, it stoked resentment at both union officials and the procedures. Some industries and workplaces lacked any form of trade union representation whatsoever, and others (including the docks, shipping and railway industries) had trade union organisation which the employer refused to recognise for the purposes of bargaining. As a result, accumulated grievances tended to explode into widespread revolts by both union members and unorganised workers alike.

Overall, the Labour Revolt involved two main concurrent revolts: one in the *organised* industries (such as coal mining, cotton, building, shipbuilding and skilled engineering) was waged by workers who were members of established and recognised trade unions who often acted unofficially, without the support of their union officials and sometimes against their union's wishes and in contravention of the discipline imposed by collective agreements

32. *House of Commons Debates* (Hansard), 16 August 1911, vol. 29, cols. 1947–1948.
33. Board of Trade (1910: 431–90).

and bargaining arrangements; the other in the hitherto *unorganised and/or unrecognised* trades (such as shipping, docks, railway, manufacturing, metal-working) was of workers outside the collective bargaining framework, whose struggles over wages and conditions also involved the attempt to build collective organisation and gain union recognition, and which also often came into conflict with cautious official union structures and institutionalised channels of labour containment. While the unorganised element was crucial to the Labour Revolt, the numerical and organisational strength of the organised extended the scope of militancy and 'helped to ensure a greater likelihood of victory all round'.[34]

In sum, a paradoxical legacy of employer and state attempts at labour containment through institutionalised procedures for settling industrial grievances was that union officials' attempts to act as a stabilising and control agency cumulatively dammed up rank-and-file anger and resentment at the meagre fruits of such incorporation, which in turn found expression through independent and unofficial forms of struggle and open revolt in which both employers/government *and* union officials became the target.[35] It was the overall failure of 'orthodox' trade unionism to secure tangible material improvements for many workers, particularly unskilled workers, that encouraged the rebellion against union officials' policy of moderation and collaboration with employers, and the appeal of moving away from conciliatory collective bargaining towards militant industrial struggle.

POLITICAL CONTEXT

An underlying contributory factor to the Labour Revolt was widespread disaffection with conventional parliamentary politics as a means of addressing and remedying labour grievances, or achieving political change more generally. Apart from the denial of the franchise to all women, approximately four out of every ten men remained debarred from the electoral register (in 1911 representing 42 per cent of adult men, or 4 million) as a result of a complex system of registration, residence qualifications and exclusions.[36] Not surprisingly it was precisely those disregarded from the parliamentary process – young unskilled and unmarried men who lived with their parents – who were particularly likely to be inclined towards militant industrial struggle as an alternative approach to address their grievances.

34. White (1982: 79–85).
35. Gore (1982: 66).
36. Pugh (2002: 135–6).

The early twentieth century ushered in a move away from the Liberal Party's previous laissez-faire approach to political economy in favour of a 'New Liberalism' philosophy that advocated the need for state intervention to tackle adverse social and economic conditions which were now viewed as the root cause of poverty. It aimed at providing a 'safety net' – a basic minimum benchmark of assistance for those unable to 'stand on their own two feet'. In part this approach reflected the perceived threat to the 1906 Liberal government from the newly formed Labour Party's 29 independent MPs, representing Labour's first real parliamentary breakthrough. While it was true that Labour owed its gains mainly to an electoral pact with the Liberals, Liberal leaders were only too well aware of the risk if they alienated Labour by neglecting social reform. Hence, the government quickly passed the 1906 Trade Disputes Act reversing the Taff Vale judgement by granting unions immunities from prosecution providing the action was in furtherance and contemplation of a trade dispute, thereby winning support from the unions and Labour Party.[37]

'New Liberalism' philosophy also prepared the ground for a concentrated burst of relatively ambitious social reform legislation enacted between 1906 and 1914 by the Liberal government, led by Lloyd George (Chancellor of the Exchequer), Winston Churchill (President of the Board of Trade) and Herbert Asquith (Prime Minister).[38] These included Acts to provide compensation to workers for industrial diseases or injuries (1906), an eight-hour working day in the mines (1908), weekly pensions funded from government taxation (1908), minimum wage rates in a number of 'sweated industries' (1909), and labour exchanges for the unemployed to secure employment (1909). Important as these were, they were overshadowed by a 1909 Finance Bill which aimed at raising the revenue to pay for the social reforms via a new graduated system of income tax, plus a 'super tax' on very high earners – a redistributive budget that became known as the 'People's Budget'.

Such proposals met opposition from powerful vested interests, with the obstructive tactics of a Conservative-dominated hereditary (and landed gentry) House of Lords that resulted in a two-year-long constitutional crisis. The Lord's rejection of the budget forced Asquith to dissolve Parliament on the issue and fight a general election in January 1910 as the champion of 'representative government' against the 'rule of the aristocracy'. But although the Liberals were re-elected to office and able to enact their Finance Bill, they

37. Powell (1996: 11–22); Saville (1996).

38. It should be noted there is a difference between the spelling of names for Prime Minister Herbert *Asquith* and Board of Trade conciliator George *Askwith*.

lost heavily to the Conservatives and now became dependent on the support of Labour Party and Irish Nationalist MPs for their parliamentary majority.

In March they introduced a Parliament Bill that proposed the Lords' veto over finance bills be abolished and that other bills if passed by the Commons on three occasions would become law, even if rejected by the Lords. When the Lords sought to block this new bill, Asquith called another general election in December on the matter, although the outcome was more or less the same result as the January election, inaugurating an even more bitter spell of inter-party warfare (amidst the height of nationwide transport workers' strikes that paralysed the economy in June–August 1911) until the Lords eventually capitulated following intervention by the King. It was followed by the most ambitious of the Liberal government's welfare reforms, the 1911 National Insurance Act, which created a contributory state insurance system to provide an income for workers when they were sick or unemployed, allowing them to escape the provisions of the Poor Law.

For many commentators, the Liberal reforms of 1906–14 were a considerable legislative achievement that established new levels of state responsibility to relieve the causes of poverty and remedy some of the deep-rooted imbalance of wealth and opportunity inherited from the Victorian era.[39] However, arguably the social welfare legislation was essentially merely a palliative for the fundamental problems of the Edwardian economy and society, and had serious limitations.[40] Despite such measures as the Trade Boards Act and Mines' Minimum Wage Act, wage rates for many groups of workers remained stubbornly low. There were a large majority of workers, including millions of women workers, who were not covered by the unemployment insurance provisions. Many casual unskilled and semi-skilled workers (heavily concentrated in the transport sector, especially dock employment), whose subsidence wages made them most vulnerable to the rising cost of living, were least likely to benefit from welfare legislation like old age pensions, with its disqualification clauses, and were not covered at all by unemployment insurance despite the risk of irregular employment.

With reference to the National Insurance Act, many workers were aggrieved that unlike earlier measures of social reform – which had consistently given something without asking for anything in exchange – they were now faced with a tax imposed on them by the state, which was, except for the poorest, uniform in amount, and with the burden of contributions required by the Act falling most heavily on working-class families with incomes of less than 30 shillings per week who were least able to afford the additional

39. Powell (1996: 27–9).
40. O'Day (1979: 5).

expense.[41] Such objections found support from the radical left, who felt that sickness and unemployment relief should have been met entirely from taxes upon the rich.

Overall, poverty and hardship remained deeply ingrained facts of working-class life, with the Liberals' social reforms having only little effect for many and 'arous[ing] no feelings of gratitude' amongst many workers.[42] At the same time, there was working-class suspicion of, and even hostility towards the state's increasing interference in their social lives, notably its compulsory and punitive character – with regulations and restrictions, and a growing army of government inspectors of various kinds that many working people bitterly resented. Thus, the experience of those who were state welfarism's supposed beneficiaries was often one of frustration and disillusionment.[43]

Meanwhile, the perceived ineffectiveness of the Labour Party also helped to shift the focus away from Westminster towards direct action and industrial struggle. In 1900 a Labour Representation Committee (LRC), a federation of a number of trade unions with socialist bodies – Independent Labour Party (ILP), Fabian Society and Social Democratic Federation (SDF) – had been launched for the purpose of getting independent Labour representation in Parliament and local authorities. With the employers' counter-offensive in the 1890s following the 'New Unionism' strike wave and 1901 Taff Vale judgement, growing numbers of union leaders became convinced that political action through Parliament was likely to be more effective than industrial action, encouraging a willingness to affiliate to the LRC. In the 1906 general election, the LRC won 29 seats helped by a secret 'Lib-Lab' pact between Parliamentary Labour Party leader Ramsay MacDonald and the Liberals that aimed to avoid splitting the opposition vote. With the advent of a Liberal government with an enormous majority in the House of Commons, the LRC's new MPs adopted the name 'Labour Party', based on a compromise whereby both the socialist and trade union affiliated bodies would work together to advance labour movement interests, and scored an important legislative victory when the Trades Dispute Act reversed the Taff Vale judgement.

But one of the largest and most powerful unions in the country, the Miners' Federation of Great Britain (MFGB), did not initially affiliate. Having been pioneers in sending their own men to represent them in Parliament long before the Labour Party came into being, they continued to put forward their own candidates under the auspices of the Liberal Party; and their MPs sat as 'Lib-Labs' together with a few other trade union members. Only in 1909 did

41. Burgess (1980: 141).
42. Halévy (1961: 440).
43. Burgess (1980: 141).

the MFGB finally decide to join the Labour Party, and Labour emerged from the December 1910 general election with 42 MPs, a gain which was entirely due to the transfer of Miners' Federation MPs from Liberal to Labour ranks, with the miners contributing 17 to this total.

Indeed, the ranks of the Labour Party now included a considerable number of people who were fundamentally Liberals, and had changed their allegiance at the behest of the MFGB without altering their political attitudes.[44] Moreover, Labour's dependence on its growing affiliated trade union membership and their organisations' funds, and concern with its electoral and parliamentary appeal ensured that the pursuit of socialist objectives was firmly subordinated to the immediate and limited legislative needs of the unions' leaders, even though there were many socialists in the party's ranks, notably from the affiliated ILP.

Concern with parliamentary effectiveness also dictated an electoral accommodation with the Liberals. Labour felt it could not press home its own distinctive demands, or vote against the Liberals, without running the risk of endangering the position of the government and its programme of social reforms, Home Rule Bill for Ireland, and legislative removal of a December 1909 Osburne legal judgment that declared it illegal for unions to spend their funds on financing the Labour Party (which crippled the party of its main source of income).[45]

Not surprisingly there was strong criticism from left-wing socialists – both inside the Labour Party (such as ILP members) and outside (such as the SDF that quickly exited the Labour Representation Committee) – who denounced the party leadership for 'having given up its independence and consented to becoming a mere tail wagged by the Liberal dog'.[46] With its overriding concern to hold in check adherents of any 'new-fangled Socialist doctrine' the Labour Party 'was predominately a Trade Union and not a Socialist, party',[47] essentially the political expression of trade union officialdom.

But while trade union membership affiliation to Labour increased substantially from 855,000 in 1906 to 1,858,000 by 172 affiliated unions in 1912 (out of total membership of 1,895,000), the party never polled more than 7.6 per cent of the vote in a general election before 1914 or received more than 506,000 votes (Tables 13–14) and the party's organisational machine was limited to only about 150 or more constituencies (usually a federation of

---

44. Cole (1946: 201–3).
45. Only in January 1913 did a Trade Union Act largely reverse the Osborne judgment to allow unions to set up separate funds for political purposes – which were then used to strengthen the financial basis for Labour Party organisation.
46. Cole (1946: 240).
47. Ibid.: 226.

local trade union branches, trades councils and ILP or other socialist society branches), but with no regular Labour Party ward meetings. It was left mainly to the ILP with about 28,000 members to act as the active agency of the party in the localities.

Moreover, with the onset of the strike wave in 1910, not only did the Labour Party not become a vehicle or channel for labour discontent, but its leaders often castigated militant strike action as a fruitless means for alleviating workers' grievances and subversive of Labour's parliamentary electoral objectives. Philip Snowden MP told the House of Commons the strikes had produced 'an exceedingly trying time' for both the union leaderships and Labour Party, and that the way forward was through conciliation, not by means of 'an … irresponsible movement'.[48] Ramsay MacDonald, chairman of the Parliamentary Labour Party from 1911–14, announced it supported 'the general community' not the battles of capital and labour,[49] and argued 'there is one kind of strike utterly valueless, and I would beg all my friends of the Trade Union movement not to place any reliance upon it, at all. I mean the sympathetic strike.'[50] And a group of senior Labour Party MPs – including Arthur Henderson, the party's secretary from 1911 – even proposed legislation to make strikes illegal unless a process of conciliation was first exhausted, with the imposition of a 30-day cooling off period of notice of strike action.

Not surprisingly, the Labour Party was often effectively ignored during the industrial unrest, much to the chagrin of Sydney Buxton, President of the Board of Trade, who reported to the Cabinet 'the almost complete collapse of the Labour Party as an effective influence in this new development of labour disputes', with 'their elimination … a distinct loss to industrial peace'.[51] One historian has claimed that whatever the causes of the 'spirit of revolt' in the years between 1910 and 14, the Labour Party was not among them.[52] Yet we can only fully appreciate the causes, nature and dynamics of the strike wave and the growing influence of syndicalist ideas – with its doctrine of 'direct action', industrial unionism and class struggle in the *industrial* field instead of relying on *political* activity – in the wider context of the widespread perceived failure of the Labour Party and ineffectiveness of Parliament. The significance of the period precisely lay in the polarisation that developed between constitutional Labour politics of gradualist reform from above and the notion

48. Cited in Askwith ([1920] 1974: 145–6).
49. Cited in Middlemas (1979: 55).
50. MacDonald (1912b: 12).
51. Buxton, Memorandum to Cabinet, 'Industrial Unrest', 13 April 1912, TNA/CAB 37/110/62; TNA/CAB 37/110/66.
52. Callaghan (2012: 9–10).

that the working class could achieve its goals through industrial militancy from below.

In other words, industrial militancy was an expression of discontent with *both* existing strategies for advancing Labour's case, reflecting not only a growing awareness of the failures of 'orthodox' trade unionism and collective bargaining in the industrial sphere, but *also* of parliamentary support for moderate social reform in the political sphere. Neither of these two strategies had prevented the fall in real wages and the deterioration of working conditions, and hence the appeal for shifting the focus of action away from Westminster and the Labour Party, on the one hand, and conciliatory trade union bargaining, on the other, to the workplace and industrial militancy.

BARGAINING CAPACITY

Adding to the mix of contextual and casual factors contributing to the Labour Revolt was the enhanced bargaining capacity of workers, their relative potential ability to exert influence over employers in a context in which the balance of power between the two parties became more favourable to workers. This was reflected in a new willingness to engage in militant forms of strike mobilisation by both rank-and-file trade unionists and unorganised workers alike.

Against the backcloth of rapid price rises and falling real wages, there had been a threatened national railway strike in 1907 when the Amalgamated Society of Railway Servants voted overwhelmingly in favour of strike action in pursuit of a substantial improvement in pay, a reduction in hours and union recognition. It required the intervention of Lloyd George, at the time President of the Board of Trade, to get the action called off with a deal agreed with the companies and union leaders to accept a seven-year arbitration scheme, although this provided only minimal improvements in pay and did not secure union recognition. This was followed by a severe economic recession in 1908–09, with unemployment levels rocketing to 7.8 per cent in 1908 and then 7.7 per cent in 1909.[53]

In the depression year of 1908 there was an outbreak of disputes amongst Lancashire cotton spinners and Clyde and Tyne shipbuilding and engineering workers; and in 1909 there were threatened strikes by South Wales and Scottish miners. Most of these strikes came in response to demands for wage cuts, and were largely restricted to workers who were already well organised; they occurred without any expansion of trade union membership, involved some prolonged and bitter defensive strikes, and in time died

53. *Labour Market Trends*, Office for National Statistics, January 1996, p. 8; Bain and Elsheikh (1976: 134); Cronin (1979: 229).

away as trade unionists became reconciled to the adverse conditions. And although there were some signs of a rising mood of industrial unrest, with strikes in 1909–10 including Northumberland and Durham miners, North-East railway workers and South Wales dockers, what prevented an explosion of militancy was the overarching impact of recession and rise in unemployment (Chapter 3).

Only with economic recovery and the consequent dramatic fall in unemployment from 1910 onwards – from 4.7 per cent in 1910, to 3 per cent in 1911 and 2.1 per cent in 1913[54] – did workers react to a decade of falling real wages and accumulating grievances by engaging in a surge of strike militancy and union membership expansion. A favourable labour market heightened workers' bargaining capacity, their incentive to seek to take advantage of this strengthened power, and their collective confidence in the possibility of success to make demands for higher wages, better conditions and union organisation.

Another important element was the 'demonstration effect'[55] in which strike successes in one workplace and industry inspired other sections of workers, showing the value of collective union organisation and what could be achieved through industrial militancy. The realisation that powerful groups such as the seamen, dockers, miners and railway workers were capable of national strike action that could bring important sections of the whole economy to a halt reinforced the appeal of strike action. Workers in many other sectors, including unorganised workplaces and industries, took action, resulting in a huge increase in the number of strikes. Likewise in the West Midlands metal-working industry, when strike action in 1913 by many hitherto unorganised groups of workers in isolated workplaces achieved unexpected success, it sparked off a chain reaction in which strikes spread like a 'prairie fire' across the area, resulting in a collective breakthrough for trade unionism.[56]

Also strengthening workers' bargaining capacity was the way the strike wave led to the development of new forms of organisation and action that could leverage greater pressure on employers by extending the field of combat and undermine sectional divisions between workers and their unions. Notably, there was the 'sympathetic strike' in which groups of workers took action in solidarity with those in dispute, often then proceeding to formulate their own demands. Such solidarity strike action invariably overflowed the bounds of established bargaining and conciliation procedures and agree-

54. Ibid.
55. Hyman (1989: 226).
56. Hyman (1971: 191–5).

ments, and was seen as a 'calculated repudiation of the contemporary labour leadership' within the unions.[57]

Recognition of the way such solidarity action considerably enhanced workers' collective bargaining position was expressed in a memorandum written for the Cabinet in April 1912 by George Askwith, who was both surprised and frightened by the new spirit that gripped rank-and-file workers: 'Their strength is greatly increased by united activity.' He feared that in the future, 'action is likely to be more sudden that heretofore', and warned against ignoring 'the grave danger of united action' which 'took the leaders of the men themselves by surprise'.[58] In the process, the 'strike fever' embraced many thousands of workers outside the network of trade union organisation, with union leaders having to work overtime to draw up lists of bargaining demands with which to capture workers' sense of grievance.[59]

Underpinning this strengthened bargaining position was the rapid demographic growth of semi-skilled and unskilled labour as a proportion of the total labour force that had occurred over the preceding years. The growth in the ranks of semi-skilled and unskilled workers resulted from an expansion in the number of non-apprenticed workers in trades like engineering, printing, iron and steel, new manufacturing industries requiring small numbers of skilled men for maintenance and much larger numbers of unskilled workers for production, and from the enhanced economic importance of transport, communication and services. All this added greatly to the amount of semi-skilled employment, with a continual increase in the size of manufacturing plants, and industrial concentration spread across larger cities and factory towns. While such a development often involved a more intensive pace of production, it also provided some stability of employment and the material bedrock for collective organisation, resistance and solidarity. So while strikes occurred and organisation deepened among skilled workers (for example, over the process of deskilling in engineering), the truly novel phenomenon was enrolment of the semi-skilled and unskilled that accounted for the massive growth in strike activity and union membership growth.[60]

Accompanying this was the impact of generational change, with the 'critical mass' of young workers within the labour force, notably amongst the growing ranks of the semi-skilled and unskilled, encouraging the emergence of new layers of workplace activists and militants willing to challenge both the employers and the state, as well as the entrenched official union leaderships.

57. Cronin (1979: 100).
58. Askwith, Memorandum to Cabinet, 'Labour Unrest', 14 April 1912, TNA/CAB 37/110/63.
59. Cronin (1979: 100–1).
60. Cronin (1982a: 82–4); Hyman (1985: 261).

LEADERSHIP AND MOBILISATION RESOURCES

While specific objective structural and contextual factors served as both provocations and opportunity for the Labour Revolt to occur, they did not, in and of themselves, necessarily generate a sense of injustice or collective identity, nor explain why the strike wave happened. To fully understand this, we have to consider the importance of the role of subjective agency – of organisation and leadership in the collective mobilisation of discontent.

Ironically, many contemporary commentators and historians have viewed the explosion of rank-and-file workers' self-confidence, organisation and militancy during the 1910–14 period as essentially a 'spontaneous' phenomenon. As George Dangerfield commented: 'the greatest impulse in the great strike movement of 1910–14 was an unconscious one, an enormous energy pressing up from the depths of the soul'.[61] But it was not only the slow deterioration in real wages, gradual intensification of the pressures of work, constraints of existing union organisation, limitations of political options, and changing trade cycle with its lowering of unemployment and strengthened bargaining capacity, which explains the way workers' accumulated material grievances suddenly exploded into strike action. Workers' readiness to engage in militant strike action critically depended upon the encouragement they received from leaders and activists within their own ranks, with the perception of possibilities of success and the means to seize them a matter of practical argument and debate inside every workplace. Certain individuals and/or groups acted as a crucial catalyst by taking the initiative to walk off the job and then provide a lead to encourage the mass of workers to do likewise, even though sometimes this leadership was improvised and/or unplanned. It involved not merely established union figures, but also inexperienced grassroots leaders and activists (irrespective of whether or not a union existed) who were not weighed down by pessimism about what could not and what should not be attempted.

Of course, that workplace activists and leaders played an indispensable role as *catalysts* of strike activity does not mean accepting the 'agitator theory of strikes' with its emphasis on the alleged *manufacture* of discontent. Agitation would have been unlikely to fall on receptive ears unless there were genuine grievances and justifiable demands to agitate about.[62]

But even if we deny 'agitation' as a cause of the strikes we cannot deny the role of workplace leaders in identifying, articulating and stimulating workers' growing awareness of grievances as well as of potential collective strength

61. Dangerfield ([1935] 1997: 194).
62. Cole (1973b: 39–40); Darlington (2006).

to achieve redress of such grievances; encouraging a belief in the desirability and feasibility of militant strike action; taking the lead in proposing or initiating such action and pulling into action more hesitant and least confident groups; shaping the definition of the meanings, purposes and objectives of strikes; influencing both the ability and willingness of workers to either bypass the perceived 'class collaboration' of official union leaders to take the initiative themselves independently from below, or respond to union officials' appeals to take strike action; channelling and influencing the overall direction of strikes once started; spreading the action to other workers and generating support for militant trade unionism and solidarity action generally; and providing some cohesion to the general movement of discontent by generalising from workers' specific economic grievances to broader class-wide and more political concerns.

At the same time, we also need to understand the way in which many strikes developed with a rank-and-file/union officialdom dynamic at their heart, in which both rank-and-file initiative *and* official action was sometimes crucial, even though overall the restraining influence of national union leaders often undermined rank-and-file potential. On the one hand, many full-time union officials were emphatically opposed to strike action advocated by militants within their ranks and did what they could to stymie rank-and-file initiatives and unofficial action, even though they were not always successful in this endeavour. They often viewed spasmodic unofficial stoppages as undesirable, undermining their credibility with employers with whom they had struck agreements on behalf of their members.

On the other hand, the problem for trade union officialdom during this period was that their restraint in the years that had followed the 1892 economic downturn and collapse of the 'New Unionism' had clearly not paid off, either in obtaining higher wages or increased respect from employers, many of whom were hostile to collective bargaining and unions and insisted on hiring non-union labour. As a result, even moderate union officials sometimes felt obliged to threaten or organise strike action.[63] They were also subject to significant pressures from their rank-and-file union members, with the perceived failure to deliver some improvements in pay and conditions raising the danger of workers bypassing them by acting unofficially. It was such pressure from below that had the effect of pushing some union leaders to themselves call strike action, even though they often viewed this not only as the means to retain legitimacy, but also to assert officially sanctioned control with a view to restraining the struggle.

63. Darlington (2014a: 5–7, 11).

In other words, national union leaderships were confronted with both a *threat* and an *opportunity*.[64] The new militant workers' movement from below threatened many of the conservative habits they had developed over the years, with the alarming prospect of it boiling over into something more radical and politically threatening. However, it also offered them the opportunity of establishing the authority of both their unions generally and their own bargaining role specifically vis-à-vis the employers and government more powerfully than ever before, as well as their credibility amongst and control over members.

So while often it was not the established trade union leaders who initiated the strikes of 1910–14, some officials – notably those on the left such as Ben Tillett of the dockers and Robert Williams of the National Transport Workers' Federation, but also some otherwise moderate and right-wing officials, such as James Sexton (dockers) and Jimmy Thomas (railwaymen) – took the opportunity to expand their influence by occasionally identifying with, giving official support, and even encouraging some struggles.[65] Relatedly, there were some national full-time officials in the smaller unions, as well as local or district-based officials who could more accurately be described as union 'organisers', who because they were closer to rank-and-file members tended to be more responsive to militant pressure from below and supportive of strikes, including women such as Mary Macarthur of the National Federation of Women Workers and Julia Varley of the Workers' Union. And the syndicalist leader Tom Mann's position straddled the official/unofficial divide, such that although opposed to conservatism and bureaucracy within unions in general, he believed it was important to work alongside union officials (including Havelock Wilson and James Sexton) within a personal full-time official union capacity and role, in the day-to-day battle to establish union organisation.

To reiterate, it is necessary to balance recognition of the 'unofficial' outbreak of militant strike action, in which local activists and rank-and-file workers took the initiative, on the one hand, against an appreciation of the role of some national union and local leaders, on the other.[66] Ironically, sometimes when hesitant union officials found themselves obliged to support strike action and articulate their members' demands against their initial inclinations, it then in turn opened up possibilities for the rank-and-file to escalate the action even further than such officials were willing to approve or able to prevent.

64. Smith (1971: 18–22).
65. Darlington (2014a: 5–7, 11).
66. Holton (1976: 89–110); Coates and Topham (1994: 342–3); Wilson (2008: 262).

Meanwhile, despite only forming a small minority of the labour movement, there was the ideological and organisational influence of radical left activists and groups. These were to be found inside a variety of different unions, as well as the unofficial rank-and-file Amalgamation Committee Movement that emerged in different industries campaigning for industrial unionism. Some were left-wing members of the Independent Labour Party, or the two main Marxist political parties, the Social Democratic Federation (that became the British Socialist Party in 1911) and Socialist Labour Party. Others were supporters of Tom Mann's Industrial Syndicalist Education League and its various offshoots in different industries (including the Unofficial Reform Committee within the South Wales Miners' Federation). And there was also a wider layer involved in the radical working-class education body, the Plebs League and Central Labour College, as well as independent Socialist Societies and the support groups around the newspapers *The Clarion* and *Daily Herald*.

Chapter 2 provides a more detailed examination, but suffice to say at this stage that in a similar way that socialists had played a leadership role during the 'New Unionism' strike wave, notably in the matchgirls', gas workers' and dockers' battles,[67] 20 years later during the Labour Revolt the impact of syndicalists, Marxists and socialists, and others influenced by their ideas, including figures such as Noah Ablett, Tom Mann, Jim Larkin and James Connolly, was also to be significant in varied ways. For example, with its emphasis on anti-parliamentary 'direct action' that bypassed the orthodox bargaining machinery and 'class collaboration' of official labour leaders, and its advocacy of revolutionary industrial unionism with the objective of overthrowing capitalism and building a new social order, the syndicalist message fell on fertile ground as rank-and-file dissatisfaction led to an increasing incidence of militant strike activity.

Ironically while syndicalist 'agitators' were often accused by employers and the conservatives press of being the direct instigators of the Labour Revolt,[68] historians such as Hugh Clegg, Henry Pelling and Keith Laybourn[69] have suggested syndicalism's role was not particularly significant. Clearly the syndicalist movement was only one of many stimuli to workers' militancy and was in many respects itself a *response* to the growing labour unrest and political radicalisation that occurred, rather than its *cause*, such that to entirely or

67. Charlton (1999: 64–81).
68. Brown (1974: 22); Askwith ([1920] 1974: 294).
69. Clegg (1985: 22–74); Pelling (1987: 130; see also 1968); Laybourn (1997a: 119).

even mainly attribute the industrial and political militancy of the period to syndicalist 'agitators' would undoubtedly be to exaggerate their influence.[70]

On the other hand, there is clear evidence of the direct influence of syndicalist – and other radical left-wing activists and leaders – in the leadership of some important strikes and the solidarity initiatives that sustained them, as well as in a more diffuse ideological and organisational fashion around rank-and-file developments inside unions. It follows that the experience of the radical left cannot simply be dismissed as some sort of irrelevant 'sideshow'. If the strike wave revealed the capacity of workers to mobilise in combative ways, it also reflected the importance of left-wing leadership inside the movement but quite different to the union officials and Labour Party parliamentarians who so often attempted to control and stymie militant rank-and-file action.

BROADER *ZEITGEIST* OF DEFIANCE

Throughout the period of the Labour Revolt the Liberal Cabinet's authority was simultaneously assailed by the escalating conflict in Ireland arising from the government's Home Rule Bill and by the militant suffrage campaign that tried to force the government to grant women the vote. Both in varying ways were to have some influence during the strike wave.

While the battle for Irish independence from British imperialism had led to extreme coercion to suppress popular unrest, the 1906 Liberal government began to search for a framework of political compromise that could reconcile the Nationalist majority to the retention of Ireland within the Union. Although it pursued a cautious 'step-by-step' approach to Irish affairs, immediate policy showed little change from its Unionist predecessors. Pressure to adopt 'Home Rule' came from the Irish Parliamentary Party, whose moderate constitutional means of seeking limited autonomy within the framework of the supremacy of the British Parliament contrasted sharply with the militant republican forces grouped around the newly formed Sinn Fein dedicated to overthrowing British imperial rule in Ireland.[71] But following the December 1910 general election, the loss of the Liberal's overall Common majority enabled the Irish Nationalists to secure a high price for their contribution to the maintenance of the Liberals' authority, namely the introduction in 1912 of a Home Rule Bill establishing an Irish parliament.

Even though it proposed only a highly limited measure of devolution in the North, the proposed bill foundered on the position of Ulster, whose largely

70. Darlington (2013b: 82–6; 2014a: 14–16; 2013a).

71. Powell (1996: 138, 142); Aikin (1972: 99).

Protestant population were not prepared to accept an Irish settlement that it was feared would place them under the jurisdiction of a Catholic-dominated Dublin parliament. It resulted in a reactionary counter-mobilisation led by the Irish Unionist MP Edward Carson, who spearheaded a mass campaign of Protestant resistance and set up a separate provisional government, along with an armed Ulster Volunteer Force, to resist Home Rule.[72]

Crucially, Ulster's defiance of the Liberal government received the imprimatur of the official leadership of Conservative MPs and peers in Britain, with their leader Andrew Bonar Law ominously warning at a rally in Blenheim Palace there were 'things stronger than Parliamentary majorities' and that, in this particular conflict, Ulstermen 'would be justified in resisting ... by all means in their power, including force'.[73] Upper echelons of the British military mutinied at the Curragh barracks in March 1914, indicating they would resign their commissions rather than serve in Ulster and face the possibility of being asked to lead their men into what could develop into a civil war. Such extra-parliamentary defiance and undisguised use of armed force against the Liberal government forced Asquith into a 'compromise' proposal to partition the country but with some Ulster counties able to 'opt out' of Home Rule, albeit events were to be overtaken by the onset of war.[74]

Meanwhile, there was the sustained struggle to force the Liberal government to give women the vote mounted by the suffragettes (the Women's Social and Political Union) and suffragists (including the National Union of Women's Suffrage Societies), which involved many thousands of women in activity that also challenged the legitimacy of existing forms of parliamentary democracy, and which peaked during the period of the Labour Revolt. Following the 1906 landslide election victory of the Liberals, hopes for franchise reform were constantly dashed with a succession of proposed bills dropped with Asquith fearing (on the basis of the existing franchise property qualifications) it might benefit the Conservatives by giving votes to propertied women alone.

In response, the suffragette leaders escalated their militant campaign of civil disobedience by appealing for a new burst of militancy, with Emmeline Pankhurst declaring: 'The argument of the broken pane is the most valuable argument in modern politics'.[75] It resulted in activists smashing the windows of famous department stores in London's West End, physically attacking government ministers (including Asquith, Churchill and Lloyd George), blowing

72. Powell (1996: 148).
73. *The Times*, 29 July 1912.
74. Powell (1996: 146–7); Aikin (1972: 104–5).
75. *Votes for Women*, 23 February 1912.

up letter boxes, setting fire to well-known buildings and country houses, and slashing art works in galleries. During its height, in one month alone in 1913, there were 52 violent attacks across the country, including 29 explosives and 15 arson attempts at churches, railway stations, post offices, banks, newspaper offices and MPs' homes.[76] As a result of this escalating militant campaign, the suffragettes were to be at the receiving end of extreme repression and violence from the government and police, with over 1,000 activists across the country arrested and imprisoned for their actions, with many subject to systematic force-feeding torture.[77]

Yet there was insufficient unity of purpose between the disparate labour, Irish Home Rule and women's suffrage movements to enable them to make common cause. The strike wave did not coalesce with the battle for Irish independence – in part because, unlike the suffrage and workers' rebellions that were both part of developing militant social movements from *below*, the Ulster crisis over the Home Rule Bill on the British 'mainland' was a counter-mobilisation from *above* by reactionary sections of the ruling establishment, with the Nationalist movement one step removed across the Irish sea, despite some localised Catholic constituency support for Home Rule.

By contrast, there were some important areas of dialogue, overlap and activity that highlighted the potential for cross-fertilisation between the suffrage and labour movements and for the broader linking of class and gender issues, even if these were not always necessarily consciously recognised, pursued or developed.[78] For example, Sylvia Pankhurst and her East London Federation of suffragettes played a key role in creating a tradition of struggle that linked female suffrage to trade union organisation to improve working women's wages and conditions as part of a wider struggle in society, for which the East London Federation was expelled from the WSPU (Chapter 9). At the same time, the independent left-wing national daily newspaper, the *Daily Herald*, which played an important role in regularly reporting on and supporting both the women's suffrage campaign as well as workers' strikes, and was supported by a network of League branches that drew into its orbit both sets of activists, was another manifestation of the potential for bridges between the different militant movements. And there was a somewhat more

---

76. Riddell (2018: 66–7); Atkinson (2018).
77. Atkinson (2018); Meers (2014); Pankhurst (1977). If the 'suffragettes' were regarded as extremely militant and law-breaking, the 'suffragists' around the NUWSS generally adopted a more constitutional but nonetheless crusading approach to take the argument for women's suffrage to men and women across the country, galvanising some activists whose affiliations spanned participation in the trade union and labour movement.
78. Darlington (2020).

diffuse and amorphous link between the labour and suffrage movements manifest by the way in which among the rapidly growing numbers of women workers who took strike action during the Labour Revolt some appear to have been emboldened by the militant suffragette movement's dramatic so-called 'Deeds Not Words' forms of protest in a context in which philosophies based on the notion of militant 'direct action' become widespread (Chapter 9).[79]

However, there remained a yawning gulf between the militant labour (including radical left) and suffrage movements, with a number of problematic dimensions to their respective strategic policy orientations that had the effect (even though not all individuals in either group necessarily adhered to their organisations' leaders' views) of negatively impacting on the development of linkages. As a result, even though there were some important interconnections, this did not fundamentally overcome the way in which the labour and suffrage revolts generally remained on separate parallel tracks (Chapter 12).

Nonetheless, even though the labour, women and Irish independence issues did not coalesce, their *aggregated* impact undoubtedly created a series of crises for the Liberal government and contributed to an undermining of popular respect for the legitimacy of parliamentary institutions, 'law and order' and constitutional behaviour. The broad *zeitgeist* of extra-parliamentary 'direct action', widespread civil disobedience, threats and use of violence, and defiance of the authorities was reflected in the way in which many strikes during the Labour Revolt were marked by aggressive behaviour. This was exemplified in mass picketing aimed at spreading the action to other groups of workers, preventing 'blacklegs' from breaking the strikes, physical assaults on strikebreakers, and street-fighting with police and troops. In sum, as George Dangerfield suggested, the three rebellions combined led to a marked weakening of the tendencies towards moderation, compromise and social harmony which had been among the distinguishing characteristics of the 'liberal England' of the nineteenth century and first decade of the twentieth century.

CONCLUSION

In conclusion, a multifaceted set of contextual and casual elements contributed to the 1910–14 Labour Revolt. Ironically, despite his disdain for strike action, Ramsay MacDonald provided a vivid portrayal of the 'heaving' of this unrest:

79. Thom (1998: 103; 1986: 269); ibid.

By 1910 everyone in touch with the masses felt the heaving of unrest. General unhappiness moved the working classes. They were like the beehive before swarming. The impelling forces ... were the protests of men wronged in pocket and spirit, feeling the injustice of society, like a persecuting malignity, at the end of their patience because their experience had not taught them that though right was worsted wrong would not triumph. The fight was forced upon them, and they entered it determined to carry it through whatever the cost was to be. Whoever stood for peace and negotiation was for the time being put upon one side ... Men thought of but one thing – their common grievances against employers. Everyone was prepared to come out because someone else was out.[80]

80. MacDonald (1912c: 95–6).

2
Influence of the Left

Politically the forces that grouped within the British labour movement in the pre-First World War period under the broad banner of the 'left' held a range of viewpoints and were fragmented in a multitude of different (and in some cases mutually hostile) organisations. However, there were common threads that were held by significant elements of the more 'radical left' forces, notably disaffection with the inadequacies of the Labour Party and trade union officialdom, and the view that workers' emancipation lay in industrial union organisation, solidarity and action, and ultimately in the control of industry by workers themselves.

In Robert Tressell's *Ragged Trousered Philanthropists* his eponymous hero, Frank Owen, powerfully argues the case for socialism in the face of the scepticism of his workmates who think that trade unionism and socialism is not for them.[1] Yet paradoxically, in the years after Tressell's death and the subsequent publication of his book, the explosive strike wave of 1910–14 was to completely transform the role and influence of many thousands of individuals like Frank Owen, both male and female. As broader social forces threw old assumptions and relationships into disarray, left-wing activists and militants were able to articulate workers' growing sense of grievance and take the lead in collective strike action, acting as catalysts in the ensuing general upsurge of class and political consciousness. Socialist policies never 'conquered' the labour and trade union movement, but they resonated with the activities and outlook of many workers.

INDEPENDENT LABOUR PARTY LEFT

The Independent Labour Party (ILP), formed in 1893, was by far the largest socialist organisation in Britain, with over 700 branches and a paying membership of 28,000 by 1913, and 1,070 local government representatives by 1914.[2] It identified its political future in an alliance with the trade unions and pivoted its strategy on converting the newly formed Labour Party to social-

1. Tressell (1973).
2. Crick (1994: 198).

ist policies and goals. However, significant sections of the ILP membership became increasingly dissatisfied with Labour's timid performance in Parliament and the way in which any socialist aspirations were being sacrificed in the interests of an alliance with trade union officials and links with the Liberals, as well as with the contrast between the ILP's left rhetoric and the pragmatic practice of its leadership.

Tensions grew after Victor Grayson's successful election as an Independent Socialist in the 1907 Colne Valley by-election (despite every effort to stand as an official Labour candidate). This demonstrated it was possible for socialists to win against the Liberals on their own merits.[3] And over the next four years some on the left of the ILP began to consider the formation of a socialist breakaway from Labour, a new independent party that could bring together Britain's splintered left-wing groups on the basis of full-blooded socialist policies.

While most Parliamentary Labour Party members, including MacDonald, Henderson and Snowden (the last two also ILP leaders) were hostile to the Labour Revolt, some ILP leading figures such as Keir Hardie, as well as the party's paper *Labour Leader*, professed sympathy for the strikes, albeit always insisting the only way to change society was through parliamentary means.[4] And sections of the ILP's heterogeneous membership (which ranged from temperance campaigns, ideas of working-class self-help, religious dissent, left Liberalism and Marxism) were active in unions and campaigned in support of strikes in many areas of the country. As the party's National Administrative Council noted in 1912: 'No small part of the work of the ILP during the last twelve months has been to aid the organised workers in their splendid industrial battles and to give legislative expression to their demands.'[5]

Leading national union officials who were members of the ILP included Robert Smillie (Scottish Miners' Federation) and Mary Macarthur (National Federation of Women Workers) – the latter of whom served on the ILP's National Administrative Council along with other Federation organisers. Some leading South Wales coalfield syndicalists had been members of the ILP, with a monthly *Rhondda Socialist* newspaper that embraced local ILP and South Wales Miners' Federation branches, and achieved a circulation that reached 6,000 copies, acting as the 'bomb' of workers. In the Durham coalfields ILP activists influenced by syndicalist ideas (if not ultimate ends) led a rank-and-file movement that endorsed industrial militancy.[6] And in Glasgow the ILP's paper *Forward* was the galvanising hub of the local labour movement,

---

3. Groves (1975); Taylor (2021).
4. *Labour Leader*, 23 June 1911.
5. ILP Twentieth Annual Conference Report, Merthyr, 27–28 May 1912, p. 9.
6. Mates (2016: 274–5).

mobilising solidarity for different strikes, with ILP members active in industrial work in their workplaces, unions and Glasgow Trades Council.[7]

In the 1911 United Turkey Red strike in the Vale of Leven, Dunbartonshire, George Dallas, secretary to the Scottish Divisional Council of the ILP, played a leading role, and three of the leaders of the 1911 Dundee carters' and dockers' strike, including syndicalist-sympathetic Peter Gillespie, were all members of the ILP. In Cardiff during the 1911 transport strikes the ILP branch afforded the opportunity for the seamen's case to be presented at several of their Sunday meetings in the public parks attended by thousands of people.[8] In Salford, ILP members were very active around the docks and transport strikes, as well as the railway labourers' dispute whose strike committee was housed in ILP rooms.[9] And in Hull, women members of the Central branch of the ILP played a key role in organising relief for the women and children of dockers on strike.[10]

SOCIAL DEMOCRATIC FEDERATION/BRITISH SOCIALIST PARTY

The largest revolutionary Marxist organisation in Britain, the Social Democratic Federation (SDF) founded in 1881 (as Democratic Federation), resigned from the embryonic Labour Party in 1901 after failing to secure the adoption of a socialist programme, and changed its name to the Social Democratic Party (SDP) in 1908 and then British Socialist Party (BSP) in 1911. Ironically, the 'old guard' leadership of H.M. Hyndman and even Harry Quelch (who had been involved in supporting the 1889 London docks strike and was chair of London Trades Council), viewed strikes with disapproval and condemned unofficial action, insisting that workers would be better occupied directing their energies towards the ballot box and political action to achieve change through revolutionary-led parliamentary means. While they believed the party should support strikes on principle, they also insisted unions were of limited value in the struggle for socialism, with the impossibility of making any real gains while the capitalist system lasted.

However, amidst the impact of the Labour Revolt, growing left-wing discontent inside the ILP, wider desire for socialist unity between different left groups, the campaign for a new and explicitly socialist party advocated by the SDP, Victor Grayson and others received wide support. It led in late

7. Smyth (2000: 73–7); Smith (1991: 62).
8. *Labour Leader*, 18 August 1911.
9. Ives (1986: 26, 34); ibid.
10. *Labour Leader*, 18 August 1911.

September 1911 to a 'Socialist Unity' conference that brought together representatives of the SDP, some left-wing branches of the ILP, the network of clubs associated with *The Clarion* newspaper, and various local independent socialist societies,[11] resulting in the formation of a new united British Socialist Party (BSP), which held its first annual conference in May 1912. The unified party declared that it was 'prepared to give its sincere sympathy and active support to the industrial organisation of the workers, as well as in the task of consolidating their forces as in the conduct of any struggles in which they may be engaged'.[12]

For a brief moment it looked as if it might eclipse the ILP and become the main force on the left of British politics, but (as with the ILP) there was an internal crisis inside the BSP – which was still dominated by the veteran SDP leadership whose insistence on the primacy of political action, with trade unionism as merely auxiliary, alienated many members (Chapter 12). If the BSP could claim 40,000 members in 1912, by 1914 this figure had fallen to 13,755 (the majority of whom were merely card-holders),[13] with the 'falling to pieces of a number of branches which sprang into existence on the formation of the BSP'.[14]

Yet despite the inflexibility of its leadership, and inability to effectively grow despite the explosion of trade union militancy, many SDP/BSP members were involved in trade union and strike activity and solidarity work, including Jack Wills (London-based building worker who became secretary of the Amalgamation Committees' Federation), and A.A. Purcell (organiser for the National Amalgamated Furnishing Trades Association and Salford Borough Councillor, who chaired the 1910 founding conference of the Industrial Syndicalist Education League and was an influential figure around the 1911 Manchester transport and railway strikes). The 1911 and 1912 London dockers' strike leader Ben Tillett was elected to the SDP's executive committee at its conference in April 1911, and Harry Quelch, full-time editor of the party's paper *Justice*, wrote the introduction to Tillett's 1911 *History of the London Transport Workers' Strike*. Even Tom Mann, who had been an SDF member in the 'New Unionism' period, rejoined when he returned to Britain after travelling abroad in 1910 to launch the ISEL, before leaving in May 1911 on the basis that 'my experiences have driven me more and more into the non-parliamentary position'.[15]

---

11. Official Report of the Socialist Unity Conference, Salford, 30 September–1 October 1911, BSP (Provisional Executive Committee).
12. BSP First Annual Conference Report, Manchester, 25–27 May 1912, p. 15.
13. Kendall (1969: 310).
14. BSP Third Annual Conference Report, London, 12–13 April 1914, p. 30.
15. *Justice*, 11 May 1911.

At the same time, many branches of the SDP/BSP became important centres for political education and working-class agitation, particularly in Scotland due largely to the efforts of the schoolteacher John MacLean who lectured at a series of education classes on economics and Marxism.[16] Although initially, in keeping with SDF orthodoxy, he was pessimistic about the role of unions and the value of strikes, he became more and more drawn towards workers' struggles, including the Singer Clydebank and national miners' strikes, and keen to relate to them politically.[17] Meanwhile in the 1912 national miners' strike, the BSP distributed 150,000 copies of its manifesto at strikebound pits,[18] and during the 1913–14 Dublin lockout held solidarity meetings in numerous towns across the country.[19] It also jointly organised a support meeting in Trafalgar Square together with the London Trades Council – within which the BSP had influence.[20]

SOCIALIST LABOUR PARTY

The other main revolutionary Marxist organisation, the Socialist Labour Party (SLP), had been formed out of a breakaway from the SDF in 1903 by Scottish branches influenced by the ideas of Daniel De Leon (leading theorist of the American Socialist Labor Party and founder member of the Industrial Workers of the World) and the Irish revolutionary James Connolly. The SLP rejected working within the existing trade unions on the grounds that they were hopelessly craft-based and led by bureaucratic and conservative leaders who sabotaged workers' struggles. Instead, they advocated the formation of entirely new separate revolutionary industrial unions ('one union for each industry') which could serve both as a means of fighting capitalism and as the basis of a future socialist society.

The principles of industrial unionism as set out in Connolly's 1908 pamphlet *Socialism Made Easy* were reprinted by the party's press in Glasgow and became one of its most popular publications. It insisted that although political action and organisation was important, the main battle the working class had to fight was to organise industrially until it became strong enough to 'crack the shell of the political state and step into its place'. The political struggle of the ballot box was merely an 'echo of this struggle'[21] that would legitimise the revolutionary conquest of power by the working class. The

16. Gordon (1991: 275–6).
17. Sherry (2014: 36); Milton (1978: 49–65).
18. Kendall (1969: 41).
19. Newsinger (2013b: 53).
20. *Justice*, 13 September 1913.
21. Connolly (1974a: 265, 283, 280).

SLP's Industrial Workers of Great Britain (IWGB) (set up on the America model) had considerable success in recruiting sections of the Clydebank Singer sewing machine workforce in the lead-up to their 1911 strike.

But while the SLP, with its emphasis on the importance of struggle at the point of production, adopted a more supportive stance towards the Labour Revolt than the SDP/BSP, it was a miniscule organisation with no more than 200 members by 1910 and perhaps 300 by 1914 – the majority based in Scotland – albeit 22 members were involved in the Singer strike. Although the IWGB could succeed temporarily in an unorganised factory like Singer, it made no real progress where other trade unions were firmly based. Ironically the SLP's 'dual unionist' strategy of replacing existing unions with new revolutionary industrial unions led it to become a vocal bitter sectarian opponent of Tom Mann and the syndicalist movement who advocated 'boring from within' in order to encourage existing unions' transformation towards industry-wide and revolutionary forms.[22]

Yet, despite the way SLP doctrine severely limited the party's membership growth, the rising tide of industrial discontent provided fertile soil for dissemination of its propaganda on the principles of industrial unionism amongst a layer of working-class activists and militants. Treating the question of political education seriously, SLP classes were held in a number of local shipyards and engineering workshops on Clydeside, producing worker-tutors that included William Paul and Tom Clark.[23] Students studied material such as Marx's *Wage, Labour and Capital* and *Value, Price and Profit*, as well as industrial history, with classes involving two-and-a-half hours of tuition each week and short discussions and examination of homework.[24] SLP propaganda, circulated in a series of pamphlets by Marx, De Leon and SLP members on a variety of industrial issues, acquired a national audience and helped to mould the theoretical principles of some leaders of the pre-war industrial revolt.[25] Indeed SLP theories developed in opposition to labour movement leaders were a factor in the students' strike which took place at Ruskin College, Oxford, in 1909, and produced the Plebs League and Central Labour College.

PLEBS LEAGUE AND CENTRAL LABOUR COLLEGE

Rebelling against the class content of the education syllabus at Ruskin's residential college for working-class students, which it was believed inculcated

22. *The Socialist*, December 1910; January, March 1911; November 1912.
23. Bell (1941: 55).
24. Challinor (1977: 114); Macintyre (1986: 72–3).
25. Woodhouse (1995: 26–7); Challinor (1977: 88).

acceptance of the basic tenets of capitalism, students established a Plebs League in October 1908 with their own journal *Plebs* to promote the principles of 'independent working-class education'.[26] The leading figure was the Rhondda miner Noah Ablett who attended Ruskin during 1907–08 along with other young miners from South Wales and elsewhere, as well as workers from other industries sent by their unions. Aspiring to learn about exploitation, the history of class struggle, materialism and Marxism, the Plebs League advocated the need for a labour college which could turn out a cadre of class-conscious trade unionists. Those 'scientifically trained to adapt themselves to the needs of the workers, with a knowledge of the economics of Labour coupled with the ability of speech and the pen, would naturally be expected to wield a great influence in their respective localities'.[27]

Ablett was responsible for converting several ILP branches in the Rhondda Valley coalfield into de facto branches of the Plebs League, a South Wales wing of which was set up under his chairmanship in January 1909.[28] And later that year, Ruskin students, having called a strike and boycott of lectures in protest at the sacking of their college principal who was broadly sympathetic to their views, created their own adult education organisation, the Central Labour College (CLC) which worked closely with the Plebs League to organise country-wide classes in Marxist economics and industrial history, with some trade unions providing scholarships. Ablett campaigned throughout the Rhondda lodges to rally support for the new institution, and by late 1910 the movement was strong enough to have its own full-time organiser and a Plebs Social Club located in Tonypandy, which became the focal point of all League activities.[29] Other Rhondda Plebs included his protégé Charlie Gibbons and rank-and-file miners' militants such as W.F. Hay, W.H. Mainwaring (prominent member of the Cambrian Combine lodge), George Dolling, A.J. Cook, and another former Ruskin rebel in 1907–08, Noah Rees (secretary of the Cambrian Combine lodge). It was to be from amongst this group that the syndicalist-influenced Unofficial Reform Committee of the South Wales Miners' Federation emerged out of the protracted 1910–11 South Wales miners' strike.

In the neighbouring Aberdare Valley, ex-Ruskin student, Wil Jon Edwards, organised evening classes in economics attended by up to 300 students who studied Marx's *Capital* 'to understand the true nature of the capitalism which exploited their Labour', and thereby created 'a nucleus of intelligent young

---

26. Pitt (1987: 3); Rose (2001: 258–9).
27. Pitt (1987: 3).
28. Davies (1987: 11).
29. Hebert (1975: 88).

men who understood what they were up against and ready to fight when the time came'.[30] And two North-East miners, George Harvey, SLP member, and Will Lawther, ex-ILP member, who attended Ruskin and the CLC in London, respectively, went on to play an important contributory role in the militant Durham miners' rank-and-file movement.[31]

Some Plebs/CLC students went on to teach classes in their own localities across the country. This movement for independent working-class Marxist education enjoyed wide support, providing a forum where supporters of the ILP left, BSP, SLP, syndicalists and independent socialists could all agree on their hostility to the nature of capitalist society and ineffectiveness of the official labour movement leadership. Many used the knowledge they acquired to take a prominent part in the industrial battles that raged in the pre-1914 period. As Rowland Kenny observed in his *English Review* article entitled 'The Brains Behind the Labour Revolt': 'During the railway strike of 1911, the chief agitators in the most militant mining districts were ex-Ruskin students, who are now Central Labour College propagandists.'[32]

INDEPENDENT SOCIALIST SOCIETIES, *THE CLARION* AND *DAILY HERALD*

Across the country there were also a number of independent Socialist Societies that acted as discussion and activist forums, drawing together different varieties of left-wing opinion whether unattached or formally committed to ILP or radical left groups. On Merseyside this included a Liverpool Marxist Socialist Society, South Liverpool Socialist Society and Birkenhead Socialist Society, all of which served as centres of wider debate about different conceptions of socialism.[33] Likewise in Manchester, the Openshaw Socialist Society, with about 300 members at its peak, including the boilermaker union member Harry Pollitt (future general secretary of the Communist Party of Great Britain), was very active with propaganda and educational meetings, and supported the call, along with Victor Grayson and others, for a united socialist party.[34] Other groups existed in Bristol, Birmingham and many smaller northern towns, and included a Rhondda Socialist Society whose members advocated a mixture of industrial unionism and syndicalism. And between 1913 and 1914 the organisation that was built up by Sylvia Pankhurst

30. Edwards (1956: 205–6, 212).
31. Challinor (1977: 116); Mates (2016).
32. *English Review*, vol. 27, no. 105, March 1912.
33. Holton (1973a: 302–3).
34. LHASC (CPGB): CP/IND/POLL/1/4; Mahon (1976: 17–33).

by linking the campaign for female suffrage with actively supporting working-class women's strikes in the East End of London was also important.[35]

Two left-wing newspapers were of significance during the period of the Labour Revolt. *The Clarion*, a socialist weekly edited by Robert Blatchford, became an open forum for different socialist groups and individuals, with a circulation that grew far beyond socialist circles to reach over 80,000 by 1908. The paper's supporters set up a network of local groups and different types of social organisation which propagandised for socialism and drew many thousands into its orbit, including Clarion Vans which toured the country with itinerant speakers, as well as cycling, scouts and rambling clubs. The paper supported many strikes during the Labour Revolt, and public meetings were organised by the Clarion Scouts addressed by speakers drawn from the wide spectrum of left-wing politics and attended by hundreds, with Clarion groups also directly involved in the 'Socialist Unity' Conference.[36]

Even more important was the role of the *Daily Herald*, which had first appeared as a news-sheet of the London printing unions' strike committee during a protracted strike in 1911, and then launched as a permanent daily paper in April 1912 by a committee which included Ben Tillett (dockers' union) and George Lansbury (left Labour MP for Bow and Bromley, London). From the outset the *Herald* functioned in an independent manner, outside the control of either the established leadership of the labour movement or the parties/groups of the socialist left. But the paper's editorial policy was keenly orientated to inviting dissident and militant opinion from a wide range of backgrounds to debate the various issues raised,[37] giving pride of place to those in active opposition to the official policies of the trade unions and Labour Party and creating a milieu where syndicalist ideas in particular came to exert a considerable influence.[38]

The paper became known as the 'rebel paper' because, as Lansbury explained, it 'always found itself supporting workers who were out on strike ... all men and women struggling to better their conditions instinctively turned to the *Daily Herald* for help during these first years; and never came in vain'.[39] The paper was not merely unofficial, it was assuredly anti-official, with typical *Herald* supporters, while not doggedly aligned to a particular socialist 'position', attracted away from the parliamentary arena and reliance

35. Connolly (2013); Jackson and Taylor (2014); Holmes (2020); Winslow (2021).
36. Blatchford (1931); Cole (1948a: 252, 311).
37. Holton (1974: 350–2).
38. Tanner (2014: 99).
39. Lansbury (1925: 48–9).

upon the state as agencies for socialist agency, and opposed to the direction of the Liberal government's social and industrial reform legislation.[40]

The mass circulation of the *Daily Herald* fluctuated between 50,000 and 100,000 subscribers (and possibly twice as many individual readers), with an upsurge in circulation to 230,000 during the 1912 London transport strike when the paper acted as an official strike organ.[41] A 'Herald League' network with about 50 local branches collected money for the paper and for strikers, embracing BSP, ILP, syndicalist and union militants. Prominent national speakers like Lansbury, Tillett and Mann toured *Herald* branches to speak on topics such as 'Socialism v Syndicalism', 'Socialism and Strikes' and 'Industrial Unionism'.[42] And the paper led the solidarity campaign in Britain during the 1913–14 Dublin lockout, calling for sympathetic industrial action, attacking the union and Labour Party leaders unsympathetic to Larkin, and organising a series of mass rallies attended by many thousands across the country.

INDUSTRIAL SYNDICALIST EDUCATION LEAGUE

Perhaps the most important left-wing organisation to play a role in the Labour Revolt was the Industrial Syndicalist Education League (ISEL) led by Tom Mann, one of the leaders of the 1889 London dock strike who returned to England in May 1910. His experiences in Australia convinced him that the pitfalls of sectional trade unionism and parliamentary politics could only be overcome through militant industrial unionism. Mann launched the monthly journal the *Industrial Syndicalist*, which became known as *The Syndicalist* from early 1912 and reached a peak of 20,000 copies. In November 1910 he organised the first conference of the ISEL in Manchester, attended by 198 delegates from over 70 union branches, trades councils and other radical groups, including figures like Noah Ablett and Jim Larkin. Two further conferences were held in 1912, in London and Manchester, at which it was estimated representatives of some 150,000 workers attended.[43]

The ISEL advocated revolutionary industrial union organisation and strike action as the central means to overthrow capitalism and achieve the economic and social emancipation of the working class. Industrially, this meant a reappraisal of existing trade unions with their craft sectionalism and conciliatory bargaining policies, towards a fighting unionism that utilised 'direct action' (including the sympathetic strike and general strike) and the reorganisa-

40. Holton (1973a: 476–9).
41. Postgate (1951: 135–6); Holton (1976: 185, 375).
42. Holton (1974: 370).
43. *The Syndicalist*, December 1912.

tion of trade union structures towards all-embracing industrial unionism (as we have seen, differentiated from the SLP's version by an insistence it could only be achieved by working *within* the existing trade unions to encourage a process of amalgamation). Such revolutionary industrial union organisation was visualised not only as a weapon of class conflict, but also as the nucleus of a future new social order. Politically, syndicalism involved a rejection of gradualist social reform through Parliament based on electoral politics via the Labour Party, the more resolute 'state socialism' of radicals in the ILP, and also the more sterile versions of Marxist politics developed within the SDP/BSP, which tended to reject the potential of industrial militancy as a means of revolutionary change. For these reasons, syndicalists described themselves as 'non-political' or 'anti-political'.[44] Their ultimate objective was to secure the overthrow of the capitalist system 'by taking possession of the means of production and distribution through an economic organisation outside the control of any parliamentary party'.[45]

Mann 'was at, or near, the centre of many of the episodes of the labour unrest of 1910–1914,[46] speaking at literally hundreds of meetings held not only under the auspices of the ISEL, but also strike committees, the SDP/BSP, ILP and local socialist bodies.[47] His record as a prominent socialist and trade union figure of 25 years standing led union officials to accord him a certain degree of respect, and he played a key role (through the support of Ben Tillett's dockers' and Havelock Wilson's seamen's unions) in forming a National Transport Workers' Federation (NTWF) that helped bring together 15 unions, with Tillett and Robert Williams (NTWF general secretary) showing some signs of commitment to syndicalist ideas of militant direct action and industrial unionism.

Although the ISEL had probably no more than a few thousand activists, its widespread influence inside the labour movement was disproportionate to this modest numerical strength. By September 1910 the *Industrial Syndicalist* could list the names of several Rhondda Plebs as 'advocates' of syndicalist principles, with the South Wales syndicalists finding fertile ground for the propagation of their ideas in the protracted 1910–11 Cambrian Combine strike in which they played a leading role.[48] Following the strike, the syndicalist activists and members of the Unofficial Reform Committee (URC) of the South Wales Miners' Federation were involved in the writing and publication in early 1912 of the pamphlet *The Miners' Next Step*, the clearest statement

44. Darlington (2013b: 22–8).
45. *Solidarity*, September 1913.
46. Brown (1974: 17).
47. Ibid.: 17–18.
48. Pitt (1987: 7).

of revolutionary trade unionism to be written during these years, and were at the forefront of the wider campaign for a national miners' minimum wage that culminated in the 1912 national strike.

The 1911 Liverpool general transport strike committee was also significantly influenced by syndicalists, with Mann chairman, Frank Pearce (Liverpool and National Ships' Stewards' Union) secretary, and others, including Joe Cotter (Ships' Stewards), Peter Larkin (Liverpool docker) and James Murphy (Liverpool Trades Council representative), and with other local syndicalists providing back-up propaganda and solidarity.[49] Following the strike in August 1911 Mann established and co-edited a local monthly newspaper *Transport Worker* (attaining a circulation of 20,000 throughout Merseyside and the North-West) that reflected the syndicalist emphasis on 'direct action' and consistently attacked attempts to reform social problems through Parliament.[50]

In the 1911 national railway workers' strike, syndicalist railwaymen operated in several key areas (including Sheffield, Manchester, Wakefield and Gateshead). Charles Watkins of Clay Cross and later Sheffield, a former Ruskin College student, member of the Plebs League and strong supporter of the ISEL, was the leading opponent of official Amalgamated Society of Railway Servants' (ASRS) policy, and spoke to railwaymen up and down the country on issues of industrial unionism and workers' control. *The Syndicalist Railwayman* newspaper was launched in September 1911 and ran to four issues before being merged into the ISEL's *Syndicalist* from January 1912.[51] The strength of syndicalist support was reflected in the election of George 'Smiler' Brown of Hull as general organiser of the union. The radicalisation of the 1911 strike, combined with a vigorous campaign for syndicalist principles within local branches and the union's 1912 Annual General Meeting, helped pave the way in 1913 for the formation of the National Union of Railwaymen (involving the amalgamation of three existing organisations) as an all-encompassing 'industrial union' of railway workers, which declared its official policy to be in favour of 'workers' control' and the construction of an 'industrial commonwealth'.[52]

By the autumn of 1912, the ISEL had linked up with a growing Amalgamation Committee movement that brought together militants within their respective different industries who, frustrated with the futility of craft-based forms of union organisation and sectional bargaining when confronted with

49. Holton (1973b: 138–9).
50. Holton (1973a: 381–3).
51. Gordon (2010: 2).
52. Pribicevic (1959: 109–10); ibid.: 6–7).

the coordinated power of federated capital, campaigned in favour of the amalgamation of existing organisations into industrial unions. It led to the establishment of a Federation of Amalgamation Committees to coordinate the activities of the different groups, which elected Jack Wills, ISEL member, as its full-time secretary.[53] As well as changing the name of its journal to *The Syndicalist and Amalgamation News*, the ISEL exerted considerable influence within this amalgamation movement, seeking to leaven the movement's programme of organisational reform with a definite revolutionary syndicalist perspective.

In the lead-up to the 1914 London building workers' lockout, syndicalists had succeeded in organising a considerable body of opinion in favour of union amalgamation and the need for 'fighting policies' to defend living standards and above all to secure control of industry by the workers themselves through wider strike action.[54] The Metal, Engineering and Shipbuilding Amalgamation Committee, led by syndicalists like W.F. Watson and Jack Tanner (who occupied the positions of general secretary and assistant general secretary, respectively), established a network of local committees in the main engineering and metalworking centres, including Birmingham, Tyneside, Sheffield, London, Erith, Coventry and Derby,[55] that united skilled, semi-skilled and unskilled militants from the various engineering unions; 10,000 copies of its pamphlet, *One Union for Metal, Engineering and Shipbuilding Workers* written by Watson, sold out within ten weeks.[56] The importance of the engineering industry as a growth point for syndicalist influence was also reflected in the support generated for Tom Mann who stood for the general secretary position in the Amalgamated Engineering Union in 1913 on a platform of 'one union for engineering working-class solidarity and direct action', polling a creditable 8,771 votes out of 34,507 cast.

In Ireland, it was the syndicalist-influenced Jim Larkin and James Connolly who led the Irish Transport and General Workers' Union (ITGWU) during the 1913–14 Dublin lockout, with the ITGWU's weekly paper *Irish Worker*, edited by Larkin, imbibed with syndicalist content. In many respects, the enormous level of support the Dublin workers received inside the British labour movement stemmed not merely from basic notions of trade union solidarity and humanitarian concern, but also out of a strong mood of sympathy for the essence of 'Larkinism' – with its uncompromising anti-capitalism,

53. *The Syndicalist*, December 1912.
54. Holton (1976: 156–9).
55. *Solidarity*, January–July 1914.
56. *Solidarity*, April 1914.

indictment of the compromises and betrayals of trade union leaders, celebration of militancy and faith in rank-and-file workers.[57]

In addition, as previously mentioned, the meaning and utility of syndicalism was a topic for debate within the *Daily Herald* from its inception. Mann, Bowman and A.D. Lewis (a prominent ISEL member who became national secretary of the Herald Leagues) were involved as contributors and *Herald* publicists, and in 1913 conducted extensive speaking tours within branches across the country, many attracting over 1,000 people,[58] thereby ensuring syndicalists' objectives received wider national publicity than was possible within the ISEL's own monthly press and outdoor agitation.[59]

INFLUENCE

Overall, it is clear the left – including both syndicalists and 'political socialists' – exercised influence amongst significant, albeit minority, sections of the labour movement during the Labour Revolt. Although the combined membership of the different left groups was small and fragmented, and often scarred by sectarianism, socialist propaganda and activity reached a much broader constituency than formal fee-paying members. There was a large periphery of informal allegiances and interlocking networks of activists who engaged in a continuing dialogue with each other, with joint forums addressed by speakers drawn from the wide spectrum of left-wing politics attended by hundreds, and occasionally thousands, who contributed to the mobilisation and solidarity of the Labour Revolt. While it is impossible to accurately calculate their overall total numbers (Table 15), one credible estimate is that there were 50,000 or more (broadly defined) socialists in 1914.[60] And crucially, the 1910–14 strike wave provided opportunities for those on the radical left who wanted to outflank the trade union and Labour Party leaders and enlist the support of workers for more militant industrial and political policies, not only against the employers but also the government (Chapter 12).

What follows in Part II, Chapters 3–7, is a brief chronological narrative of some of the most important and/or characteristic individual strike movements between 1910 and 1914, concentrating attention on their origins, nature of development and overall impact.

57. Newsinger (2004: 97).
58. *Daily Herald*, 26 February 1913; 1 May 1913.
59. Holton (1973a: 484–8).
60. Laybourn (1997b: 63).

PART II

REVOLT

3

Scope, Harbingers and Springboard

The official statistics for strike activity between 1910 and 1914 in the 'United Kingdom' (which at the time included the whole of Ireland)[1] that were collated by the Board of Trade's Labour Department underestimated the actual number of strikes and thereby presented only a partial picture of the extent of strike action generally (Tables 2–5).[2] Partly this was because only those strikes that came to the Board's attention were counted, and partly because strikes that involved less than ten workers and lasted less than one day (except when the aggregate duration exceeded 100 days) were omitted. The scale of underrepresentation can be gauged from the 36 strikes in the cotton trade over 1910–14 that were not included in the Board's annual *Report on Strikes and Lockouts* despite being clearly within the inclusion criteria. Likewise, a series of unprecedented short lightning strikes that took place in various hotels in London and elsewhere in 1913 (Chapter 6) were too small to be included in the statistics.[3] Other problems arose from the way the Board's records consisted only of those disputes which were confined to a single district or region, which understated the incidence of strike action in industries which were nationally organised or where disputes tended to spread rapidly. For example, while the Board classified the national transport strike movement of 1911 as 'one' UK dispute, it could have been disaggregated to record the many separate but overlapping constituent strikes that took place in different ports across the country involving seamen, firemen, stewards and cooks, dockers and carters and other transport workers.[4] In sum, there was a higher level of strike activity between 1910 and 1914 than official Board of Trade records suggested.[5]

Nevertheless, the official data undoubtedly provided evidence of the extensive overall level of strike activity during the Labour Revolt, which is

1. Rather than 'United Kingdom' use will be made of the names 'Britain' and 'Ireland'.
2. Davidson (1985: 242, 256).
3. White (1978: 184); Board of Trade (1914: xvi).
4. Lyddon (2012: 246–7).
5. Glasgow Labour History Workshop (1996a: 24); Gordon (1991: 238); Outram (2008).

discussed below, before we turn attention to the harbingers and springboard of this strike wave.

SCOPE OF LABOUR REVOLT 1910–14

The years between 1910 and 1914 saw an annual average strike rate that was four times greater than that recorded in the previous decade (Tables 1–5). In each of the years 1910, 1911 and 1913 there were around 10 million *working days lost* due to stoppages; in 1912, with a national miners' strike, the figure rocketed to nearly 41 million, and then in the seven months (January–July) of 1914, before the commencement of war, remained extremely high at 9.9 million; overall between 1910 and 1914 there were no less than 82.7 million working days lost through strike activity. The *number of strikes* rose from 531 in 1910 to 903 in 1911 (more than twice the level of 1909), and then dropped slightly to 857 in 1912 before jumping again to 1,497 in 1913, and then to 848 between January and July 1914. The *number of strikers* followed a somewhat different pattern: in 1910, 385,000 workers took part; this increased to 831,000 in 1911 and still further to 1,233,000 in 1912 when the figure was inflated by the national miners' strike, then fell to 516,000 in 1913, with the previous year's large confrontations in major industries stimulating more widespread smaller-scale action across many different sectors; and between January and July 1914 there was a similar pattern of smaller strikes involving 308,000 workers. Reflecting on the period 1910–13 in Britain and Ireland as a whole, the Board of Trade's *Labour Gazette* commented: 'There has never before been a series of three consecutive years marked as a whole by such widespread industrial unrest.'[6]

One notable feature was the number of what the Board termed 'great disputes' that involved 5,000 or more workers or 'lost' at least 100,000 working days – 1910 (14), 1911 (22), 1912 (15), 1913 (26) and 1914 (8) – often taking place in strategically important industries that threatened the basic fabric of the economy and challenged the power of government.[7] On the other hand, in every year between 1910 and 1914 strikes involving less than 1,000 workers formed the great majority of all disputes, with less than 100 workers involved in a large proportion of cases. Yet historically, the size of the average strike doubled from 350 workers during the years 1889–92 to 780

6. Board of Trade (1914: ii).
7. Ibid.: 80–93); Lyddon (2012: 242–3). Although no equivalent series of 'great disputes' was produced by the Board after 1913, the 1914 figure was provided in *Labour Gazette*, July 1925.

workers during 1910–13.[8] Overall, it can be calculated that the total number of different workers who engaged in strike action (excluding double-counting of those who took action more than once) was about 2.58 million, which represented around 17.67 per cent of all industrial workers.[9]

A very wide range of industries were affected during the Labour Revolt involving 'practically all main groups of trade'[10] (Tables 3–5) with strikes not only in coalmining, textiles, railways, docks, shipping, metal, engineering and shipbuilding, and building industries, but also many other sectors, including non-unionised clothing, food-processing, foundry and laundry industries. Not surprisingly, there were considerable variations in the distribution of strikes *between* different industries. On the basis of all three traditional measures of strike activity, number of strikes, number of strikers and number of working days lost, coalmining dominated the statistics,[11] graphically illustrated in Wales where miners, who represented about 33 per cent of the male labour force and 25 per cent of the labour force in general, accounted for three-quarters of the total number of strikes in Wales during the period.[12] Across Britain as a whole, miners were almost three times as strike-prone as the next group, railway workers, followed by textile, transport, and metal and engineering workers, who were all more predisposed to militancy than others.

While it is difficult to explain such variation, the most strike-prone industries tended to have some common economic features.[13] They were all large, strategically important sections of the economy where imperatives of market forces and business cycle fluctuations made employers highly sensitive to labour costs, and therefore attempted to increase efficiency through work intensification and control over pay, which in turn generated collective resistance. High unionisation (although not always recognition by employers for collective bargaining) was also important, with membership figures showing that by 1913, over 900,000 miners were union members, with over half-a-million in unions in both the metalworking and textile industries, and almost three-quarters of a million in various branches of transport. Therefore, the strike wave was shaped by occupational or industrial-based unions – miners, transport, textile and railway workers – drawing into their ranks enormous numbers of new members. In the case of the miners and dockers,

---

8. Cronin (1979: 90–1, 51).
9. Routh (1980: 6, 9–10, 34); Bain, Bacon and Pimlott (1972: 113); Bain and Elsheikh (1976: 134).
10. Askwith ([1920] 1974: 347).
11. Board of Trade (1914: 55); Board of Trade, *Labour Gazette*, January 1915.
12. Hopkin (1989: 255).
13. Cronin (1979: 171–8, 187).

it seems likely that relatively cohesive occupational and geographic communities played some role in fostering traditions of militancy and solidarity.[14]

There was also a geographical pattern of strikes, with some areas more strike-prone than others. The industrial North and South Wales were much higher than the national average, while London and the South was considerably lower.[15] In part, variations reflected differences in regional industrial structure, with some highly concentrated industries with larger-sized workplaces accounting for a significant portion of strike activity, especially coalmining, engineering, shipbuilding and textile manufacture.[16] However, even *within* the same industry there were considerable regional differences, for example, between the particularly strike-prone coalmining area of South Wales compared with other areas in the country.[17] And within Wales, not only were strikes more common in Glamorgan compared with Monmouthshire, but strikes in Glamorgan were largely concentrated in certain areas, such as the Rhondda and Pontypridd.[18] This suggests the nature of local working-class organisation and political traditions were also important factors.

Liverpool had a weak manufacturing base, with relatively less firmly entrenched institutionalised and bureaucratic forms of organisation and leadership in the labour movement than some areas, although conservative and religiously divided political elements were also important. It was Britain's second largest port, characterised by casualised employment on the docks and associated transport industries, with workers facing poor working conditions and pay, and employers who were extremely hostile to union activity. Within this context, a combination of factors – an energetic (official) union organising drive conducted among seamen, dockers and other transport workers, an unofficial strike dynamic that drew into action huge numbers of hitherto unorganised unskilled workers, and the influence of a sizeable layer of local syndicalist activists led by Tom Mann, all contributed to the way in which explosive, militant and aggressive strike action could erupt and collective union organisation was able to gain a strong foothold.[19]

HARBINGERS 1907–10

While the Labour Revolt did not take off until 1910, there were important harbingers, with some of its main features presaged as early as 1907 by a dockers'

14. Ibid.: 171–84.
15. Board of Trade (1914: 64).
16. Charlesworth et al. (1996: 132).
17. Church (1987).
18. Hopkin (1989: 270–1).
19. Physick (1998: 2–3).

and carters' strike in Belfast, led by Jim Larkin. Larkin had arrived early that year in Belfast as an official of the British-based National Union of Dock Labourers (NUDL) headed by James Sexton, and within three months had launched a union organising drive on the docks – where the majority were casually employed and on low wages – that resulted by April in the establishment of an NUDL branch that included 2,900 of Belfast's 3,100 dockers. Between May and November 1907, Larkin waged a continuous series of individual struggles involving dockers, carters, coal-heavers and many other waterfront workers, which the employers eventually countered by locking out union members in a full-scale attempt to break union organisation. Larkin responded by bringing out the dockers and then carters en masse.

Although 2,600 British troops occupied the Belfast docks and strikebreaking labour was brought in from Britain and Southern Ireland, the strike grew in strength and succeeded in uniting Protestant and Catholic workers, with more than 100,000 workers marching down the Protestant Shankill Road in a demonstration involving both Orange and Nationalist flute bands. During several days in August the police baton-charged strikers and troops shot dead two people.[20] The strike was eventually broken by the intervention of the NUDL leader James Sexton, who crossed over from England to agree an unfavourable deal with the employers above the heads of the strikers, resulting in the euphoria of the strike being quickly replaced by bitter demoralisation. Yet despite defeat, the strike made a considerable advance in building the unity and solidarity of Belfast workers, and opened up a period of labour militancy that shook Ireland from one end to another, with Larkin subsequently leading strikes of Dublin carters in 1908 and Cork dockers in 1909 that won major concessions and built union organisation.

It was an approach that clashed with Sexton's preference for joint negotiations and compromise between employers and union leaders to settle industrial problems. By the end of 1908 Sexton and the moderate NUDL leadership felt threatened by Larkin's semi-autonomous Irish campaign, and suspended him from office. Larkin promptly responded by establishing a breakaway union, the Irish Transport and General Workers Union (ITGWU) with himself as general secretary. When James Connolly returned from America, he became the ITGWU's Belfast organiser.

Meanwhile, across the Irish Sea on the British 'mainland' in the autumn of 1907, members of the Amalgamated Society of Railway Servants (ASRS) voted overwhelmingly in favour of strike action in pursuit of a substantial improvement in pay, reduction in hours and union recognition. Lloyd George, at the time President of the Board of Trade, was apprehensive about the possible

20. Gray (1985: 59–60, 143, 154–68).

repercussions of a strike on the entire industrial life of the country, and intervened to find a way out of the impasse by meeting with the companies and unions separately. It resulted in an astonishing abnegation by the ASRS leadership, who agreed to the regulation of industrial relations and diffusion of militancy by a system of sectionally based Conciliation Boards that were to run for seven years, with no union recognition and only minimal, if any, improvements in pay and conditions.[21] Lloyd George and the Board of Trade also successfully intervened when strikes broke out by Lancashire cotton spinners over demands for increased pay in November 1907 and Clyde and Tyne engineering and shipbuilding workers over wage reductions in January 1908, in both cases securing compromise agreements.[22] In 1909 threatened strikes by miners in both the South Wales and Scottish coalfields over the way in which the government's Coal Mines Regulations Act, with its planned institution of an eight-hour working day, would impact on wage agreements, were averted with some slight modifications agreed.[23] Most of these disputes, which were restricted to workers who were already well organised, died away amidst the adverse economic conditions in which British industry had been suddenly plunged, with further action postponed until there was greater prospect of success.

But by early 1910, coinciding with the trade cycle becoming more favourable, there were early signs of a rising mood of labour unrest. Although the number of stoppages during 1910 (531) was not greatly in excess of the average of the ten previous years, the number of workers involved (515,165) was the highest recorded since the 1893 mining lockout.[24] The high figures for 1910 began to accumulate with unofficial miners' strikes over large sections of the Durham and Northumberland areas between January and April, involving 85,000 in the former and 30,000 in the latter. The strikes arose out of the way coal owners changed working patterns following the 1908 Eight Hours Act, including replacing two shifts with a three-shift system in many collieries that reduced wages. In both counties Miners' Federation advice to accept the new system was strongly opposed, and union officials were criticised for refusing strike pay.[25] Amidst the threat of the industrial economy of the whole North-East being paralysed, 12,000 South Wales and Monmouthshire miners joined the walkout, also fearing lower wages because of the regulatory regime. The union called a coalfield-wide ballot which voted to accept new

21. Bagwell (1963: 262–88).
22. Board of Trade, *Labour Gazette*, December 1907; February 1908.
23. Halévy (1999: 300–1).
24. Board of Trade, *Labour Gazette*, October 1915.
25. Mates (2016: 101–44).

negotiated agreements, and in turn both the Durham and Northumberland disputes ended.[26]

The second major dispute of 1910 was a cotton workers' industry-wide lockout. This was sparked off in June at a Lancashire cotton mill, in Shaw near Oldham, when all the workers walked out on strike over the dismissal of a union member who had refused to undertake work outside his duties. The dispute dragged on through the summer, eventually leading in September to an ultimatum from the owners that unless the workers agreed to arbitration, the Federation of Master Cotton Spinners would declare a general lockout of the whole trade affecting 700 mills. *The Times* reflected that if the employers 'overlook the disobedience of the man … they will be troubled with endless acts of insubordination of a similar character and they will lose control of their mills'.[27] While workers agreed to arbitration, they refused to go back to work unless their colleague was reinstated – and on 3 October, 102,000 mill workers were locked out, despite efforts by the Board of Trade's George Askwith to find a compromise deal. The cotton workers' cardroom union, helped with subventions from the General Federation of Trade Unions, paid strike pay to those locked out, thereby hardening the strikers' resolve, and finally the owners agreed to re-employ the discharged man, albeit at another mill, in order to bring the dispute to an end.[28]

Ignoring their ASRS union officials, 9,000 North-Eastern railway workers took strike action in July 1910 over a shunter being sacked for refusing to be assigned to a particular goods yard. Freight traffic around Newcastle was brought to a standstill, stopping the movement of coal to the ports and livestock to market. The drivers of passenger trains also walked out. According to *The Times*, the strikers let it be known that the *casus belli* was 'the general attitude displayed by [union] officials towards certain men throughout the northern district'.[29] Signalmen then joined the strike, severely disrupting rail services from London to Edinburgh through Newcastle, and the dispute spread as far as Carlisle and York, only being called off after the company agreed to a full inquiry into the case, although the sacking decision was not rescinded. As with the miners' dispute the previous winter, the railway workers had proved that organised labour could cause serious economic harm.[30] At the same time, faced with a number of local disputes in the principal centres of the shipbuilding industry, involving over 15,000 workers on the Clyde

26. Board of Trade, *Labour Gazette*, January 1911.
27. *The Times*, 29 September 1910.
28. White (1978: 112–25); Heffer (2017: 667–8); Askwith ([1920] 1974: 137–40).
29. *The Times*, 20 July 1910.
30. Board of Trade, *Labour Gazette*, August 1910; Heffer (2017: 664–6).

and Tyne, in September 1910 the employers imposed a national lockout of members of the Boilermakers' Society in federated shipyards. After abortive negotiations between the parties, the government intervened in the dispute, with Askwith once again called upon to try to resolve the dispute; eventually on 15 December both parties accepted an agreement that embodied new provisions for the settlement of differences.[31]

Another important dispute took place in May 1910 when dock workers in Newport took strike action in opposition to the threat by the shipping company Houlder Brothers to change the system of payment for loading ships from piece-rates to day rates. The company, strongly backed by the fiercely anti-union Shipping Federation, imported so-called 'free labour' to load and unload its vessels, and requested police protection for its strikebreakers.[32] Attempts by the imported 'blacklegs' to load Houlder's vessel was met by a strike on the docks which spread to the river wharves and other works in the town, and with mass picketing which led to outbursts of fighting.[33] But once the company had agreed to go to arbitration, which went in Houlder's favour, the local authority authorised the importation of 150 police officers to augment the local forces. And despite strikers voting by 2-1 against the arbitration terms that had been signed, they ended their dispute after national union official Ben Tillett demanded they return to work.[34]

While all these disputes were evidence of a growing mood of workers' resistance, it was to be the stunning victory achieved by one of the most exploited and unorganised groups of workers in the autumn of 1910, involving hundreds of women chain-makers in the Black Country, that was to provide a powerful object lesson of how conditions could be improved through strike action.

CRADLEY HEATH CHAIN-MAKERS' STRIKE: AUGUST–OCTOBER 1910

The 'Black Country' is an industrial area to the north-west of Birmingham (lying within parts of the modern-day metropolitan boroughs of Dudley, Sandwell, Wolverhampton and Walsall) whose name described the impact of industrialisation upon the area with its landscape scarred with the blackness of pits and furnaces and the air often choked in a thick black smoke.[35]

31. Cole (1948a: 320); Askwith (1920 [1974]: 141–2).
32. Weinberger (1991: 21–2).
33. 'Strike at Newport Dock', 19 May 1910, TNA/HO 45/10608/192.905/1; *The Times*, 19 May 1910.
34. Weinberger (1991: 26–9, 43, 230).
35. Barnsley (2010: 23).

Within this geographical area, Cradley Heath had become the centre of the chain-making industry in Britain, with heavy and higher-quality small chains produced by men in union-organised foundries and large workshops, while large numbers of unorganised women were employed in small cramped forges in outbuildings next to their home, using little more than a domestic hearth to produce small chains. The work was hot, physically demanding and extremely poorly paid – with women unable to earn 7 shillings a week (at a time when the Board of Trade estimated a male labourer's wage at over 25 shillings) for working a 54-hour week in unsanitary, often dangerous conditions, a classic example of a 'sweated' trade.[36] Children often accompanied their mothers to work, sitting in the corner of the workshop, and once old enough, helping in the production of the chain.

The Liberal government's 1909 Trade Boards Act legislated to establish and enforce minimum rates of pay for workers in sweated industries like the domestic chain trade. However employers, organised in a Chain Manufacturers Association (CMA), alongside 'middlemen' with whom each individual chain-maker had to negotiate a price for their work, attempted to subvert the new minimum wage due to come into effect in August 1910. This led to the strike and provided a test case for the Act's implementation. When the small all-grades National Federation of Women Workers (NFWW), led by its general secretary Mary Macarthur and to which some 400 women chain-makers in Cradley Heath belonged, demanded the minimum rates were enforced, employers in about 30 small factories in the areas responded with lockouts. Macarthur organised a mass meeting of all the domestic chain-makers in the area, including both those working in small factories or in their own backyard, which attracted some 1,000 women and children, and within days hundreds of women were on strike.[37]

Aware of the imminent hunger and hardship the strikers faced, Macarthur left the immediate running of the strike in the hands of local union organisers Julia Varley (who had recruited many of the women to the NFWW) and Charles Sitch, while she threw her energy and considerable talent into using every outlet available to raising support for the strike.[38] Leaflets, letters and numerous meetings were organised across the country, including ones where strikers themselves spoke with chains hung around their necks. Macarthur stimulated the interest of many national newspapers and even utilised the power of the cinema, which was in its infancy at this time, with a short *Pathé News* film that was shown in the principal music halls in London and in over

36. Sloane (2018: 166).
37. Barnsley (2010: 40–1); ibid.: 168.
38. Hunt (2019: 89–94).

Figure 3.1 Mary Macarthur, the National Federation of Women Workers' leader, addressing a crowd during the Cradley Heath chain-makers' strike of August–October 1910.

Credit: Black Country Living Museum.

500 picture theatres throughout the country, and seen by an estimated 10 million people.

At the same time, the women strikers themselves organised collections outside churches, chapels, football grounds, factories and trade union meetings, with over 200 trade union bodies donating to the strike fund by the second week of the strike.[39] So successful were attempts to raise support that a remarkable £4,000 (£482,000 today) was received by the end of the dispute, thereby making it possible to provide all the women with strike pay

39. Barnsley (2010: 42, 46).

of 5 shillings per week, as well as handouts of food and a milk ration for those with children.

The dispute gained momentum with daily strikers' processions with banners and bands, and by 3 September the numbers on strike increased to 800. A delegation of women chain-makers attended the annual TUC conference in Sheffield, and were invited to appeal for support from the platform, with a collection raising over £11 (£1,300 today).[40] The combination of strikers' defiance and the level of solidarity generated dented the employers' and middlemen's early confidence, creating divisions among them that led virtually all employers to concede the minimum wage of 2½ pence an hour. After ten weeks on strike the dispute ended victorious on 22 October 1910. NFWW membership in Cradley Heath grew from 400 before the strike to 1,700 by its end, and the huge surplus from the strike fund was used to build a local Workers' Institute. The victory also boosted the confidence of other local workers, with thousands of unskilled, poorly paid and unorganised male and female workers in factories and workshops across the Black Country subsequently able to win wages increases and build trade union organisation (Chapter 6).[41]

But if the chain-makers' strike acted as a harbinger to wider militancy, what decisively opened the floodgates, and would become the main springboard for the 1910–14 Labour Revolt, was the South Wales miners' strike.

SOUTH WALES MINERS' STRIKE: SEPTEMBER 1910–AUGUST 1911

Unlike engineering, the mining industry experienced no significant technological change before the First World War, due to a lack of capital and the difficulties of introducing mechanisation, together with a very conservative management. But there was centralisation of ownership, particularly in the exporting areas, such as South Wales, where the Cambrian Combine in the Rhondda Valley (formed in 1908 from companies owned by D.A. Thomas, Liberal MP in Cardiff)[42] exploited existing techniques to drive down labour costs and speed up production by greater physical exertion. These major changes established working practices that spread across the country after the introduction of the Eight Hours Act 1909 and the Wages Agreement of

40. Sloane (2018: 169).

41. Barnsley (2010: 45–8); Hunt (2019: 94–6).

42. Owner of the Cambrian Combine, Thomas was elected a Liberal MP for Merthyr Tydfil 1888–1910, where he topped the poll even when Keir Hardie was standing. In 1910 he won a seat in Cardiff.

1910. However, both local and national leaders of the Miners' Federation of Great Britain (MFGB) failed to mount any effective resistance, which was left to unofficial rank-and-file militancy.

In South Wales militancy centred on the Cambrian Combine coalfield where 70 miners at the Ely colliery refused to accept the proposed reduced piece-rates for working on difficult geological seams ('abnormal places'). When no agreement was reached, the company dramatically escalated the dispute by locking out all 950 miners at the pit on 1 September. This led to unofficial sympathy strikes by miners employed at other pits also owned by the Cambrian Combine. Although the owners had rejected proposals for compensatory payments, the moderate South Wales Miners' Federation (SWMF) leadership remained committed to the established Conciliation Agreements as a means of settling coalfield grievances, and William Abraham (known as 'Mabon'), SWMF President and Liberal-Labour MP for Rhondda since 1885, pleaded for a return to work, as notice of the action had not been served. But following a ballot, the SWMF executive committee was forced to agree to call out on official strike 12,000 miners employed by the Cambrian Combine, commencing on 1 November.

Meanwhile, in the neighbouring Aberdare Valley, another particularly bitter unofficial dispute was precipitated by the employers' withdrawal of the customary practice of allowing miners to take home broken pieces of timber for use as firewood, along with a variety of other grievances relating to wages and conditions, including the 'abnormal places' payments.[43] By the end of the first week in November there were 12,000 miners on strike in the Rhondda Valley and 11,000 in the Aberdare Valley; by early December up to 30,000 miners were either on strike or locked out in the South Wales coalfield.[44]

Despite the widening of the dispute, the SWMF leadership were able to use their influence to secure a coalfield-wide ballot vote rejecting a general sympathetic strike (by 76,978 to 44,868) to support the Cambrian Combine strikers, in favour of a financial levy instead. Workers who had taken sympathy action, and those in the Aberdare Valley, returned to work in December, leaving the Cambrian miners to fight on alone.

As noted in Chapter 2, syndicalist ideas had developed within some South Wales ILP branches which aligned with the new Plebs League that had been built by ex-Ruskin College young miners who circulated revolutionary industrial literature.[45] Prominent syndicalist figures within this network played an influential role in the miners' strike. These included Noah Ablett, Noah

43. Mor-O'Brien ([n.d.] 2019); Barclay (1978).
44. Arnot (1954: 60).
45. Holton (1973a: 120; 1976: 80–1).

Rees, secretary of the Cambrian Combine Strike Committee, W.H. Mainwaring and Tom Smith, and two other members of the strike committee; and W.F. Hay, who with Ablett wrote articles on the strike for *Industrial Syndicalist* that were widely distributed.[46] A.J. Cook (future general secretary of the MFGB) was also involved. There was evidence of a fairly close rapport between this group of militants and Tom Mann and the ISEL.[47]

Apart from Mann himself, who was a constant visitor to the Rhondda Valley in early November,[48] other syndicalist figures present in the early phases of the dispute were 'Big Bill' Haywood of the American IWW, a former miner who addressed large meetings on the same platform as Mann in both Tonypandy and Aberdare, and Antoinette Cauvin, widely known as Madame Sorgue, who was connected with the French anarcho-syndicalist *Confédération Générale du Travail* and attended a meeting of the Aberdare Strike Committee.[49]

Faced with coal owners' plans to utilise 'blackleg' miners and safety and maintenance men still working in the pits to break the strike, the Cambrian Combine Strike Committee, made up of representatives from the pit lodges, won support at mass meetings of up to 10,000 miners to mount mass pickets and demonstrations. As one of the strike leaders, William John, told a mass meeting in Tonypandy: 'The Combine Workmen's Committee will strain every nerve to bring the fight to a successful issue, and it is our intention to stop any man from doing any work at the collieries.'[50] The strikers' strategy concentrated on stopping all 'blacklegs' as well as preventing colliery officials, including winding men, enginemen and stokers who were members of three other unions, from attending to the ventilating and water-pumping machinery, so as to force management to concede their demands under threat of flooding the works.[51]

Pickets took up positions at street corners, with the main body of strikers congregating at the entrances to the various pits, thereby making it practically impossible for anyone to get to work unobserved, and with an impassable barrier of bodies. 'Blacklegs' were harangued, ostracised and sometimes attacked in the streets or at their homes and frog-marched back home. The

46. *Industrial Syndicalist*, November 1910; February 1911.
47. Holton (1973a: 149). Mann spoke in Tonypandy on the eve of the 1910 strike, and again in the coalfield in the company of 'Big Bill' Haywood, leader of the Western Federation of Miners, the strongest union affiliated to the American IWW, who was touring Britain: Haywood (1929: 234–6).
48. *Justice*, 5 and 12 November 1910; 14 January 1911.
49. *The Times*, 15 November 1910; *Western Mail*, 15 November 1910.
50. Cited in Arnot (1967: 183).
51. Pitt (1987: 7).

Figure 3.2 Tonypandy miners, members of the South Wales Miners' Federation, involved in the protracted 1910–11 Cambrian Combine miners' strike.
Credit: Levi Ladd © Amgueddfa Cymru - National Museum Wales.

letters 'B', 'BL' and Scab' were painted on the doors of houses, while crowds of pickets, including women and children, threw stones to smash the windows of the empty homes.[52] Likewise trains bringing in strikebreaking labour from other areas were intercepted, their windows broken and the occupants sent home. *The Times* noted the successful use of mass picketing to stop non-strikers:

> ... so well had the strikers placed their pickets that it was impossible for any ['blackleg'] to gain access to the colliery without being detected. When one of these men was seen on his way to work, with his 'jack' of food, the strikers formed a cordon around him very much in the same way as a scrummage is formed in Rugby football. By this method of 'persuasion' man after man was turned back amid more or less excitement, which was proportionate to the amount of effort which he made to force his way through the crowd.[53]

Mass picketing succeeded in halting production in all the local pits except one – the Glamorgan Colliery in Llwynypia, which employed over 3,000 men

52. Evans (1911: 84); *The Times*, 8 November 1910.
53. *The Times*, 8 November 1910.

and where about 60 officials and 'blacklegs' kept the machinery running. The colliery was important to both strikers and the mine owners as its powerhouse controlled a huge pumping plant that kept the mines free of water and enabled the maintenance of a minimum level of production. It had been transformed into a near fortress by the general manager of the Cambrian Combine, Leonard Llewellyn, who had arranged to have stationed at the mine a large contingent of police – including police who were drafted in from Swansea, Bristol, Cardiff and elsewhere – under the personal command of the Chief Constable of Glamorgan, Captain Lionel Lindsay. The police were placed at the service of the mine companies and responded ferociously to mass picketing attempts to stop the pit operating. When some 9,000 miners marched from the Mid-Rhondda Athletic Ground and encircled the pit at 10.30 pm on Monday 7 November, Lindsay ordered his officers to draw their batons and to charge the crowd, resulting in sharp skirmishes between the two groups that lasted until midnight, before the police were finally able to clear the roadway and disperse the pickets.

Alarmed by the events of the evening, and fearing that the police would not be able to repel further attacks, the Chief Constable immediately telegraphed the War Office to request troops be sent to the area, to which an order was given to dispatch two companies of soldiers. On learning of this development early in the morning of Tuesday 8 November, the Home Secretary Winston Churchill countermanded the order, stopping the infantry at Swindon and the cavalry at Cardiff, and instead dispatched 70 mounted and 200 foot constables of the Metropolitan Police to reinforce existing police forces. Yet even though Churchill did not specifically agree to the deployment of troops at this stage, he made it clear they were to remain in reserve 'unless it is clear that the police reinforcements are unable to cope with the situation'.[54]

Later that day there was the renewal of mass picketing outside the Llwynypia pit, with a demonstration of between 7,000–9,000 miners and their supporters, including women and children. Following some stone throwing that shattered powerhouse windows, the Chief Constable ordered several baton-charges by the police, including mounted officers. The battle, with fierce hand-to-hand fighting, lasted for over two hours, and led to numerous casualties, with many strikers injured from head wounds inflicted by police batons.

The Times reported that all members of the crowd became targets for the police batons irrespective of whether or not they had actually committed an

54. Telegram from Churchill to Lindsay, 8 November 1911, cited in Smith (1988: 122).

offence: 'That the police are using their batons with effect is obvious from the number of bandaged and it is a case of "whenever you see a head hit it".'[55] According to another pro-employer contemporary account, pickets were 'struck down like logs' with 'scores, if not hundreds, of rioters prone on the ground or staggering along the road groaning from the pains of injured shoulders, arms and heads'.[56] One miner, Samuel Rays, was killed by blows to the head by a blunt instrument, almost certainty a police baton. Ironically the police were forced to order 300 batons to replace those broken or lost in the battle.[57]

Repulsed and driven back once again from the Llwynypia pit by the police, the strikers and their supporters expressed their frustration and bitterness with three hours of rioting, damaging 63 shops along the whole length of the nearby Tonypandy town centre. Shop fronts were smashed and goods of every description, including drapery, millinery and grocery provisions, littered the streets, with looters carrying away rolls of cloth, hats, umbrellas, bundles of clothing and even shop fittings.[58] The Cambrian Combine Strike Committee played no active part in the looting, although they confessed their inability to control their supporters if 'blacklegs' were imported into the district.[59] Syndicalists and socialists excused, but did not condone the attacks on shopkeepers by many local supporters as well as strikers.[60] Yet it would be a mistake to dismiss the riot as 'an orgy of naked anarchy' by a rampaging outcast mob of drunken youths, drunks and strangers as *The Times* and others claimed.[61]

Of particular interest was the purposeful way shops 'were smashed systematically but not indiscriminately'.[62] The shopkeepers whose stores were ransacked were 'bastions of the local business community'[63] who were known to be sympathetic to the local coal owners, some renting out houses in which strikers lived, while other individual shops were left untouched, notably that of chemist Willie Llewellyn who had been a famous Welsh international rugby footballer. The crowd 'expressed contempt and resentment rather than greed and fear ... The amount of looting was not so important as the display

55. *The Times*, 9 November 1910.
56. Evans (1911: 47).
57. Ibid.: 48.
58. *Daily Mirror*, 10 November 1910; Evans and Maddox (2010: 76).
59. Macready (1924: 146–7).
60. Smith (1988: 118).
61. *The Times*, 9 and 10 November 1910; Smith (1980: 167).
62. Smith (1988: 114).
63. Pitt (1987: 5).

of bravado enacted on the streets in a festival atmosphere.'[64] As one haberdasher recalled:

> People were seen inside … handing goods out … afterwards walking in the Square wearing various articles of clothing which had been stolen and asking each other how they looked. They were not a bit ashamed and they actually had the audacity to see how things fitted them in the shop itself.[65]

In response, Churchill authorised the dispatch of a squadron of the 18th Hussars to the South Wales coalfield under the command of Major-General Sir Nevil Macready, who was given control of both the police and military to finally restore 'order'. The two-day riots, in which nearly 80 police and over 500 miners and supporters had been injured, attracted national news and the name of Tonypandy was to become notorious throughout the labour movement.

Churchill's role in allowing troops to be sent to Tonypandy has been of much historical contention, with Churchill himself attempting to create his own legend of countermanding the troop movements, instead dispatching Metropolitan Police forces to the area.[66] Likewise some historians[67] have argued that he directed the troops to 'assume a policing role,'[68] with the military not directly involved in quelling disturbances so as to avoid strikers coming 'up against the rifles with consequences of the utmost gravity'.[69]

Nonetheless, alongside the many hundreds of officers from the Metropolitan and other police forces that were drafted into the Rhondda and Aberdare Valleys, Churchill's overall deployment of two squadrons of Hussars and two infantry companies constituted a formidable, and in many respects decisive, force, aimed at intimidating and overawing the miners. The coalfields remained under military occupation for months, which prevented the strikers from using mass picketing to prevent 'blackleg' labour and safety officials from working, thereby ensuring the employers' victory.[70] General Macready imposed severe constraints on picketing by informing the strike committee that if more than six miners were present on any one picket line this would

64. Smith (1988: 114).
65. *Draper's Record*, 19 November 1910, cited in ibid.: 126–7.
66. *Colliery Strike Disturbances in South Wales: Correspondence and Report, November 1910*, Parliamentary Papers, Cd. 5568, HMSO, 1911.
67. Mor-O'Brien (1994; [n.d.] 2019); Sheldon (2013).
68. Morgan (1987: 47).
69. Addison (1992: 143).
70. Smith (1988: 111–12).

constitute obstruction and the police would move them on, enabling him to claim that by the end of November 'picketing had practically ceased'.[71]

In reality, sporadic clashes continued for several months, with a number of instances in which troops were utilised to prevent effective picketing. On Monday 21 November the signal box at Llwynypia was targeted by about 400–500 strikers in an attempt to stop incoming trains, allow scrutiny of passengers and remove scab labour. That evening there was the 'battle of Penygraig', a village near Tonypandy, as a crowd hurled stones and sticks at the police, who repeatedly made baton charges. Strikers ran around a warren of terraced streets attacking the police from the rear and the sides, with many women joining the strikers and from bedroom windows showering buckets of hot water and household utensils onto the police. Attacks and counter-charges continued for four hours with considerable injuries on both sides until police reinforcements arrived followed by two detachments of Hussars who quelled the protest.[72]

The presence of soldiers was stepped up with military pickets posted at all railway stations to prevent pickets searching trains for scabs. Mass picketing at the Gilfach Goch pit on 25 November had to be abandoned when a large detachment of troops was sent to allow 18 colliery officials to enter the pit to restart the pumps and end its flooding.[73] According to one of the Aberdare strikers, Wil Jon Edwards:

> ... our area was invaded by soldiers ... we believed that the soldiers had been sent to intimidate the people and, in consequence, to break the strike ... they were in our valley and in the Rhondda, and what with them and the police, the area was like an armed camp. The soldiers and their horses were billeted on the colliery owners' properties, and, from these centres, they embarked on regular patrols to look for trouble, and to make it, if they could not find it.[74]

Keir Hardie, the local Labour MP for Merthyr Tydfil, who raised the conduct of the police in the House of Commons, complained they had bludgeoned pickets in a 'reign of terror',[75] with the use of troops amounting to 'Russification' similar to that exercised by the oppressive Tsarist regime. His demand for an inquiry into their conduct was refused by Churchill. Further

71. Macready (1924: 153).
72. Evans (1911: 90–5).
73. Ibid.: 99.
74. Jon Edwards (1956: 223).
75. *Labour Leader*, 2 December 1910.

clashes took place in March and April 1911, with the last major confrontation occurring on 25 July at the Ely pit, when a crowd of 3,000-plus miners, from positions on the mountainside above the pit, threw stones at police escorting a 'blackleg' into work. They were supported by women who collected loose stones in buckets and their aprons to provide relays of ammunition. Police baton-charges failed to dislodge the pickets until 80 soldiers arrived from the Somerset Light Infantry, armed with fixed bayonets and ball cartridge.[76]

The Cambrian Combine strike came to an end in August 1911 following a ten-month battle. While in the earlier phases of the dispute few arrests were made, between December 1910 and September 1911 over 500 alleged offenders were brought before magistrates,[77] with many, including two strike committee leaders, receiving prison sentences. The miners and their families found themselves at war not only with the coal owners and police and military, but also with their own local and national union leaders. At the request of the SWMF officials, a Miners' Federation of Great Britain Special Conference was held in January 1911, which confirmed the proposed terms of settlement and to 'accept no further responsibility in this dispute'. Despite this, the Cambrian miners continued on strike throughout the whole summer and autumn of 1911.[78] But while the MFGB provided weekly financial support of £3,000 to supplement the small amounts of strike pay that had been provided by the SWMF during the first few months of the strike, they resisted demands raised by South Wales militants (after the police and military had frustrated their attempts to close down the Cambrian collieries) for the dispute to be escalated into national strike action for a guaranteed minimum wage for miners in every coalfield.[79]

At a mass meeting of over 5,000 strikers on Wednesday 22 March 1911 the executive council of the MFGB and two members of the SWMF executive were strongly criticised for trying to persuade the strikers to accept a compromise settlement based on terms previously negotiated in October 1910. Rejection was overwhelmingly confirmed in a ballot by 7,041 to 309 (although 5,000 did not vote).[80] Another attempt at ending the strike in May was also rejected. As a consequence, the strikers were left isolated by the union leadership, with financial support from the MFGB withdrawn in July 1911. Eventually in August 1911, following a decision by the SWMF officials to recommend a return to work, the strikers went back on terms which were

76. Evans (1911: 111).
77. Ibid.: 208.
78. Arnot (1954: 76).
79. Pitt (1987: 9).
80. Evans and Maddox (2010: 146).

no better than those offered at the beginning of the strike, with some 3,000 men losing their jobs.

Yet despite its defeat, the Cambrian strike proved to be of fundamental importance in generalising the issue of special payments for miners working in 'abnormal places' into the campaign for a guaranteed national minimum wage, which became the rallying cry for miners across Britain's coalfields and paved the way for the national strike of 1912 (Chapter 5).[81]

It also laid the basis for a broader campaign to challenge the moderate SWMF leadership that miners held mainly responsible for the defeat, with the establishment in May 1911 of the Unofficial Reform Committee (URC). It was this Committee which later produced the seminal syndicalist pamphlet *The Miners' Next Step* (1912) that provided a devastating critique of union officialdom and called for the reconstruction of the miners' union on 'fighting lines' with the objective of workers' control of the industry (Chapter 9). The change in temper became evident in October 1911 when elections were held for the three places on the SWMF executive council, with the sitting moderates voted out in favour of URC militants, including Noah Ablett and Noah Rees (and in 1913 Frank Hodges and William John of the URC joined the same body).

The South Wales miners' strike also became the main springboard for a broader industrial insurgency in Britain as a new phase of unrest broke out within the transport and railway industries.

81. Edwards (1938: 49).

4

Spirit of Revolt

The year 1911 saw unprecedented levels of workers' struggle sweep across Britain with 903 strikes involving almost 962,000 workers, and with an increase in quantity leading to an accompanying qualitative change in the nature of struggle towards mass insurgency. Although the majority of disputes involved comparatively small numbers of workers, 22 large strikes involving either over 5,000 workers and/or 'losing' at least 100,000 working days accounted for 67 per cent of the total number of workers involved. Nearly half of workers affected were transport workers, with 400,000 involved in the strike wave that took place between June and August in what was the second main phase of the Labour Revolt.[1] It began with insurgent strike action by 120,000 seamen, dockers and other workers employed on various waterside jobs, which closed most of Britain's principal ports and led to generalised strikes in Hull, Salford/Manchester and Cardiff. This was followed by an all-out strike on the hitherto unaffected London docks involving 77,000. Meanwhile unofficial strike action by Liverpool railwaymen spread across the country leading to the first ever national railway strike involving 140,000, and a Liverpool general transport strike involving 66,000. As the Webbs noted: 'Suddenly ... the pot boiled over. There was a spirit of revolt in the Labour world.'[2] And as the militancy and revolt gathered pace, union leaders found themselves either swept aside or desperately trying to 'ride the wave'.[3]

WATERSIDE TRANSPORT WORKERS' STRIKES: JUNE–AUGUST 1911

The first bout of waterside transport strikes began in June, involving the small and weak National Sailors' and Firemen's Union (NSFU) under the leadership of its President, Havelock Wilson (who had been a Liberal MP between 1906 and 1910). Seamen's real wages were falling, but the NSFU was confronted by an extremely belligerent employers' body, the Shipping Federation, which

1. Board of Trade (1912: 11).
2. Webb and Webb (1920: 528).
3. Newsinger (2015: 20).

operated a permanent strikebreaking organisation transporting scabs ('free labour') to ports across the country, and insisted on the right to employ only those who accepted the Federation's 'ticket' to work as directed, including with non-unionised crew.[4] In the face of such well-coordinated antagonists, Wilson felt there was no alternative but to call a 'do-or-die' national strike with the aim of attempting to force the employers to recognise the union for collective bargaining over pay and conditions.[5]

Exceptionally busy summer business trading, low unemployment and consequent tightened labour markets, and the coronation of King George V on 22 June with its anticipated influx of large numbers of overseas dignitaries by sea, provided favourable conditions for strike action. But also important was the union organising campaigns throughout the winter and spring of 1910–11, with meetings at all the principal ports in support of the Seamen's Union's programme of demands, which successfully stimulated a combative mood among the largely unorganised workforce. Tom Mann (who had been one of the leaders of the 1889 London docks' strike), newly returned from Australia, was employed by Wilson (whom he had previously helped establish an international federation of ship, dock and riverside workers) as an organiser in the official NSFU campaign. It was a 'marriage of convenience' given their contrasting political philosophies; the moderate Wilson valued Mann's outstanding talents in helping to secure union recognition, while Mann valued Wilson's official backing for his advocacy of industrial unionism involving a federation of the numerous separate waterside transport unions.[6]

The second issue of the Industrial Syndicalist Education League's *Industrial Syndicalist* contained a letter from the veteran dockers' leader Ben Tillett of the London-based Dock, Wharf, Riverside and General Labourers' Union (DWRGWU) urging support for a federation.[7] March 1911 saw the formal inauguration of a National Transport Workers' Federation (NTWF) with 17 affiliated unions, embracing the NSFU, two major dockers' unions – Tillett's DWRGWU (whose main strength outside London was in the Bristol channel ports) and James Sexton's National Union of Dock Labourers (NUDL) (mainly based in Liverpool, Glasgow, Scotland and Ireland) – and other unions with interests in the docks.

4. Powell (1950); Saluppo (2019).
5. *The Seaman*, June 1911.
6. Torr (1956: 37); Hebert (1975: 164).
7. *Industrial Syndicalist*, August 1910.

Federation supporters carried out intensive publicity and mass union recruitment campaigns aimed at building up workers' organisational strength.[8] Mann, already working with the seamen's union in 1910 and the first half of 1911, agreed to devote part of his energies to assisting Tillett (with whom he had helped win the 1889 victory of London dockers) and the DWRGWU (of which he had been elected its first full-time President in 1890–92). During his nationwide speaking campaign thousands of dockers and seamen came into contact with Mann's syndicalist case for industrial unionism and 'direct action' through workers' own power rather than through Parliament.[9] Such emphasis blended well with the philosophy of Tillett who, while by no means an out-and-out syndicalist, nevertheless publicly expressed commitment to industrial unionism and vigorous non-parliamentary class conflict.[10]

Under the auspices of the NTWF, an active union organising movement in the ports and docks went side-by-side with the vigorous national strike mobilisation of the NSFU. Faced with a casual labour system with more applicants than jobs, both seamen's and dockers' unions needed to secure a closed shop to restrict labour supply to union members only. As long as employers could choose non-union labour, the unions were powerless to demand wage rises or better conditions, and therefore were unable to attract more than a small percentage of workers into membership.[11] Evidence that the agitational activities of Mann, Wilson, Tillett and others began to bear fruit became evident in April 1911 when *The Seaman* reported over 800 had joined the Manchester branch of the NSFU during the previous twelve months,[12] and in June the recently established Salford DWRGWU branch announced it had recruited 1,200 members.[13]

Wilson hoped for an international seamen's strike as a means of preventing the International Shipping Federation using foreign 'blacklegs' to defeat strikes. But although a recently formed International Committee of Seafarers' Unions agreed to present simultaneous claims in several European countries over wages, manning and union recognition, and to call for an international strike on 14 June, it went largely unheeded apart from in Britain.[14] Moreover, the National Transport Workers' Federation decided, with less than a week before the proposed strike's scheduled start, not to participate with the NFTW's secretary Robert Williams dismissing it as 'a gambler's last

8. Marsh and Ryan (1989: 55).
9. *Docker's Record*, September 1910.
10. Schneer (1982: 155, 159).
11. Ives (1986: 18–19).
12. *The Seaman*, April 1911.
13. *Dockers' Record*, June 1911.
14. Clegg (1985: 33).

chance'.[15] Tillett's DWRGWU's attention was focused primarily on London, and the moderate Sexton's NUDL was even less inclined to join the seamen's ambitious strike plans.[16]

Nonetheless, willingness to take on the port employers was so strong that, although the strike had officially been planned to commence on 14 June, seamen in Southampton on the White Star Line's *RMS Olympic* jumped the gun and stopped work on 9 June.[17] Each day afterwards the strike spread across the country, and by 20 June had affected 20 ports, including Goole, Hull, Grimsby, Glasgow, Newcastle, Liverpool, Salford, Bristol, Cardiff, Newport and Belfast, although not initially London. Significantly, large numbers of non-union seamen responded as enthusiastically to the strike call as NSFU members and flocked to join the union in order to improve their pay and conditions and constrain the autocratic powers of managers and foremen.

Despite Wilson's willingness to compromise with employers over wages and conditions in return for union recognition and establishment of a Conciliation Board, the situation rapidly escalated when seamen called on dockers (themselves often employed by the same shipping companies) to take solidarity action in defiance of their own reluctant national DWRGLU, NUDL and NTWF union officials (despite previous organising campaigns). Wilson blamed agitators, noting that 'when working men find they have some power, it is easy for anyone to encourage them to go beyond what is reasonable'.[18] Rank-and-file dockers' pressure, exercised in defiance, played a crucial role in this escalation. Yet as the ILP's *Labour Leader* reported:

> The original purpose of their strike was purely sympathetic, but the completeness of response to the cry 'stop work' emboldened them to advance demands of their own. An extraordinary feature of this phase of the dispute was the keenness of the non-Union men. Members of the Dockers' Union awaited instructions from their officials, but the non-Unionists joined the revolt at the first appeal of the seamen. The strike-fever swept the docks with the rapidity and all-inclusiveness of a prairie-fire.[19]

15. Mogridge (1961: 381).
16. Wilson (2008: 268–9).
17. Marsh and Ryan (1989: 55).
18. Havelock Wilson to Hermann Jochade (general secretary of the International Transport Workers' Federation), 6 July 1911, MRC MSS/159/3/B63, cited in Ives (1986: 51–2).
19. *Labour Leader*, 7 July 1911.

Solidarity action quickly developed its own dynamic, spreading to all-out strike action by dockers and carters, as well as many other groups of workers employed in the dock districts. Across the country some 120,000 waterside transport workers became directly involved at one stage or another in a series of overlapping strikes between June and August.[20] Within two weeks the Shipping Federation found it could not cope when seamen's strikes hit every major port at the same time, thereby undermining its ability to supply sufficient 'free labour' strikebreaking resources, and in a context in which no one had foreseen the level of support given to the seamen by other transport workers.[21] Shipowners were forced to grant substantial increases in pay and standardise local rates, and grant union recognition to the NSFU (although only Liverpool and Cardiff established effective collective bargaining arrangements), with national union membership rising from 20,000 in 1911 to 60,000 by 1912.[22] And union leaders generally were forced to support dockers' and other waterside workers' strikes which also won major gains, with the NUDL – whose national membership rose from 12,000 in 1911 to 24,000 by 1912 – transformed into a major presence in many ports with full union recognition and representation on joint employer-union bodies.[23]

A flavour of the strike movement can be gleaned from some of the main sites of conflict in Liverpool, Hull, Salford/Manchester and Cardiff.

Liverpool

Tom Mann went to Liverpool on the day before the seamen struck work, following an invitation from Wilson, where he quickly formed a strike committee and addressed mass meetings. The striking seamen were joined by members of the National Union of Ships' Stewards, Cooks, Butchers and Bakers, resulting in united action of workers 'above' and 'below' the ships' decks. Some employers (including Cunard, White Star Line and the Booth Line) quickly conceded considerable wage increases and recognition of both the NSFU and Ships' Stewards Union, because their profit derived from both passenger lines and cargo transport.

But these agreements did not apply to the smaller shipping firms which were intent on keeping wages at the old levels, and whose hostility was buttressed by membership of the Shipping Federation and its strikebreaking system. In order to increase pressure on smaller non-federated shipping

20. Board of Trade (1912: 114–15).
21. Mogridge (1961: 382); Powell (1950: 22).
22. Powell (1950: 26); Marsh and Ryan (1989: 57, 306).
23. Coates and Topham (1994: 374, 378).

companies, the strike committee under Mann's chairmanship issued 50,000 copies of a manifesto calling on all Merseyside dock workers, carters and other waterfront workers to refuse to handle goods of firms affected in solidarity with the seamen.[24] The objective 'was to unite the transport workers on the sea with those on the land'.[25]

Initially the NUDL executive committee, whose Liverpool (predominately Catholic) membership of about 7,000 were confined to smaller firms berthed at the south end of the docks, had been reluctant to become directly involved. However, there was a surge of rank-and-file sympathetic action outside of union structures, with *The Pointer*, a vessel crewed by scab firemen, blockaded by non-union dockers who (acting without any authority from the NUDL), refused to touch the cargo, and demanded the removal of the scabs and reinstatement of the sacked union crew.[26] Sexton and the Mersey Quay and Railway Carters' Union (predominately Protestant) agreed to give official support to Mann's call for the 'blacking' of all goods affected by the seamen's dispute.[27] Within a few days this solidarity action forced most of the remaining shipping employers to concede a general wage increase of 10 shillings per month.[28] Liverpool's Head Constable noted that: 'the failure of the Shipping Federation to stand out against the men's demands by importing labour proves pretty well that there is no free labour available'.[29]

On 28 June there was further escalation which took the strike committee by surprise, when thousands of north-end Liverpool dockers (previously a weak spot for NUDL organisation), carters and other dock workers took strike action, partly in solidarity with the seamen, but then for their own demands for better pay and conditions and union recognition. Within a few days there were about 15,000 dockers involved, with hundreds of recruits joining the union each day.[30] And about 2,000 of the newly victorious seamen now walked out again in sympathy with the dockers as a way of reciprocating the support dockers had provided them.[31]

An extended joint strike committee now embraced representatives from the unions of seamen, dockers (including Sexton himself), ships' stewards (including ISEL syndicalists Frank Pearce and Joe Cotter), carters and the

24. Taplin (2012: 27).
25. *Liverpool Daily Post and Mercury*, 15 June 1911.
26. Ibid., 20 June 1911.
27. Holton (1973a: 317).
28. Board of Trade (1912: 22).
29. [TNA]/HO 45/10654/212470/1a, cited in Physick (1998: 20).
30. Board of Trade (1912: 22).
31. Ibid.; *The Times*, 29 June 1911.

Liverpool Trades Council (including another syndicalist James Murphy).[32] The *Liverpool Daily Post* was amazed at the 'incredible solidarity' bringing together not only different sections and different unions but also unionists and non-unionists: '"All hands" throwing sectionalism to the winds and joining hand-in-hand for the furtherance of the common cause. It was a remarkable – even historic – event in trade union progress.'[33] As *Labour Leader* reported:

> It was no longer a strike of the seamen with the dockers supporting them; it was a strike of the dockers with the seamen supporting them. And the seamen stood by the dockers as loyally as the dockers stood by the seamen.[34]

With the docks at a standstill and with all waterfront workers solidly behind the dock labourers, the employers were forced to back down and make an interim port-wide *White Book Agreement* to grant full union recognition to the NUDL, with a virtual closed shop, union rates of pay and a joint employer-union body to negotiate wages and conditions. But an attempt by strike committee leaders to obtain a return to work before the new port-working rules had been implemented was greeted with considerable opposition by many rank-and-file dockers who had flocked into the unions.

Even Mann himself, who 'was the darling of the proletariat of the entire city',[35] could not induce the workers to return to work, and was heckled and shouted down, with dockers tearing up copies of the strike committee's manifesto and 'flinging them contemptuously about the Dock Road'.[36] It took a week of mass meetings addressed by Mann, Sexton and Tillett (representing the NTWF) to overcome this resistance,[37] and to convince the men that strike action would be resumed if the employers refused to abide by the agreement.[38]

Such developments finally ended the waterfront dispute in Liverpool on 4 August, with both the seamen's and dockers' unions recognised by the employers and union conditions and rates of pay successfully negotiated. It resulted in an enormous increase in union membership, with the local NUDL

---

32. Holton (1976: 90; 1973b: 133); Coates and Topham (1994: 383).
33. *Liverpool Daily Post and Mercury*, 21 June 1911.
34. *Labour Leader*, 7 July 1911.
35. Hyndman (1912: 464).
36. *Liverpool Daily Post and Mercury*, 1 July 1911.
37. Physick (1998: 62–3); Taplin (1986: 91–2).
38. *Liverpool Daily Post and Mercury*, 3 July 1911.

growing by 17,000 and the NSFU by 4,500.[39] During this period a growing number of different other groups of workers across Liverpool also took strike action, partly in support of the dock workers and partly in support of their own wage claims, including tugboat men on the River Mersey, coopers and labourers at the Stanley Dock tobacco warehouse, scalers at Wallasey Ferries, Cotton Exchange porters, oil workers, and young women workers at Walton rubber works. And just as the conference of shipowners and dockers was reaching its final agreement, a strike by railwaymen spread to engulf the city in generalised strikes of even greater proportions (see below).

Hull

Striking seamen in Goole were joined by seamen from the nearby totally unorganised port of Hull on 20 June. Mass picketing by strikers and their supporters involved an attack on 50 'blacklegs' from Cardiff who had been brought in by the Shipping Federation to unload cargoes and were being escorted through the town by police. A striker was seriously wounded by gunfire from a strikebreaking cargo ship,[40] and 500 Metropolitan Police reinforcements were dispatched to the city to bolster the local force in an attempt to subdue the unrest.[41] By 27 June there was a sympathetic strike by all dock workers in the port, with picketing extended to other workers in Hull, including railwaymen (acting without official union authority) and timber, cement and flour-milling workers.[42]

A joint strike committee, chaired by a young syndicalist-inclined docker John Burn, represented all sections involved (the DWRGWU emerging as the major union on the waterfront).[43] The mood of insurgent direct action, combined with total hostility towards mediation initiatives, meant shipowners who wanted to unload cargo had to apply to strike leaders for authorisation. This was usually rejected with permits to allow goods through the picket lines only issued for use by hospitals and workhouses. It was a powerful display of union power. An estimated 300,000 pounds of perishable cargoes were held up by the strike, resulting in grain stocks running dangerously low.[44]

George Askwith rushed to Hull, and was told by a shipowner that the dockers and other transport workers had new unknown leaders with whom

39. Mann (1923: 277-8); ibid., 4 July 1911.
40. *Hull Daily Mail*, 21 June 1911.
41. 'Shipping Strike Disturbance at Hull', 28 June 1911, TNA/HO 45/10648/210.615/9; Brooker (1979).
42. *Hull Daily News*, 29 June 1911; *Hull Daily Mail*, 28 June 1911.
43. Taplin (1986: 84); Coates and Topham (1994: 353–4).
44. Weinberger (1991: 72); Coates and Topham (1994: 354).

employers were at a loss to deal with.[45] Although he helped the shipowners to negotiate a settlement with the seamen, this was held up when it was discovered that the dockers who had initially struck in sympathy with the seamen, and many of whom were not union members, now wanted a wage increase for themselves. Askwith described the uproar which greeted attempts by the strike committee to seek endorsement of the settlement:

> It was estimated there were 15,000 people there when the leaders began their statement. They announced a settlement; and before my turn came, an angry roar of 'No!' rang out: and 'Let's fire the docks!' from outskirts where men ran off. [46]

Fears that a ship was being unloaded led men to rush to the docks and rioting followed involving about 2,000 dockers, during which the windows of the Shipping Federation, offices of Wilson Line and depot of the 'Free Labour Association' were smashed. A pitched battle lasting several hours ensued, involving police baton-charges and strikers launching fusillades of stones and bricks.[47] Askwith reported the presence of a mood of almost revolutionary intensity in the city, adding that 'the union leaders have little control and are now frightened'.[48] A town councillor, who had been in Paris during the 1871 Commune, told him he 'had never seen anything like this, and … not known that there were such people in Hull – women with hair streaming and half nude, reeling through the streets smashing and destroying'.[49]

In response, Churchill placed two squadrons of cavalry (up to 400 soldiers) on standby,[50] although Askwith eventually managed to broker a deal involving concessions for all sections of workers, including a wage increase of halfpenny an hour for dockers, that resulted in a return to work.

Salford and Manchester

On 27 June, following the seamen's walkout, dockers employed at the Manchester Ship Canal also ceased work.[51] At a series of mass meetings the syndicalist Salford Borough Councillor and furnishing trade union organ-

45. Askwith ([1920] 1974: 149).
46. Ibid.: 150.
47. TNA/HO 45/10649/210.615; *Hull Daily Mail*, 30 June 1911; *Daily Mirror*, 30 June 1911.
48. Askwith to Board of Trade, 2 July 1911, cited in Holton (1976: 93).
49. Askwith ([1920] 1974: 150).
50. Brooker (1979: 20).
51. Board of Trade (1912: 21).

iser A.A. Purcell, and local NFSU secretary, R.H. Capner, urged dockers who had already agreed to refuse to cargo vessels manned by 'blacklegs' to strike in support of the seamen.[52] National DWRGWU officials, notwithstanding a rapidly growing local membership, were hostile to any suggestion of a strike and warned the Salford branch the union would accept no responsibility for any such action.[53] But Capner took up the recent appeal Mann had made in Liverpool for united action by all transport workers, and the Salford dockers responded with an all-out strike that involved many non-unionists.[54] James Wignall, local DWRGWU organiser 'was at some pains to explain the position of his organisation in the struggle in which it had become involved',[55] although the union quickly realised that in order to retain credibility it had to declare the strike official, and Wignall drew up a list of demands to redress dockers' own grievances that were presented to the employers. Even Tillett, whose initial reaction had been to warn against the strike, felt obliged to identify himself with the action.[56]

Other groups of workers quickly became infected by the spirit of revolt, with 200 carters employed at the Oldham Road Goods Depot of the Lancashire and Yorkshire Railway Company, and members of the General Railway Workers' Union refusing to handle goods from the Ship Canal and walking out. They marched from one goods yard to another and by the end of the day there were 5,000 carters on strike demanding pay increases, bringing most of road transport throughout Manchester and Salford to a standstill.[57] By 5 July, 12,000 carters and dockers were out, and on 6 July, about 1,500 coal miners in Pendleton and Agecroft in Salford unofficially downed tools in support of the carters.[58]

A joint strike committee organised regular mass meetings attended by up to 6,000 workers (including one addressed by Mann), with seamen, firemen, dockers and carters joining together on picket lines at docks, goods yards, large factories and warehouses to stop all goods and food being transported by scabs.[59] As in Hull, special dispensation by the strike committee was permitted in certain cases, but otherwise scab horse-drawn carts under police protection were met by mass pickets, stoned and overturned, with their

52. *Salford Reporter*, 24 June 1911.
53. *Manchester Guardian*, 27 June 1911.
54. Frow and Frow (1990: 9).
55. *Salford Reporter*, 1 July 1911.
56. Ives (1986: 26); Frow and Frow (1990: 11).
57. *Manchester Guardian*, 4 July 1911.
58. *Labour Leader*, 14 July and 18 August 1911; *Daily Mirror*, 7 July 1911.
59. Ives (1986: 29); Frow and Frow (1990: 12).

goods tipped into the street.[60] According to the local Chief Constable's report to the Salford Borough Watch Committee: 'The Carters and their sympathisers threatened and intimidated men willing to work, and desperate measures were adopted to paralyse the trade and business of the Borough and City.'[61]

With an estimated 40,000 workers idle as mills and factories closed down due to lack of fuel, thousands of pounds worth of perishable goods left rotting in ships' holds, and a serious food shortage developing, the local Chambers of Commerce and other employers' associations sent letters to Prime Minister Herbert Asquith demanding assistance to secure the passage of goods and food across the city.[62] Police reinforcements were drafted into Manchester from across the North-West and Birmingham, along with 200 Metropolitan Police.[63] But repeated confrontations between groups of up to 3,000 strikers and the police took place, with pickets holding up all produce at Shudehill wholesale market aided by large crowds of women who pelted officers with peas and raspberries, to which police responded with baton-charges. It was reported 'as the day wore on the city seemed to be under martial law almost. No vehicles moved except under police protection.'[64]

Over a period of 48 hours both Manchester and Salford were embroiled in what the *Daily Despatch* described as 'a series of riots ... carried on in defiance of the advice of the leaders of the union, and ... conducted with the aid of all kinds of illegal action. It is a kind of war on society.'[65] According to the *Daily Mirror*:

> All day long there was constant rioting, each outbreak becoming more serious than the last. Pitched battles between strikers and police, mounted and on foot, were frequent, the strikers meeting baton charges with showers of stones, brickbats, and other missiles. Many were injured on each side ... It is estimated that the number of casualties during the rioting of the last two days totals about 100.[66]

Strikers placed the blame for the violence firmly on police shoulders,[67] with Capner declaring: 'If it comes to violence, for God's sake do it well. If

60. *Manchester Guardian*, 4 July 1911; *The Times*, 5 July 1911.
61. Special Report to County Borough of Salford Watch Committee from Captain Godfrey, Chief Constable of Salford, 10 July 1911, WCML: F12 Box 62; *Salford Reporter*, 8 August 1911.
62. Ives (1986: 30); Frow and Frow (1990: 12).
63. Macready (1924: 160–1).
64. *Daily Mirror*, 5 July 1911.
65. *Daily Despatch*, 5 July 1911.
66. *Daily Mirror*, 6 July 1911.
67. *Manchester Guardian*, 5 July 1911.

it comes to a fight and the police use their batons, then by God we will use something too. If it comes to batons, then let them have batons for all you are worth.'[68] The *Manchester Guardian* condemned the transport workers' strike as a 'weapon of social brigandage' against society,[69] and the Mayor of Salford sent a report to the Home Office requesting 'a force of cavalry be sent immediately'.[70] The following day two squadrons of Scots Greys and a battalion of infantry from the Staffordshire Regiment were dispatched under the command of General Nevil Macready (previously involved in the South Wales miners' strike),[71] and by Thursday there were 750 soldiers in Manchester to help the police restore 'order'.[72]

As elsewhere, an important feature of the strike dynamic was the support provided by the wives of seamen and dockers, who regularly addressed mass meetings, on one occasion with over 100 assembling at the docks' gates to encourage strikers to remain firm.[73] On Friday 7 July a demonstration of about 2,000 women 'in their tattered shawls and gowns', many of them carrying children in their arms, marched from Salford to Manchester city centre with banners carrying slogans such as 'Our Poverty is Your Danger – Stand By Us!'[74]

When George Askwith was sent to try to reach a settlement, he was confronted with no less than 18 different unions representing a variety of workers who pledged no section would return to work until all had reached a satisfactory settlement. He was forced to spend five days in simultaneous negotiations in Manchester Town Hall, attending innumerable conferences, 'debating, discussing and almost fighting',[75] until eventually agreeing a settlement between the Manchester Ship Canal Company and the victorious strikers who won huge concessions over wages and union recognition from their employers.[76] These events were followed in August by even more extensive strike action lasting for about three weeks across Salford and

---

68. 'Strike Riots: Manchester and Salford', TNA/HO 45/10648/210.615/43a, 6 July 1911.
69. *Manchester Guardian*, 28 June 1911.
70. Telegram from Mayor of Salford to War Office, 5 July 1911, TNA/HO 45/10648/210.615/42.
71. Telegram from Churchill to Secretary of State for War, 5 July 1911; TNA/HO 45/10648/210.615/42a; CHAR 12/12/1-3, CHAR 12/12/5-6; *Manchester Guardian*, 7 July 1911.
72. 'Strike', *Daily Mirror*, 7 July 1911.
73. *Manchester Guardian*, 6 July 1911; Frow and Frow (1990: 11).
74. *Manchester Guardian*, 8 July 1911; Roberts (1990: 94–5); Frow and Frow (1990:15); Ives (1986: 33).
75. Askwith ([1920] 1974: 152); *Labour Leader*, 18 August 1911.
76. *Manchester Guardian*, 10 and 11 July 1911.

Manchester involving railway labourers, carters, dockers and miners at a number of pits, together with workers at a range of copper and wire factories and about a dozen engineering companies,[77] almost all of whom achieved some success.[78]

Cardiff

Cardiff seamen took strike action from 14 June, but experienced greater difficulty in making their strike effective than those in other ports because, as a coal export port, it already made widespread use of low-wage foreign crews, who were now used to act as 'blackleg' labour. When the Shipping Federation brought the *Lady Jocelyn* into the docks on 10 July containing primarily (though not exclusively) Hong Kong Chinese seamen, who were seemingly prepared to work for lower wages and worse conditions than union standards, mass picketing followed, which made it impossible for the ship to unload its scabs. This mass picketing was galvanised by the local NSFU organiser, 'Captain' (Edward) Tupper, part swashbuckling militant and part collaborator with the shipping bosses, who had been deployed by Wilson to work for the union.[79] And despite the decision of the NTWF not to call a sympathetic strike, dockers and many other unskilled waterfront workers, including tippers and trimmers who supplied coal to the ships, began to walk out on strike in support of the seamen, and then raise their own demands on local employers.[80] According to the Secretary of Cardiff Trades Council:

> The Seamen's cause was immensely popular throughout the city. Opportunity was afforded Captain Tupper by the local I.L.P. to present the Seamen's case at several of their Sunday meetings in the public parks, when thousands of people were present at each gathering. A conference of delegates from various Trade Union Branches was summoned, at which a resolution was passed pledging all societies engaged in work at the Docks to immediately hold meetings to consider the question of the sympathetic strike. The result of all this was that craft after craft ceased work at the Docks.[81]

---

77. *Labour Leader*, 18 August 1911; *Salford Reporter*, 19 August 1911.
78. Frow and Frow (1990: 26).
79. Tupper (1938: 27–8); Evans (1988: 155). There is no evidence that Tupper was ever a 'captain' in the navy, military or merchant navy. Balfour (1970: 63–4).
80. Weinberger (1991: 79–80); Griffiths (2012: 4–5).
81. *Labour Leader*, 18 August 1911.

As the dispute became more prolonged, with repeated picketing attempts to stop the Shipping Federation's strikebreaking supply ships, and with the police stoned and a warehouse set alight, the Chief Constable applied to the Home Office for the importation of 320 officers from the Metropolitan Police and 90 from neighbouring forces.[82] A demonstration of 15,000 and assembly of 40,000 in Cathays Park underlined the extent of solidarity being generated. But when on the night of 19 July, Chinese strikebreakers were imported by train from London, and escorted by the police to the docks where they were placed on board a ship, a large crowd of strikers and their supporters, including women and children, captured several charabancs of luggage belonging to the scabs, and looted and burnt them.[83]

This was followed on 20 July by a racist-tinged attack on all but one of Cardiff's 30 Chinese laundries in the belief – largely if not wholly erroneous – that they were housing strikebreakers, and police were pulled from their horses while struggling to restore order, although local press reports claimed that few strikers took part in the violence.[84] The attack brought a detachment of soldiers to Cardiff on 21 July, with 600 Lancashire Fusiliers used to guard power stations and gas works, while the Metropolitan Police and other imported officers were kept at the sharp end as a mobile force.

Yet despite this presence, strikes extended with a number of 'marching gangs' of pickets touring the docks and surrounding streets to spread the strike against the advice of their union officials to many other of Cardiff's myriad of dockside workplaces. These embraced non-transport industries, including brewery workers, coal washers, foundry workers, wagon builders and repairers, flour mill workers, railway workers, timber yard operatives, storemen and warehousemen, manufacturing and engineering workers, laundry assistants, and wire-rope and brattice cloth workers. The police complained about intimidation 'by bodies of men and women going from place to place with a view to inducing those inclined to remain at work to join their ranks'.[85]

When women factory and workshop workers joined the strike wave, the *South Wales Daily News* reported 'the feminine strike was not without its exciting incidents', as women and girls on the potato wharves forced entry to other premises, including Hancock's brewery where they pitched casks of beer into the dock and Frank's sweet factory where it was alleged 'several

82. Evans (1988: 150–1); Griffiths (2012: 6–7); Weinberger (1991: 81–3).

83. Griffiths (2012: 8); Evans (1988: 152).

84. Cardiff City Police Superintendent Report, 29 July 1911, TNA/HO 45/10649/210.615/134; Griffiths (2012: 9).

85. Cardiff Chief Constable's report on the seamen's strike, 10 August 1911, cited in Morgan (1991: 166).

employees complained that they were literally dragged out'.[86] In reporting on the strike escalation, the *Labour Leader* observed:

> Conditions were bad in these places, and the feeling developed that now was the chance to strike a blow for better wages, more decent conditions, and recognition of the manhood and humanity of the workpeople …
>
> In many [cases] … there was not a single member of a Trade Union. But these poor, disorganised workers seemed to grasp the principle of unity as though they had been gifted with a new vision, and from all such disorganised work-places we saw the men and girls in their Sunday best marching in fours to a Trade Union lodge-room in order to enrol themselves, for the first time, as members of a battalion in the industrial army fighting in the conflict of Labour against Capitalism.[87]

As in other ports, a joint strike committee was formed with representatives from the different unions involved (covering about 15,000 workers, in addition to the seamen), committed to resolving the grievances of all groups of workers before any strikes were called off,[88] and with its own permit system for the unloading and carriage of goods from the docks, including the distribution of flour, which threatened a shortage of bread across the city.[89]

Persistent clashes took place between strikers and the Metropolitan Police, who became the target of popular hostility. On one occasion a crowd of 2,000 gathered outside the skating rink where police were quartered, and over two nights showered them with stones and engaged in street fighting.[90] *The Times* reported 'a city under siege'.[91] With escalating violence prompting fears of social disintegration, frantic negotiations eventually led to a settlement of the seamen's dispute, which in return for some concessions on wage demands by the strike committee, the shipowners (distancing themselves from the Shipping Federation) conceded union recognition.[92] Many other groups of workers also made important gains, and there was an enormous increase in trade union membership, notably amongst the DWRGWU.[93]

In summary, the hitherto effective strikebreaking organisation of the Shipping Federation was virtually powerless in the face of strikers' fierce

86. *South Wales Daily News*, 22 July 1911.
87. *Labour Leader*, 18 August 1911.
88. Griffiths (2012: 7).
89. Weinberger (1991: 84).
90. Evans (1988: 156).
91. *The Times*, 22 July 1911.
92. Evans (1988: 152–3).
93. Coates and Topham (1994: 438).

determination and the simultaneous closure of most of the country's ports. Employers had to accept settlements that would have been unthinkable only a short time before. Reflecting on the nationwide industrial strife, Askwith highlighted the rank-and-file dynamic of the strikes:

> In almost every port the movement started with unorganised men, generally young men. The labour leaders were taken by surprise. Some quickly headed the movement and tried to regain lost authority. Others frankly expressed astonishment, and could not understand the outbreak and the determination ... [as] new men came to the front.[94]

During the strikes, he submitted a memorandum to the Cabinet titled 'The Present Unrest in the Labour World' which considered the way in which the speed and success of the transport workers' movement, and readiness with which other workers had lent their support, reflected a marked advance in workers' organisation. If the 'New Unionism' strike wave had been 'largely spasmodic and had little cohesion: the present one is essentially national and frankly aims at a complete stoppage, with all the advantage of organised bodies in the separate trades acting in unison'.[95]

The escalating nature of transport strikes across the country was of particular concern to Home Secretary Winston Churchill, who condemned the 'growing readiness to resort to violence' that was 'imposing heavy labour and responsibility both on the police and military'.[96] Yet no sooner had this phase of the Labour Revolt subsided than the huge Port of London, hitherto unaffected by the strike wave, erupted into conflict in the first two weeks of August.

LONDON TRANSPORT STRIKE: JULY–AUGUST 1911

The absence of a mass walkout on the London docks upon the declaration of the seamen's strike in June reflected the willingness of employers to pre-empt action by making concessions that would not threaten the competitive position of individual port employers. Throughout July, negotiations took place between the Port of London Authority (PLA) – chaired by Lord Devenport – and the NTWF executive. Consequentially, instead of calling for strike

94. Askwith ([1920] 1974: 177).
95. Askwith, Memorandum to Cabinet, 'The Present Unrest in the Labour World', 25 June 1911, TNA/CAB 37/107/70.
96. Herbert Asquith's Cabinet Report to King George V, 21 July 1911, TNA/CAB 41/38/3; Wrigley (1976: 62).

action on 3 July as anticipated, the NTWF continued discussions and utilised the threat of a total stoppage to extract a 'Devonport Agreement' offering significant wage increases to most groups of waterfront workers, along with a port rate. Although the proposed increases did not consistently apply to all sections of workers and the vital question of hiring procedures was left undecided, NTWF leaders felt unable to hold out for better terms against the backcloth of over 20 years of weakness on the London docks.[97]

But while both Tillett and Harry Gosling, the secretary and President of the NTWF, respectively, recommended the deal as an important advance achieved without a strike, they completely misjudged the mood of the men who vigorously rejected it at a mass meeting. On 29 July unofficial strike action by coal porters, one of the groups excluded from the Devonport Agreement because they were not employed by the PLA, spread to between 4,000 and 5,000 dockers in the Albert and Victoria Docks.

Strenuous efforts to induce the men to return to work were made by Gosling and Harry Orbell, a local DWRGWU official, with Tillett, also concerned to establish stable bargaining structures, publicly regretting the action.[98] Yet the strength of rank-and-file resistance to the settlement was such that the NTWF officials 'decided to bend with the wind and accept the inevitability of a stoppage', declaring the strike official and the following day announcing a general strike of the whole port involving everyone whose work was connected to the docks.[99]

On 3 August the Port of London stopped work (some six weeks later than waterside stoppages elsewhere), in a strike that had all the hallmarks of its 1899 forerunner, albeit on this occasion exceeding it in magnitude.[100] This time it involved not only dock and wharf labourers, but also lightermen, tugboatmen, ship repairers, sailing bargemen, coal porters, carmen and stevedores, granary workers, crane porters, and railway workers connected with the docks. By 10 August around 77,000 London transport workers, belonging to different unions were on strike,[101] with many non-unionists joining until the stoppage was practically complete. Daily mass meetings were held on Tower Hill, and as in other ports, a joint strike committee was set up that issued permits to restrict movement of goods, with only essential supplies to hospitals, orphanages and public health bodies.[102] Again it represented a vivid display of the power exercised within the transport disputes.

97. Lovell (1969: 163).
98. *Daily News*, 2 August 1911.
99. Lovell (1969: 168); Holton (1976: 95–6).
100. Coates and Topham (1994: 371).
101. Board of Trade (1912: 116–17); *The Times*, 11 August 1911.
102. *The Times*, 12 August 1912.

The unofficial, apparently spontaneous, onset of the strike had (as elsewhere) been preceded by months of propaganda and agitation in which Tillett, Mann and others had been active, and the establishment of a Port of London Organising Committee in 1910 covering all the different unions. Moreover, during the course of the strike, a number of the more radical local leaders continued the earlier campaign for industrial unionism, direct action and the sympathy strike, including Ted Leggatt, an official of the London Carmen's Union and committed anarcho-syndicalist, who became prominent.[103]

The heatwave in early August 1911, with exceptional continuously high temperatures that reached up to 98.6F (36.7C) in London on 10 August, meant perishable goods, especially butter, meat, vegetables and fruit, quickly rotted in ships and on the wharves. On 6 August an arbitrator, Sir Albert Rollit, nominated by the London Chamber of Commerce, recommended the men be paid eight pence an hour and a shilling an hour overtime. The arbitrator's announcement was relayed to a huge Sunday afternoon rally of 13,000 strikers that filled Trafalgar Square, and when they were told by Gosling they had won 'hats were thrown in the air, sticks and handkerchiefs were waved, and cheer after cheer was given'.[104] But the men were told not to return to work until the NTWF Strike Committee had been assured that all other claims had been met. According to Tillett:

> During our negotiations a spirit of revolt had seized even those of whom we had the least hope, and, as if by some great magic wave of electric telepathy that moved the minds of the people, unrest manifested itself by the stoppage of vessels and by a new demeanour of the men towards the managers and foremen ... All these were portentous signs, symbolical of the revolutionary tendencies. The effect of this new spirit, almost unknown to the powers that be ... were manifestations of the new growth.[105]

From various parts of the country 1,600 'free labourers' were dispatched through the agency of the Chief Office of the Shipping Federation in London and the outports.[106] In response, mass pickets thronged the streets around the Tower of London and out towards Wapping docks, stopping vehicles they thought might contain strikebreakers, unharnessing horses from carts and leaving overturned carts to block roads. Police frequently attempted to intervene, with baton-charges taking place in the East India Dock. And a

103. Holton (1976: 96).
104. *The Times*, 7 August 1911.
105. Tillett (1912: 6–7).
106. Saluppo (2019: 586).

Figure 4.1 The front cover of Ben Tillett's account of the 1911 London transport strike in which the veteran dockers' leader played a prominent role.

Credit: Working Class Movement Library.

100,000-strong march of strikers and their supporters was held through the heart of the City of London.[107]

Fish, meat and fruit shortages were further exacerbated by strikes of meat porters at Smithfield Market and fish porters at Billingsgate.[108] Food

107. Tillett (1912: 24).
108. *Daily Mirror*, 10 August 1911.

wholesalers spoke of impending bankruptcy, and it was feared that newspapers would cease publication because of shortages of newsprint and a strike among distributors. Private and commercial motor vehicles were threatened by a worsening petrol shortage, with the London Underground in danger because of an inability to move coal to the power stations. It was estimated the strike directly and indirectly caused nearly 200,000 Londoners to cease work.[109] Most alarming for the authorities was a threat by London County Council Tramway workers to strike, with Sydney Buxton, President of the Board of Trade, trying to assure the House of Commons they were 'using their utmost endeavours to promote a satisfactory settlement'.[110]

The *Daily Mirror* reported London was 'almost face to face with famine, the docks of the largest port in the world a wilderness, parts of the city in a state of siege, food supplies cut off'.[111] An editorial in *The Times* complained that 'six or seven millions of people cannot be expected to submit to starvation at the behest of a comparatively small minority who have chosen to proclaim war upon their countrymen'. It was a 'vast conspiracy to bring the life of a capital to a standstill'.[112]

This was the moment when George Dangerfield, recollecting the events a quarter-century later, said that 'for four days Messrs Gosling, Godfrey and Tillett had the singular satisfaction of governing London'.[113] Tillett dramatically told strikers: 'I want to say that the workers should for ever remember that their hands are on the throat of trade and industry at all times ... and ... they ... have only to use their power ... to bring the whole activities of civilisation to an abrupt standstill.'[114] Reflecting on the strike in a short pamphlet written afterwards, Tillett claimed the 'Government on Tower Hill' became 'the hub of industrial England'. 'The seats of the mighty had shifted to Tower Hill, where the Parliament held unanimous and enthusiastic sway ... It was on the Hill our Strike Committee issued orders of war, of treaty; we governed more than the ten million people of the Thames Valley.'

Preparations were made at Aldershot Garrison in Hampshire to send 10,000 troops to London,[115] although a potentially explosive situation was defused by the Chancellor, Lloyd George, who persuaded the Prime Minister to urge Churchill to moderate his position in case his 'habit of calling in the military to settle industrial disputes should bring open warfare in the

109. Ibid., 11 August 1911.
110. *House of Common Debates* (Hansard), 10 August 1911, vol. 29. col. 1150.
111. *Daily Mirror*, 11 August 1911.
112. *The Times*, 11 August 1911.
113. Dangerfield ([1935] 1997: 213).
114. Tillett (1931: 19–20).
115. Heffer (2017: 684–5).

streets'.[116] Instead, the government intervened by sending Askwith to hold a series of mediation meetings between the employers and Gosling and Tillett in an attempt to secure a settlement.[117]

And finally, on 11 August a series of separate agreements were signed in which John Burns, Cabinet Minister (and another of the leaders of the 1889 London docks' strike alongside Tillett and Mann) was involved that conceded substantial wage increases ranging 'from 20 per cent to 40 per cent'.[118] It also included rises for most workers who had been excluded from the Devonport Agreement, and the introduction of some union regulation of employment. Even so work was not resumed until 21 August, arising from unresolved issues related to the reinstatement of labourers who had joined the strike, as well as strikers' unmet demands for a union closed shop.[119]

Although the eleven-day strike was called off, by mid-August the London membership of the DWRGWU had risen from under 2,000 to over 22,000, and its branches from 14 to 49,[120] with the NTWF's reputation flourishing and its affiliated membership leaping from 54,716 in June to 220,000 (with eleven new affiliations) by April 1912.[121] Indeed the experience of the 1911 strike undoubtedly helped to stimulate the development of further industrial militancy on the London waterfront culminating in another all-out strike the following year (Chapter 5).[122]

LIVERPOOL GENERAL TRANSPORT STRIKE: AUGUST 1911

Even before the London transport strike was settled, a new phase of conflict opened up, with unofficial strike action by Liverpool railwaymen leading to strikes by many other transport workers and climaxing in a city-wide general transport strike (lasting ten days), as well as leading to the first ever national railway strike (lasting three days). Although these two disputes overlapped, they are primarily examined separately here in order to appreciate their distinct dynamic patterns of development.

The unofficial strike action which broke out among railwaymen in Liverpool related to a number of long-standing grievances. These concerned falling real wages, long working hours, the cumbersome and ineffective operation of the four-years old functioning Conciliation Boards, and the way in which Amalgamated Society of Railway Servants' (ASRS) national officials

---

116. Askwith ([1920] 1974: 149).
117. Ibid.: 155.
118. DWRGWU, *Annual Report*, 1911, pp. 5–7, cited in Hebert (1975: 249).
119. Marsh and Ryan (1989: 60–1); Lovell (1969: 178).
120. Lovell (1969: 173).
121. Coates and Topham (1994: 378).
122. Holton (1976: 97).

prevented industrial action in the hope of securing eventual recognition by the companies. The recent success of the waterfront strikers encouraged the railwaymen to seek concessions.

Action began on Saturday 5 August with 1,200 Lancashire and Yorkshire Railway Company goods porters, many of whom (handling sea-borne cargo in dockland railway depots) had refused to touch scab goods during the earlier strike, now walked out themselves for reduced hours and increased wages. Confident of their position under the 1907 Agreement, the employers announced the effective 'blacklisting' of any railwaymen who participated in the strike. Ironically, this obdurate stance spread the dispute, with railwaymen marching from one station to another, attempting to win solidarity action. By Tuesday some 3,500 railwaymen (both unionised and non-unionised) from six other companies whose trains served Liverpool had joined the strike, with carters and shunters refusing to cross picket lines, despite condemnation by ASRS national officials. Over the next few days, the unofficial strike extended to different railway centres elsewhere across the country, including Manchester, Sheffield, Derby, Bristol, Birmingham, London and South Wales, before leading to an official national strike (see below) that coincided with what was to become a Liverpool general transport strike.[123]

In Liverpool an immediate issue was the question of solidarity action by other transport workers, despite the fact that dockers and other waterside workers had just returned to work. In response, the previously established joint strike committee headed by Tom Mann now quickly resumed its leadership role and called on all railwaymen in Liverpool to come out. On 9 August it issued a strike declaration published in *Transport Worker* (the new monthly paper of the NTWF Merseyside District edited by Mann). This called on all transport workers in the city to 'black' goods moving to or from rail depots and stations in the port, to 'demonstrate our loyalty to the principles of industrial solidarity' until the railwaymen had satisfaction.[124] The strike committee mobilised reciprocal support from the dockers and carters for the solidarity action that had been taken by local railwaymen during the transport strikes. Co-opting local officials from the ASRS and the General Railway Workers' Union, the joint strike committee became empowered to deal with all negotiations over the railwaymen's strike in the city,[125] despite the fact the national executives of the railwaymen's unions were opposed to the strikes.

By 10 August some 8,000 Liverpool dockers and carters had refused to handle 'blacked' goods destined for or arriving from railway stations, effec-

123. *The Times*, 9, 15 and16 August 1911.
124. *Manchester Guardian*, 10 August 1911.
125. Weinberger (1991: 88); Hikins (1961); Holton (1976: 98).

tively paralysing the port and all day-to-day commercial life.[126] This action soon escalated with a new wave of unofficial strike action by dockers in support of their own unresolved demands, a move that breached the *White Book Agreement* recently established by NUDL leaders with shipowners. Pleas by both NUDL officials, and even Mann, that strikers return to work pending a meeting of the strike committee were rejected at waterfront meetings.[127]

In view of the protracted and ever-expanding dislocation of the port, the shipowners issued an ultimatum to Havelock Wilson and the NUDL: control your members, get them back to work, and honour the recent agreement or all cargo operations in the port will be suspended from Monday 14 August, with a general lockout of all dockers. But Sexton was powerless against his own union dissidents, whom he described as 'men of vicious instinct who strove to exploit the ignorance of newcomers'.[128] And amidst mass picketing, attacks on 'blackleg' labour and goods in transit, and sporadic cases of arson in dock-side installations, there were violent clashes with the police at Central Station with an estimated 100 baton-charges.[129] The city authorities responded by calling in large bodies of police reinforcements from Leeds and Birmingham, and it was announced that soldiers of the 2nd Royal Warwickshire Regiment, Northumberland Fusiliers, Scots Greys, the 2nd South Staffordshire Regiment and Hussars would also be deployed to Seaforth barracks.[130]

The joint strike committee organised a huge solidarity demonstration on Sunday 13 August on St. George's Hall Plateau with an estimated crowd of 80,000 men, women and children (the largest public demonstration ever held in the city) to hear speeches from Mann and other NTWF officials in support of the railwaymen and celebrating the recent victories of the seamen and dockers. Significantly, the traditional deep religious sectarian hostility between Catholics and Protestants, which had hindered the development of Liverpool trade unionism, was marginalised, if only temporarily. Fred Bower, a syndicalist stonemason, observed:

> From Orange Garston, Everton and Toxteth Park, from Roman Catholic Bootle, and the Scotland Road area, they came. Forgotten were their religious feuds ... The Garston band ... drum-major proudly whirled his sceptre twined with orange and green ribbons as he led his contingent band, half out of the Roman Catholic band, half out of the local Orange band.[131]

---

126. *Liverpool Daily Post and Mercury*, 11 August 1911.
127. *Liverpool Courier*, 12 August 1911.
128. Sexton (1936: 224).
129. *Daily Mirror*, 11 August 1911.
130. Taplin (1986: 95); Mann (1913a: 66).
131. Bower (1936: 132).

Figure 4.2 The 80,000-strong demonstration at St. Georges Plateau in Liverpool on Sunday 13 August 1911 which was attacked by police, and followed by a city-wide general transport strike.

Credit: Modern Records Centre, University of Warwick.

But in what became known as 'Bloody Sunday', police used a scuffle on the outskirts of the rally as an excuse for launching indiscriminate baton-charges that provoked hand-to-hand street fighting and rioting. The *Manchester Guardian* reported that:

> ... the police ... used their truncheons mercilessly and some could be seen taking deliberate aim at the backs of men's heads before giving them blows which despite the din could be heard yards away ... Dozens of heads and arms were broken and many shoulders and arms received blows ... IT WAS A DISPLAY OF VIOLENCE THAT HORRIFIED THOSE WHO SAW IT.[132]

Around 350 people were injured and treated in hospitals and clinics, while 95 were arrested and charged.[133] But the strike committee remained defiant.

132. *Manchester Guardian*, 14 August 1911.
133. Davies and Noon (2014: 64, 67).

Street fighting and rioting spread to the inner working-class north-end suburb of Liverpool and continued for the next two days. In Christian Street protestors stretched barbed wire across the road and made a barricade of dustbins. The *Liverpool Daily Post* reported:

> The residents in many instances took sides with the rioters against the police, throwing bottles, bricks, slates and stones from the houses and from the roofs. The whole area was for a time in a state of siege.[134]

Peace was only restored in the early hours of Tuesday 15 August when soldiers fired shots over the heads of crowds and later charged them with fixed bayonets.[135] What *The Times* called 'guerrilla warfare' continued later in the day when a 'mob of 3,000 persons' attacked a convoy of five prison waggons transporting convicted Bloody Sunday prisoners to Walton Gaol under the protection of mounted police and soldiers of the 18th Hussars. The troops opened fire, shooting five civilians, two fatally (Michael Prendergast, a Catholic dock worker, and John Sutcliffe, a Catholic carter). Ten others were injured, some with bayonet wounds.[136]

Although the strike committee disclaimed any responsibility for the protest, arguing that 'none of the men who took part in the attack on the van were strikers', the records of those hospitalised and arrested reveals it involved not only dockers and carters, but also local workers, and women and children.[137] The subsequent funerals for those killed were attended by both Catholic and Protestant workers.

In the course of the next few days Liverpool came to a virtual standstill. With the shipowners carrying out their threat to close down all cargo operations, the strike committee now called for a general transport strike, which began from midnight on Tuesday 15 August and lifted the total number on strike to an estimated 66,000 across the city and Birkenhead over the next few days.[138] In addition to railwaymen and dockers, there were carters, tugboatmen, coalheavers, ancillary waterfront workers (such as cold storage men and boiler scalers), and scavengers (dustmen and cleaners) on strike, aroused by

---

134. *Liverpool Daily Post and Mercury*, 14 August 1911.

135. *The Times*, 15 August 1911; *Justice*, 19 August 1911.

136. *The Times*, 16 August 1911; Davies and Noon (2014: 75). Only four days later, on Saturday 19 August, two more strikers were shot by troops in Llanelli during the national railway strike.

137. Holton (1976: 101–2); Davies and Noon (2014: 69–72).

138. Taplin (1986: 95).

support for the railway workers as well as by long-standing grievances of their own.[139]

Divisions of occupation, trade and organised/non-organised status, as well as inter-union demarcations, were all pushed to one side in remarkable acts of solidarity.[140] And with the local unofficial railwaymen's dispute rapidly spreading elsewhere across the country, union leaders finally agreed to give official support and call a national railway strike from Thursday 17 August unless the employers negotiated (see below).

Apart from several hundred police reinforcements from elsewhere, by 15 August some 3,500 troops had poured into Liverpool, with many involved in guarding railway stations with loaded rifles, placing the city 'practically under martial law'.[141] Two days later the warship HMS *Antrim* suddenly appeared anchored on the River Mersey near the landing stage with its guns trained over the approaches.[142] At the same time, Special Constables, enrolled from employees and managers of large commercial and trading companies, were issued with batons and deployed to patrol streets and railway lines, guard power stations and cold storage depots, man police stations, convey goods, and quell disturbances and disperse crowds.[143] But with liners idle in the Mersey, hundreds of tons of food rotting in the docks, and both passenger and goods train services halted, Liverpool was effectively paralysed. As Mann defiantly declared:

> The presence of Mounted Police with long bludgeons, and fire-arms, and of Cavalry and Infantry with bayonets fixed, will not prevent the workers engaged in this Industrial struggle from still being in it, and conducting their fight with the utmost vigour.
>
> And more, let Churchill do his utmost, his best or his worst, let him order ten times more Military to Liverpool, and let every street be paraded by them, not all the King's horses with all the King's men can take the vessels out of the Docks to sea. The workers decide the ships shall not go, what Government can say they shall go and make the carters take the freight and the dockers load same, and the seamen the steamers? Tell us

139. Taplin (1994: 12).
140. O'Brien (2012: 46).
141. Weinberger (1991: 93); Taplin (1994: 18); *Daily Mirror*, 15 August 1911.
142. *Daily Mirror*, 18 August 1911; another warship, HMS *Warrior*, was sent to Douglas, Isle of Man, to prevent a strike of the crews of the Packet Company's boats. Report from Isle of Man Lieutenant Governor to Home Office, 25 August 1911, TNA/HO 45/10656/212.470/329.
143. *Liverpool Courier*, 31 August 1911.

> that, gentlemen? Is there really a stronger power than that of the workers in proper organised relationship?[144]

Once again there was a system of official permits issued by the strike committee to stop the movement of non-essential goods without special dispensation. Goods such as milk and flour for hospitals and other public institutions were brought out for delivery by union-driven lorries, with each accompanied by a couple of committee men and bearing a large placard that declared 'By Authorisation of the Strike Committee', and cheered on by thousands.[145] With heavy police and military escorts required for any carriage of goods without permits, the Lord Mayor sent a telegram to the Home Secretary:

> We are only able to arrange for one daily convoy of perishable foodstuffs such as vegetables, fruit, fish, from the Railway Stations ... No meat can be delivered from the fifteen Cold Storage Depots. Flour cannot be delivered from the mills to bakers, excepting by some few special permits granted by the Strike Committee. Food must be getting very scarce ...[146]

As the food supply increasingly failed to meet the needs of the population, persistent looting occurred; in one incident 'a crowd of women raided a lorry loaded with bacon, carrying off many sides of bacon to their homes'.[147] According to the journalist Philip Gibbs, the city was 'as near to revolution as anything I had seen in England ... nothing moved in Liverpool',[148] and likewise, Liberal Cabinet member, Herbert Samuel, wrote to his wife in a panic that 'Liverpool is verging on a state of revolution'.[149]

After a further six days of sporadic conflict the Liverpool general transport strike was finally settled on 25 August. Once the railway strike had become official, Mann had entered into an undertaking with the joint national railway union executives based in London that neither the Liverpool trans-

---

144. Mann (1923: 275).
145. Mann (1913a: 80–1).
146. Telegram from Lord Mayor of Liverpool to Home Secretary, 17 August 1911, TNA/HO 45/10654/212.470/130; Weinberger (1991: 97).
147. *Liverpool Daily Post and Mercury*, 22 August 1911.
148. P. Gibbs, *The Pageant of the Years* (1946), p. 125, cited in Taplin (1994: 12).
149. Wrigley (2004: 58). Churchill was informed that the Mayor of Liverpool was afraid there would be a revolution and wholesale looting in Liverpool, 15 August 1911: CHAR 12/12/35. King George V sent a letter to Churchill concerned it was 'more like Revolution than strike' and recommending troops 'be given a free hand' so that 'the mob should be made to fear them', 16 August 1911: CHAR 12/12/37.

Figure 4.3 The legendary trade union and syndicalist agitator Tom Mann addressing a mass meeting of dockers during the 1911 Liverpool general transport strike.

Credit: Liverpool Record Office.

port workers nor the railway workers would return to work until both had settled their disputes. But the national union leaders agreed a settlement after a three-day national strike that left the Liverpool transport strikers on their own, unconvincingly claiming they had understood the Liverpool strike had been called off with all workers to be reinstated.[150] In fact, 250 uniformed City Corporation tramwaymen remained out and it was only when Mann and the strike committee threatened to appeal to the NTWF for a national sympathetic transport strike that Askwith managed to persuade the City Corporation to forego the penalties they intended to impose and reinstate sacked strikers that the strike committee ordered a general return to work.[151]

In sum, for nearly three months between June and August, Liverpool workers successfully withheld the pressures of employers, local authorities and police and military to achieve significant concessions, transforming one of the country's key industrial areas – which previously had formally no stable or effective unions – into the best organised port in the country.[152] By

150. Report and Decisions of the Joint Conference of the Executive Committees of the ASRS, ASLEF, GRWU and UPSS, Liverpool, 15–16 August 1911, and London, 17–24 August 1911, pp. 30–1; *The Clarion*, 25 August 1911.

151. *Liverpool Daily Post and Mercury*, 24 August 1911; Clegg (1985: 36, 39).

152. Taplin (1986: 85).

October 1911, Mann's new *Transport Worker*, a 'Non-Parliamentary' organ devoted to furthering direct action within the trade union movement, had attained a circulation of 20,000 throughout Merseyside.[153]

NATIONAL RAILWAY STRIKE: AUGUST 1911

Although the Liverpool general transport strike had grown out of the sympathetic action by dockers and others in support of the railway dispute, leaders of the main railway union – the ASRS – had intervened early on to repudiate the unofficial action of their members and attempt to achieve a speedy return to work on the basis of a 'no strike' clause in the 1907 agreement. But with action quickly spreading to numerous other main railway centres involving some 50,000 workers,[154] *The Times* reported members of the ASRS were 'on the verge of striking in every corner of the United Kingdom'.[155]

While the underlying cause of the strike was growing dissatisfaction with the operation of the company Conciliation Boards, the railwaymen's action can only be understood in the context of the preceding wave of strikes, during which seamen, dockers and others had won significant concessions from employers, with railwaymen drawn into sympathy action in many areas. They now put forward their own demands for a 2 shillings a week pay rise, reduction in the working week from 60 to 54 hours, and union recognition.

The *Industrial Syndicalist* published a special issue devoted to the railway industry in May 1911 titled 'Conciliation or Emancipation?', written by a prominent member of the ASRS.[156] Charles Watkins, a railway worker from Clay Cross and later Sheffield, an ex-Ruskin College student, argued that by agreeing to the 1907 settlement, the union leaders had ensured 'the immediate result was the dispersion of the men's forces, the dissipation of energy generated by the national movement, and the indefinite postponement of consideration of the men's grievances'.[157] He presented a critique of the strategy of the ASRS and Labour Party in calling for state ownership of the railways, and instead advocated workers' self-management and control of the industry.

Syndicalist railwaymen were to be found in several areas, including Wakefield and Gateshead. In Manchester, the impact of agitators like Reuben Bebbington, a member of the ASRS executive committee, secretary of the Man-

153. Holton (1973a: 140; 1976: 102–3).
154. *Liverpool Daily Post and Mercury*, 4, 5 and 7 August 1911.
155. *The Times*, 14 August 1911.
156. Gordon (2012).
157. *Industrial Syndicalist*, May 1911.

chester Strike Committee and attendee at the ISEL conference in November 1910, was increased by an informal network of syndicalists amongst railwaymen in the city, with 18 other delegates from all grades present at the conference.[158] As the historian of the railway unions has argued:

> ... it would be a mistake to over-emphasise the importance of the spread of syndicalism as an influence in the consolidation of railway trade unionism, it would be just as much a mistake not to take it into account as a doctrine fervently held by a minority of active and influential members of the ASRS ...[159]

J.H. Thomas, assistant general secretary of the ASRS and Labour MP for Derby, reflected in his memoirs on the way the situation 'assumed ugly proportions' and that he was 'not prepared for the restfulness that was displayed by the strikers towards the Union or, rather, our interference'.[160] W.G. Lorraine, the Manchester ASRS official, sought to distance his union from the growing strike movement: 'I want to make it perfectly clear that ... the present dispute is not sanctioned by the executive authority of the organisation, and that the action taken by the men places them outside the financial benefits of the union.'[161] However, such disapproval and warnings were ignored as the unofficial action spread across the country.

In a desperate attempt to gain control of the escalating rank-and-file defiance, the executives of the four manual worker railway unions – the ASRS, the Associated Society of Locomotive Engineers and Firemen (ASLEF), General Railway Workers' Union (GRWU) and United Pointsmen's and Signalmen's Union (UPSS) – hurriedly met in Liverpool on Tuesday 15 August. They unexpectedly issued an ultimatum to the railway companies to meet them within 24 hours to agree to enter into negotiations on improvements in pay and conditions, failing which an official national strike would be declared.[162] Such a combined union stance was largely a response to the impressive degree of industrial unity that had been forged between different grades of railwaymen (drivers, firemen, shunters, cleaners and per-

158. Ives (1986: 41).
159. Bagwell (1963: 327).
160. Thomas (1937: 32).
161. *Manchester Evening News*, 14 August 1911; *The Times*, 15 August 1911.
162. Report and Decisions of ASRS Special Meeting in Liverpool, 15 August 1911, and Ordinary Meeting, London, 11–15 September 1911, p. 6; Report and Decisions of the Joint Conference of the Executive Committees of the ASRS, ASLEF, GRWU and UPSS, Liverpool, 15–16 August 1911, and London, 17–24 August 1911, p. 3.

manent-way men) hitherto deeply fragmented by sectional interests and grievances.[163]

News of the strike ultimatum was received with surprise by the railway companies, if not with incredulity: 'I do not think the majority of the men, even if nominally members of the [ASRS], will come out', said Sir James Inglis, general manager of the South-Western: 'they have too much to lose and too little to gain by it ... In any case, it is unlikely that the companies will give way to the men at all. We would rather close down the whole system.'[164]

However, while the railway companies continued to point-blank refuse to meet directly with the unions, the government was sufficiently concerned at the prospect of a widespread strike in an industry central to the economy to quickly intervene. Herbert Asquith met separately with leaders of both the companies and unions, along with Board of Trade officials, including the ubiquitous George Askwith. The Prime Minister offered the unions a Royal Commission to enquire into the unions' complaints over the working of the 1907 conciliation scheme, but with no guarantee of its outcome or of how soon it would report. Yet as much as the union leaders might have liked to have accepted such an offer, with more and more men coming out on unofficial strike every day, they felt unable to do so. When informed of their rejection in their joint meeting, Asquith ominously murmured: 'Then your blood be on your own head',[165] and later that afternoon of Thursday 17 August the first ever national railway strike in Britain was declared.

Government assurances to the railway companies that they would be given every assistance in ensuring that the supplies of food, fuel and other essentials would be maintained, thereby breaking the strike, led Sir Guy Granet, general manager of the Midland Railway Company, to feel confident to divulge to the *Daily Mail*:

> The Government at our conference today have undertaken to put at the service of the railway companies every available soldier in the country. In this dispute the Government and the railway companies are necessarily working together ... We have got to stand firm, and if the men wish it, there will be a fight to a finish. The companies are prepared even in the event of a general strike to give an effective, if restricted service.[166]

163. *The Times*, 15 and 16 August 1911.
164. *Daily Mirror*, 16 August 1911.
165. Askwith ([1920] 1974: 164).
166. *Daily Mail*, 17 August 1911; *Railway Gazette*, 18 August 1911. In a letter to Churchill on 17 August 1911 Granet claimed his words in the *Daily Mail* had been 'distorted', CHAR 12/10/75.

In the face of such opposition, the unions sent out 2,000 telegrams to their branches: 'Your liberty is at stake. All railwaymen must strike at once. The loyalty of each means victory for all.'[167] Within twelve hours of its official commencement at 5 pm on Thursday 17 August up to 145,000 workers had responded to the strike call, with around 200,000 joining the strike altogether during the course of the dispute.[168] The magnitude of the response astounded the employers, press and politicians, and also 'staggered the executive committee [of the ASRS] themselves'.[169] As in previous strikes, the railway workers received widespread support from dockers, miners and others, and women often played a strong supportive role, for example, with strikers' wives holding a mass meeting in Stockport 'determined to stand by the men'.[170]

The strike movement was not a complete national stoppage, remaining largely confined to areas of industrial, and especially coal production, in the North, Midlands and South Wales. Support in London and the South was very uneven and the dispute barely registered in Scotland, while in Ireland significant action only occurred in September. Nonetheless, even though sporadic passenger services were maintained, the transport of goods was almost completely halted in large parts of the main striking areas,[171] causing the Liberal government to claim that the 'national interest' demanded military intervention.[172]

If the wave of strikes over the summer had already ushered in civil strife and public disorder, the turmoil reached a new height with the national railway strike. The Cabinet met frequently on Thursday 17 and Friday 18 August, being particularly concerned about the shortage of perishable food supplies. In Manchester, the inability to move coal from the sidings was causing factories and mills to close across the North-West, with retailers warning the situation was 'critical' with a fast-approaching famine in the city.[173]

The unprecedented scale of military mobilisation to reinforce local police forces reflected the government's concern.[174] General Nevil Macready was put in charge of the organisation of 'practically the whole of the troops of Great Britain on duty scattered along the railway system'.[175] Churchill sus-

---

167. Report and Decisions of the Joint Conference of the Executive Committees of the ASRS, ASLEF, GRWU and UPSS, Liverpool, 15–16 August 1911, and London, 17–24 August 1911, p. 10; Bagwell (1963: 293).
168. Bagwell (1963: 296).
169. *Railway Review*, 25 August 1911.
170. *Manchester Evening News*, 17 August 1911.
171. *Railway News*, 26 August 1911.
172. Howell (2012: 71).
173. *Manchester Evening News*, 15–19 August 1911.
174. Davies (2012: 97).
175. Macready (1924: 163); *Employment of Military during Railway Strike: Correspondence between Home Office and Local Authorities*, London: HMSO, 1911, TNA/

pended the Army Regulation which only permitted troops to be dispatched following a specific requisition from a civil authority, allowing the War Office to unilaterally send 50,000 troops to industrial areas and strategic railway centres.[176]

The Daily Mirror

THE MORNING JOURNAL WITH THE SECOND LARGEST NET SALE

No. 2,438. FRIDAY, AUGUST 18, 1911 One Halfpenny.

GENERAL RAILWAY STRIKE DECLARED YESTERDAY: SENTRIES WITH FIXED BAYONETS GUARD THE LIVERPOOL TERMINI.

Liverpolitans, whose city has been reduced to a parlous state by the hooligan element, woke up yesterday morning wondering whether their troubles were to be increased by a general railway strike. Unfortunately, their fears proved well grounded, as during the afternoon the news that the strike had been declared was made known throughout the country. The crowds who gathered at the Liverpool termini saw an unusual spectacle—namely, a sentry with fixed bayonet, an outward and visible sign of the assurances given by the Government that the various systems would receive ample protection. The photograph shows the sentry on duty at Lime-street Station, the terminus of the London and North Western Railway Company.

Figure 4.4 Troops with fixed bayonets dispatched to Liverpool Lime Street station during the national railway strike in August 1911.

Credit: Mirrorpix.

HO 45/10657/212.470/421; War Office Daily Reports, 18–21 August 1911, TNA/HO 45/10657/212.470/390; Home Office, *Railway Strike of August 1911: Confidential Memoranda and Reports*, TNA/HO 45/10658/212.470/451.

176. Morgan (1987: 54); TNA HO 45/10660/213025.

Notwithstanding the government's pretence that it was only intervening to safeguard law and order, food and mail supplies, and 'prevent the paralysis of trade', and was not taking sides in an industrial dispute, telegrams and memorandums sent by Churchill and the War Office to Chief Constables and Mayors made clear the determination to utilise the army as a crucial mechanism for strikebreaking, for 'protection to ... all railwaymen within their jurisdiction who wish to work'.[177]

In the process, Churchill placed 'large parts of the country ... under martial law'.[178] In London, 20,000 troops were mobilised, with bayonets fixed, and positioned at every station, as well as many viaducts and bridges, in a graphic show of force, with camps established in Hyde Park, Battersea Park and elsewhere.[179] The Liberal MP Charles Masterman, Parliamentary Under-Secretary to Churchill, recorded in his diary: 'Winston was in a very excited state of mind. He has got rather a whiff-of-grape-shot attitude towards these matters; and he enjoyed intensely mapping the country and directing the movement of troops ... [he was] longing for blood.'[180]

With railway companies offering strikebreakers extra pay, the stoppage was not absolute even in the most solid districts. Many non-unionists, often older men, were willing to work, and police and troops were deployed to protect them.[181] Despite advice from local union officials to refrain from violence, there were many instances of physical attacks on non-strikers and their homes, as well as the stoning of trains and signal boxes manned by 'blackleg' labour.[182] At Portishead near Bristol, 1,000 men launched a midnight attack on a signal box still in operation. Similar attacks occurred at Ilkeston, Derby and Mold, North Wales, and in Lincoln attacks on signal boxes and the Midland Railway's goods office were followed by the ransacking of shops.[183] Likewise, in many other areas across the country attempts were made to disrupt railway services by placing obstacles on the line, tearing

177. Memorandum from General Macready to Chief Constables, TNA/HO 45/10655/212.470/162; *House of Common Debates* (Hansard), 22 August 1911, vol. 29, col. 2332.
178. Bagwell (1963: 295).
179. *Daily Mirror*, 19 August 1911.
180. Masterman (1939: 205).
181. Bagwell (1963: 295).
182. Howell (2012: 71).
183. Chief Constable of Bristol to Home Office, 22 August 1911, TNA/HO 45/10655/213.470/243a; Chief Constable of Lincoln to Home Office, 21 August 1911, TNA/HO 45/10655/212.470/250; Chief Constable of Derby to Home Office, 21 August 1911, TNA/HO 45/10654/212.470/84; *Daily Mirror*, 21 August 1911; ibid.: 72; Nurse (2001: 18).

up tracks, cutting telegraph wires and damaging engine sheds.[184] At Chesterfield, where the railway station was attacked by a crowd of 4,000 and partly burnt down, 50 troops of the West Yorkshire Regiment were called in to supplement the local police force, and the crowd was only repulsed after repeated bayonet-charges by the army.[185]

The most violent conflict involving military intervention developed in Llanelli,[186] where on Thursday 17 August 1,500 strikers and their supporters, notably dockers and tin-plate workers, flocked to the railway station, some of them occupying the signal boxes, while others blocked the level crossing to prevent any movement on the track. The following day social conflict intensified with the deployment of police and troops to clear the pickets off the tracks and take back control of the signal box and level crossing.[187] But in defiance of local strike committee officials, the pickets successfully mounted the footplate of two trains and convinced the drivers to extinguish the engines' fires and evacuate their trains. Further troop deployments were now dispatched, with the local train drivers' union official Richard Squance appealing to the pickets, who by this time numbered some 2,000:

> There is sufficient military at hand to clear this crossing tonight. Is it worth shedding blood for the sake of preventing a few trains passing through? Don't allow the dignity of Llanelli to be dragged into the mire by having bloodshed without cause.[188]

Such entreaties were to be of no avail, and that evening the police and military authorities moved decisively to open the gates and enable trains to go through. The reaction was swift and furious, with an army of pickets swelling to 5,000 as charge after charge was launched against the police, until the level crossing was regained following a bloody battle. Only with the arrival of a bigger contingent of Worcester Regiment troops was it enough to force the pickets to yield the crossing and gates back to the authorities.[189]

---

184. *The Times*, 19 August 1911.
185. Chief Constable of Chesterfield to Home Office, 23 August 1911, TNA/HO 45/10656/212.470/279; Williams (1962: 393); Holton (1976: 104–5); *Daily Mirror*, 21 August 1911.
186. Known as 'Llanelly' at the time.
187. Hopkin (1983: 494).
188. *South Wales Press*, 23 August 1911, cited in Griffiths (2009: 44).
189. Memorandum from Carmarthen Chief Constable to Home Office, 18 August 1911, TNA/HO 45/10655/212.470/171; Report from Col. Freeth to the War Office, 19 August 1911, TNA/HO 45/ 10655/212.470/206; Griffiths (2009: 43–5).

The next day, Saturday 19 August, a crowd of pickets, most of whom no longer recognised the strike committee's authority, successfully stopped and immobilised an Irish mail train which had passed through Llanelli station. When soldiers arrived, they were attacked on both sides by a fusillade of stones, slates and railings thrown by a crowd of pickets and their supporters on the railway embankments, with one soldier struck. Eventually, soldiers fired into the crowd, with two young men, John John (tinplate worker) and Leonard Worsall (labourer) shot dead and two others wounded.[190]

The killings provoked a violent response, bringing most of Llanelli out onto the streets with hours of rioting in which the town centre was wrecked and shops looted. Great Western Railway Company goods depots were assailed and 96 carriages looted, with many set alight.[191] Some railway carriages that were later attacked contained explosive material that blew up and killed another four people and injured others.[192] Mass protest meetings were held in Llanelli and throughout South Wales, and Keir Hardie, the Labour MP for Merthyr Boroughs, told Parliament that 'the men who have been shot down have been murdered by the Government in the interests of the capitalist system'.[193] Hardie penned a pamphlet entitled *Killing No Murder! The Government and the Railway Strike*, which for a time was one of the most popular books in the country, and such was the public pressure that a Commission of Inquiry was established.

Even though there were accusations of purposeless rampaging by a violent underclass of anti-social and criminal elements, court and casualty records show that many of those who took part in the rioting were local workers, and there was clearly a high degree of purpose and direction in the specific attacks made on the railway company and army property.[194] A senior magistrate who brought in the troops, and was a shareholder in the Great Western Railway, saw his shop looted and arson raids made on two of his farms.[195] Yet the inquest into the deaths and Commission of Inquiry reported with a verdict of 'justifiable homicide'.[196]

By Friday it had become clear the government's policy of repression via military intervention was not producing the hoped-for victory. Each day more railway workers joined the strike, 'violent disorder' was widespread, and the inability to move coal was not only affecting food and other essen-

190. Hopkin (1983: 497–9); Edwards (1988: 55–97).
191. Hopkin (1983: 498–9).
192. Griffiths (2009: 52); *Daily Mirror*, 21 August 1911.
193. *House of Common Debates* (Hansard), 22 August 1911, vol. 29, col. 2340.
194. Griffiths (2009: 54–7).
195. Holton (1976: 106).
196. *The Times*, 30 August 1911; Griffiths (2009: 75).

tial supplies but threatening the rapid closure of much of industry.[197] For example, the steel works in Consett had stopped production because of a shortage of ore, resulting in many thousands of miners in the North-East being laid off. Men in the Rhondda coalfields were also laid off.[198]

Churchill confided: 'The men have beaten us ... We cannot keep the trains running. There is nothing we can do. We are done!'[199] In a debate at the House of Commons two days after the strike ended, Churchill claimed:

> Had the strike proceeded for a week ... there must have been practically a total cessation of industry ... a continuation of the railway strike would have produced a swift and certain degeneration of all the means, of all the structure, social and economic, on which the life of the people depends ...[200]

This underlined the extent to which the government felt threatened. After fruitless efforts to intervene in the dispute with four days of separate talks with employers and unions involving the Board of Trade's Sydney Buxton, Labour leader Ramsay MacDonald and government Chief Whip Arthur Murray, a new initiative was taken. Chancellor of the Exchequer, Lloyd George – with the Prime Minister's seal of approval – opened up direct joint negotiations with employers and unions late on the Saturday evening. After informing them in confidence of a threatening international crisis – with an alleged imminent danger of war arising from Germany's military intervention to uphold her interests in Morocco by dispatching the warship HMS *Panther* to seize the port of Agadir – Lloyd George appealed for patriotic compromise in the national interest to agree to settlement terms and end the strike.

But the terms of the compromise that were quickly agreed by 11 pm that evening, at what was the first ever joint meeting of employers and union officials, accompanied by Board of Trade official George Askwith, merely repeated the promise of a Royal Commission into the working of the 1907 Conciliation Boards (with the added provision that it would report its findings very rapidly), proposed no wage increases and left the Conciliation Boards intact in the interim. The ASRS union leaders – who had only made the strike official so they could gain control over it – now promptly surrendered, accepting what were essentially the same terms the Prime Minister

197. Davies (2012: 109).
198. Board of Trade (1912); ibid.: 111–12.
199. Masterman (1939: 207).
200. *House of Common Debates* (Hansard), 22 August 1911, vol. 29, cols 2325-2327.

had offered only a few days previously. They sent out a telegram to all centres: 'Strike settled. Victory for trade unionism. Men to return to work at once.'[201]

Lloyd George's relief was palpable as he burst into the War Office exclaiming: 'a bottle of Champagne! I've done it! Don't ask me how, but I've done it! The strike is settled!'[202] But according to Charles Masterman, when Churchill heard that the strike was settled, he telephoned Lloyd George and told him: 'I'm very sorry to hear it. It would have been better to have gone on and given these men a good thrashing.'[203] With the end of the strike, Churchill now encouraged the police to take firm action against rioters and looters in disturbed areas, with police raids conducted in Llanelli resulting in 23 men and one woman being charged with looting, and all but three receiving heavy sentences.[204]

A return to work, bringing to an end the three-day official strike, was achieved by presenting the surrender as an historic victory, and at mass meetings across the country the men were told their unions had won recognition. But at numerous union meetings, for example, in Newcastle, Sunderland, South Shields, Middlesbrough, Hull and Salford, the settlement was condemned as a 'sell-out'.[205] In Manchester a mass meeting of 4,000 railwaymen voted against with only six in favour,[206] with *The Times* reporting:

> Some of the men could scarcely control themselves, so great was their anger at the suggestion that they should return to work before they had realised all their hopes. They treated the members of the Strike Committee with scant courtesy and occasionally one heard insinuations of 'Price' and 'Treachery'.[207]

Labour MP George Barnes, who was involved in recommending the deal, admitted that: 'If the men … had known the full text and character of the settlement, no restarting would have taken place.'[208] As *The Clarion* argued:

> … the bitter truth is that the workers have once again been *sold*. There is no escaping from the cold fact … Their 'leaders' have arranged another 'settlement' for them.

201. Newsinger (2015: 28).
202. Jenkins (1978: 234–5).
203. Masterman (1939: 208).
204. Morgan (1987: 173–4).
205. Physick (1998: 47).
206. *Manchester Evening News*, 21 August 1911; *Daily Mirror*, 21 August 1911.
207. *The Times*, 21 August 1911.
208. *House of Commons Debates* (Hansard), 22 August 1911, vol. 29, cols 2317-8.

However, with many local union branches accepting the settlement, and with no national rank-and-file organisation able to mount an effective challenge to the sell-out, the railwaymen returned to work unbeaten but betrayed.[209]

When the Royal Commission's recommendations were published on 18 October there was a hostile reception to the predictably retained conciliation system (albeit in modified form) as a means of settling grievances.[210] Even union leaders (excluding the drivers' union) who might otherwise have been happy to accept the scheme felt under membership pressure to reject it, and proceeded to organise a referendum (as opposed to ballot) of three unions on the question of whether there should be a second national railway strike. The voting figures were never made public, although it appeared the Royal Commission's findings only had limited support.[211] But utilising the vote as a negotiating ploy, government mediation secured some marginal improvements, sufficient to obtain union leaders' acceptance, even though some 100 branches of the ASRS strongly criticised the conciliatory policy of their leadership.[212]

Despite this ignoble ending, Askwith acknowledged: 'For good or evil, practical recognition of the unions [within the Conciliation Boards], and the principle of negotiations with the railway companies as a body, were the chief results of the railway strike of 1911.'[213] Moreover, there was a spectacular increase in ASRS membership from 75,153 in 1910 to 116,516 by the end of 1911.[214]

Syndicalist ideas and propaganda were increasingly brought to bear, with Charles Watkins, who remained the leading opponent of official union policy, speaking to railwaymen across the country on issues of industrial unionism and workers' control.[215] There was the election of a staunch advocate of revolutionary industrial unionism and prominent member of the Plebs League as general organiser of the ASRS.[216] The new monthly newspaper, *The Syndicalist Railwayman*, was launched in September 1911,[217] with branches

209. Newsinger (2015: 28).
210. *Report of the Royal Commission on the Railway Conciliation and Arbitration Scheme 1907*. Cd. 5922 (1911).
211. MRC: MSS 127/AS/3/1/2A, cited in Howell (2012: 79).
212. Holton (1976: 108); Bagwell (1963: 304).
213. Askwith ([1920] 1974: 169).
214. Bagwell (1963: 698).
215. Gordon (2010).
216. Holton (1976: 109).
217. The paper ran for four issues (until December 1911) before being merged into the ISEL's *The Syndicalist* from January 1912.

circularised and militant speakers invited to expound revolutionary industrial methods. The clearest indications of syndicalist influence were felt at the 1912 ASRS AGM with the union's formal adoption of the objective of workers' control of industry, and in 1913 contributing to the amalgamation of three railway unions into a new 'all-grades' and genuinely industrial union, the National Union of Railwaymen, which by 1914 had recruited half the workers in the industry.

5
Gathering Momentum

With *The Times* warning that 'the public must be prepared for a conflict between Labour and Capital, or between employers and employed, upon a scale as has never occurred before', the level of workers' struggle rocketed to a new high level in 1912.[1] Although the 857 disputes recorded as commencing in 1912 were slightly less than in 1911, the total number of workers involved increased to 1,463,000, and the number of working days 'lost' increased to nearly 41 million. Nearly half of all strikes involved less than 100 people, 782 involved less than 1,000, but 15 strikes involved 5,000 or more workers or 'lost' at least 100,000 working days, and two of these larger disputes dominated events of the year.[2] The first ever national miners' strike (lasting for seven weeks between February and April) in pursuit of a national minimum wage involved altogether over one million workers and accounted for nearly 70 per cent of the total number of workers involved in strikes that year. Then between May and August attention turned back to the transport industry with another London docks' strike, this time over joint union bargaining rights and pay, involving about 80,000, and briefly spreading to a few other ports involving another 20,000 workers. In both disputes the Liberal government became directly involved in attempting to find settlements, with the threat and/or use of the military.

For a time afterwards, the momentum of the strike wave seemed to waver, but then in 1913 it surged back once again, with a workers' offensive that branched out into an unprecedented series of smaller strikes, pushing the annual total number of strikes to 1,497. The number of workers involved declined compared with 1911 and 1912 to 689,000, and the number of strike days also fell back to 11.6 million, with no single dispute directly involving more than 50,000 workers. But 26 strikes involved 5,000 or more workers or 'lost' at least 100,000 working days, and these accounted for about 32 per cent of the total number involved.

While in 1913 there were no very large or national strikes like in 1911 and 1912, there were continuing numerous local strikes in the coalfields, and

1. *The Times*, 6 January 1912.
2. Board of Trade (1913a: x, xii).

textile and transport industries.[3] Moreover, apart from the Dublin lockout (examined in Chapter 7), there was a strike wave in the spring and summer of 1913, on a scale of magnitude and seriousness similar to the earlier episodes of the Labour Revolt, that centred on largely unorganised West Midlands engineering and metal workers, a so-called 'prairie fire' that involved an aggregated 40,000.

NATIONAL MINERS' STRIKE: FEBRUARY–APRIL 1912

Even though there had been rapid economic recovery in 1911 and wages had increased in many industries, this had not been reflected in coalmining, where no less than 370,000 miners had suffered pay cuts, and only 13,000 secured increases. As we have seen, the ten-month Cambrian Combine strike was sparked off by miners working in difficult seams ('abnormal places') earning considerably less than others. Although only South Wales went on strike, many districts experienced declining piecework earnings caused by falling productivity. But it was the syndicalist-influenced South Wales militants who were largely responsible for converting 'abnormal places' agitation into a general national demand for a minimum wage for *all* miners.

Following publication of their 1911 pamphlet *The Miners' Next Step*, with its critique of bureaucratic union leadership and advocacy of rank-and-file democratic accountability, South Wales 'missionaries', including W.H. Mainwaring and Noah Rees of the Unofficial Reform Committee, were sent to other coalfields in England and Scotland to address union lodge meetings. Their visits collecting funds for the Cambrian Combine strikers were also used as occasions to sell their pamphlet, propagate industrial policies, and publicise the minimum wage campaign and urge a national strike. While there was nothing specifically syndicalist in the minimum wage demand, the lukewarm attitude of many within the Miners' Federation of Great Britain (MFGB) leadership helped the Welsh militants' arguments make considerable headway across the coalfields, given the lack of progress made by Labourist or Lib-Lab union officials in satisfying grievances.[4] Persistent agitation by rank-and-file militants pressurising official union structures from below led the union's annual conference in October 1911 (held following the defeat of the Cambrian strike) to support the claim for a minimum wage.

Although the MFGB leadership now demanded a minimum wage as official policy, negotiations with the employers' body, the Mining Association of Great Britain, failed – owing to resistance to national negotiations from

3. Board of Trade (1914: xi).
4. Holton (1976: 111–12).

mine owners in Scotland, South Wales, Northumberland, Durham and elsewhere who insisted on district-by-district negotiations. This failure added fuel to the syndicalist arguments for 'direct action'. At another conference in November, MFGB leaders were pressed into agreeing to ballot members on national strike action, albeit they stipulated that under union rules any strike action would require a two-thirds majority vote in favour. The result of the ballot was an overwhelming 80 per cent majority (445,801 for, and 115,921 against) and notices were tendered in every district for action to commence at the end of February. Moreover, a new demand was now put forward, that all underground workers should receive no less than 5 shillings per shift for men and 2 shillings for boys – the 'five and two'.

The country was now faced with the prospect of a coal stoppage of a size hitherto unknown. Manufacturing industry, railways and power stations were all coal-fired, and coal was the heating fuel for most houses. Consequently, the Liberal government quickly intervened to try to avert a strike that it feared would be economically and socially catastrophic. The Prime Minister and three Cabinet Ministers (Sir Edward Grey, Foreign Secretary; Lloyd George, Chancellor of the Exchequer; and Sydney Buxton, President of the Board of Trade) met with 170 Miners' Federation delegates, as well as with the employers. Asquith submitted proposals to both parties that recognised the principle of a minimum wage, but specified that this must be determined in the various districts by special agreements that would differ from coalfield to coalfield; in each district a joint conference would be set up on which the government would be represented, and if it failed to reach an agreement the government representative would act as umpire.

The employers rejected the government's terms, on the basis that a minimum wage would cause a fall in profits and that only the inducement of piecework would ensure miners worked productively. The terms were also rejected by a national MFGB conference on 27 February which sanctioned the national strike and now demanded not only the acceptance of the principle of a national minimum wage but that the 'five and two' should be *legally* fixed. Even before the union's conference had ended, miners in Derbyshire, Leicestershire and South Wales had walked out on strike.

As talks continued, the Prime Minister made an impassioned speech to MFGB representatives, telling them that coal production provided 'the life blood' of industry and that they would bear 'a terrible responsibility' if the strike proceeded, because of the effect on 'the great mass of people outside whose livelihood, comfort, welfare, even existence, very largely depended upon you'.[5] He also met privately with the owners who remained steadfastly

5. *The Times*, 1 March 1912.

opposed to accepting any kind of minimum wage or negotiation, and with the South Wales mine owners' leader, D.A. Thomas, not wanting any compromise or the strike to be postponed.[6] After four days of desperate talks, Asquith had to admit the two sides were still too far apart and nothing could be done, and by 1 March no less than 93 per cent of British miners had walked out.

The 1912 strike was by far the largest strike that had ever occurred in the coalmining industry (with all coalfields across the country simultaneously included), or in any other single industry in Britain (or any other country),[7] involving over one million miners, apart from the 'safety men' whose continued employment was sanctioned by the Federation. Behind it, apart from the desire to enforce the universal adoption of the minimum wage, was the will to secure fuller recognition for the MFGB as the representative body for the industry at national level. Over the course of the next seven weeks the strike effectively paralysed whole swathes of industry affecting about a million workers, with railwaymen, transport workers and factory workers in different industries temporarily laid off, and with large numbers of other workers having their hours cut.[8]

Despite, or perhaps because of, the widespread nature of the miners' strike there was, relative to the transport strikes of the previous year, little violence, in part explained by deep-rooted collective loyalties and the way in which every colliery was brought to a standstill. In some districts, such as Lancashire, the strike was so solidly supported there was no need to picket at all. Nonetheless, the new Home Secretary, Reginald McKenna, made arrangements for the rapid deployment of troops to coalfield areas in response to a deluge of anxious requests from local Chief Constables, magistrates and local employers about the development of militancy among miners and the expectation of violence.[9]

In a few areas, where attempts were made to reopen pits with 'blackleg' labour backed up by police or military, there were isolated incidents of 'disorder'. For example, in March rioting by crowds of up to 6,000 pickets and their supporters, including hundreds of women who carried their children, took place for several hours in the Cannock Chase coalfield in Staffordshire, involving 'threats of vengeance' against men who were working. Stones and other missiles were thrown, buildings attacked, and windows and plant damaged, leading to police reinforcements being hastily summoned

6. *Manchester Guardian*, 23 February 1912.
7. Arnot (1954: 101–2).
8. Home Office, *Coal Strike 1912: Confidential Memoranda and Correspondence*, TNA/HO 45/10674/218.781/22; J.B., Memorandum to Cabinet, 'Effect of Coal Dispute', 30 March 1912, TNA/CAB 37/110/56; Board of Trade (1913a: xxxiii).
9. Holton (1976: 113–14).

from various districts, and repeated baton-charges to disperse the crowd. Shortly afterwards, 500 troops from the 1st West Yorkshire Regiment arrived, although this did not prevent further disturbances the following day at Leighwood Colliery, when several hundred miners 'molested and turned back home again' scabs.[10]

There was rioting at the Cadeby Colliery, near Doncaster in Yorkshire, where the police formed themselves into an escort for scabs. They were met with 'a big rush' of pickets, encouraged again by hundreds of women, until police baton-charges 'had the effect of quietening the disturbance' in which several people were injured.[11] And there were other confrontations with scabs and police in Haydock, near St. Helens, Tamworth, Warwickshire, Chirk, near Wrexham, and Pendlebury, Salford.[12] Nonetheless, such incidents were not common and even the Home Secretary commented that 'considering the extent and magnitude of the strike, it is remarkable how few and insignificant have been the disturbances accompanying it'.[13]

On the other hand, the Cabinet was clearly determined to stamp its authority during the strike, and despite reservations expressed in memorandums to the Cabinet from both Sydney Buxton and George Askwith of the Board of Trade,[14] on 19 March Tom Mann, whose syndicalist ideas had made headway among some of the young miners' leaders, was arrested under the 1797 Incitement to Mutiny Act on the orders of the Attorney General. This was for the publication in *The Syndicalist* in January 1912 of a 'Don't Shoot' leaflet, an 'Open Letter to British Soldiers' which appealed to troops not to fire on striking workers during industrial disputes.

This had been authored (unsigned) by Fred Bower, a Liverpool syndicalist stonemason, and first appeared in the *Irish Worker* (edited by Jim Larkin) in July 1911, and then reprinted in *The Syndicalist*.[15] The appeal, which was also reprinted and distributed as a leaflet to soldiers at Aldershot Barracks by a syndicalist ASRS train-driver, Fred Crowsley, led to the government prosecuting Crowsley, Guy Bowman (*The Syndicalist* editor), and printers (Charlie

10. 'Disturbances at Cannock Chase', 27–28 March 1912, TNA/HO 45/10675/218.781/130; *Daily Mirror*, 28 and 29 March 1912; *The Times*, 28 March 1912.
11. *Daily Mirror*, 29 March 1912.
12. TNA/HO 45/10675/218.781/117 and 128, 170a, 177 and 190; *The Times*, 28 March 1912.
13. Arnot (1967: 294).
14. Buxton, 'Industrial Unrest', 13 April 1912, TNA/CAB 37/110/62; LG/C/21/1/10; Askwith, 'Labour Unrest', 14 April 1912, TNA/CAB 37/110/63; LG/C/21/1/11.
15. Bower (1936: 121–3).

HALT! ATTENTION!!

Open Letter to British Soldiers.

This letter to British soldiers, reprinted from *Sheldrake's Military Gazette* (Aldershot), of March 1st, 1912, is the subject of the charge against Crowsley, Guy Bowman, the Buck brothers, and Tom Mann. Read and judge for yourself. Let the voice of the PEOPLE be heard.

Men! Comrades! Brothers!

YOU are in the Army

So are WE. YOU in the Army of Destruction. We in the Industrial, or Army of Construction.

WE work at mine, mill, forge, factory, or dock, producing and transporting all the goods, clothing, stuffs, etc., which make it possible for people to live.

YOU ARE WORKING MEN'S SONS.

When WE go on Strike to better OUR lot, which is the lot also of YOUR FATHERS, MOTHERS, BROTHERS, and SISTERS, YOU are called upon by your officers to MURDER US.

DON'T DO IT!

You know how it happens always has happened.

We stand out as long as we can. Then one of our (and your) irresponsible Brothers, goaded by the sight and thought of his and his loved ones' misery and hunger, commits a crime on property. Immediately YOU are ordered to MURDER US, as YOU did at Mitchelstown, at Featherstone, at Belfast.

Don't YOU know that when YOU are out of the colours, and become a "Civy" again, that YOU, like US, may be on Strike, and YOU, like US, be liable to be MURDERED by other soldiers.

BOYS, DON'T DO IT!

"THOU SHALT NOT KILL," says the Book.

DON'T FORGET THAT!

It does not say, "unless you have a uniform on."

No! MURDER IS MURDER, whether committed in the heat of anger on one who has wronged a loved one, or by pipe-clayed Tommies with a rifle.

BOYS, DON'T DO IT!

ACT THE MAN! ACT THE BROTHER ACT THE HUMAN BEING!

Property can be replaced! Human life, never.

The Idle Rich Class, who own and order you about, own and order us about also. They and their friends own the land and means of life of Britain.

YOU DON'T. WE DON'T.

When WE kick, they order YOU to MURDER US.

When YOU kick, YOU get courtmartialed and cells.

YOUR fight is OUR fight. Instead of fighting AGAINST each other, WE should be fighting with each other.

Out of OUR loins, OUR lives, OUR homes, YOU came.

Don't disgrace YOUR PARENTS, YOUR CLASS, by being the willing tools any longer of the MASTER CLASS.

YOU, like US, are of the SLAVE CLASS. WHEN WE rise, YOU rise; when WE fall, even by your bullets, YE fall also.

England with its fertile valleys and dells, its mineral resources, its sea harvests, is the heritage of ages to us.

YOU no doubt joined the Army out of poverty.

WE work long hours for small wages at hard work, because of OUR poverty. And both YOUR poverty and OURS arises from the fact that Britain with its resources belongs to only a few people. These few, owning Britain, own OUR jobs. Owning OUR jobs, they own OUR very LIVES.

Comrades, have WE called in vain? Think things out and refuse any longer to MURDER YOUR KINDRED. Help US to win back BRITAIN for the BRITISH, and the WORLD for the WORKERS.

Figure 5.1 The famous 'Don't Shoot' leaflet, published in *The Syndicalist* in January 1912, which led to the arrest and imprisonment of Tom Mann and others under the 1897 Incitement to Mutiny Act.

Credit: Working Class Movement Library.

and Ben Buck), as well as Mann as ISEL President who had publicly read out the letter in a speech to a meeting in Pendleton, Salford. It read:

> Men! Comrades! Brothers!
>
> YOU are in the army.
>
> So are WE. YOU, in the army of Destruction. WE in the Industrial, or Army of Construction.

> WE work at mine, mill, forge, factory, or dock, producing and transporting all the goods, clothing, and stuffs which makes it possible for people to live.
>
> YOU ARE WORKING MEN'S SONS.
>
> When WE go on strike to better OUR lot, which is the lot also of YOUR FATHERS, MOTHERS, BROTHERS and SISTERS. YOU are called upon by your officers to MURDER US.
>
> Don't do it! ...
>
> ACT THE MAN! ACT THE BROTHER! ACT THE HUMAN BEING![16]

The appeal expressed the general anger of the trade union movement at the repeated determination of Churchill to employ troops in industrial disputes – an anger that had been brought to a climax by the shooting dead of strikers in Liverpool and Llanelli in 1911, as well as the use of drawn bayonets during the Cambrian miners' strike. The trial and harsh sentences, in Mann's case of six months imprisonment, were widely reported in the newspapers and there was a groundswell of national protest and mass solidarity meetings, including two demonstrations of 7,000–8,000 each in Trafalgar Square, with Labour MPs Keir Hardie and George Lansbury leading protests in Parliament.

Ironically, while the Liberal government's action was aimed at trying to quell any repeat of the levels of social unrest of 1911 spilling over into military insubordination, the publicity and protests helped to make 'syndicalism' a household name up and down the country and encourage the view that the Labour Revolt was caused by syndicalist 'agitators'.[17] And the mounting broad-based campaign of opposition quickly resulted in Churchill, in consultation with the Attorney General, reducing the length of all sentences, with Mann released from Strangeways Prison in Manchester after serving only seven weeks.[18]

With the economy grinding to a halt, Asquith attempted to break the impasse by announcing to the House of Commons that he hoped an act of *force majeure* would bring the miners' dispute to an end. He proposed 'with great and unaffected reluctance' a Coal Mines (Minimum Wage) Bill to establish a statutory minimum wage for miners employed underground (but not

16. *The Syndicalist*, January 1912; Mann (1923: 289–90).
17. Brown (1975: vii). *The Times* carried a series of articles condemning syndicalism in March 1911, and in a long feature on 16 April 1912 stated: 'The existence of a strong Syndicalist movement in this country can no longer be denied, though attempts have been made up till quite recently to deny it.'
18. TNA/HO 144/7062/220.603/87; *The Syndicalist*, June 1912; Holton (1973a: 414–18).

for surface workers), to be fixed under conditions that would vary with each class of worker and be established via new District Boards of employers and workers' representatives with 'independent' arbitrators. Passing such a Bill 'within a very short period of time', Asquith insisted, was 'absolutely imperative in the best interests of the country', so as to end the strike as 'a matter of paramount urgency'.[19]

In effect the government, which had initially assumed the role of mediator in the dispute to bring the two sides together for talks, albeit to no avail, then acted as arbitrator only to see its decision rejected, now utilised its final weapon, legislation, to force a settlement.[20] Asquith had not wanted a Bill to introduce a minimum wage, partly because it would be precisely the sort of 'coercion' of employers to which he was opposed, and partly because of the precedent it would set of government intervention in the relation between 'masters and men' in a labour market where liberal theory had it that wages were set by supply and demand. But he pressed forward the Bill as 'affording the best possible solution in the great emergency with which we are confronted',[21] and by 29 March it had successfully been rushed through all its stages in Parliament and received its Royal Assent, despite opposition from many employers, the conservative press and even some Cabinet members.

Although the new Act contained the principle of the minimum wage, the chief union demand of the 'five and two' was absent and it contained no clause fixing specific wage rates in the different coalfields; district minima were to be settled only after a return to work by the District Boards. The MFGB leaders agreed to ballot their members, resulting in a narrow but significant majority (244,011 to 201,013) in favour of continuing the strike, with several of the larger areas, including Lancashire and Yorkshire, recording considerable majorities against a resumption of work, as did the two North-Eastern counties of Northumberland and Durham.[22] The only major coalfield to vote in favour of a return to work was South Wales (by a margin of 62,538 to 31,127). This opposition to continuing the protracted national strike reflected strike weariness following the 1910–11 dispute, growing hunger, and depletion of local union financial reserves for strike pay, but was nevertheless a setback for the syndicalists of the Unofficial Reform Committee.

The MFGB executive committee overruled the ballot decision and called the strike off by utilising another newly instituted union rule change that required a two-thirds majority for its continuation. The failure of the Act

19. *The Times*, 20 March 1911; Heffer (2017: 697).
20. Moss (1983: 78).
21. Heffer (2017: 699).
22. Arnot (1954: 109); *The Times*, 1 April 1912.

to specify rates led to rank-and-file miners refusing to return to work in the Lancashire coalfields, and resistance spreading across the North of England, with riots in Golborne (between Wigan and Manchester) where the army was sent in after a police baton-charge failed to restore order. But by the end of April practically all pits were working normally, albeit with many miners believing they had been cheated of an assured victory.

Nonetheless, even if they had not won everything they demanded, the miners had obtained, for the first time in the history of labour legislation, the establishment of the principle of the minimum wage, with general wage increases almost everywhere, as well as the assurances to faceworkers that they would not suffer badly from working in abnormal places. Moreover, the Miners' Federation had powerfully demonstrated its offensive power, with union membership increasing from 586,000 in 1912 to 645,000 by 1913 and 761,184 by 1914.[23] As the suffragettes' *Votes for Women* acknowledged:

> The miners in fourteen short days have brought the Government, to legislation-point, whereas women have in nearly fifty years of agitation failed to achieve as much. Why is this? The reason obviously is that the miners' methods have been more effective ... It is only under pressure of sheer and stern necessity that [the government] have decided to run counter to their own inclinations by carrying such a measure.[24]

LONDON TRANSPORT STRIKE: MAY–AUGUST 1912

Within a few weeks following the settlement of the national miners' strike, the government's attention had to turn back again to the transport industry, notably with a 10-week London transport workers' strike that took place between May and August 1912. Unlike most of the 1911 transport strikes, it began as official union action and resulted in defeat. Its origins lay in the way complex sectional settlements that had terminated the London transport strike of 1911 generated constant friction over interpretation. The National Transport Workers' Federation (NTWF) complained that employers, if they could not dispense with union recognition altogether, insisted on dealing with its individual affiliated unions separately rather than a Federated bargaining body, and only consider a joint board representing employers and workers as a purely consultative body without any powers for settling disputes.[25]

23. Arnot (1954: 545).
24. *Votes for Women*, 22 March 1912.
25. Heath (2013: 145).

The trouble came to a head over the employment of non-unionists when a lighterage company employed a watchman who refused to join the Amalgamated Society of Watermen, Lightermen and Bargemen. On 16 May the Lightermen's Union, led by Harry Gosling (NTWF President), called out on strike all their members employed by the company. In response, the Association of Master Lightermen and Barge Owners, fearing 'their heads were to be chopped off one by one',[26] arranged for other firms to undertake the work of the firm involved in the dispute. When union members in these companies 'blacked' the work, they were dismissed by their employers and the dispute quickly escalated, with the Lightermen's Union calling out all its 6,000 members across the port.

Two days later the London district committee of the NTWF, and the DWRGWU (headed by Ben Tillett) and Stevedores' Union promised not to do the work of the Lightermen, and the NTWF executive met in London and, under pressure from members, called a total stoppage of all transport workers on the Thames and River Medway on the basis that 'upon your solidarity depends the whole issue of the dispute'.[27] It resulted in the Port of London being brought to a halt within a few days as some 100,000 workers, representing almost every trade, including dockers, stevedores, tugboatmen, seamen and many other sections, responded to the strike call or were indirectly involved.[28]

Taking the strike at face value, Askwith's immediate reaction was that 'the main cause of the dispute is the question of union and non-union labour'.[29] But Harry Gosling claimed this issue was only one of a series of other grievances and that a strike would have taken place anyway, it was merely a 'match to a fire already laid'.[30] In the process, the NTWF was to play a considerable role because no one union had emerged as the dominating force in the London docks. The decision to call a port-wide strike under the auspices of the Federation reflected a series of earlier confrontations between different affiliated groups anxious to extend the gains of 1911, as well as the fear that employers might launch an organised counter-attack similar to that which had occurred following the victorious 1889 strike, and which had come close to destroying trade unionism in the ports.[31]

26. Askwith ([1920] 1974: 221).
27. *Daily Mirror*, 28 May 1912.
28. Board of Trade (1913a: xxxix, 104–5).
29. Letter from Askwith to the King, 24 May 1912, cited in Pratten (1975: 230).
30. Gosling (1927: 158).
31. Holton (1976: 122); Clegg (1985: 53).

NTWF leaders issued two demands: recognition of the Federation as the representative of its constituent unions, and uniform pay at all grades at an average increase of 'tuppence' an hour. The *Daily Herald* served as the 'official organ' of the strike committee, with Tillett – one of the paper's leading sponsors – writing most of the material dealing with the dispute.

A series of 'monster' processions were organised from the East End into central London at least once a week, with sporadic clashes between strikers and police occurring along the route, and on occasions when food convoys were being escorted from the docks. An official report of one of a number of attacks upon a convoy carrying 'blackleg' cargo through Rotherhithe underlined the widespread participation of strikers' families:

> On June 11th a crowd of 3,000 lined the streets prior to the movement of good from the docks. There was a considerable proportion of women and children in the crowd and the disorder took place to some extent under the protection of their presence. Superintendent Waters stated that a woman with a baby aloft in her arms stood in front of a van proceeding along the Jamaica road, compelling the driver to stop while two or three men endeavoured to pull the driver from his seat.[32]

The Shipping Federation arranged for over 2,000 strikebreaking dockers from various centres to be brought into London and housed on ships being worked or in sheds ashore, with a volunteer vigilante group assisting them in escorting large bodies of local willing workers to the docks.[33]

Despite protests made by the NTWF strike committee to Reginald McKenna, who had been appointed the new Home Secretary in October 1911, that the police's rough handling of pickets and protection of imported labour represented the government taking sides, McKenna insisted police protection would be given to 'free labour' unloading and moving provisions. On 27 May, a special train of strikebreakers and men from the meat market arrived at the dock to unload the *Highland Brae*, with the goods then conveyed to Smithfield Market in convoy, accompanied by 1,000 police including 100 mounted men, with troops held in reserve. The Home Office meticulously recorded that: 'Protection was afforded by the Metropolitan police daily, Sunday excepted, throughout the strike', and between 27 May and 31 July 'they protected en route to Smithfield 187 convoys, comprising

32. 'Certain Disturbances at Rotherhithe on June 11th 1912, and Complaints against the Conduct of the Police in Connection Therewith', *Parliamentary Papers 1912–13* xlvii (Cd 6367), p. 4; TNA/HO 144/1211/223.877/725.

33. Saluppo (2019: 588).

8,600 vehicles'.[34] With the employers determined not to make concessions, and some 13,000 imported labourers working under 'protection' in the port by the end of June,[35] the protracted strike became increasingly characterised by numerous violent episodes in the Royal Albert, West India, Surrey Commercial and Tilbury Docks, with many striking dockers charged with assault on 'blacklegs' and either fined or sentenced to several months hard labour. With significant numbers on both sides carrying revolvers, a serious gun battle took place on the steamship *City of Colombo* in the Victoria Docks with 'several men … afterwards removed to hospital suffering from shot wounds'.[36]

Tillett, who had initially opposed the strike, but been outvoted and overruled, became impatient at the employers' continuing refusal to talk and increasingly became combative in his stance as the dispute wore on. At a mass meeting of over 20,000 on Tower Hill, he dramatically called on God to 'strike dead' Lord Devonport (chair of the Port of London Authority), to which the crowd responded with hands held up 'Oh God, strike Lord Devonport dead'.[37] Tillett, whose rousing oratory was often far more militant than his actions,[38] caught the temper of his members when he told them at a demonstration in Hyde Park on 7 July that he 'did not want to utter any threats':

> … but if they could not win by peaceful methods, if the capitalists and Government said they should not have the right to live, then they must take the power into their own hands. We must use other means, and I openly state here that the only means we have to use is violence and the use of every physical power we have …[39]

Meanwhile, in the absence of the Prime Minister, who was on holiday in Sicily, a group of Cabinet Ministers led by Lloyd George stepped into the fray by announcing a Commission of Inquiry to be conducted by Sir Edward Clarke to look into the causes of the dispute. The Clarke report, promptly presented on 27 May, recommended recourse to the Board of Trade and suggested the question of enforcing agreements on employers who were not

34. Superintendents' Daily Reports to Home Office from 25 May–8 August 1912, TNA/HO 144/1211/223.877; Home Office, *London Dock Strike 1912: Confidential Memoranda and Correspondence*, TNA/HO 45/10674/218.781/22; Weinberger (1991: 109, 110).
35. Weinberger (1991: 110).
36. TNA/HO 144/1211/223.877/692; *The Morning Post*, 1 August 1912.
37. *Daily Mirror*, 25 July 1912.
38. Schneer (1982: 160).
39. *Glasgow Herald*, 8 July 1912, cited in Holton (1976: 123).

members of their associations could only be dealt with by legislation.[40] Ministers made attempts to arrange a conference with both sides, putting forward proposals for a joint board consisting of representatives of both employers and unions that would have appeal panels with the power to impose penalties for breach of agreement.

But the employers flatly refused to consider any proposals without an unconditional return to work, and made it clear they were emphatically opposed 'under any circumstances' to recognition of the NTWF as the negotiating body for the mass of small unions to which the workers of the Port of London belonged.[41] As Lord Devonport saw it, the strike was on an issue 'on which no compromise is possible'.[42] Against this determined resistance, government ministers made no progress and exercised little subsequent influence.[43]

In this situation the Transport Workers' Federation's national executive on Monday 10 June played what it believed would be its trump card – to send out a telegram recommending an immediate national sympathetic strike of transport workers in ports across the country.[44] It issued a manifesto to its members appealing for their support, stating that, as well as ignoring agreements and spurning the government's proposals, the owners 'depend upon the brutal weapons of starvation and intimidation, police and military repression, to beat us'.[45] But the response to the strike call was very poor and quickly collapsed.

To some extent, the meagre response can be explained by the failure of Tillett and other Federation officials to make practical preparations for national action outside the capital. There was no concerted campaign of agitation in the provinces; instead, they mistakenly assumed the militant pattern of 1911 would be repeated. Another problem was the way in which it was only in London that employers' resistance to collective bargaining and the issue of union control over hiring had been maintained intact, whereas outside London most transport workers had achieved higher wages and union bargaining rights as a result of the 1911 strikes. This meant that by 1912 the London dispute could appear to some in the provinces as of only sectional advantage to those directly involved, with no common set of grievances that could unite all transport workers on the different waterfronts, as there had been the previous year.[46]

---

40. *Daily Herald*, 29 May 1912.
41. Clegg (1985: 54); Heath (2013: 146); Askwith ([1920] 1974: 223).
42. Kearley (1935: 175).
43. Lovell (1969: 200–1); Redman (2013: 44).
44. *Daily News*, 11 June 1912; *Daily Herald*, 11 June 1912.
45. *The Times*, 11 June 1912.
46. Holton (1973a: 441–2; 1976: 125).

An additional problem was that whereas in London the NTWF brought together twelve unions covering almost every trade within the docks, canals and shipping lines, in the provinces the influence of the Federation was negligible, with some two-thirds of its affiliate members in the NSFU and NUDL. Officials within these two unions were reluctant to jeopardise permanent collective bargaining systems and associated gains in union recognition from port employers by encouraging solidarity strike action for London men who were, in the case of the dockers, largely organised in the DWRGWU. For example, in Leith NUDL officials had signed an agreement which ruled that 'no strike shall in any case take place ... on account of the action of any employer not a member' of the local employers' association, and Sexton's national executive committee rejected the Federation's recommendation.[47]

Likewise, the NSFU's national executive, who had already considered the prospect of a national strike at an emergency meeting on 7 June, albeit in the absence of both Havelock Wilson (on tour in America until the end of July) and Tom Mann (in prison for most of June and July), decided that as it was already paying out £1,000 a week strike benefits to its 4,000 London members it would be unable to meet the costs of a national strike, quite apart from concerns over the threat to their provincial agreements. They informed the NTWF that the calling of a national strike 'would be detrimental to all concerned' and they would hold a ballot of their members to ascertain their support for any strike.[48] The ballot recorded a majority of 3,678 to 2,137 against a national strike, with a large section of the minority located in London.[49]

This lack of official support from the two major Federation-affiliated unions inevitably undermined the potential basis for solidarity action. It meant that, although the majority of transport union leaders and rank-and-file members sympathised with the London strikers, they failed to respond to the national strike call, with the exception of those ports organised within Tillett's DWRGWU, such as Manchester, Southampton, Plymouth, Bristol and South Wales – where strike action was taken by some workers, involving a total of about 20,000. But this action lasted only for a few days, while the ports in Liverpool and Hull (where Sexton's NUDL was the main force), Glasgow and elsewhere remained at work.[50]

47. Clegg (1985: 55).
48. Marsh and Ryan (1989: 63); Mogridge (1961: 385).
49. Marsh and Ryan (1989: 63); Clegg (1985: 55).
50. *Daily Herald*, 12 and 13 June 1912; Holton (1976: 125; 1973a: 435–9). In Glasgow the main union was the Scottish Union of Dock Labourers.

As a result, the London port workers were left isolated and their bargaining position considerably undermined – being unable to effectively prevent ships being diverted to other ports, and without the threat to the capital's food supplies that had put pressure on employers the previous August. Yet despite disappointment at the abortive national strike, the intransigence of the employers produced in turn a determination to fight to the bitter end, and on 23 June about 100,000 men, women and children participated in another march several miles-long from the East End to Hyde Park.[51] The strikers continued to resist for another six weeks, with Tillett making efforts through his rousing oratory to bolster spirits at the daily mass meetings at Tower Hill.

A growing availability of 'blacklegs' who were 'offered extra wages … for the purposes of accommodating the masters … from 5s an hour to 30s a day' increasingly became a crucial challenge.[52] The Shipping Federation's *Lady Jocelyn* sailed up the Thames into the port and was used as a floating hostel for 'free labourers', and it was reported that 'by 17 June there were 9,600 imported labourers and the numbers continued to increase week by week until by the beginning of July, they reached the numbers required to keep the port going'.[53] This huge influx of scabs, combined with the financial privation and gradual drying up of union relief funds, led some strikers, concerned for the sheer survival of their families, to begin to return to work. The numbers of men at work in the port (including both workers abandoning the strike and those imported) increased to 19,000 by 23 July.[54]

Notwithstanding solidarity funds being generated by different union bodies (as well as from Australia, United States and Germany), there were advanced signs of hardship among the strikers' families, with many children being fed by charities. Extensive rioting broke out on the docks, with fires lit and wagons of food looted. Tillett condemned the way employers 'contributed to the murder by starvation of their children, their women, and their men'.[55] As Sylvia Pankhurst observed:

> The strike was maintained to the point of starvation … Misery was intense, homes were sold, children died … Thousands of sympathisers lent their aid, but the area and extent of the poverty was too great for volunteer help to avail; the people were starved into submission.[56]

---

51. *Daily Herald*, 24 June 1912.
52. Ibid., 29 May 1912.
53. Broodbank (1921: 453).
54. Clegg (1985: 56).
55. *The Times*, 25 July 1912.
56. Pankhurst (1977: 366).

In other developments, George Askwith persuaded Lord Devonport to meet Gosling, the Lightermen's Secretary, and Harry Orbell, DWRGL official (both members of the NTWF executive) in behind-the-scenes talks aimed at resolving the dispute. Yet while Devonport gave some assurances on employers not breaching existing agreements concerning hours and wages which had existed before the strike, he also made it clear the 'Federation ticket' issued by the NTWF through its affiliated unions would not be recognised.[57] And although the Cabinet discussed the possibility of legislation to resolve the dispute, the Prime Minister was unconvinced; with the docks partially operating unlike the mines which had been completely closed down, direct government intervention did not appear to be necessary.[58]

In the meantime, Mann, newly released from prison, spoke in support of the strike at a mass meeting at Tower Hill and made a last-ditch effort to salvage the situation in a 'stirring appeal' titled 'How to Win' printed in the *Daily Herald*, which declared:

> ... after a magnificent eight weeks, it is the duty of all workers to help to win the fight for the workers ... All the pressure needed could and would be provided by a two days' stoppage of all in the shipping and railway industries ...
>
> To stand by indifferently will be a social crime ... I put in my plea for Solidarity.[59]

In a very late initiative, Havelock Wilson, who had returned from America, joined forces with Mann (as in 1910–11), this time to promote a campaign in support of London, visiting four or five provincial ports to try to persuade workers to make the strike a national one.[60] Within a few days the seamen's leader had persuaded a group of 1,000 transport workers in Hull to back a national stoppage.[61] But shortly afterwards, Wilson, facing some opposition elsewhere, reported to his NSFU executive that the London strike was hopeless, and induced them to tell the Transport Workers' Federation strike committee that unless the strike was called off their members would be ordered back to work.[62] While an earlier more energetic NTWF campaign outside London from the outset of the strike might have generated a much

57. *The Times*, 18 July 1912.
58. Pratten (1975: 246–7).
59. *Daily Herald*, 22 July 1912.
60. Marsh and Ryan (1989: 63).
61. *Daily Herald*, 24 July 1912.
62. Mogridge (1961: 385–6); Marsh and Ryan (1989: 63).

greater level of provincial support, this belated effort was inevitably destabilised by the loss of momentum.

The poor response to calls for sympathetic strike action and consequent isolation of the London strikers, combined with the resolute hostility from the port employers, growing number of 'blacklegs' and hardships endured by strikers and their families, eventually prompted the NTWF Strike Committee to call a return to work on Saturday 27 July, with no provision even for reinstatement. At first this was rejected by a mass meeting of strikers, to the extent that when Gosling asked: 'Are you prepared to go back tomorrow? I want a show of hands', not a single hand of an estimated 30,000 was raised in support. They declared instead that 'they would return to work if the conditions were the same as those which prevailed prior to the strike, and on those conditions only'.[63] But by Monday considerable numbers of dockers and stevedores had drifted back and a general return to work had occurred by 6 August.

With the London strikers starved into a submission 'a sense of defeat and weariness hung over [the men] for many weeks and months after the summer of 1912'.[64] It represented a damaging reversal of fortune for the NTWF – which lost 30,000 members – and affiliated unions – notably the DWRGWU whose membership declined from 50,000 to 37,000 over the following year.[65] However, membership losses were confined to London and there was no general offensive against the unions in other ports.[66] And defeat and failure of national strike action brought the issue of *amalgamation* to the fore, rather than *federation* to the NTWF. A national rank-and-file Amalgamation Committee was formed in September 1912, supported by a number of syndicalist activists and other militants. This Committee campaigned for a single national transport workers' union to overcome the sectional identities that had remained intact inside the NTWF. Moreover, despite the severity of the 1912 defeat, it by no means extinguished the broader movement of working-class militancy that continued to gather pace and reach across other industries.[67]

WEST MIDLANDS METAL WORKERS' STRIKES: APRIL–JULY 1913

The engineering industry did not experience any national strike action in contrast to waterside transport, railways and coalmining. Nevertheless, there

63. *Daily Herald*, 29 July 1912.
64. Gosling (1927: 164).
65. Coates and Topham (1994: 437–8); Clegg (1985: 56).
66. Clegg (1985: 66).
67. Lovell (1969: 209); Holton (1976: 129–30).

were 92 strikes between 1910 and 1914, almost triple the number in the 1905–09 period.[68] Grievances, notably among skilled workers, centred on the general decline in real wages and changes in technology and work methods as mechanisation replaced craftsmen with rapidly increasing numbers of semi-skilled workers employed as 'machine-minders'. Employers reduced labour costs through low wages, hostility towards unionisation, and the exploitation of women workers who were sometimes employed at half of adult male wages.

While a progressive minority within the Amalgamated Society of Engineers (ASE) recognised the need to control competition by lower-paid rivals by admitting women to the Society, the fears of skilled engineers was so great that most branches simply refused to recruit them into membership. As a result, the small engineering all-grades Workers' Union (WU) had been founded in 1898 for the express purpose of organising traditionally neglected groups of unskilled, semi-skilled and women workers ignored by the ASE.[69]

Like most industries before the war, engineering lacked any system of national wage determination – wages and conditions were instead founded on a system of 'district rates' determined by ASE District Committees who enforced these as far as possible across the local area. Likewise, district organisation became the WU organisational unit. By 1913, the West Midlands – the home of the most rapidly expanding sections of engineering – became an important base for a series of small-scale local stoppages that culminated in a vast wave of strike action.[70]

The West Midlands district WU official, John Beard, helped to organise semi-skilled and unskilled engineering workers in Birmingham from 1904, and during 1911–12 the union established a foothold in the 'Black Country,'[71] expanding its local organising staff to five, including the ex-National Federation of Women Workers' organiser Julia Varley. It developed a campaign for a minimum wage of 23 shillings a week for male workers and 12 shillings for adult female workers, and for union recognition.[72] According to Askwith:

> … the strike commenced with the small beginnings of some girls in Dudley saying that they could not live any longer on the wages paid to them. Just as years ago the London match-girls had started the London dock strike,

68. Burgess (1989: 296–7).
69. Hyman (1971: 39–41); Holton (1976: 150).
70. Hyman (1971: 48).
71. The 'Black Country' to the west of Birmingham gained its name in the mid-nineteenth century due to the smoke from the coal mines and ironworking foundries and forges.
72. Clegg (1985: 58).

so these girls lit the torch which fired the Midlands. The men followed suit in factory after factory.[73]

There were three main phases to the strike wave that subsequently swept the West Midlands, an area not regarded as militant.[74] The first strike movement took place between November 1912 and April 1913, involving a series of individual walkouts by low-paid, male and female unskilled engineering workers across Birmingham, Smethwick and West Bromwich. Invariably it involved a majority of non-unionised workers, with Beard and Varley immediately dispatched to represent the strikers and successfully forcing the separate employers to meet with them.

On Monday 14 April, a near riot occurred outside the Kenrick's 'hollow-ware' works when some 700–800 strikers and their sympathisers blocked the gates in front of the works and, despite the presence of police, prevented a much smaller number of 'blacklegs' returning to work after lunch. As elsewhere, a settlement was reached which conceded virtually all the union's demands, and success achieved at these companies led many other local firms to fall like dominos, attempting to avoid strike action before it started by announcing they would pay the 23 shillings minimum.[75] By the end of April the 23 shillings had been conceded by most of the principal firms in Birmingham, Smethwick and West Bromwich, with an average increase of 2 shillings for 10,000 workers.[76]

In the second phase, a prolonged strike started on Friday 23 April in the Smethwick works of the Birmingham Carriage Company, spreading to nearly half the company's 2,000 workers, with the WU formulating an advance of 2 shillings to apply the 23 shillings minimum. As elsewhere, most strikers entered the dispute as non-unionists and were ineligible for strike pay. A massive community effort provided relief, with charity shows at theatres, tradesmen donating food and the Town Council of Smethwick feeding children at school. Frequent meetings and demonstrations were held to maintain morale, while the union arranged special meetings of strikers' wives to ensure their support.[77]

The success of the minimum wage campaign in Birmingham encouraged the spread of the strike movement to numerous engineering firms in the Black Country, including many women WU members, and the union

73. Askwith ([1920] 1974: 252).
74. Hyman (1971: 52).
75. Staples and Staples (1990: 165).
76. Hyman (1971: 52–3); Clegg (1985: 58).
77. Coates and Topham (1994: 387–8); Hyman (1971: 53).

STRIKE COMMITTEE, MESSRS. A. KENRICK'S & UNITED HINGE CO.'S DISPUTE.
BIRMINGHAM DISTRICT.

ORGANISER MISS JULIA VARLEY, centre; ORGANISER JOHN BEARD, left hand; ORGANISER G. E. GEOBEY, right hand.

Figure 5.2 The joint male and female strike committee linking the United Hinge cold rolling mill and Kenrick's 'hollowware' works during the 1913 West Midlands metal workers' strikes.

Credit: Modern Records Centre, University of Warwick.

demanded the general minima of 23 shillings and 12 shillings. This third phase of the strike movement during the latter part of May and whole of June brought a rapid quickening of pace, and attracted national attention. Smethwick carriage strikers, still in deadlock after five weeks on strike, made a renewed surge towards victory, with 1,500 marching in formation to Oldbury and Wednesbury, where other workers in the same trade in the Metropolitan Company were persuaded to join the strike. Beard called out 200 of the Saltley members, claiming that work was being diverted there from the strikebound factories, and almost at once the firm retaliated by locking out 7,600 workers. Thus, within four days, the Smethwick dispute involved more than 10,000 additional carriage workers.[78]

The tube trade workers were equally anxious to extend the scale of their disputes, and the topography of the Black Country allowed them to march from factory to factory and town to town, bringing out new waves of workers, according to the *Wolverhampton Express and Star* 'singing with considerable

78. Hyman (1971: 53–5); Coates and Topham (1994: 388).

intimidation what became their theme song "Hello, hello, here we are again".[79] From Wolverhampton, Wednesbury and Walsall the unrest spread through Great Bridge and West Bromwich to Halesowen, where 5,000 workers at the Coombs Wood works of Stewart and Lloyd joined the strike at the end of May. As some firms conceded the 23 shillings and work was restored, new disputes broke out to take their place. The 3,000 workers at GEC, a firm with notoriously bad conditions, made an especially large addition to the total number of workers on strike.[80]

Again, even though local WU officials like Beard and Varley had often not initiated strikes, they quickly supported them, articulated workers' demands, and helped win solidarity, in the process attracting many new union members. As the ASE's Midlands Organising District Secretary wryly observed: 'The Workers' Union is not so much directing the strikers as following them, and is making members by the thousand.'[81] Local strike leaders often pushed the momentum of strikes even further, with Teddy Williams of Bilston and Joe Thickett of Walsall leading attacks on factories worked by 'blackleg' labour and upon mass police concentrations brought in to defend them. Widespread sabotage took place in the factories with 'shaft-belts cut' and 'machinery damaged'.[82]

In a typical incident at Fellows Ltd of Bilston, a large crowd of strikers tried to storm the works' gates and stoned the 150 policemen posted there, successfully preventing scabs from working in the strikebound factory.[83] Five young girl strikers, who had been imprisoned for their alleged intimidation of 'blacklegs', were met on their release by a demonstration under the auspices of the WU, with thousands of people lining the route and giving loud cheers for the girls; a large meeting was held afterwards addressed by Varley and local union reps.[84]

The intervention of Tom Mann at a number of mass meetings during the strike contributed to the general mood of unrest.[85] Mann (who had been a leading founder of the Workers' Union and Vice-President in its early years, and had stood for election as general secretary of the ASE in April 1913) took up the issue of a minimum wage for the unskilled in a pamphlet, *The Labourers'*

---

79. *The Times*, 9 June 1913; *Wolverhampton Express and Star*, 30 June 1913.
80. Coates and Topham (1994: 388); Hyman (1971: 55–6).
81. ASE *Monthly Journal and Report*, June 1913, cited in Hyman (1971: 56); Carr (1978: 34–5).
82. Midlands Employers' Federation to Asquith, July 1913, TNA/HO 45/10706/239.811/8; Holton (1976: 150–1); Barnsby (1989: 491).
83. Hyman (1971: 58).
84. *Labour Leader*, 11 August 1911.
85. *Wolverhampton Express and Star*, 11–15 June 1913.

Minimum Wage: A Demand for 25s a Week which was explicitly geared to policies of direct action and solidarity as a means of remedying poverty:

> Socialists and Syndicalists, Trade Unionists and Co-operators are requested to help in the Minimum Wage movement ... The rates of pay in the Black Country districts are awful to think of, and in some districts near West Bromwich the pay of the women is a hideous crime ... No longer must the workers accept unchallenged the domination of the capitalist class; the only way to demonstrate that we are truly conscious is to be actually engaged in the class war.[86]

As Askwith reflected, the earlier strikes of transport workers, railwaymen and miners had their 'demonstration effect' on the previously non-union men and women of the Midlands:

> The dispute in the Midlands was a sequel to the economic disputes of 1911 and 1912, but it must not be supposed that any of these disputes failed to leave a mark. They indicated to labour the value of organisation, which was being actively pressed throughout the country, and the value of propaganda, which more and more made its force felt; they increased the cohesion of labour, particularly among semi-skilled and unskilled labour; they educated both leaders and rank and file on things to be done and things to be avoided in the course of a strike.[87]

At its peak the Black Country disputes encompassed an aggregated 40,000 strikers (with some 10,000 indirectly affected) in Wolverhampton, Walsall, Bilston, Darlaston, Smethwick and Birmingham, involving 'tube works, railway carriage and waggon works, metal-rolling works, boiler and bridge works, nut and bolt works and other allied trades'.[88] Because so few of the workers at the strike-hit firms had been members of the WU more than six months, almost all were ineligible for strike benefits, and so money had to be raised to feed workers and their families. Local collections were arranged, with barrel organs touring the streets of Smethwick and West Bromwich, and on Sunday 13 April a parade was organised in West Bromwich in which 3,000 took part. In June, four contingents of strikers marched from Birmingham,

86. Mann (1913b). Mann also wrote an article 'Rally to the Fighters!' in the *Daily Herald*, 4 July 1913.
87. Askwith ([1920] 1974: 257).
88. Board of Trade (1914: p. xxiii); 'Labour Unrest at Darlaston and Wednesbury', 28 June 1913, TNA/HO 45/10706/239.811/6; *Daily Chronicle*, 28 June 1913.

respectively, to Bristol, Manchester, Doncaster, and Lancashire and Yorkshire, holding meetings and collecting donations en route,[89] with a large welcome for the marchers in London's Trafalgar Square.[90]

The parades, collections and rallies received widespread public sympathy,[91] albeit 'in spite of the activities of relief agencies, distress among the families of the strikers bec[a]me increasingly acute'[92] with strikers having to resort to Poor Law relief. Women were intimately involved with the strike, not only as affected workers themselves, but again with the WU organising special meetings of the wives of male strikers to help sustain community morale.

The employers, who had been in retreat since the first wave of strikes, formed a Midlands Engineering Employers' Federation and in early June conceded some parts of the union's claims, but insisted on a differential of 2 shillings between Birmingham's minimum of 23 shillings and the Black Country rate. A union ballot decisively rejected this offer by 4,717 to 99, with the level of violence, stone-throwing and street confrontations with police notably increasing.[93]

On 2 July Askwith intervened and within three days had managed to resolve the dispute with a settlement that granted a minimum of 23 shillings in the Birmingham district, and 22 shillings for the Black Country for six months after the resumption of work and 23 shillings thereafter; women who had come out in large numbers to support the strike also won their demand for an increased minimum wage to 12 shillings.[94] Work was resumed by the majority of workers on Monday 14 July, and by practically everybody by 18 July.

Although in general terms, the Black Country metal workers' strikes dealt a severe blow to employers' power and solidarity, evidence of continuing rank-and-file discontent was manifest after the eventual negotiation of the strike settlement between union officials and employers. Agreements included the right to union recognition at a number of target companies, and achieved significant pay increases for both male and female workers through the introduction of a universal minimum wage for a range of diverse metal trades, which would apply to the least skilled labourer, as well as at the lower level to women and young workers.

---

89. *Daily Herald*, 18 June 1913.
90. Ibid., 4 July 1913.
91. Staples and Staples (1990: 166).
92. Askwith ([1920 1974: 255).
93. Coates and Topham (1994: 388; Pratten (1975: 286).
94. Clegg (1985: 59); Heath (2013: 157).

But in a context where labourers' wages varied considerably from firm to firm, even within the same factory, the agreement caused some dissatisfaction because skilled craftsmen and semi-skilled workers on piece-rates gained little or nothing. It took some days before a complete return to work was achieved, with union officials reporting that dissenting strikers made threats of personal violence against them at a mass meeting in Walsall. Even after the return to work, there remained a strong movement in favour of direct action and more militant methods in West Midlands branches of the Workers' Union.[95] Moreover, the WU failed to challenge the practice of paying unskilled girls and women *less* than unskilled boys and men of the same age, accepting the notion of the 'family wage' that privileged male workers who the union believed were their main natural constituency.[96]

Nonetheless, the Workers' Union reaped a massive increase in union membership as a result of the strikes. Membership increases were considerable in Birmingham and even greater in the Black Country. Whereas in 1910 there had been a combined membership of only 250 in Smethwick, West Bromwich, Oldbury, Dudley, Wednesbury, Walsall and Wolverhampton, by 1914 each town had over 1,000 members, and nationally, union membership, having already leapt in 1911 from 5,000 to 18,000, saw a spectacular advance in 1913 with a gain of 68,000, raising total membership to 91,000.[97]

95. Holton (1976: 152); Hyman (1971: 59).
96. Staples and Staples (1990); Lewenhak (1977: 141).
97. Hyman (1971: 60–1, 35).

6
Diversity of Struggles

Thus far we have concentrated attention on some of the larger and nationally prominent strikes that took place during the years of the Labour Revolt. In this chapter we broaden the canvas to examine a variety of smaller, locally based and often less well-known, but nonetheless important disputes that took place during the period 1910–13. These involved not only some of the main industrial groups of workers we have already encountered, such as miners, dockers and railway workers, but also strikes by workers in a variety of other industries, including those involving women and young workers and even schoolchildren. Widening the focus of inquiry in this fashion – and less tied to a strict chronological sequencing – depicts the scale, and industrial and geographical scope, of industrial militancy, underlining its horizontality and mushrooming diversity.[1]

SOME NOTABLE STRIKES: 1911–13

To begin with we examine some notable strikes that occurred in a variety of different industries across the country, and which involved both workers' victories and defeats, as well as the characteristic features of rank-and-file/union official tensions, violent confrontations and widespread community support.

Waterside Strikes: 1911–13

In December 1911, just a few months after the national transport workers' strikes, the waterfront of Dundee became the scene of a 'declaration of industrial war'[2] when 600 carters, 700 dockers and 200 coal carters challenged the railway and general carting companies and the Shipping Federation over pay. The strike was led by the carters' leader and syndicalist sympathiser, Peter Gillespie, a founder member of the North of Scotland Horse and Motormen's

1. Lyddon (2012: 261).
2. Kenefick (2012: 202).

Association,[3] and generated widespread sympathy from other transport workers across Scottish and English ports. With the backing of the recently formed Scottish Union of Dock Labourers (SUDL),[4] NUDL, NSFU and NTWF the well-organised strike brought transport on the docks and railway depots to a standstill.

When traders attempted to move goods utilising imported scab labour it provoked widespread 'disorder' across the Dundee waterfront. As a result of the daily violence, city magistrates sent telegrams to the War Office, Home Office and the Scottish Office requesting 300 troops be sent immediately, and on 19 December three detachments of the Black Watch, accompanied by 167 additional police, arrived in the city. With local jute mills and factories soon brought to a complete standstill, thousands of laid-off textile workers joined the strikers, prominent amongst them being thousands of unionised female spinners from Lochee in the west of the city (who had been on strike between February and March 1911). They were subjected to a mounted police charge at a public meeting addressed by local and national labour leaders.[5] A 'monster procession' of around 4,000, which included 'mill lassies who took a prominent position within the ranks', was headed by the visiting Tom Mann alongside Gillespie.[6]

The Dundee strike leaders refused to allow goods to move in the city without a permit signed by Gillespie and the Carters' Union. The local press complained that employers were 'practically down on their knees … asking him [Gillespie] to allow them to drive stuff', which he steadfastly refused, except for the transportation of essential food, hospital supplies and deliveries of domestic coal. The public outcry against the mounted police charge, alongside the threat of the strike spreading to Leith and Glasgow, forced the local authorities, supported by the unions and employers, to contact the Board of Trade, and after 17 hours of meetings with George Askwith an agreement was reached that resulted in a more or less complete victory for the strikers.[7]

The waterside strike momentum then turned to the Glasgow docks, where on 29 January 1912, 7,000 dockers, carters, sailors, firemen, cooks, stewards, cranemen and riggers walked out in support of dockers who the employers had locked out in a dispute over the number of men in gangs, bringing the

3. Baxter and Kenefick (2011: 201); Kenefick (2015: 47–9; 1996: 139–43); Tuckett (1967).

4. The SUDL, which had come into existence in mid-July 1911 after Glasgow dockers left the ranks of Sexton's NUDL, extended its influence along the Clydeside waterfront. Kenefick (2000: 210–12).

5. *The Times*, 21 December 1911.

6. Kenefick (2012: 202–5).

7. Ibid., 206.

port to a halt.[8] Although this first phase of the dispute was officially ended on 10 February, following an agreement between employers and union officials, 6,400 dockers came out on strike again against their leaders' advice.[9] There was a significant degree of sympathetic action in the Clydeside region, with the seamen's union refusing to work alongside any non-union docker or 'blackleg', and the carters declaring they would stand by the dockers.[10] But following intervention by Askwith, arbitration found in favour of the employers and ended the dispute, despite some pockets of resistance.[11]

Between June and August 1912, a seven-week dockers' strike in Leith involving 4,000 workers represented by the NUDL claimed a rise of 'a penny per hour' on the day rate.[12] The powerful Leith Dock Employers' Association, with the assistance of the Shipping Federation, brought in 600 'free labourers' drawn from across England, some housed on the Federation's ships *Lady Jocelyn* and *Paris*, and protected day and night by police drawn from Edinburgh, Leith and beyond. Unable to gain entry into the docks, which were surrounded by a perimeter wall, and allowed only six pickets at a time under tight police escort, the dockers vainly attempted to persuade the scabs to stop work. Nonetheless, 200 carters and 600 seamen refused to handle any cargo or work boats operated by scab labour, dockers at Grangemouth, Granton and Kirkcaldy refused to handle cargo diverted from Leith, and Lothian miners also backed the dockers.[13]

This was followed by a 'strike epidemic' across Leith with female rope-workers and shipmasters and mates walking out over pay and conditions. Over three nights between 16 and 18 July there was serious rioting around the docks, with disturbances getting progressively more violent and numerous cases reported of alleged molestation of 'free labourers', and even an unsuccessful attempt to blow up the perimeter wall with gelignite. At the request of the Midlothian authorities, six naval gunboats were positioned in the Leith harbour, although they were withdrawn when questions were raised in Parliament.

Meanwhile, Edinburgh tramwaymen and the Leith boilermakers also took strike action, and although not directly connected to the docks' dispute, joined forces with the dockers, seamen, firemen and others on a demonstration through Leith, which ended with a rally with two platforms, around

8. Board of Trade (1913a: 104–5); Board of Trade, *Labour Gazette*, February 1912, p. 68.
9. Askwith ([1920] 1974: 193).
10. Kenefick (2000: 220).
11. Heath (2013: 141); ibid.: 219–23.
12. Board of Trade (1914: 90–1).
13. Kenefick (2007: 114–15).

which gathered crowds of 6,000 and 7,000, respectively, addressed by the French anarcho-syndicalist Madame Sorgue, and the leader of the French dockers' union.[14] But in the face of highly adverse picketing circumstances, and with reports of another Federation 'depot ship' carrying 300 new scabs on its way from Newcastle, it was decided by a large majority on the advice of the NUDL leadership to end the strike and return to work on the same conditions as before.

Nonetheless, there were relatively successful dock workers' strikes in 1912 in Manchester (3,500) and Tilbury (3,000), and in 1913 in Hull (10,000) and Manchester (3,500), amongst others.[15] In Bradford in May 1913, a carters' strike that involved attacks by a crowd of over 2,000 strikers and their supporters on police foot and mounted convoys of goods from railway depots won union recognition and a substantial pay rise.[16]

Railway Workers' and Miners' Strikes: 1912–13

Following their 1911 national strike, railway workers' discontent persisted during 1912 and 1913 over long working hours, low wages and discipline, with continuing dissatisfaction with the leadership of the ASRS (which became the National Union of Railwaymen (NUR) after its amalgamation with two other unions in the spring of 1913) and their support for conciliation and hostility to direct action. In August 1913 at a mass London rally to celebrate the second anniversary of the 1911 strike, some 20,000 listened to a platform of unofficial speakers call for a higher minimum wage and an eight-hour day, declaring 'it was no use relying on Unity House [union headquarters] – the men had to fight for themselves', and in Doncaster, J.H. Thomas was shouted down for his defence of conciliation.[17]

Discontent also manifested itself in a series of local unofficial disputes over disciplinary matters in 1912–13 such that 'it became more difficult for its full-time officers to keep fully in touch with opinion in the branches where the membership was increasingly influenced by syndicalist doctrines ... [and] were less prepared to tolerate the abuses of officialdom'.[18] For example,

---

14. Ibid.: 116–17. Antoinette Cauvin was known as the 'most dangerous woman in Europe' due to her role in spreading the ideas and methods of French syndicalism. She met with Mann and her speeches were reported in *The Syndicalist* in July and October 1912.
15. Board of Trade (1913a: 104–5; 1914: 140–3); monthly issues of *Labour Gazette*, 1913.
16. TNA/HO 45/10704/238840; *Bradford Daily Argus*, 27–30 May 1913.
17. *The Times*, 18 August 1913.
18. Bagwell (1963: 337).

in early December 1912, 3,000 railwaymen took unofficial strike action in support of an engine driver on the North Eastern Railway Company demoted after being convicted of drunkenness, prompting government intervention, a Home Office inquiry and subsequent reinstatement. And in September 1913, following a train crash involving 16 fatalities at Aisgill, Cumbria, which resulted in the conviction and imprisonment for manslaughter of the train driver, there were widespread calls for national strike action. It sparked a militant protest of almost 1,000 workers at St. Pancras station, which led an alarmed government – afraid of strike action on the railways at a time when unofficial action in solidarity with locked-out Dublin workers was very much on the agenda (Chapter 7) – agreeing to an unprecedented pardon.[19]

In the mining industry grievances also persisted on a significant scale in the aftermath of the 1912 national strike settlement, with unrest often directed against pay awards made by arbitrators under the Minimum Wage Act which involved district minima being fixed at lower levels than the MFGB demanded. There was also resentment over lengthy working hours, suspensions and dismissals, non-union labour and many other issues. In July 1913, 1,000 Cardiff miners struck for three days for being prevented from attending the funeral of a comrade who had been killed at work.[20]

Although many union officials remained wedded to conciliatory trade union policies and refused to countenance industrial action, that did not prevent recurrent strikes, albeit these were often small scale affecting single pits. Larger strikes included those in Cannock Chase (8,000), St. Helens (7,000), Rhondda Valley (6,000), Merthyr Tydfil (5,000), Ebbw Vale (4,000), Sunderland (2,000), Gateshead (1,600) and Rotherham (1,600),[21] as well as a strike in May 1913 over non-union labour which extended to 50,000 across the South Wales and Monmouthshire coalfield.[22]

North-East Lancashire Cotton Weavers' Lockout: December 1911–January 1912

Following the successful outcome of the one-week spinners' industry-wide lockout in October 1910 (Chapter 4), the production and employment boom in the Lancashire cotton industry presented the opportunity to remedy a series of cotton workers' grievances over wages and conditions, albeit most

19. Ibid.: 337–40); Cole and Arnot (1917: 32–5); Howell (1991:123–54); Pratten (1975: 257–75); Board of Trade (1913a: xvii).
20. Board of Trade (1914: xviii, 110, 90–1).
21. Board of Trade (1913a; 1914); monthly issues of *Labour Gazette*, 1913.
22. Board of Trade (1913a: 80–7, xvi–xvii); monthly issues of *Labour Gazette*, 1913.

strikes were small and locally based.[23] While the majority of spinners' strikes were official, most weavers' strikes were unofficial, although union officials also responded to the mood of workers by officially calling strikes that might have proceeded anyway.

The North-East Lancashire cotton weavers' lockout of 1911–12 was to be one of the largest disputes during the Labour Revolt and attracted nationwide attention. Following a demand by the Amalgamated Weavers' Association, the largest of the cotton unions (with a huge female membership) to the Cotton Spinners' and Manufacturers' Association for the establishment of a closed shop, weavers in Accrington walked out over the refusal of management to dismiss two non-union workers in December 1911. Mill-by-mill strikes threatened to escalate. When the employers responded by giving notice of a general lockout, the industry was brought to a standstill on 28 December with an estimated 160,000 workers involved.[24]

While weavers' union officials had been obliged to give their support to local closed shop strikes at individual mills where 85 per cent or more workers were union members, in this more generalised case they believed there was no possibility of the employers' association conceding, and so introduced a claim for a general increase of 5 per cent on the standard piecework rates, hoping the lockout would be suspended while negotiations proceeded and the Accrington issue resolved locally. With the employers steadfastly refusing to budge, Askwith held a series of conferences with both parties, and succeeded in brokering a compromise settlement that work would be resumed on the basis of the non-union issue being frozen for six months.

Although the great majority of weavers were back at work by 22 January 1912, the terms were condemned at mass meeting in many parts of Lancashire, with unofficial strikes and threats of unofficial action in several towns. Arthur Henderson, ex-chairman of the Labour Party, complained about the way 'some of the rank-and-file expect too much' from the agreement reached by union officials and 'conclude they have been "sold"' to express their disappointment.[25]

After six months the Amalgamated Weavers' Association had achieved a 5 per cent increase in piece-rates, but concluded that they could not pursue the closed shop any further. Union officials had to mollify union members who wanted to continue the struggle, with a mass meeting in Blackburn passing a resolution against the terms of the settlement, with only two dissenting voices, and two mass meetings in Nelson denouncing the settlement

23. Board of Trade (1912: 64; 1913a: 16–19, 42; 1914: 16–19, 42).
24. Board of Trade (1912: 29); Askwith ([1920] 1974: 187–8); Clegg (1985: 41–3).
25. Cited in Askwith ([1920] 1974: 199).

by booing and hissing officials.[26] Even so, this partial defeat, far from resulting in industrial peace, triggered unabated militancy continuing throughout the rest of 1912 and 1913,[27] with weavers' union membership increasing from 134,000 in 1911 to 179,000 by the end of 1912.[28]

Lancashire Agricultural Workers' Strike: June–July 1913

Between 1912 and 1914 there were numerous small agricultural workers' strikes on individual farms in which 'the issues fought out had bearings on the conditions of workers over far wider areas'.[29] In the process, the National Agricultural and Rural Workers Union, which had originally built a membership base in East Anglia, began organising in Lancashire, although it resisted rank-and-file calls in the area for strike action over pay, with general secretary George Edwards declaring: 'I have always been against the strike weapon being used until other means have failed to secure justice' and advising members to 'be very moderate in their demands and courteous to their employers, and not give them any excuse for extreme action'.[30]

But with farmers provoking action by victimising union members and evicting them from their tied cottages, and a demonstration of 2,000 calling for an increase in workers' notoriously low wages, union officials felt under increasing pressure to issue strike notices, and on 23 June 1913, 2,500 Lancashire farm labourers walked out on official strike. They elected a strike committee, held mass meetings and organised the picketing of farms to 'turn out' most of the labourers still working and stop wagons taking produce to market.[31]

Liverpool trade unions contributed to the strike fund, with dockers and ships' stewards picketing boats to ensure strikebreakers were not brought in by sea. The Ormskirk branch of the NUR – under the influence of its secretary John Phipps, a syndicalist supporter who had been a member of the 1911 Liverpool transport strike committee – refused to handle or convey any farm produce, and Liverpool NUR threatened to follow suit. The strike was marked by its bitterness and violence with extra police drafted in and billeted in farmhouses and used to escort convoys of wagons to Liverpool. The *Daily Herald* reported on various 'Scrimmages between Farm Pickets and Police', including one where foot and mounted police were met by a band of pickets

26. White (1978: 138–9, 142).
27. Ibid.: 126–7, 144.
28. Clegg (1985: 43).
29. Groves (1949: 139).
30. Edwards (1922: 177).
31. Mutch (1982/83: 56–67).

who, 'encouraged by their womenfolk', threw stones and sticks, with a number of arrests being made.[32] With less than half the usual amount of produce on sale in the Liverpool market, the strike ended on 7 July 1913 with workers successfully winning a rise of 2 shillings a week, a weekly half-day holiday and union recognition.[33]

Clydebank Singer Strike: March–April 1911

In March–April 1911, strike action broke out at the American-owned Singer Sewing Machine Company in Clydebank, one of the world's earliest multinational manufacturing companies. The huge industrial plant employed over 12,000 workers and incorporated the most up-to-date production and 'Taylorist' labour management techniques. The strike was the culmination of several years of smouldering grievances centring on de-skilling, speed-up, intensifying workloads, increased supervision and a host of other 'petty tyrannies',[34] with the fiercely anti-union Singer only reluctantly recognising two skilled craft unions in the plant.

It originated among twelve young women in the cabinet-polishing department over an attempt by management to reduce the headcount, increase the workload of those remaining and cut piece-rates. The women were immediately supported by the majority of the 2,000 other women employed in the factory, and within a couple of days the dispute had spread to other departments to involve the men, with some 9,000 of the 11,000 male workers out in sympathy, bringing the plant to a complete standstill.

Contributing to the outburst of shopfloor militancy was the role played by a group of young SLP members around Tom Bell, who had channelled and directed the radical challenge to management over the period 1910–11.[35] In early 1910, William Paul, one of the main theorists of the SLP, had begun a series of lunch-hour meetings at the Kilbowie plant and growing interest in these meetings, together with encouraging sales of SLP literature, prompted the formation of a Sewing Machine Workers' Industrial Union Group.[36] Through sustained propaganda work, the 'industrial unionists' developed a wider base, including some support from local ILP activists, and membership grew steadily to 150 by December 1910, with a name change to the Sewing Machine Group of the Industrial Workers of Great Britain (IWGB) that

32. *Labour Herald*, 28 June 1913.
33. Mutch (1982/3: 56–67); Clegg (1985: 89).
34. Gordon (1991: 255); Glasgow Labour History Workshop (1996b: 198).
35. Glasgow Labour History Workshop (1996b: 198); Gordon (1991: 256).
36. Bell (1941: 71–5); Challinor (1977: 100).

assumed the functions of a union along the lines of their American Industrial Workers of the World (IWW) counterpart.

The IWGB advocated a system of shop committees through which grievances could be reported at departmental level and then linked up through a 'General Committee of the Industrial Union Group' or Works Committee. It was effectively a shop stewards' form of organisation that could bring together representatives from each department as the means to break down barriers to solidarity, with the slogan 'An injury to one is an injury to all'. And in the early months of 1911 the shop committees in a number of departments became embroiled in a series of disputes with management, in the process boosting workers' confidence and collective power, with a meteoric growth of the IWGB membership from 150 in December 1910 to 850 in early March 1911 and 1,500 by mid-March 1911.[37]

While the IWGB had little influence on the outbreak of the dispute, they played a crucial role in extending it on the first day to four of the departments that contained the largest numbers of IWGB members,[38] which in turn encouraged the majority of the workforce, including skilled craft workers, to also walk out. At a mass meeting held in the SLP rooms in Clydebank a strike committee was formed, composed of five elected delegates from each department on strike, totalling between 150 and 190, in effect replicating the IWGB's structure as the form of representation and organisation.

The strike committee, which met twice daily in the SLP rooms and elected a small sub-committee of seven charged with negotiating with management, crystallised workers' demands into an increase in piece-rate wages for those women affected by work reorganisation in the polishing room, along with union recognition and collective bargaining rights. Strike Districts were established in other geographical areas to keep informed the 4,000 or so workers who lived outside the Clydebank area, with each district having a designated speaker and meeting place where the day's proceedings were reported each evening. To publicise their case and maintain solidarity the strike committee also organised a number of processions and mass gatherings, including one of 8,000 through Clydebank and another of 10,000 in Kilbowie Park.[39]

However, most IWGB members were confined to only four of the 41 departments in the factory, had little experience of trade union organisation or running and sustaining a mass strike. Their influence on the strike committee and the strike was limited because they were only a small minority,

37. Glasgow Labour History Workshop (1996b: 201–3).
38. *Glasgow Herald*, 24 March 1911.
39. Glasgow Labour History Workshop (1989: 31, 48).

although they contributed to building the solidarity that characterised the strike for the first fortnight.[40]

But the initial upsurge of defiance and enthusiasm was to evaporate in the face of management's threat to close the works, and their use of the strike-breaking tactic of a referendum. This was delivered via postcards sent direct to workers' homes, calling on them to agree to confirm their agreement to go back to work and to return the forms within 24 hours or be dismissed. The strike committee was caught off guard by the initiative and, amidst widespread claims of ballot rigging, the referendum resulted in a 6,527 to 4,025 vote to return to work. The dispute ended on Monday 10 April, with the union conceding defeat.[41]

Within a few weeks of the termination of the strike, there was the systematic victimisation of hundreds of strike leaders, IWGB members and many political activists in the plant, including over 20 members of the SLP, 60 ILP members and a number of SDP members,[42] with the virtual collapse of trade unionism amongst the majority of unskilled and semi-skilled workers.[43] Ironically, the forced dispersal of labour activists in search of alternative employment was to have a dramatic impact on radical socialist politics on Clydeside during the war.[44]

London Tailors' and Tailoresses' Strike: April–June 1912

In London's West End in April 1912, against the backcloth of the continuing London transport strike, 7,000–8,000 highly skilled tailors and tailoresses at 200 workshops and factories went on strike demanding more pay, shorter hours, better conditions and the closed shop. Some of the strikers were members of the Amalgamated Society of Tailors and Tailoresses. A crucial test was whether the less skilled tailors and tailoresses in the East End would take action to support the West End. These East End workers were mainly unorganised and overwhelmingly immigrant Jews from Eastern Europe.

The German-born anarcho-syndicalist Rudolf Rocker had spent years trying to convince the Jewish garment workers of Whitechapel to properly unionise. The East End workforce were already taking on work of the striking

40. Glasgow Labour History Workshop (1996b: 203, 211, 48; ibid.: 29); Gordon (1991: 257).
41. Glasgow Labour History Workshop (1989: 38–40; 1996b: 204); Gordon (1991: 258).
42. Glasgow Labour History Workshop (1989: 49; 1996b: 204–5).
43. Challinor (1977: 104).
44. Glasgow Labour History Workshop (1989: 51–2; 1996b: 206–7); Hinton (1973: 124–5).

(mainly non-Jewish) West End tailors when, on 8 May, Rocker spoke to a meeting of 8,000 in Whitechapel, with 3,000 in the street outside. They voted to join the strike, and within two days 13,000 East End tailors in 500 different workplaces had walked out, many of them non-union. With a combined total of about 20,000[45] it was the biggest East End strike since 1889. Rocker, who became a member of the Strike Committee, organised joint meetings and demonstrations on Tower Hill between the East End tailors and striking London dockers.[46]

After three weeks, the employers in men's tailoring surrendered, but those in ladies tailoring refused to concede the closed shop. A mass meeting was held at the Pavilion Theatre where Rocker urged them to reject an employers' compromise proposal, with the vote to continue the strike unanimous. The next day, employers (in both West and East End) conceded all the workers' demands. They won shorter hours, no piecework and better sanitary conditions, and the factories became closed shops.[47] After this triumph, the East End tailoring unions launched a campaign in support of the dockers who were still out on strike, placing over 300 dockers' children in East End Jewish homes.[48]

London Motor Cab Drivers', Hotel Workers' and Musicians' Strikes: January–March 1913

From 1 January to 19 March 1913, there was a strike by 6,500 London motor cab drivers, members of the London and Provincial Licenced Workers' Union, in response to proposals by employers to offset the increased cost of petrol by substantially reducing drivers' earnings.[49] Although a third of London's taxis remained running, either because their owners had agreed not to implement the wage reductions or because they were owner-driven, effective picketing ensured their drivers bought a 'ticket' from the union each day before taking their vehicles out. Extra earnings due to the shortage of taxis helped to cover the cost of the tickets and the scheme brought in £2,000 (worth £240,000 today),[50] enabling the union to finance the strike and distribute weekly food parcels to the strikers. Many of the wives of the striking taxi-cab drivers acted

45. *Sheffield Daily Telegraph*, 7 May 1912.
46. Rocker (2005); *Westminster Gazette*, 13 May 1912.
47. Fishman (2004: 294–301); Kershen (1995).
48. Rocker (2005: 131).
49. Board of Trade (1914: 142–3); *Daily Telegraph and Daily Witness*, 1 January 1913; *The Times*, 4 January 1913.
50. *Daily Herald*, 15 March 1913.

as pickets outside the cab garages and the houses of 'blackleg' drivers.[51] By 20 March the employers' federation capitulated, agreeing to withdraw the increase in petrol price, reinstate the strikers and dismiss strikebreakers.[52]

During March 1913 there were also a series of strikes by London hotel workers instigated by the Amalgamated Union of Hotel, Club and Restaurant Workers and the 'London Cooks' Union' in pursuit of their demands, including the adoption of the Shops Act 1913, giving a half-day holiday and among other things, a minimum wage, and abolition of the living-in system for anyone over 16 years old. There were successful strikes by kitchen staff at the Criterion Restaurant, Piccadilly Circus, and strikes at the Hotel Great Central, Marylebone Road, Coburg Hotel in Mayfair, and Queen's Hotel, Leicester Square. Management at the Savoy Hotel on the Strand capitulated as soon as staff threatened to strike.

There were also successful strikes at three hotels in Edinburgh and one in Glasgow, although when temporary waiters at the Adelphi Hotel in Liverpool stopped work they were paid off.[53] In November 1913 a series of lightning strikes by orchestra musicians demanding pay increases and recognition of the Amalgamated Musicians' Union closed down several London music halls, including the Euston Palace.[54]

Cornish Clay Workers' Strike: July–October 1913

Particularly violent clashes between strikers and police took place during the Cornish clay workers' strike of 1913. The Workers' Union (WU) had begun to recruit among the china clay miners and pressed local companies for a pay increase of 5 shillings a week, wages to be paid fortnightly and an eight-hour day. When this was rejected, the union called a strike on Monday 21 July of about half the workers (30 men) at one small works in Carne Stents near St Austell, and appealed to workers at other pits to join them in solidarity. By the following week, 1,000 were out on strike and the numbers continued to grow as strikers sent pickets from pit to pit in mid-Cornwall winning support. Julia Varley from the WU was sent to organise the miners' wives and families of the strikers, holding large demonstrations. The numbers on strike rose to almost 5,000 in the second week of August, a strike committee was

51. *Daily Citizen*, 27 January 1913.
52. TNA/HO 45/10696/232.677/4; *The Times*, 21 March 1913; Clegg (1985: 57).
53. Board of Trade (1914: xii, xv); Lyddon (2012: 258–9).
54. *Daily Herald*, 10 November 1913.

formed, and the union was able to pay 10 shillings a week strike pay, while local tradesmen distributed food vouchers.[55]

However, with significant numbers remaining at work, there were many confrontations between strikers and scabs. A contingent of 100 Welsh police from Glamorgan (with experience of breaking South Wales miners' picket lines), along with 60 from Bristol and 30 from Devon, were drafted in to support the local police, and on 1 September they baton-charged a 300-strong group of pickets, with strikers chased into nearby fields and attacked again. Although for a month the strike remained solid, the employers rejected an offer of mediation by George Askwith, with some companies reopening their works for those who wished to return. When a demonstration of 300–400 strikers near Bugle, which included two 'waggonettes' full of women organised by Julia Varley, was baton-charged, one eyewitness recorded:

> Crack! Crack! Crack! With startling quickness the batons fell upon the heads of those nearest. It was an indescribable and unforgettable scene. Soon a struggling and seething crowd was reduced to dazed and startled units as one by one they fell bleeding and groaning to the ground and shrieks and screams of the women onlookers, and yells of protests from the rapidly dispersing strikers.[56]

The attack attracted the attention of the national press and a resolution at the annual TUC conference protesting at the violent conduct of the police imported into Cornwall.[57] Although the strikers voted in a ballot to stay out by 2,258 to 558, there was a slow and continuous increase in 'blacklegging', with many strikers running out of money resorting to selling family possessions. The strike became increasingly violent with some attacking an engine house, and one of the strike's teenage leaders shooting a local police officer in the thigh. In October, with the employers feeling strong enough to announce their intention to reopen *all* their works and warning that those who did not reapply for their jobs within three days would not be employed, the strike committee recommended a return to work. Yet despite the fact the clay workers returned without a deal, they remained loyal to the WU and within three months of the end of the strike, many companies had granted union recognition and substantial pay increases.[58]

55. Board of Trade (1914: 114–15); Costley (2013: 18–19, 27–8).
56. *Cornish Guardian*, 5 September 1913, cited in Costley (2013: 37).
57. Report of Proceedings of the Forty-Sixth Annual Trades Union Congress, Manchester, 1–6 September 1913, pp. 237–9.
58. Clegg (1985: 89); Hyman (1971: 66).

Leeds Corporation Strike: December 1913–January 1914

The most important public services dispute during the Labour Revolt was a strike by Leeds Corporation workers in 1913, organised by a Federal Council of Municipal Employees of eight affiliated unions and spearheaded by the National Union of Gas and General Workers (NUGGW) who organised workers involved in the production of gas for the Corporation.[59] Their claim for 2 shillings a week across-the-board pay increase brought an offer from the Conservative-Liberal led Corporation of increases grade by grade, but this was rejected as being divisive, and on 11 December, 3,000 Corporation workers walked out on strike, with another 1,000 thrown idle. Their ranks were swelled later in the day by the tramwaymen (who had a separate agreement), lifting the numbers on strike to 4,434. Within a short period, thousands of Leeds clothing, engineering and boot and shoe industry workers were placed on short-time because their factories depended on gas for illumination, and at night many streets were unlit.[60]

The Corporation responded by pressing its clerks and supervisory staff to maintain a skeleton municipal service, and 200 out of the 660 students from the recently established Leeds University, backed by the Vice-Chancellor, were also utilised as strikebreakers. Scabs employed on the trams and at gas works and electrical power stations were provided with food and living accommodation at their place of work, and protected by police drafted in from Liverpool, Huddersfield, Bradford and elsewhere. A number of clashes ensued in which strikers laid siege to installations being worked, tram windows were broken and the city tramway's electricity supply was sabotaged. When 300–400 strikers marched to the New Wortley gasworks where scab labour was being employed, they were scattered by police baton-charges,[61] with a number of strikers charged with assault, and 25 gas workers convicted of throwing missiles at tramcars receiving 14 days hard labour.[62]

Although the Gas Workers' Union's support for the strike remained firm, the strike was undermined by the systematic mounting of police guards at various termini, junctions and depots, combined with a Corporation ultimatum that tramway strikers would be dismissed if they had not returned to work by 19 December, resulting in 500–600 returning on condition of not having to cover power station work.[63] Similar offers sent out to water-

59. Board of Trade (1914: 156–7); Radice and Radice (1974: 66).
60. Williams (1971: 79–80); Dalton (2000: 276).
61. Williams (1971: 81); Dalton (2000: 270).
62. Dalton (2000: 269).
63. Ibid.: 276; *The Times*, 19 December 1913.

works, gas, street-cleaning, electricity, sanitation, sewerage and street lighting sections also brought some returnees, and undermined the united front among the workforce as 2,028 workers (mostly tramwaymen) were reinstated while others (mainly from the NUGGW) remained on strike.[64]

By Christmas only 1,000 jobs had not been filled by either those returning to work or scabs given permanent jobs. Amidst the growing frustration and despair there was a notable increase in violence, with more strikers arrested and sent to prison for assaults or intimidation. On 6 January an explosive was thrown at the door of the boiler-house in an attempt to wreck an electricity station, and a bomb was thrown at the local barracks housing police from Liverpool and Huddersfield.[65]

Finally, on 13 January 1914 Gas Workers' Union President (and North-East Manchester Labour MP) J.R. Clynes agreed a return-to-work deal largely on management's terms that failed to secure the reinstatement of all strikers.[66] By a large majority a mass meeting accepted the terms, resulting in a significant proportion of the strikers being dismissed, although the defeat of the municipal workers had relatively little effect on the organised labour movement generally in the city.[67]

High Wycombe Furniture Trade Workers' Strike: October 1913–February 1914

When the National Amalgamated Furnishing Trades Association began organising workers in the small industrial town of High Wycombe, north-west of London, and refused to accept the employers' schedule of wage rates, 32 federated firms responded by locking out 3,000 workers.[68] Extraordinary levels of violence occurred with riots and the importation of mounted Metropolitan Police. Women workers, organised by the NFWW, played a prominent part in the strike, standing side-by-side with the men on the picket lines.[69]

A *Daily Herald* solidarity rally in early January was held with Tom Mann, Ben Tillett and Robert Williams, as well as Fred Bramley, the organising secretary of the Furnishing Trades Association,[70] and was followed a few days later with a 5,000-strong solidarity demonstration in Trafalgar Square.[71]

64. *Yorkshire Post*, 23 December 1913.
65. Williams (1971: 86); Dalton (2000: 285).
66. Dalton and Dominguez (2013).
67. Dalton (2000: 286, 292).
68. Board of Trade (1914: 92–3).
69. Heath (2013: 163).
70. *Daily Herald*, 15 January 1914.
71. Ibid., 19 January 1914.

Askwith organised a conference in London with both parties, at which the dispute was settled with a favourable schedule of wages and other terms of employment, with women workers especially benefiting with a 50 per cent pay increase.[72]

WOMEN WORKERS' STRIKES: 1910–13

In the pre-war period many trade unions still displayed an indifference or even opposition to the inclusion of women as members, with women's increasing participation into industries previously dominated by men often viewed as threatening the male breadwinner's 'family wage'.[73] Partly as a consequence of such predominant negative attitudes, over 90 per cent of all trade unionists were men in 1914, even though there was a significant increase in union membership among women in the period 1910–14.

Some of the general labour unions that emerged from the 'New Unionism' strike upsurge (such as the Matchmakers' Union and Gas Workers' and General Labourers' Union) welcomed the recruitment and organisation of women workers, and there was a notable concentration of women union members in cotton, jute and boot and shoe industries. A Women's Trade Union League (WTUL) fostered the organisation of women in the same unions as men in predominately female trades. Yet by its very nature, the WTUL ignored the many thousands of women in both male-dominated industries where they were excluded from existing unions, as well as in trades where there was no union. Moreover, it was committed to social peace in industry, as opposed to 'tirades against the bourgeoise' which were 'unreal'.[74]

It was to address this problem that the National Federation of Women Workers (NFWW), an all-female organisation, was founded by Mary Macarthur in 1906. It organised women working both in predominately male-dominated industries where they were refused admission to the existing unions, as well as women working in unorganised trades where there was no union. Macarthur regarded a separate national women's federation as a necessary temporary form of organisation through which women could gain a sense of solidarity and overcome their fragmented and isolated position. But the NFWW cooperated as far as it could with established unions and gave its active support to a policy of joint organisation.

Integral to its success in growing from an initial 2,000 members in 1906 to over 20,000 before the outbreak of the First World War was the evangel-

72. Heath (2013: 164).
73. Lewenhak (1977); Soldon (1978); Boston (1980).
74. Hamilton (1925: 99).

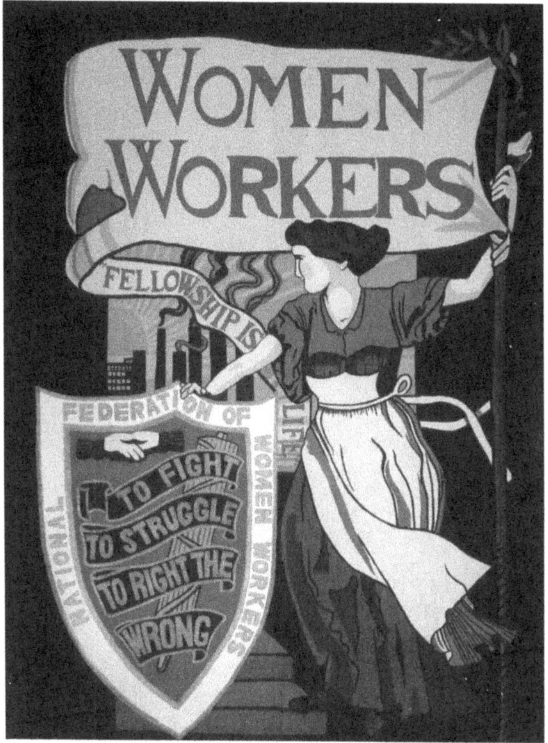

Figure 6.1 A replica of the 1914 banner of the National Federation of Women Workers with its design by the radical artist and illustrator Walter Crane (see also Figure 4.1).
Credit: People's History Museum.

ical style of trade unionism that made supporting strike action the chief means of organising unorganised women workers, as with the chain-makers in Cradley Heath.[75] We can examine a handful of other important strikes involving women in which the NFWW was central, before then considering some women's strikes in which other unions were involved.

Neilston Textile Strike: May–June 1910

One of the largest concentrations of NFWW organising was in Scotland where, according to official statistics, nearly 55,000 women were involved in

75. Ibid.: 42; Drake (1984: 45); Boston (1980: 62, 69); Hunt (2011: 175–6; 2014: 45; 2019: 55–100).

industrial protest between 1911 and 1913.[76] In May 1910, a strike over pay rates by 150 non-union women textile workers in the copwinding department of the English Sewing Machine Company's Crofthead thread mill in the village of Neilston in East Renfrewshire rapidly spread to other nearby thread workers. NFWW organisers Esther Dick and Kate McLean, and the Glasgow Trades Council had been instrumental in establishing a branch of the union in the factory. Once the dispute had begun the Federation drafted in Dick to assist the women in negotiations with management, and within days the majority of workers in the mills were NFWW members. The Trades Council also sent representatives and organised financial assistance, as did the ILP, while John Maclean of the SDP provided advice on how the women could win and wrote in the local ILP paper *Forward* to appeal for support from the rest of the Scottish labour movement.[77]

When company directors refused to speak to the NFWW, other departments in the factory struck in sympathy with the copwinders and for recognition of the union. In response, the employers declared a lockout, by which time some 1,700 women (many aged between 15 and 18 years old) were embroiled in the dispute and playing a leading role in its organisation. The manager of the works was mobbed and had to take refuge in the booking office of the local railway station to avoid a hail of missiles thrown by angry strikers, and windows of the mills were smashed, with the house of the manager of the turning shop also becoming a target for many missiles.[78] By 8 June the foremen were forced out by the strikers so that the withdrawal of labour became total.

The dispute continued with frequent mass solidarity demonstrations to the accompaniment of singing, dancing and banner waving, with mass meetings held in the afternoons and evenings addressed by an array of representatives from the Scottish labour movement, and with collections taken regularly outside the local mills that yielded considerable sums and helped to sustain the struggle. On 10 June there was a 5,000-strong march of strikers and their supporters to the home of the manager of the mills at Barrhead some seven miles away, with pipers, singing and banner-waving, and the carrying of effigies of the manager.[79] Eventually the employers were forced to accept Board of Trade intervention, which resolved in the women's favour to guarantee an increase in wages, with the strike called off.[80]

76. Gordon (1991: 136).
77. Ibid.: 242–3); Knox and Corr (1996: 101–28).
78. Gordon (1991: 243); Knox and Corr (1996: 120).
79. Gordon (1991: 244); Knox and Corr (1996: 120–1).
80. Board of Trade, *Labour Gazette*, July 1910.

Vale of Leven United Turkey Red Strike: December 1911

In the Vale of Leven, West Dunbartonshire, in December 1911, there was a strike by 2,000 women workers in the United Turkey Red (UTR) Combine, a dye company in which there was a marked differentiation between the company-recognised skilled workers organised in their own union and the unorganised semi- and unskilled workers whose attempts to improve pay rates were met with demands for work intensification. During a series of disputes earlier in the year, workplace activists and the NFWW's Scottish organiser, Kate McLean, succeeded in organising mass meetings and building branches of the union with an estimated membership of 2,000. Together with the male-organised Amalgamated Society of Dyers (ASD) they submitted a claim for a 10 per cent wage increase, reduction in the working week to 55 hours, and time-and-a-half for overtime. In November, a ballot of the workforce resulted in 91 per cent in favour of strike action, and on 9 December the strike commenced and was to last two weeks.[81]

On the first day of the strike crowds numbering 7,000 were at the gates bringing the works to a 'virtual standstill'. Workers formed an impromptu band, behind which men and women marched, with pickets lining the streets to jeer strikebreakers with banners declaring 'White Slaves, Vale of Leven, No Surrender'. Over the next week the strike continued with well-organised mass meetings and picketing, and received the support of the SUDL, Glasgow Trades Council and ILP, with Madame Sorgue addressing the strikers. A carnival atmosphere within the Vale was evidenced when a 5,000-strong march escorted by four bands displayed two effigies, one representing the director of the company and the other the firemen-clerks. The *Glasgow Herald* reported how:

> … the Clerks from head office in Glasgow were subjected to a lively time by female strikers, who threw flour and peasemeal at them, and a number were carried to the river and thrown in …[82]

The UTR strike was brought to an end on Christmas Day 1911 following intervention by the Board of Trade, with a partial victory, including recognition for the two unions, albeit the original claim, which had been for the same rise for both men and women, was reneged on by the ASD who accepted an offer of 1 shilling for men and 6 pence for women per week. Nonetheless,

81. Rawlinson and Robinson (1996: 175–8, 181–2); Hunt (2014: 53–4); Kenefick (2015: 42–5).
82. *Glasgow Herald*, 14 December 1911.

not long afterwards, the ASD opened its ranks to women members, and the NFWW turned their branches over to the union.[83]

Kilbirnie Curtain Net Workers' Strike: April–September 1913

The longest recorded strike of women workers in Scotland during the Labour Revolt was the curtain net workers' strike in Kilbirnie, Ayrshire, which lasted from April to September 1913 involving 390 workers in seven different factories in the town.[84] They took action over the demand for a pay increase, albeit the issue of union recognition became the focal point of the women's grievances. Once again trade union and socialist organisations rallied to the women's cause, with Kate McLean of the NFWW undertaking the task of organising support for the strikers, Glasgow Trades Council sending speakers to factory gates to appeal for donations, and considerable local support generated by men and women in the surrounding area, as well as the ILP.[85]

In the sixth week, a 4,000-strong trade union procession was followed by a rally of some 10,000, providing a bedrock of support for the women's strike. The local ILP paper *Forward* noted that 'strikes in Kilbirnie [were] akin to village carnivals' and came to involve the whole community.[86] When six strikers were tried in Kilmarnock for intimidation of 'blacklegs', they were accompanied by 'about sixty sympathisers, including pipers and night-shift workers from Glengarock'.[87] Four of the women were found guilty and fined, and on their return to Kilbirnie the whole town turned out to welcome them. The strike was resolved after 21 weeks with the women obtaining a pay increase, which although less than the initial demand, was regarded as a victory, and union recognition, with the NFWW enrolling almost 1,000 new members. This dispute triggered a number of pay claims from other local workers.[88]

Bermondsey Strikes: August 1911

The NFWW were also involved in a number of strikes in England, one of the most important of which occurred in the hot summer of August 1911 when some 15,000 unskilled women and girls working in 20 different local food-processing, glue and box-making factories in Bermondsey, London,

83. Rawlinson and Robinson (1996: 181–6).
84. Board of Trade (1914: 134–5).
85. Gordon (1991: 247–8).
86. *Forward*, 19 May 1913, cited in Kenefick (2015: 53).
87. Gordon (1991: 249).
88. *Forward*, 31 May 1913, cited in Gordon (1991: 254).

walked out. Bermondsey was defined by its high population density, overcrowded housing and extreme poverty. The strikes pivoted on the very low average wages for women of between 7 to 9 shillings a week, with many girls receiving only 3 shillings,[89] and the 'almost indescribable' poor working conditions, with many working 'ten and a half hours a day, pushed and urged to speed'.[90] The women's revolt was also inspired by the simultaneous London transport workers' strike that involved many dock labourers whose wives and daughters now took action themselves.[91]

The Bermondsey strikes began when a group of women workers in a large confectionary factory suddenly left work and marched down the street. *Labour Leader* editor Fenner Brockway recalled it was the release of suppressed frustration that gave the strikers their wild enthusiasm: they 'could not even voice their grievances, they knew nothing of how to run a strike; they just knew that the conditions of their existence were intolerable, and they would no longer put up with them without protest'.[92] The women marched past factories calling on more and more workers to join them, with women from Pink's jam factory in the forefront with a banner inscribed, 'We are not white slaves, but Pink's slaves'.[93] With 20 separate strikes joining together the *Daily Chronicle* reported on a demonstration:

> The women seemed to be in the highest spirits. They went laughing and singing through Bermondsey, shouting, 'Are we downhearted?' and answering the question by a shrill chorus of 'No!'. It was noticeable that many of them had put on their 'Sunday Best'. In spite of the great heat, hundreds of them wore fur boas and tippets – the sign of self-respect.[94]

George Dangerfield considered it was as though 'their strike [was] some holiday of the soul, long overdue'.[95]

The strikers immediately turned to the NFWW for assistance and both Mary Macarthur and Marion Phillips of the Women's Labour League threw themselves into setting up headquarters in the local Labour Institute and ILP base, helping to coordinate the setting up of strike committees, organisation of daily strike meetings and conduct of negotiations with a list of

89. Hamilton (1925: 102).
90. Cited in de la Mare (2008: 69).
91. *Labour Leader*, 18 August 1911.
92. Cited in de la Mare (2008: 72–3).
93. *Daily Chronicle*, 15 August 1911.
94. Ibid.
95. Dangerfield (1997: 216).

Figure 6.2 Women from the Pink's jam factory in Bermondsey, London, during the August 1911 successful strike wave by 15,000 unskilled women workers from 20 different factories.

Credit: TUC Library Collection.

wage demands.[96] Macarthur wrote to the press to appeal for donations to support the strikers, while strikers' public meetings and processions passed through the streets with collecting boxes. Hundreds of pounds were raised, which contributed to the provision of 25,000 loaves of bread, along with sterilised milk, that was distributed daily.[97] A strike rally held on 14 August in Southwark Park, at which the speakers included Ben Tillett and Macarthur, attracted an audience of 10,000.

Trade by trade, Macarthur and her colleagues negotiated agreements, such that within ten days of strike action, wage rises ranging from 1 to 4 shillings a week and improved working conditions, along with union recognition, had been gained from most of the 20 employers. In the process, the NFWW recruited 2,000 members.[98]

Bridport Gundry's Strike: February 1912

In February 1912 the NFWW were also active during a strike by 35 women workers in Gundry's net and rope manufacturing factory in Bridport, Dorset,

96. de la Mare (2008: 73).
97. Barnsley (2010: 61–2); Hunt (2019: 97); *Daily Mirror*, 17 and 18 August 1911.
98. NFWW, *Fifth Annual Report*, 1912, p. 5.

against a proposed readjustment of wage scale which increased the rates of the lowest paid at the expense of the higher paid. Both groups of workers, mainly in their mid-teens, joined forces and walked out, mounting a regular picket line outside the factory, as well as a flying picket at the nearby Folly Mill to win support. Many men from other factories in the town congregated in the streets to support the women's protest.

The *Bridport News* reported that the 'girls' marched through the streets of the town singing the suffragette anthem 'Shoulder to Shoulder'.[99] The strikers, who refused arbitration from a banker and local Conservative MP, kept up their strike for a week, with Ada Newton, a NFWW official from London, holding meetings with the strikers, signing most up to the union and leading negotiations with the company that led to a favourable agreement.[100]

Dundee Jute Workers' Strike: January–April 1912

During the Labour Revolt many strikes by women involved unions other than the NFWW. An important example was the 1912 Dundee jute workers' strike.[101] The jute industry directly employed almost half of the city's workforce and influenced the lives of many others. No other substantial city in Britain had such a high dependency on one single sector of the economy and such a high female workforce, with more than 43 per cent of Dundee's labour force female by 1911. There were specialist textile workers' unions in the city, but the newly formed Dundee and District Jute and Flax Workers' Union (DDJFWU) was a mixed-sex union with a predominance of women whose membership increased rapidly from 1910 onwards.[102] Concerned to be recognised by the employers within formal collective bargaining procedures, the DDJFWU was reluctant to call strikes, but this did not stop a number of strikes being initiated by rank-and-file members, some of which subsequently obtained union support, or occasional wildcat strikes by the 'unorganised' majority.[103]

In January–February 1912, Dundee female weavers went on strike at Grimond Bowbridge jute works over pay reductions, which set in motion a strike wave by textile workers in the city involving some 2,000 DDJFWU members at different mills. While most strikes were resolved by an increase in wages, the great majority of unorganised workers' wages and conditions

99. *Bridport News*, 16 February 1912, cited in Guarita (2015: 14).
100. Guarita (2015: 1–29); Rabbetts (2019).
101. Board of Trade (1913a: 98–9).
102. Gordon (1991: 195); Soldon (1978: 57, 60).
103. Gordon (1991: 200–1, 204).

remained the same. The DDJFWU, sensing an opportunity to expand its membership, threatened a city-wide general strike after having secured some financial support from the General Federation of Trade Unions in London.[104] By 3 March 1912, 18,000 mill workers were on strike from 24 separate mills and factories as Dundee 'came under a strike spell', and this grew to some 25,000 workers in a city-wide general strike, involving mainly non-union members.[105]

With the level of financial distress increasing daily, the Dundee Trades Council, ILP and other bodies intervened to provide breakfasts for between 1,200 and 1,300 hungry children. Despite employers' threat of a lockout, 4,500 female spinners (2,000 in the DDJFWU) and 500 male Calendar Workers' Union members at the Lochee factory, in west Dundee, refused to return, in defiance of being instructed to do so by the DDJFWU. In response, the Lochee owners closed the factory, as did 30 other firms who were members of the employers' association, representing 20,000 workers. With the Baxter Works and another firm previously unaffected by the strike joining the lockout on 4 April, there was a city-wide lockout of 30,000 Dundee textile workers, only 10,000 of whom were organised. In the face of strikers' attempts to exhort 500 female weavers to join the strike, large detachments of police were drafted in to maintain control,[106] and almost every demonstration in March resulted in some form of disturbance.

The worst took place at Lochee where a crowd attacked a jute lorry, and when police reinforcements attempted to break up the demonstration they were 'pelted with sticks, stones and other missiles', resulting in several officers being injured. Eventually in April 1912, the Dundee general strike and lockout was finally brought to an end, with an agreement between the employers and textile unions which represented an unexpected breakthrough, conferring union recognition and the establishment of collective bargaining procedures for the industry, although there was only a slight advance in wages.[107]

Chipping Norton Bliss Tweed Mill Strike: December 1913–June 1914

The mixed-sex Workers' Union was also active in supporting strikes in which women workers were involved. Apart from the Midlands metal workers' strikes, this included a six-month strike at the Bliss Tweed Mill in Chipping Norton, a small market town in Oxfordshire, that involved 237 woollen-tex-

104. Kenefick (2012: 207–8; 2015: 49–52).
105. Kenefick (2012: 208–9); *Scotsman*, 2 March 1912.
106. *Dundee Courier*, 9 March 1912; *Dundee Advertiser*, 13 March 1912.
107. Kenefick (2012: 209–13); Knox, and Corr (1996).

tile workers – 125 women and 112 men. Confronted by a new forceful style of management and refusal to increase wages to levels paid elsewhere in the industry, the WU mounted a recruitment campaign and enlisted around 230 workers employed at the mill. When management responded by sacking three prominent male union activists, workers walked out demanding their reinstatement despite the fact that Christmas was only one week away.[108]

Just over a third of the workforce continued to work, the mill's manager hired new labour and 40 extra police from Oxford were brought in to provide protection for the strikebreakers. An elected strike committee established a daily picket of the mill, and utilising WU's resources, organised meetings and demonstrations around the country to gain financial support from the labour movement. Young workers formed the majority of the strikers – with 77 per cent of those employed at the mill aged between 18 and 34 joining the action.[109]

Effigies of 'blacklegs' were paraded through the town, and during one of the nightly processions, the strikers and their supporters targeted the house of the mill's general manager, smashing windows. A number of incidents of assault on 'blacklegs' and police went to court with fines and imprisonment for those convicted. Annie Cooper, who had worked at the mills for 26 years, was found guilty of assaulting a strikebreaker and sentenced to 14 days in prison after refusing to pay the fine. On her release on 28 February 1914, Cooper was met with 1,000 jubilant supporters, presented with a silver teapot inscribed to commemorate the occasion from the WU's Julia Varley, and paraded through the streets in a wagon pulled by the strikers accompanied by a brass band and greeted by a packed meeting at the Town Hall.[110]

However, despite six months of resistance, by the end of May there was a fall in the number of strikers to 168, and the union finally conceded defeat in June, with only 100 strikers taken back, and even many of these not rehired until after the start of the war.[111]

Garston Wilson's Bobbin Workers' Strike: May–August 1912

Another important strike involving women workers took place at the Wilson bobbin and shuttle factories in Garston, Liverpool, and Cornholme, near Todmorden in West Yorkshire.[112] The company had become the largest

108. Richardson (2008: 84–90; 2013: 7–17).
109. Ibid.: 92–4.
110. Ibid.: 96–7; Richardson (2013: 23).
111. Richardson (2013: 99).
112. Board of Trade (1913a: 106–7); Rees (2020: 45–51; 2017: 41–6).

bobbin manufacturer in the world, supplying the Lancashire cotton industry and also exporting 60 per cent of its product to the Empire. At the Garston site there were five unions in total, including the Amalgamated Warehouse and General Workers' Union which had been formed in 1911 and organised unskilled workers, many of whom were women. The union employed Mary Bamber (a Liverpool suffrage supporter who spoke at Women's Social and Political Union (WSPU) meetings) as a full-time local official with special responsibility for organising women workers. Although there was also a skilled male sawyers' union and the WU, which organised some unskilled and semi-skilled male and female workers, many workers were not members of any union.

The five unions came together via a Joint Council of Trades and approached the company with demands for better wages and for union recognition. When this was refused, a strike at the two sites began on 4 May 1912,[113] which at Cornholme was solid with 400 workers out. By contrast at Garston, although pickets assembled outside the plant about 400 workers went into work and hundreds of police, some on horseback, were mobilised to escort the strike-breakers. Nonetheless, the strikers organised parades around the district and meetings on street corners, and by the end of the first week there were between 600 and 700 out, with local dockers and carters refusing to handle material from the bobbin factory.

This led the company to close the gates and both sides dug in for a long struggle, with strikers sent to address meetings and raise money across Merseyside and Lancashire. A Distress Committee was set up and run by women strikers and hardship pay provided to 1,100 workers, including those at Cornholme. And a meeting was organised with Tom Mann as the keynote speaker, with a lunchtime crowd of 5,000 people.

In week twelve, on Monday 22 July 1912, the company reopened the gates and under police protection a large body of 'blacklegs' were escorted into the plant, albeit the attempt to break the strike failed. A month later another attempt was made, with strikebreakers travelling to Garston by tram where they were met with mass pickets. After work, there were a number of violent confrontations as the scabs were escorted by police to their waiting trams in nearby Speke, with one woman striker beaten unconscious. Finally, after 15 weeks the company surrendered, agreeing to recognise the unions, increase wages and reinstate all strikers, with the unions claiming a complete victory.[114]

---

113. *Manchester Guardian*, 6 May 1912.

114. Rees (2020: 45–51).

YOUNG WORKERS' AND SCHOOLCHILDREN'S STRIKES: 1911

As previously noted, another important feature of the Labour Revolt was the enthusiastic involvement of young people in strikes, in what has been termed 'an effervescence of youth'.[115] For example, in the mining industry in July 1911 there were sporadic strikes by 'haulage lads' (mainly aged 15–21) over different rates of pay for the same work at a number of collieries in Swinton, near Manchester, and also by 'pit lads' at Yorkshire collieries such as Rotherham, Mansfield and Nottingham.[116] In 1913 in Yorkshire a pit was stopped for one day as a result of pit lads striking in sympathy with their comrade who had refused to work because of the insufficient amount of compensation paid to his father for an accident.[117] These and similar strikes elsewhere were usually in defiance of local union leadership, with some lasting a day or two, others longer, and with adult miners being laid off.

Other industries that had strikes by young male workers – 'lads' or 'boys' – included the tinplate industry in South Wales, where there was a one-day strike of 110 'cold-roll boys' in five firms around Briton Ferry and Swansea in September 1911 which laid off over 1,000 workers but won wage increases. In August 1911, 200 Dublin *Evening Herald* delivery boys went on strike for increased pay with '[e]xtraordinary scenes, including truncheon charges and the galloping of mounted police … [as the] … newsboys set upon distribution vans, seized the papers, and threw them around … Repeated attempts were made on the office of the *Evening Herald*, and … the Sunday issue … was not printed.'[118] Also swept up in a wave of strikes across the country in August 1911 were golf caddie boys, aged between 12 and 16, and there was even a strike by 130 boys in the printing department of the Bank of England in September 1912.[119]

Apprentices' workers' strikes over demands for wage increases also occurred sporadically in different areas of the country, including a two-week walkout by 3,000 in 50 Leeds engineering companies in August 1911.[120] The most important dispute was a series of overlapping engineering and shipbuilding apprentices' strikes from August to October 1912 across Scotland and the North-East and North-West of England. It began in Scotland where 5,000 apprentices became involved from August to September, with 60,000 days lost; the strike spreading from Kirkcaldy to Dundee, Glasgow,

115. Kenefick (2012: 189–221).
116. Board of Trade (1913a: 82–5).
117. Board of Trade (1914: xviii–xix).
118. *Manchester Guardian*, 21 August 1911.
119. Lyddon (2012: 248–52).
120. Board of Trade (1912: 100–1); Lyddon (2012: 252).

Aberdeen, Coatbridge, Kilmarnock, Edinburgh, Arbroath, Renfrew and elsewhere. While the bulk of the strikers were engineering apprentices, they were joined by some shipyard apprentice carpenters and joiners, and apprentice moulders from foundries, as well as platers and other shipyard apprentices. Also on strike in August and October 1912 were 1,400 Tyne, Wear, and Tees engineering apprentices, and then 6,500 engineering apprentices in south-east Lancashire and Cheshire became involved in September and October. In the Manchester area an estimated 53 firms experienced strikes, with picketing gradually extending the dispute to a large geographical area that included works in Ashton, Oldham, Bredbury and Newton-le-Willows. Strikes even spread to Liverpool and Birkenhead.[121]

In September 1911 there was also a wave of schoolchildren's strikes in protest against corporal punishment, for a reduction in the length of the school day and other concerns. The strikes started in Bigyn Council School in Llanelli on the morning of Tuesday 5 September when a deputy headmaster physically punished a boy for handing round a piece of paper in class calling on his classmates to strike. In protest, a group of 30 or so boys walked out of their playground and paraded the streets singing and visiting neighbouring schools to call on pupils to join them, with New Dock, Lakefield and Old Road Schools coming out in solidarity.

On 8 September children in Liverpool struck, and by 11 September the strive wave had reached Manchester and London. During the next three weeks, school strikes spread in a rapidly accelerating wave, affecting some 66 different towns and cities across Britain.[122] Even very young children were affected by the strike epidemic, with strikers in Bermondsey in London including 'tiny tots' aged between six and eight.[123] Some strikes lasted only a few hours, a token protest that ended with the appearance of a teacher enough to send them back to their desks, while others lasted a few days; they ranged from a few children to hundreds being involved; and while some were largely peaceful, light-hearted affairs, others became violent.

While the strikes spread locally by word of mouth and across the country courtesy of the press, in some areas the role of 'flying pickets' seeking support from pupils in neighbouring schools was important. For example, in Manchester it was reported:

---

121. Lyddon (2012: 253–4); Knox (1984: 22–36).
122. Marson (1973): Humphries (1981: 94); Adams (1991: 217–18).
123. *Hull Daily News*, 16 September 1911, cited in Marson, *Children's Strikes in 1911*, 1973, pp. 8–9.

> The young disputants desiring to extend the fight ... appointed pickets who, labelled with papers pinned to their caps bearing the word 'picket' marched in a body to the Holland Street municipal school ... to induce ... a sympathetic strike ... teachers prevented the pickets from entering [but] the strikers ... assumed quite a militant attitude, having on the way secured sticks which they brandished fiercely, but an even more terrifying display was made by others who were the possessors of toy pistols.[124]

The level of organisation and determination varied significantly. For example, in Dundee on 14 September no fewer than eight schools were involved and it was calculated that by the afternoon around 1,500 boys had 'mutinied', attacking teachers and breaking at least 100 windows. Likewise in Hull, schools were described as being 'besieged' by crowds of pickets shouting at the pupils who had returned to their classrooms 'come out!' and 'blacklegs'.[125] In the Edgehill district of Liverpool, gangs of strikers smashed street lamps and school windows as they marched, with '"loyal scholars" beaten with sticks',[126] and in Glasgow, Bradford, Leicester, Sheffield and elsewhere, there were attacks on school buildings.[127]

Across the country schoolchildren formed strike committees, painted banners, organised mass meetings, produced leaflets and marched through the streets with placards. Although girls played only a very small part in the strike, they joined boys in Kirkcaldy and Cambuslang in Scotland, as well as Nottingham, Portsmouth and Sunderland – where they even stayed out after most boys had returned to school – and Hull where newspaper photographs captured pictures of girls next to the boys.[128]

As with their young worker counterparts, the school strikes were influenced by the wider industrial militancy that had been taking place across the country, with many of the children involved coming from areas that had experienced mass strikes in the dock, railway, mining and other industries in which police and military action had led to riots and casualties.[129] Not only had some of their parents and siblings been directly involved as strikers within their respective industries, but children had *themselves* been involved directly in the street protests of their adults, including attacks on the police and military in Llanelli, Liverpool, Hull and elsewhere.[130]

---

124. *Northern Daily Telegraph*, 9 September 1911, cited in Marson (1973: 6–7).
125. *Manchester Guardian*, 12 September 1911.
126. *School Government Chronicle*, 16 September 1911, cited in Marson (1973: 9).
127. *Manchester Guardian*, 13 September 1911.
128. Marson (1973: 19).
129. Humphries (1981); Marson (1973); Baker (2010).
130. Cunningham and Lavalette (2016: 76–7).

But if the Labour Revolt acted as a source of inspiration, with the tactics used by adult strikers at times appropriated, the strikes also reflected school students' own immediate grievances in a context in which dilapidated buildings, huge classes, poor teaching, a lack of provision and physical violence were common experiences for many children. The strikes petered out after three weeks,[131] and while in the short term they failed to achieve their principal demands, they helped to create a national debate on the uses and abuses of corporal punishment within the school system.

131. Baker (2010: 35–6).

7
Challenges and Expectations

As well as being the most important industrial struggle in Irish history, the six-month Dublin lockout between August 1913 and February 1914 was one of the most important struggles of the Labour Revolt of which it was an integral part, with the fight for solidarity with the Dublin workers carried into the heart of the British labour movement. The decisive defeat inflicted on the Dublin workers provided encouragement to some employers in Britain, reflected in the six-month London building workers' lockout between January and August 1914, which exacted another defeat. However, these reverses did not have a generalising impact on the overall momentum of the unrest in the first seven months of 1914, with strikes by 12,000 munitions workers at the Woolwich Arsenal and 150,000 South Yorkshire miners, nor did it diminish government fears of an 'impending clash'[1] involving a newly formed Triple Alliance between the miners', transport and railway workers' unions before the First World War intervened.

DUBLIN LOCKOUT: AUGUST 1913–FEBRUARY 1914

The 1907 Belfast dockers' and carters' strike led by Jim Larkin opened up a period of labour militancy in Ireland, with Larkin leading strikes by Dublin carters and Cork dockers in 1908 and successfully establishing branches of the National Union of Dock Labourers (NUDL) in every port in Ireland. But his militant methods had brought him into conflict with the moderate union leadership of James Sexton. As a result, he established an alternative Irish Transport and General Workers' Union (ITGWU) in December 1908, with the majority of the NUDL's Irish membership joining the new union of which he became general secretary.

Larkin urged a campaign of militant class struggle to organise all unskilled workers in Ireland into the ITGWU. In 1910 James Connolly returned to Ireland from America, where he had been strongly influenced by the syndicalist IWW, and Larkin immediately made him an official in Belfast where he became a powerful advocate of creating 'One Big Union' in the form of the

1. Meacham (1972: 1343–64).

ITGWU. Larkin and Connolly argued that ultimately, the problems of the working class would only be resolved with the fundamental transformation of capitalist society to create a workers' republic, and a free and independent Ireland from British imperialist rule.

The union played a major part in organising a wave of industrial militancy that swept over Ireland.[2] While Larkin led a strike of dockers, carters and coal labourers in Dublin in 1911, there was also a protracted Wexford foundry strike in 1911–12, two major dock strikes in Galway and Limerick in 1912 and 1913, and two general local strikes in Galway and Sligo in 1913.

One of the most novel features of the ITGWU's strike mobilisation was its solidaristic nature, exemplified by Larkin's advocacy and use of the 'sympathetic strike' and boycott of 'tainted goods' handled by scabs as the means by which individual sections of workers in dispute could rely on the active support of the rest of the union as a crucial instrument for breaking down employers' resistance. This was particularly important in a context in which a surplus of unskilled labour enabled employers to often break strikes by the wholesale replacement of strikers with scabs. The ITGWU rapidly grow its membership from 3,000 in 1910 to over 30,000 by the summer of 1913, with Larkin claiming that Dublin was the best organised city in the world, and the union producing a weekly *Irish Worker* (that he edited) with average sales of around 20,000 covering the bulk of the Dublin working class.

Though not predominantly an industrial city, Dublin was a trading centre in which transport work provided the vast majority of the jobs, albeit the majority of workers were either unskilled or employed casually. Existing trade unions covered mainly skilled workers, while unskilled labourers suffered low wages (16 shillings a week on average) and terrible conditions, sometimes working up to 70 hours a week. Half of the working class resided in tenement housing, with many families occupying only one room, and with unemployment at around 20 per cent.[3]

It was in this context that an employers' counter-attack to the growing strength of the ITGWU was mounted by Catholic Ireland's most powerful capitalist, William Martin Murphy, the fiercely anti-union owner of the *Irish Independent* newspaper and of the Dublin tramways on which the ITGWU was organising a strike. He was determined not just to exclude the union from his own concerns, but to destroy it throughout the city, shifting the balance of power between capital and labour. The Liberal government in London

2. O'Connor (2005: 101–21; 1992: 67–83).
3. *Report into the Housing Conditions of the Working Classes in the City of Dublin*, Parliamentary Papers, HMSO, Cd 7273, 1914, vol. xix, cited in Hattersley (2012: 179); Ryan (1913: 15).

promised Murphy whatever police and military support he might need to defeat the union, which enabled Murphy to convince other employers that the ITGWU could be broken, and that the time was ripe to crush 'Larkinism'.

In August 1913 Murphy locked out all the tramworkers, saying they would only be taken back if they left the ITGWU. The lockout spread to the *Irish Independent* newspaper and Jacob's biscuit factory also owned by Murphy. Although workers across the city retaliated by 'blacking' Murphy's goods, notices appeared in the Dublin papers for non-ITGWU men to fill the places of the dismissed union members. The Dublin Castle government moved quickly to demonstrate its full support for Murphy, with Larkin arrested and charged with 'seditious libel' and 'conspiracy', although he was released on bail and went into hiding.

On Friday 29 and Saturday 30 August there were serious clashes in different parts of the city between pickets and police. Attempts to stop trams manned by 'blackleg' crews brought violent counter-attacks from foot and mounted police, with two workers (James Nolan and John Byrne) killed, 200 injured and scores taken to hospital and arrested.[4] On the following day, after Larkin had been smuggled onto the balcony of the Imperial Hotel on O'Connell Street overlooking a mass ITGWU demonstration of 10,000, the police moved with indiscriminate violence to clear the union off the streets in what became known as Dublin's 'Bloody Sunday'. As news of the police attack spread, so fighting broke out elsewhere across the city with over 400 people receiving hospital treatment for injuries suffered at the hands of the police, and hundreds more arrested.[5] The subsequent funeral procession of one of those beaten to death by the police attracted 10,000, including 1,000 women workers.[6]

Encouraged by this dramatic display of state support, and with Larkin back in prison, other Dublin employers felt confident to follow Murphy's lead, with workers required to handle 'tainted goods' and/or sign an undertaking not to be a member of the ITGWU, and when they refused being promptly locked out. By the end of September Dublin was in the grip of a general lockout with some 25,000 workers, by no means all of them ITGWU members, locked out by 404 employers. As William Partridge, speaking on behalf of Dublin Trades Council, told the annual TUC conference in Manchester in September, the employers had 'declared war on the trade unions'.[7]

4. Yeates (2000: 51–3).
5. Newsinger (2004: 48–9); Nevin (2006: 179–89).
6. *Freeman's Journal*, 4 September 1913.
7. Report of Proceedings of the Forty-Sixth Annual Trades Union Congress, Manchester, 1–6 September 1913, p. 70.

Moreover, the ITGWU found itself fighting for its life not just against the employers, but also the police, the Unionist establishment, the Catholic hierarchy and even the Home Rule party. The Liberal government intervened by appointing a Board of Trade 'court of inquiry' led by George Askwith, with both independent trade unions and employer representation, which quickly reported and made proposals to resolve the dispute that were rejected by both the ITGWU and employers.[8]

Working-class resistance was stimulated throughout by the syndicalist-influenced leadership of Larkin and Connolly, with the ITGWU extending its strike organisation functions to become the focus of social life for families and individuals affected by the lockout, including the distribution of food and clothing.[9] However, if the union's great strength had been working-class solidarity whereby individual employers found themselves confronting the strength of the whole union, the lockout effectively countered this with working-class solidarity now matched by employers' solidarity. The ITGWU was confronted with a prolonged battle of attrition designed to bleed away its resources, both financial and moral.[10]

At the same time, the Shipping Federation began importing hundreds of scabs into Dublin on depot ships, many of them from Britain, with Connolly's rallying call to union members to stop the 'English blacklegs' by joining mass pickets effectively going unheeded.[11] Partly this was because the police had already demonstrated they were prepared to violently bludgeon workers off the streets, and partly because Dublin was put under 'the Iron Heel' with three companies of troops called out to protect the scabs in 'a deadly attack on picketing' designed to 'bend and break Trade Unionism'.[12] With the successful implantation of scabs into Dublin to keep the port open, the employers were able to transform the balance of power in their favour. And Connolly's formation of a 'Citizen Army', a disciplined force of 1,200 union members armed with pickaxe handles to protect meetings and demonstrations and prevent police attacks on strikers, did not stop armed scabs shooting two women and escaping prosecution.[13]

Confronted with a battle for its very existence, it became clear that financial and food assistance from the TUC, no matter how generous, was going to win the dispute. Hence the ITGWU, Larkin argued, needed urgent solidar-

8. Askwith ([1920] 1974: 262–70); Board of Trade (1914: xxvii–xxx); Heath (2013: 159–61).
9. Holton (1976: 189–90).
10. Newsinger (2004: 54–5).
11. Saluppo (2019: 588); Newsinger (2004: 80).
12. *Daily Herald*, 14 November 1913.
13. Newsinger (2013a: 59).

ity *industrial* action in Britain – specifically 'blacking' of all goods in transit to Dublin or 'tainted goods' from Dublin handled by imported scabs – so as to break the employers' solidarity and force individual companies to settle on terms dictated by the union. After his release from prison, Larkin toured Britain, speaking at a series of huge meetings in an attempt to secure such solidarity: 'We say all your money is useful, but money never won a strike. Money can't win a strike. Discipline, solidarity, knowledge of the position, and the strength to carry out your will – these are the things [with which] you could win in Dublin tomorrow if you mean to.'[14] The ITGWU, which had always refused to touch 'tainted goods' from Britain, and displayed a high level of solidarity for both the seamen's and railwaymen's unions during their respective national strikes in 1911,[15] now called for reciprocal action.

In the process of appealing for British labour movement support, Larkin excoriated individual trade union and Labour Party leaders for their refusal to sanction sympathetic industrial action. Even after the Parliamentary Committee of the TUC, under pressure from union branches across the country, took the unprecedented decision to call a special conference to be held on 9 December (following its earlier annual congress in September) to consider the unions' support for the Dublin dispute, Larkin published a manifesto in the *Daily Herald* appealing directly to union members, warning that union leaders were preparing a settlement of the lockout inimical to trade union principles:

> Comrades in the British Labour movement ... Tell your leaders now and every day ... that they are not there as apologists for the shortcomings of the Capitalist system, that they are not there to assist the employers in helping defeat any action of workers striving to live, nor to act as a brake on the wheel of progress.[16]

Larkin lambasted J.H. Thomas of the new NUR as 'a double-dyed traitor to his class' and accused Havelock Wilson of actively assisting the Shipping Federation in pouring in strikebreakers to Dublin; they were union leaders who had 'neither a soul to be saved nor a body to be kicked'. He claimed the official British labour leaders were about as 'useful as mummies in a museum',[17] and urged the rank-and-file to compel them to agree to mobilise an official union boycott of Dublin traffic.

---

14. *Freeman's Journal*, 10 December 1913; Yeates (2000: 470).
15. Devine (2012: 176); Greaves (1982: 59, 62); O'Connor (2015: 91).
16. *Daily Herald*, 22 November 1913.
17. Ibid., 13 October 1913.

The British labour movement had rallied to the cause of Dublin workers, with an enormous level of solidarity expressed in various ways. There was unprecedented financial assistance generated by the TUC and its affiliated unions, which was undoubtedly crucial in allowing the ITGWU to continue to fight over the months of the lockout. According to one estimate,[18] the British labour movement raised around £150,000 (£18 million today), with numerous trades councils and local union branches organising solidarity meetings and collections. Financial donations were also generated by the various different political strands within the British labour movement, notably the *Daily Herald*.[19] There were numerous specially chartered food ships (notably the *SS Hare*), which carried thousands of packages of food, with crates of jam, tea, butter, margarine and groceries that were sent to the Dublin strikers in very public displays of support organised under the auspices of the TUC.

The enthusiastic response to solidarity appeals for the Dublin workers was evidenced by the huge attendances at many public rallies held across Britain, many of which Larkin addressed as part of a so-called 'Fiery Cross'[20] propaganda crusade organised by an amalgam of radical left groups, including *Daily Herald* Leagues and Clarion Clubs. At the Free Trade Hall in Manchester on 16 November, where he spoke alongside Tillett, Connolly and the American IWW leader 'Big Bill' Haywood, there were 4,000, with upwards of 20,000 thronging the streets outside.[21] A huge rally was held at the Albert Hall in London three days later that was filled to capacity with over 10,000 in attendance and thousands again gathered outside.[22] Other meetings were held in Sheffield (2,000), Leicester (3,000), Liverpool (3,000), Bristol (4,000), Glasgow (4,000), Edinburgh (7,000) and other towns and cities.

Larkin's arrest and seven months' imprisonment for 'seditious libel' also provoked grassroots protests across Britain, with another Albert Hall *Daily Herald* rally drawing a packed audience to hear platform speakers drawn from different sections of the labour, left and suffrage movements (Chapter 9). The adopted pledge from the rally to campaign against the Liberals at three pending parliamentary by-elections until he was freed, combined with the impact of rioting in Dublin, led the government to order Larkin's release after just 17 days. It was a significant victory which helped identify him ever

18. Moran (1978: 44).
19. Sweeney (1980: 107–8); Yeates (2000: 321–3).
20. The burning cross was a traditional call to war of the Scottish clans, popularised in England by Sir Walter Scott's narrative poem *The Lady of the Lake*.
21. *Liverpool Daily Post and Mercury*, 17 November 1913; *Daily Mirror*, 17 November 1913.
22. *Daily Herald*, 20 November 1913.

more closely with the Irish struggle and underlined the level of support for the Dublin workers.

Meanwhile, there was a so-called 'Kiddies Scheme' devised by socialist-suffragist Dora Montefiore in association with supporters of the *Daily Herald*, which aimed at alleviating distress by sending 350 of the Dublin strikers' children to stay with sympathetic families in Britain for the duration of the dispute. Modelled on the successful children's holiday organised the previous year by the IWW during the Lawrence textile workers' strike, the plan was short-circuited in Ireland in the face of full-blown opposition mounted by Catholic priests, with allegations that the children would be sent to Protestant homes resulting in a mob physically attacking the children and their mothers, and preventing them from boarding ships taking them to Britain.[23]

Most significantly, there were two bouts of unofficial sympathetic strike action by railway workers across the country following Larkin's 'Fiery Cross' campaign. In September 1913, after a small group of Liverpool railway workers, members of the newly formed NUR, were suspended for 'blacking' Dublin traffic, strike action rapidly spread from Liverpool to some 13,000–14,000 goods traffic railwaymen in Birmingham, Crewe, Derby, Sheffield, Gloucester, Nottingham and Leeds.[24] In early December, after two Llanelli train drivers were sacked for refusing to handle trains with 'tainted' coal bound for Dublin, some 2,300 railway workers of different grades walked out on official strike, indirectly laying off thousands of other workers, notably miners,[25] and with 2,500 miners also refusing to proceed to work at Penygraig in trains worked by 'blacklegs'.[26]

More than 300 NUR branches, representing some 85,000 members, had already passed a vote of no confidence in their union leaders for tolerating 'tainted traffic', and hundreds of branches demanded an executive meeting to discuss the advisability of a joint solidarity strike of miners, transport workers and railway workers 'as the only means of ending the dispute'.[27] A member of the NUR's London District Council commented: 'I have never seen enthusiasm as there is among our men in the London branches. They are ready for anything in the way of sympathetic action.' The only obstacle was the union

23. Hunt (2013: 107–44); Cowan (2013: 138–44); Montefiore (1927: 159–70).

24. Holton (1976: 191); Cole and Arnot (1917: 34–5); *Liverpool Daily Post and Mercury*, 10–23 September 1913.

25. *Daily Herald*, 6 December; Board of Trade, *Labour Gazette*, January 1914; Yeates (2000: 459).

26. *Daily Herald*, 4 December 1913.

27. Ibid., 14 November 1913; Yeates (2000: 304, 377).

leadership, but he thought it likely 'the whole of our forces' will be 'ranged behind the men of Dublin before many days are over'.[28]

Meanwhile, solidarity strike action was taken by some dockers in Liverpool against Irish firms importing strikebreakers, and in Salford striking dockers took action as a means of ensuring the ship *SS Hare*, which had just arrived from Dublin, took back food packages for the city's locked-out workers.[29] There was also considerable support for the ITGWU on the London docks, where Dock, Wharf, Riverside and General Workers Union (DWRGLU) official Harry Orbell reported:

> In all my experience I have never known a time when there has been manifested such a desire to help any union in dispute as there is among dockers both in London and the provincial ports towards their Dublin comrades. We have had to rearrange the whole of our paid officials in London, placing them in certain centres with the express purpose of preventing any disorganised move ... It has been with the greatest trouble – and some of us have received rather strong words – that we have so far been able to hold the men in check.[30]

At the annual conference of the Miners' Federation delegates supported a proposal to approach all transport unions with the aim of coordinating a general strike to support the Dublin workers. Numerous resolutions sent to the TUC from union branches calling for consideration of a general 'down-tools' policy,[31] along with the *Daily Herald*'s campaign supporting a general strike, indicated the extent of pressure building up from below. And as with other disputes, radical left activists and their supporters inside the working-class movement were important in building support for the Dublin workers and encouraging a mood of sympathy for the aggressive syndicalist-influenced aims of the TGWU, thereby helping to make 'Larkinism' (along with 'syndicalism') a household word in Britain during the winter of 1913–14.[32] However Tom Mann, who straddled the official/unofficial divide within the trade union movement and might otherwise have played a pivotal role, was in America on a speaking tour during this crucial period from August to December 1913 and therefore unable to lend his authority and influence to the campaign.

---

28. *Daily Herald*, 10 November 1913.
29. Yeates (2000: 183).
30. *Daily Herald*, 10 November 1913.
31. TUC Parliamentary Committee, 18 November 1913, cited in Moran (1978: 42).
32. Holton (1976: 191).

Despite such widespread support by grassroots union members for Larkin's appeal, most national union leaders were emphatically opposed to the aggressive industrial tactic of sympathetic industrial action. On the railways, faced with the first bout of unofficial action by his members, Thomas directly intervened in union districts in the North, Midlands and Wales to assert his authority and denounce sympathetic strike action as 'ruinous'.[33] The NUR executive issued a manifesto, signed by its general secretary J.E. Williams, denying that traffic from Dublin was 'blackleg traffic',[34] and NUR officials were sent to Liverpool and Birmingham to instruct their members to work their 'ordinary duties'. In the absence of official support, the strikers were eventually persuaded to return to work.[35] Likewise, with the second wave of unofficial action, Thomas directly intervened and 'turned the table on the malcontents',[36] instructing his members back to work and denouncing the two victimised train drivers as 'a disgrace to the trade-union movement'.[37]

This setback, coming just three days before the TUC special conference met in London to formally consider the dispute, considerably undermined the momentum for sympathetic action. Other union leaders matched this opposition to solidarity industrial action for Dublin workers, with James Sexton deploying NUDL officials in all ports where it had members to discourage unofficial walkouts, and Havelock Wilson publicly condemning 'Larkinism'.[38] As a result, 'blacked' cargo was loaded in Dublin by NSFU members onto ships crewed by NSFU members, and then discharged in Liverpool by NUDL members.

The 9 December TUC conference voted 11 to 1 against sympathetic industrial action, deploring and condemning the 'unfair' attacks upon the leaders of the British trade union movement, and expressing confidence in those who had been 'unjustly assailed'.[39] Ironically it was Ben Tillett, who had shared a 'Fiery Cross' platform with Larkin on a number of occasions, that struck the fatal blow, proposing the motion condemning Larkin and thereby opening the floodgates for a score of attacks from Wilson and others. As the *Daily Mirror* exclaimed: 'Mr Larkin's "Fiery Cross" is extinguished.'[40]

33. Blaxland (1964: 85).
34. *Railway Review*, 19 and 26 September 1913.
35. Ibid., 12 December 1913.
36. Alcock (1922: 475).
37. *Daily Herald*, 10 December 1913; *Railway Review*, 12 December 1913.
38. Wilson (1913: 3).
39. TUC Parliamentary Committee Report of Special Conference Held at the Memorial Hall, 9 December 1913; *Daily Herald*, 10 December 1913; *Labour Leader*, 11 December 1913.
40. *Daily Mirror*, 10 December 1913.

Arguably, the conference arrangements were stacked against Larkin's position, since most delegates did not reflect the growing clamour for sympathetic industrial action,[41] but were 'largely made up of the obedient official element of their own stamp'.[42] Many union leaders felt that such action would deplete their strike funds, disrupt bargaining and conciliation arrangements, jeopardise union recognition agreements, and be ineffective. Their preferred solution was a compromise settlement, which they unsuccessfully tried to foist, but were unable to overcome the hostility of the Dublin employers to any deal. They were also wary of unleashing rank-and-file militancy inside their own unions which they would be unable to control, and of a victory for 'Larkinism' increasing support for the syndicalist objectives and methods they were so opposed to.

In addition, notwithstanding the enormous sympathy for Dublin workers inside the British labour movement, rank-and-file organisation was insufficiently coordinated and confident enough to overcome the opposition of trade union officials by acting unofficially en masse and providing an alternative leadership, a problem compounded by the political limitations of the radical left (Chapter 12).

As a result of the TUC decision, the momentum for unofficial action was decisively halted. Left to struggle on alone, the Dublin workers suffered a crushing defeat some weeks later, with hundreds falling victim to the blacklist and those who retained their jobs returning on humiliating terms. Yet although a blow to the British labour movement, the Dublin dispute highlighted the widespread militancy and willingness to take solidarity action that existed, with Connolly acknowledging: 'I say in all solemnity and seriousness that in its attitude towards Dublin, the Working-Class Movement of Great Britain reached its highest point of grandeur – attained for a moment to a realisation of that sublime unity towards which the best of us must continually aspire.'[43]

LONDON BUILDING WORKERS' LOCKOUT: JANUARY–AUGUST 1914

The defeat of the Dublin workers seems likely to have encouraged employers in the building industry to seek to emulate the lockout tactic as a counter-attack against the rank-and-file militancy that had been gaining momentum since 1913. During a flourishing period for the construction industry, the

41. Moran (1978: 43–4).
42. Ryan (1913: 176).
43. *Forward*, 9 February 1914.

growing demand for building labour increased workers' bargaining leverage, producing numerous small stoppages.

After an average of under 35 strikes a year during the period 1901–10, the number rose to 198 in 1913, with the number of workers involved increasing from an average of just under 6,100 between 1901 and 1910 to 40,002 in 1913.[44] The high level of strike activity was caused by employers utilising skill-displacing technology to undermine craftsmen's job control and status and further cut labour costs by imposing more intensive work schedules.[45] Additional factors fuelling strike action were a combination of discontent with wage awards, leading in July 1913 to the Operative Bricklayers' Society's withdrawal from the joint Conciliation Boards scheme (with echoes in other unions),[46] and the perceived failure of most union officials and the joint body of the London building unions' branch delegates – the London Building Industries Federation (LBIF) – to provide effective opposition to the well-organised London Master Builders Association.[47]

As unrest developed, many employers reverted to overtly antagonistic policies, including enforcing a 'no-disability rule' which allowed employers to undermine union bargaining power by employing non-union labour. This was an especially powerful weapon in a casual industry in which union organisation had to be established from scratch on each new building site. Out of 48 strikes in London between May 1913 and January 1914, no less than 17 affecting 20 firms were against subcontracted non-union labour.[48] London employers' attempt to impose individual contracts requiring union members to work with non-unionists only helped to intensify discontent uniting both skilled and unskilled.

Meanwhile, syndicalist influence was expanding within the building industry, reflected in the prominent role of Jack Wills and George Hicks (London) of the Operative Bricklayers' Society (OBS), and Fred Bower (Liverpool) and Jack Hamilton (Leeds) of the Operative Stonemasons (OM), with significant syndicalist minorities developing in both unions over the course of the unrest. At the same time, a Provisional Committee for the Consolidation of the Building Industries' Trade Unions (embracing plumbers, painters, joiners, labourers, plasterers, masons and bricklayers) and an OBS Consolidation Committee were both influenced by the activities of Industrial

44. Board of Trade (1913b: xii).
45. Holton (1976: 154).
46. Clegg (1985: 65); Drucker (1980: 73).
47. Holton (1976: 154, 158).
48. Price (1980: 258).

Syndicalist Education League members, with the former linked to the Amalgamated Committees Federation and established by an ISEL initiative.[49]

Centred in London with some support from larger industrial districts elsewhere,[50] the Provisional Committee rejected existing craft-based trade union organisation (in which numerous different unions engaged in sectional bargaining) and advocated the need for amalgamation and industrial unionism to unite all building trade workers. The need for organisational reform reflected a rejection of conciliation and moderate trade unionism and its replacement with 'fighting policies' of direct action to defend living standards, as well as fighting for the ultimate objective of securing control of industry by the workers themselves through wider strike action.[51]

But although consolidation committees' pressure throughout 1911 and 1912 resulted in the TUC's agreement to hold a conference on amalgamation in the summer of 1912, only 11 of the 21 unions immediately proceeded to a ballot on a general draft scheme for amalgamation. Two subsequent ballots held in October 1912 and July 1913 failed to secure the required 'two-thirds' majority to proceed, despite winning overall majorities.[52] While syndicalist influence remained significant within some building unions, notably the stonemasons and bricklayers, it was not sufficiently widespread to overcome the vested interest of most full-time union officials in the status quo. They preferred 'closer unity' by federations of kindred trades to amalgamation.[53]

Even so, the amalgamation campaign inspired a general desire to strengthen trade unionism by the elimination of non-unionism, with all of the 48 strikes in London between May 1913 and January 1914 unofficial and in violation of the 'no-disability rule' and conciliation procedures, although some London building unions did not regard themselves bound by these rules.[54]

At a joint employers and union meeting on 23 December 1913, the London Master Builders warned the unions to discipline their members engaged in strike action against non-union members in breach of the conciliation procedure, and to deposit financial guarantees against such strikes. Conflict erupted when a small minority of radical union leaders, led by the OBS delegates on the LBIF, refused to accept such proposals, although the vast majority of union officials were not prepared to support a militant oppositional stance. But their conciliatory response merely encouraged the London employers' federation to announce in early January 1914 that they were with-

49. Holton (1976: 155).
50. Drucker (1980: 77–8).
51. Holton (1976: 156, 158–9).
52. Postgate (1923: 407–13).
53. Holton (1976: 158).
54. Price (1980: 258).

drawing from the conciliation agreement and would henceforth be requiring each worker to sign an individual contract 'document' – to be enforced by a financial penalty of £1 – binding them to work peaceably with non-unionists, and with the banning of all strikes on the issue.[55]

When the unions revealed they could not meet these demands, the employers issued their own union general lockout notices, effective on 24 January, resulting in over 40,000 London building workers being locked out or on strike.[56] Union officials refused to accept the employers' ultimatum, but their response to the lockout was extremely timid, with some blaming the leaders of unofficial strikes, and while the LBIF insisted on the abolition of the no-disability and conciliation rules and the Federation to be the only bargaining agent in London, national union officials merely wanted the withdrawal of the 'document' and the return to the old conditions for each craft. Despite authorising strike pay, officials made few preparations to mobilise rank-and-file support.

In this situation, it was left to syndicalists and other militant activists – through the auspices of the newly formed Industrial Democracy League (which had emerged from the disintegration of the ISEL in late 1913), its paper *Solidarity* and the building trades' Amalgamation Committee – to provide an alternative pathway to rank-and-file forces. It successfully exerted pressure on the LBIF to call a branch delegate conference to discuss strategy, with a proposal that all negotiations should be conducted centrally through the Federation rather than sectionally by individual unions (with any future settlement put to a ballot of members), and a demand that employers must not only withdraw their anti-union 'document', but also concede wage increases and reductions in hours of work.[57] Branch delegate agreement to all these proposals created the basis of strike policy during the next five months of struggle, with rank-and-file control of the strike further achieved with local strike committees set up to implement the programme, supervise picketing and maintain morale.

Building employers were determined to put an end to industrial militancy and saw their stance in almost zealous terms. They expected an easy victory, but workers' resistance to the employers' demands or even any compromise settlement was also considerable. Significantly, the lockout failed to generate the extent of violence and social confrontation in other strikes during this period due to the relative absence of large numbers of 'blacklegs', with many

55. Drucker (1980: 84); Clegg (1985: 65–7).
56. Holton (1976: 159); Clegg (1985: 67); Postgate (1923: 415).
57. Holton (1976: 160).

non-unionists refusing to sign the 'document'.[58] Where building sites continued working, mass pickets were mobilised to close them down. A site on the Kingsway Road in north-west London was shut down despite clashes with the police when it was invaded by over 1,000 pickets, with those imprisoned greeted by cheering crowds on their release.[59]

Confronted with such militancy, on 16 April the employers withdrew their 'document' and offered a compromise settlement – involving the withdrawal of individual contracts in return for no union card inspections on site without employer's permission and with union enforcement of the new rules, including disciplinary action. Building union leaders, determined to end the strike, recommended acceptance of these terms and a return to work.[60] But a ballot overwhelming rejected the employers' terms by 23,481 to 2,021, with workers determined not to go back without the withdrawal of the non-union labour 'document', a closed shop and improved pay and conditions.

In response, the employers made some minor concessions, which were then submitted to further ballots in May and June. Despite full-blown hostility from the mainstream press, the building unions' leaders urging acceptance, and the executive of the National Federation of Building Trade Employers threatening a *national* lockout if the London dispute was not settled, the men voted again to stay out. On the first occasion the new terms were rejected by 21,017 to 5,824, and on the second by 14,081 to 4,565. No national lockout followed, but a breach was opened in the solid front with the stonemasons voting by a majority for a return to work along with the members of several smaller unions.[61]

When union officials attempted to meet employers in secret on 14 and 15 May, they were greeted with a protest that held aloft a banner 'WARNING TO OFFICIALS: NO SURRENDER', and mass pickets mobilised to prevent a return to work.[62] At the Marylebone Town Hall site in early July, attempts by the Princess Royal to lay the foundation stone were interrupted by locked-out building workers singing *The Red Flag* and the *Marseillaise*, followed by three cheers for the social revolution, three boos for 'blacklegs' and three boos for royalty.[63] Despite this persistent militancy, and the majority ballot decisions, individual national union leaders actively tried to end the strike by securing sectional bargaining settlements. At the same time, officials blocked attempts by London union activists to pressure employers by spreading strikes to

58. Postgate (1923: 416).
59. Newsinger (2015: 36).
60. Clegg (1985: 68).
61. Postgate (1923: 418–20); Drucker (1980: 86).
62. *Daily Herald*, 16 May 1914.
63. Ibid., 9 July 1914.

firms working on subcontract for members of the London Master Builders Association.[64]

The abandonment of industrial solidarity by union officials produced a flood of hostile resolutions from local strike committees to union headquarters, and unofficial militants took over the platform and prevented officials from speaking during a mass meeting of 7,000 in Trafalgar Square during mid-July.[65] But with employers signalling a national lockout to commence on 15 August, national union leaders agreed to new terms, including reinstatement as soon as practicable of those who had gone on strike. And regardless of a proposal for a further ballot from the London district committees of the Operative Bricklayers and the Amalgamated Carpenters and Joiners, their executives settled over their heads.[66]

The growing realisation that union officialdom posed a far greater obstacle than had hitherto been appreciated led many militants to support the creation of an entirely new revolutionary building workers' union rather than continuing to attempt to reconstruct existing unions along industrial lines. It led to the formation of a Building Workers' Industrial Union (BWIU) that involved most of the leading syndicalists from the amalgamation movement, including Jack Wills and Jack Hamilton, who became secretary and general organiser, respectively,[67] although George Hicks was opposed to this new initiative.[68] However, although four small local building unions immediately joined the BWIU, the new body was overtaken by the onset of the war, which broke out on the very weekend the union was established, and which allowed the officials to finally carry the day by playing the patriotic card to secure a return to work and end the five-month dispute.[69]

ENDURING INDUSTRIAL MILITANCY: JANUARY–AUGUST 1914

Despite the defeats inflicted on the Dublin transport and London building workers the pattern of industrial militancy during the first seven months of 1914 prior to the outset of war showed little reduction from the previous year. The 848 strikes between January and July were only slightly less than in the whole of 1912, and involved close to half-a-million workers with nearly ten million working days lost (Table 2).[70] As Askwith recalled:

64. Clegg (1985: 69).
65. *Daily Herald*, 20 July 1914.
66. Clegg (1985: 68).
67. *Daily Herald*, 13 July and 5 August 1913.
68. Postgate (1923: 421).
69. Ibid.: 423.
70. Board of Trade, *Labour Gazette*, October 1915.

> Day after day was taken up in travelling to all parts of Great Britain by my officers and myself to answer the numerous calls to preside at conferences, with a view to settlement of sporadic disputes.[71]

In the mining industry, there were almost as many local strikes in 1914 as there had been in 1910–13, with grievances over low wages, lengthy hours and non-union labour. Between February and April there was a strike involving 150,000 miners in South Yorkshire over a demand for the minimum wage rates fixed under the Act of 1912 to include the percentages awarded under the Conciliation Board – 6 pence per day for some men and 5 pence for others. Although MFGB officials tried to persuade their members to stay at work until the conciliation board had delivered its decision, a Rotherham strike[72] spread throughout the district and lasted five weeks, with many pits in West Yorkshire stopping in sympathy, and the MFGB eventually granting full financial backing to the Yorkshire Miners' Association.[73] Finally, the conciliation board and minimum wage board jointly proposed that the percentages should be added to the new, higher rate except where a pit could be proved to be unprofitable, terms which were accepted by the men.[74]

In January, 13,000 coal porters and carmen took strike action over pay in a dispute with coal dealers, although the joint strike committee granted permits to hospitals, workhouses and similar institutions.[75] In March, 300 women workers at Morton's, a food preparation factory in Millwall, east London, walked out in protest at management's plan to undercut wages by recruiting young girls to work at lower rates than adult women. Soon all the 900 women and girls, and 300 men who came out to support them, were on strike demanding better pay and conditions. A strong picket line was established, with enthusiastic regular meetings held outside the factory and local halls. Mary Macarthur (NFWW) helped to organise the women strikers, alongside the Gasworkers' Union in a display of cooperation and solidarity between women and male workers.[76] When strikers marched around Millwall the *Daily Mail* published a photograph under the headline 'Tango Dancing Girl Strikers'.[77] A march to Trafalgar Square was accompanied by a band and piper and NFWW banner, and was joined at Blackfriars by women

71. Askwith ([1920] 1974: 347).
72. *Daily Herald*, 28 February 1914.
73. Ibid., 18 March and 31 March 1914.
74. Clegg (1985: 71).
75. *Daily Herald*, 22 and 27 January 1914; *Daily Mirror*, 27 January 1914.
76. *Daily Herald*, 25 March 1914; *Woman's Dreadnought*, 21 and 28 March 1914.
77. *Daily Mail*, 19 March 1914.

workers from Camberwell who were also on strike.[78] The dispute lasted twelve days before management, having been overwhelmed by the strikers' public support and embarrassed by the media coverage, agreed to the strikers' demands, including a general wage increase of between 10 and 25 per cent; 960 women were enrolled by the Federation.[79]

In April, following the dismissal of two teachers at a small Church of England school in Burston, Norfolk, for complaining about unhygienic conditions and inadequate heating and lighting, 66 of the school's 72 children went on strike in their support, singing and marching around the village waving flags. Underlying the dismissals was the two teachers' encouragement of the organisation of local agricultural labourers and their refusal to be deferential to the school's rector and managing body who were generally supportive of farmers' interests. None of the children returned to school, but instead received lessons in a marquee on the village green with the full backing of their parents, and financed by donations from the labour movement. The Burston School strike would become the longest-running strike in British history, with the teaching of local children lasting until 1939.[80]

In June, women employed in small fish factories in North Shields to gut herrings with razor-sharp knives walked out on strike in protest at their wages and took the ferry to South Shields, where 150 of them marched from the landing stage to call out the workers of Robertson's, Brough's and Fuller's to join them, with an immediate and enthusiastic response. Although the women were not members of a trade union, they found energetic support from James Wilson of the National Amalgamated Union of Labour who helped them organise daily meetings at the union offices and formulate demands for 6 pence an hour and overtime pay for evenings and weekends. They received financial support from the Harton Lodge of the Durham Miners' Federation, while the local NUR 'blacked' the handling of fish at the ports. The strike continued until 4 August 1914 when war was declared and the herring trawlers were commandeered for naval use and fishing ended for the duration.[81]

In July Mary Bamber, the Liverpool local organiser for the Amalgamated Warehouse and General Workers Union, led a strike of 6,000 laundresses in pursuit of a 50-hour working week, a substantial pay rise and an end to the system of fines. There were large mass meetings, pickets, visits to individual

78. Hunt (2011: 180).
79. *Daily Herald*, 28 March 1914; Jackson and Taylor (2014: 138–9); Boston (1980: 70); Drake (1984: 46–7).
80. Jeffery (2018).
81. Gorman (1980: 94–5).

scabs' homes to persuade them to join the strike, and a seven-mile march of 1,200 women to form a mass picket to close down a laundry in Formby, in the north end of Liverpool. The strike was partially successful in securing a minimum rate, a five-hour reduction in the working week and an end to the system of fines.[82]

A momentous three-day strike took place at the huge, highly unionised and government-owned Woolwich Arsenal in July, just days after the assassination of Archduke Ferdinand in Sarajevo, when a fitter and member of the Amalgamated Society of Engineers (ASE) was dismissed for refusing to erect some machinery on a concrete bedding which had been prepared by non-union labour. A union meeting later that day decided, with no sanction from ASE officials, to call out all the union members employed in the factory, and to urge all unskilled unions to join in.

This was so successful that by the following day over 7,000 men had stopped work, and within three days production at the Arsenal was brought to a complete halt when men in the Army and Navy Ordnance Department joined the strike, lifting the numbers involved to about 12,000.[83] An 'all-grades' shop stewards' committee embracing craftsmen and unskilled labourers (established the previous year by Tom Rees, London district secretary of the ASE, and ex-Ruskin College and Central College student)[84] mobilised mass picketing to keep the works shut, and workers at Plymouth, Portsmouth and Enfield voted to take sympathy action.

The Prime Minister believed the strike was entirely subversive of discipline in an institution that was, in effect, part of the British Army, and that giving way to its 'unreasonable demands would set an example which might have disastrous consequences for the country'.[85] But in the face of a total halt to production, and with war looming, he quickly established a Court of Inquiry with Askwith as chairman and two employers and two union representatives.[86] An agreement that the dismissed man would be reinstated and not punished if the Court's result went against him ended the three-day stoppage.[87]

Most significantly in the summer of 1914, there was the possibility of national strike action in other strategically important industries. In the

82. Rees (2017: 44); Grant (1987).
83. *Daily Herald*, 5 July 1914; *Yorkshire Post*, 8 July 1914; Board of Trade, *Labour Gazette*, August 1914.
84. Holton (1973a: 613).
85. *The Spectator*, 11 July 1914.
86. Phelps Brown (1959: 331).
87. *Sheffield Evening Telegraph*, 8 July 1914; Heath (2013: 165); Askwith ([1920] 1974: 356–7).

mining industry, where Scottish employers' profits were being squeezed by falling prices and rising costs, wage cuts were anticipated. The issue had already been raised by Scottish delegates at the MFGB annual conference in October 1913, where they had been given an assurance that 'all possible assistance' would be provided in the event of any wage reduction. Throughout the spring and summer of 1914, the Scottish mining situation became increasingly tense as union officials resisted owners' demands for pay cuts of 1 shilling a day, and threatened a four-day working week, even though this risked the prospect of a lockout.[88] A special conference of the MFGB in July agreed to support the Scottish miners if they took strike action, but there was disagreement over what form this support should take.

Eventually it was agreed to provide financial support and to ballot the entire MFGB membership on a national strike.[89] It was decided that, if a general stoppage were decided, outstanding grievances among other groups would be brought forward as part of a national set of demands. That this final step was so seriously contemplated suggests (assuming a ballot vote would have been supported by other regions of the union) there was the possibility of another national miners' strike, until the outbreak of war in the middle of this mining crisis brought negotiations to a standstill.[90]

At the same time, there was the prospect of a national railwaymen's strike over NUR demands for a national programme involving full union recognition, the 48-hour week and a 5 shilling pay rise for all grades.[91] And national confrontations also loomed on the horizon in other industries. As Askwith had warned in November 1913:

> There is a ... spirit and a desire for improvement, of alteration ... that nobody can be surprised at. And which is bound to continue ... Within a comparatively short time there may well be movements in this country coming to a head of which recent events have been a small foreshadowing.[92]

Reflecting on this prognosis, Askwith later wrote that 'the comparative placidity of the summer of 1914 seemed in a measure to be deceptive'. He explained it was known that the miners, transport workers and railwaymen were all preparing new claims and organising fast, and with the three-year agreement in the engineering industry due to end, claims for shorter hours,

88. *Daily Herald*, 4 July 1914; *Manchester Evening News*, 22 July 1914.
89. *Manchester Evening News*, 27 July 1914.
90. Holton (1976: 171); *Daily Herald*, 4 July 1914.
91. *Liverpool Daily Post and Mercury*, 20 June 1914; Halévy (1961: 478).
92. Askwith ([1920] 1974: 348–9).

increased wages and improved conditions were expected. 'The cost of living appeared to be on the upward trend. There was a spirit of unrest that vaguely expressed itself in an oft-heard phrase, "Wait till the autumn".'[93]

With the simultaneous deterioration of relations in several important industries, and with severe economic recession anticipated in the summer of 1914, reports reached the Cabinet Committee on Industrial Unrest predicting a resurgence of large-scale national strikes in the autumn of 1914. As the Chancellor, Lloyd George, recalled: 'in the summer of 1914 there was every sign that the autumn would witness a series of industrial disturbances without precedent'.[94] Addressing an audience of financiers and merchants in the City of London on 17 July, he expressed concern that if the 'insurrection' of labour should coincide with the Irish rebellion, which everyone feared, 'the situation will be the gravest with which any government has had to deal for centuries'.[95]

TRIPLE ALLIANCE: 1914

One of the main factors encouraging many contemporary participants (Board of Trade, government, employers, newspapers and union activists alike) to anticipate a resurgence of national-level strikes in the autumn of 1914 was the formation in April of a 'Triple Alliance' uniting the miners' (MFGB), transport (NTWF) and railway (NUR) workers' unions, with its prospect of coordinated action. In a formal institutional sense, the Triple Alliance resulted from the Miners' Federation annual conference of October 1913 at which a resolution requesting the union executive approach other unions with a view to cooperative action in support of each other's demands was enthusiastically supported.

This initiative resulted in a joint delegate conference of the three unions which met in London in April 1914, followed by an organising conference in June at which officers of the new Triple Industrial Alliance were elected.[96] The plan was that, as Robert Smillie, who had become MFGB President, explained: 'each of these great fighting organisations, before embarking upon any big movement, either defensive or aggressive, should formulate its programme, submit it to others, and that upon joint proposals joint action should then be taken'.[97]

93. Askwith ([1920] 1974: 356).
94. Lloyd George (1938: 1141).
95. *The Times*, 18 July 1914.
96. *Daily Herald*, 24 April 1914.
97. Smillie, 'The Triple Industrial Alliance', in *The Labour Year Book*, 1915, cited in Arnot (1954: 175).

But less organised grassroots undercurrents were also partly responsible for the foundation of the Triple Alliance. With strikes by dockers, railwaymen and miners between 1911 and 1912 highlighting their mutual interdependence, and the belief in solidarity action by one section for another widely accepted among rank-and-file activists, it encouraged the momentum for a campaign of industrial unity between them. Syndicalist advocacy of the sympathetic strike, refusal to touch 'tainted goods', and active support of amalgamation and industrial unionism played an important part in nurturing this widespread interest in unity. It was further developed during the 1912 London transport strike, when joint action between transport workers and railwaymen occurred on a considerable scale in the East End, where many railwaymen demanded that union officials authorise a strike in support of the transport workers.[98] Although officials refused to sanction this move, the East London initiative helped to stimulate wider rank-and-file interest in joint action among local railwaymen's branches.

The defeat of the London transport strike, far from thwarting moves for joint action, led to it being more widely canvassed, with radical opinion now beginning to consider the possibility of a *permanent* body linking transport workers, railwaymen and miners, such that industrial solidarity might be more effectively pursued in the future.[99] In the process, the concept of the Triple Alliance as a weapon to fight employers and government was advocated in syndicalist publications, and by the *Daily Herald*. Rank-and-file activists and militants within all three industries enthusiastically supported the idea of a Triple Alliance, sending a stream of union branch resolutions calling for joint action to their respective executives and officials.[100]

Against this backcloth, the Triple Alliance came into being, albeit with varied degrees of backing and contrasting interpretations as to its function amongst leaders within the three unions, with the most enthusiastic backers Tillett and Williams of the NTWF and Charlie Cramp of the NUR.[101] A draft scheme was devised that suggested each union arrange their collective agreements so that they all terminated at the same time. Each body would simultaneously submit its own demands for improvements in pay and conditions, and agree they would not settle unless the others had also reached agreements. On this basis, it was hoped either the employers would give way before the massed industrial power of the three groups, with no strike needed, or if a strike did occur all three industries would be stopped at once, with

98. *The Syndicalist*, June 1912.

99. Holton (1973a: 585–90; 1976: 173–4).

100. Coates and Topham (1994: 553).

101. *Daily Herald*, 24 April 1914; Bagwell (1971: 104).

each union striking for its own programme as well as in support of others.[102] Although not constituting a majority of the British trade union movement, they numbered about 1.3 million workers (268,000 railwaymen, 800,000 miners and 163,000 transport workers) with the consequence that any joint action would threaten to disrupt the economy like a general strike, probably forcing the government to intervene to bring about a settlement.

In their classic *History of Trade Unionism*, the Webbs wrote: 'British Trade Unionism was, in fact, in the summer of 1914, working up for an almost revolutionary outburst of gigantic industrial disputes, which could not have failed to be serious ... when, in August 1914, war was declared, and all internal conflict had perforce to be suspended.'[103] Likewise, a few years later George Dangerfield reflected:

> The disputes of 1911 and 1912 ... were bitter and frequent, they had convulsed the country, they had humbled Parliament, and they were leading – with a disconcerting speed and directness – towards the final assault of a General Strike. One by one, the transport workers, the miners, and the railwaymen had come out; one by one they had returned, not merely with a sense of grievance, but with a sense of power: it was simply a question of time before they joined forces.[104]

It was assumed by many contemporary participants and subsequent historians that the Triple Alliance anticipated or entailed the 'great General Strike of 1914', only to be 'forestalled by some bullets at Sarajevo'.[105] But a more realistic assessment of the role the Triple Alliance might have played suggests it could have been highly problematic in terms of restraining rather than leading rank-and-file workers' struggles (Chapter 9).

Part III turns towards a thematic and analytical assessment of the 1910–14 period, exploring the rank-and-file/union official dynamic, striking organisation, counter-mobilisation and violence, political radicalisation, and relationship between industrial struggles, political action and the radical left.

---

102. Cole (1948a: 350); Halévy (1961: 477–8); *Daily Mirror*, 29 July 1914.
103. Webb and Webb (1920: 690).
104. Dangerfield ([1935] 1997: 249).
105. Ibid.: 320.

PART III

Assessment

8

Rank-and-File/Union Official Dynamic

David Shackleton, ex-textile workers' union leader and Labour MP, who was appointed Labour Advisor to the Home Office by Winston Churchill, observed in a July 1911 memorandum to the Cabinet: 'The most serious feature of the labour unrest is the failure of the accredited leaders of Trade Unions to hold their men in hand; this is largely because the leaders stand for arbitration and conciliation as the best means of settling disputes.'[1] It was an acknowledgement of the way in which, as we have seen, throughout the Labour Revolt there were internecine battles inside unions, as a new generation of young militants emerged who were prepared to challenge incumbent full-time trade union officials that often seemed unresponsive to their members' discontents, and wanted to develop more aggressive forms of struggle.

In many respects, this rank-and-file challenge signalled a serious crisis for both employers and government precisely because it represented an undermining of the recently constructed institutionalised procedures of labour incorporation, containment and control.[2] However, even though trade union structures and internal relations were considerably transformed during this period, there were also important continuities in the way in which full-time officials were often able to stymie rank-and-file initiatives and organisation, and in the process successfully reassert their authority and control.

TRADES UNION CONGRESS

In the decades following its formation in 1868, the main function of the Trades Union Congress (TUC), reflected in the title of its executive body – the Parliamentary Committee – was not organising in support of industrial struggles, but politically lobbying Parliament and ministers over legislative

1. Memorandum from David Shackleton to the Cabinet, 22 July 1911, TNA/CAB: 37/107/78.
2. Gore (1982: 66).

matters related to the protection of workers and providing legal security for unions. It viewed all industrial disputes as the concern of affiliated individual unions over which the TUC had no jurisdiction, and effectively played no part in strikes, although it set up in 1899 a General Federation of Trade Unions (GFTU) to provide some financial assistance to unions involved in protracted strikes.

But the TUC Parliamentary Committee's role in the 1910–14 Labour Revolt, notwithstanding some leading figures such as Will Thorne, James Sexton and Harry Gosling, was negligible. It participated in discussions on the eve of the 1911 national railway strike, but left later negotiations to try to settle the strike to Labour Party leaders Arthur Henderson and Ramsay MacDonald. Likewise, in the 1912 national miners' and London transport strikes it was content to leave the main intervention to Labour Party leaders. Even though five TUC leaders were invited to discuss the escalating levels of industrial militancy with Asquith and Buxton, and individual officials were appointed in 1911 to a short-lived tripartite Industrial Council (Chapter 10), the TUC was 'generally irrelevant' to the government's efforts to secure industrial peace.[3] And while the Parliamentary Committee's annual report to the September 1911 Trades Union Congress, held following the national wave of transport strikes earlier that year, briefly noted the substantial 'gains from recent events', it also unequivocally 'condemn[ed] the outbreaks of violence on the part of unorganised men' and insisted that 'the permanent success of the workers can only be assured through Trade Union action'.[4]

While the new militant spirit of rank-and-file workers influenced annual Congress debates (notably at the 1911 and 1912 congresses, the latter at which Noah Ablett put the case for the syndicalists in a hard-hitting speech), the weight of tradition and cautious inclination of many delegates resulted in no great change in policy. The Dublin transport strike provided the one important exception, when Congress, stirred by enormous grassroots pressure, directed the Parliamentary Committee to intervene.[5] But as we have seen, while the Parliamentary Committee encouraged trade union material relief, it refused to mobilise sympathetic industrial action to stop the movement of goods to and from Dublin, condemned Larkin and attempted to foist a 'compromise' settlement over the heads of the ITGWU.[6]

3. Martin (1980: 120, 125).
4. Report of Proceedings of the Forty-Fourth Annual Trades Union Congress, Newcastle upon Tyne, 4–9 September 1911, pp. 70–1.
5. Report of Proceedings of the Forty-Sixth Annual Trades Union Congress, Manchester, 1–6 September 1913, pp. 67–72, 849.
6. Yeates (2000: 456, 458–9; 460–2); Darlington (2016: 517–19).

Meanwhile, by the end of 1911 even the limited financial assistance provided by the GFTU in long drawn-out strikes to supplement individual unions' own dispute benefits proved unsustainable. Amidst rocketing levels of strike action and the failure to secure the affiliation of several key unions (including the miners and railwaymen), the GFTU found itself paying out more in benefits than its total annual income. Instead, for the vast majority of strikes, the financial assistance received depended on what was generated at local level by union branches, trades councils, local communities and left-wing groups.[7]

As a consequence, many rank-and-file militants who aspired to the transformation of trade unionism and its bureaucratic and conservative official structures tended to look not so much to the TUC, but to other newer union bodies. The National Transport Workers' Federation (NTWF) and Triple Alliance, along with the underlying grassroots campaign for amalgamation and industrial unionism, were viewed as a potentially more fruitful means of pursuing radical strategies of industrial confrontation and strike solidarity.

RANK-AND-FILE/UNION OFFICIAL DYNAMIC

In terms of individual trade unions, as we have seen, it was invariably an unofficial dynamic, in which rank-and-file workers took the initiative independently of national officials and acted as the central motor driving the Labour Revolt forward. It was this bottom-up militancy, with its remarkable ability at critical junctures to overcome the inertia or compromises of the official union leadership, that played a crucial contributory role in winning concessions from employers and government and building the strength of trade union organisation.

Of course, it is important to recognise that some national union officials, like Mann, Tillett and Williams, and even Wilson, Thomas and Sexton, as well as local officials such as R.H. Capener (of the Seamen's Union in Manchester) and Mary Bamber (of the Warehouse and General Workers' Union in Liverpool), could play a very important role on occasion in mobilising workers into action, or at least supporting action their members had taken on their own initiative.

Nonetheless, in many strikes official union backing for strike action only came about because of independent rank-and-file pressure that encouraged or forced officials to adopt such a stance, and which sometimes during the course of disputes extended the action in more militant ways than offi-

7. Clegg, Fox and Thompson (1964: 356); Prochaska (1982: 104–6); leaflets issued by GFTU Management Committee, MRC: GFT/5/1 1364/1.

cials were prepared to countenance. Moreover, despite variations in the balance and boundaries between official and unofficial action within specific disputes, the rank-and-file often found it necessary to attempt to prevent union officials from curbing, controlling and/or sabotaging action, with different degrees of success.

Even some of the most militant left-wing union leaders were challenged by this grassroots upsurge, at least in the short term. For example, during the 1911 Liverpool seamen's and dockers' strikes, appeals for a return to work by Mann and other officials were rejected at several crowded dockside meetings, with platforms 'besieged by a host of orators of a non-descript character'.[8] Likewise during the 1911 London transport strike, despite Tillett's organising reputation, relations with the newly radicalised waterfront workers were far from smooth, as he acknowledged:

> Whoever undertakes to write up the psychology of such a movement as ours will have an interesting study, inasmuch as the whole driving force was direct, compelling and spontaneous as the driving force of human beings suddenly aroused, unconscious of their strength. I have no other reason to give for the miracle. The leadership, however splendid, the organisation, however conscientious, did not and could not account for the great upheaval.[9]

This non-institutional locus of militancy was also manifest even in those contexts where militant strike committee leaders had supported mass picketing against 'blacklegs', with action sometimes going far beyond the nature and level that had been sanctioned, including street rioting that involved a wider framework of social community support. On occasion it was striking non-unionised workers who refused to accept compromises proposed by union officials, as during the 1911 Liverpool and London dockers' strikes when recommended agreements were opposed by non-union workers with little allegiance to official union authority and procedures.

Additionally, strike action was often taken by non-unionised rank-and-file workers in *unorganised* workplaces – such as in the 1913 West Midlands metal workers' strike, and 1911 Bermondsey and 1913 Bridport Gundry's women's strikes. Significantly, in these cases, officials of the relatively much smaller general labour unions – such as Macarthur of the NFWW and Varley of the WU – played a much more supportive role, often acting like organisers, supporting strikes as the means to recruit workers and build union organi-

8. Lovell (1969: 162).
9. Tillett (1912: 22–3).

sation. As a result, there was a blurring of conventional hierarchical tensions between officials and the rank-and-file. There was a similar picture inside Larkin's ITGWU.

Attempts by government and employers to institutionalise conflict and incorporate trade union officialdom (see Chapters 1 and 10) were checked by this 'dual revolt' during 1910–14, as union officials and conciliation procedures were bypassed by informal grassroots organisation in both organised and unorganised workplaces. It was a rank-and-file driven phenomenon that encouraged a 'unions-as-*movement*' dynamic that posed a serious, if spasmodic, challenge to 'unions-as-*institutions*'.[10] Yet conversely, the spread of workers' militancy also reinforced established formal conflict resolution systems. The enormous rise of trade union membership (both within and outside previously existing organised areas) led to unions becoming recognised in more industries and an extension of collective bargaining arrangements, which in turn increased the numbers of full-time union officials. In the process, the massive expansion of trade union coverage and official structures contributed to the broader attempts made to institutionally regulate and defuse unrest amongst the rank-and-file. It meant 'responsible' union officials, as quid pro quo of being granted union recognition and stable bargaining arrangements with employers, felt obliged to accept the obligation to control union members' militancy, with a concomitant acceptance of the legitimacy of managerial authority in a capitalist economic system whose inequity was the very *raison d'être* of trade unionism.[11]

A notable example of this process occurred on the Liverpool docks where a port-wide *White Book Agreement* granted full NUDL recognition, a virtual closed shop, union rates of pay and a Joint Committee consisting of equal numbers of employers and union representatives to negotiate wages and conditions, but also entailed commitments from the NUDL to exert a new disciplinary control over their members to ensure they abided by collective agreements and followed agreed procedures, including continuing to work while disputes were resolved.[12] Moreover, notwithstanding its rank-and-file dynamic, overall during the Labour Revolt union officials were often able to control the way disputes ended, agreeing settlements that fell short of rank-and-file objectives, and issuing instructions for a return to work either with little consultation or irrespective of membership ballot results. This happened in the national miners', and railway and London building workers' strikes.

10. Herberg (1943); Hyman (1975); Zoll (1976); Cohen (2006); Darlington (2014b).
11. Hyman (1971: 203–5); Price (1980: 252).
12. Taplin (1986: 94).

The contradictory *conflictual* and *accommodative* role of unions and their officials was personified even in the left-wing figure of Ben Tillett. On the one hand, his dramatic firebrand speeches established him as one of a handful of leaders with a militant reputation, and in the public mind he came to personify the aggressive consciousness of syndicalist philosophy. Never hesitating to attack the moderate leaders of the Labour Party, he preached direct action and the necessity of social revolution at every opportunity, actively participated in two of the major strikes of the period, and encouraged the growth of industrial unionism, establishing the NTWF.

Yet despite his radical image, Tillett had long advocated conciliation and compulsory arbitration instead of strikes as the route to union recognition, and displayed a long-standing opposition to sympathetic walkouts. He even opposed the use of the strike weapon itself, in preference to exhausting every 'reasonable' means of settling disputes through negotiation, for example, instructing DWRGWU members not to take action in the 1911 Liverpool and Manchester transport strikes.[13]

Such contradictory behaviour can be explained by the sophisticated syndicalist analysis of official trade unionism that developed. On the one hand, they criticised union officials for acting as a brake on workers' struggles, 'betraying' their members during strikes and preventing a decisive challenge to the employers and capitalist class. They accused union officials of subordinating the interests of the wider working class to organised craft or sectional interests within it, and drew attention to the collaborationist logic of formalised collective bargaining which defined the way in which union officials concentrated on improving workers' material conditions within the framework of capitalist society, rather than seeking to transform society through revolution and thereby undermining their own *raison d'être*.[14]

A connection was made between the structural features of trade union consolidation (for example, recognition by employers and the state, achievement of social prestige and acquisition of organisational assets) and the adoption of conciliatory and bureaucratic policies. As E.J.B. Allen argued: 'The capitalists recognise these gentlemen's utility to them ... Because the employers recognise these men as their chief bulwark against a revolutionary movement.'[15]

On the other hand, although they believed that the existing unions were bogged down by years of conciliation and bureaucratic domination, they were confident it would be possible to transform the structures and proce-

13. Schneer (1982: 155, 159); LASC: LP/TIL/08.
14. *The Syndicalist*, October 1912.
15. Allen (1909: 9).

dures of union organisation (towards industrial unionism) as a means to wrest effective control away from bureaucratic officialdom and encourage unions to adopt revolutionary objectives. Syndicalists proposed practical measures, notably mass action and control from below, to overcome the official stranglehold. Tom Mann assumed that union officials would not be able to withstand this pressure from below:

> ... the time has gone by when reactionary officials are to be allowed to impede working class advance; it is really a case of 'get on and lead', or 'get out and follow': and the sooner this is fully realised the better for all concerned.[16]

Many of these ideas were presented in a more fully rounded critique of union officialdom in the seminal syndicalist pamphlet *The Miners' Next Step*, published in 1912 by the Unofficial Reform Committee (URC) within the South Wales Miners' Federation (SWMF).[17] The pamphlet was very much the result of extensive rank-and-file industrial and educational activity arising from the collective efforts of the group of young syndicalist militants who led the battle against the entrenched 'Lib-Lab' old-guard on the SWMF executive.

At its heart was the theory of industrial unionism, to overcome existing sectionalism by building a single national industrial union to more effectively struggle against an increasingly organised employing class and lay the basis for the eventual control of the means of production by the workers. The pamphlet insisted 'the remedy is not new leaders',[18] but rather a radical reallocation of power, in which the rank-and-file could assert democratic control over the official apparatus of the union and direct it to their own ends. With control vested in the union lodges and union executive transformed into a rank-and-file body from which officials were excluded, the workers would become the 'bosses' of their union and the 'leaders' their 'servants'.[19]

Yet notwithstanding its pioneering attempt to understand the nature of bureaucratic union officialdom and suggest practical means of overcoming its influence, syndicalist analysis and practice was also constrained by a number of dilemmas.[20]

16. *Industrial Syndicalist*, February 1911.
17. Unofficial Reform Committee ([1912] 1973).
18. Ibid.: 16.
19. Ibid.: 21.
20. The limitations of the British Socialist Party's and Socialist Labour Party's attitude towards union officialdom are explored in Chapter 12.

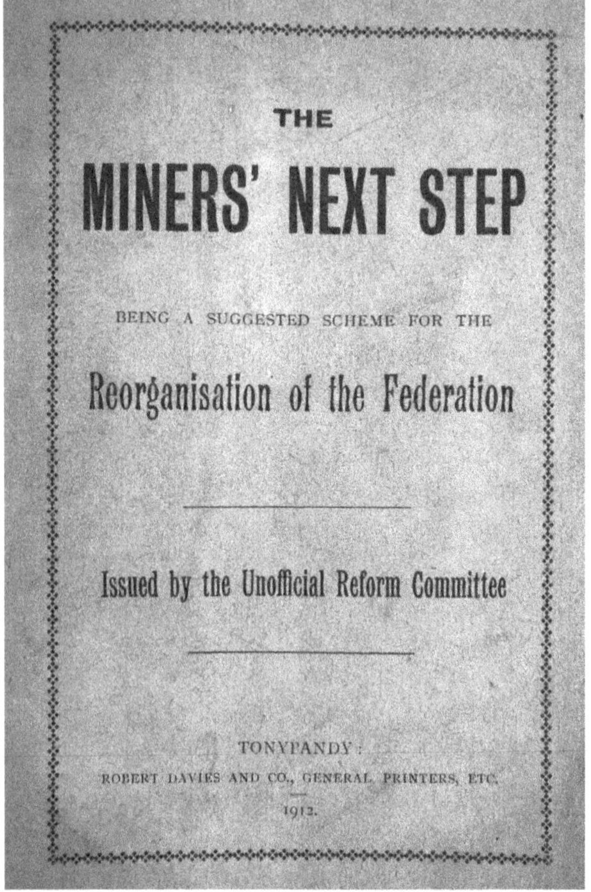
THE

MINERS' NEXT STEP

BEING A SUGGESTED SCHEME FOR THE

Reorganisation of the Federation

Issued by the Unofficial Reform Committee

TONYPANDY:

ROBERT DAVIES AND CO., GENERAL PRINTERS, ETC.

1912.

Figure 8.1 The front cover of the seminal pamphlet published in early 1912 by the syndicalist-influenced Unoffical Reform Committee of the South Wales Miners' Federation.

Credit: Working Class Movement Library.

TOM MANN AND UNION OFFICIALDOM

First, there was syndicalism's equivocation towards union officialdom. Thus, while Mann was undoubtedly opposed to the 'dead hand' of officials within unions in *general*, he never openly criticised individual officials, nor laid the blame for the ineffectiveness of strikes on the activities of officials directly involved. In this regard, Mann's attitude towards Tillett and the other NTWF leaders during and after the 1912 London transport strike is instructive.

As we examined, the woefully inadequate agitation and preparation to ensure the required action at other ports contributed to the poor response and ignominious collapse of the isolated London strike. Yet with defeat imminent, Mann insisted: 'I blame no one and raise no quibble, but I put in my pleas for solidarity.'[21] Following the defeat, he wrote a major article in *The Syndicalist* analysing the strike that said nothing about the role of the officials.[22] Instead he argued the main lesson from the failure of the strike was sectionalism between transport unions and the need to replace the NTWF with an amalgamation of all the organisations in the industry into a single union. The specific problems of Tillett's leadership and union officialdom within the industry generally were not addressed, and Mann later emphasised the 'inadvisability' of syndicalists 'singling out officers of unions for special criticism'.[23]

Of course, Mann was aware that 'officialdom is up against us, and forms a solid plank of reaction. The officials are more often to be found siding with the employers than with the rank and file.'[24] But having opted for a tactic of 'boring from within' the trade unions to win them over to syndicalist objectives, it was tactically difficult to argue, as a matter of principle, that existing named leaders were the main obstacle to workers' advance. In effect, he seemed to think that a militant rank-and-file, committed to direct action and grassroots union democracy, would be able to force incumbent union officials either to act in the interests of their members or be pushed aside from below. Yet detailed advice on the manner in which officials (including left-wingers like Tillett and Robert Williams) could manoeuvre, the difference between their rhetoric and action, the need to avoid placing any reliance on their leadership, and the type of demands that could be placed on them (let alone how to build up alternative forms of rank-and-file organisation that could act independently of them if necessary) were not really considered.[25]

The other reason for Mann's ambiguity towards officials was personal, and related to the important official union positions he himself had previously held. As noted in Chapter 4, following his leadership of the 1889 London dock's strike alongside Tillett, he had been elected President of the newly formed DWRGWU, as well of the International Transport Workers' Federation in which he worked alongside Wilson. And then in 1910–11, having returned to Britain from a nine-year spell in Australia, he had been

21. *Daily Herald*, 22 July 1912.
22. *The Syndicalist*, August 1912.
23. *Solidarity*, March 1914.
24. Ibid., April 1914.
25. Darlington (2008: 121; 2013b: 261–4).

reappointed to the upper echelons of the trade union movement, working alongside officials like Wilson and Tillett again in the day-to-day battle to establish union organisation. He would not have wanted to jeopardise this work or his position.[26] It is not that Mann did not passionately believe in, and advocate, militant action from below, but in attempting to collaborate directly with such leaders and cultivate influence more generally among union officials he came under pressures to subordinate a more independent and critical stance to the general need for unity in action to achieve common goals.

That Mann's equivocation towards union officialdom was not always merely a personal limitation, but could reflect a wider dilemma inside the syndicalist movement generally, was reflected in the way in which its newspapers abstained from any criticism of individual named officials. As one report from an ISEL meeting announced: 'It was no part of the League's policy to attack [official union] persons'.[27] By contrast, as we have seen (Chapter 7), Jim Larkin was prepared to make bitter attacks on the British union leaders during the 1913 Dublin lockout for their failure to organise solidarity strike action.

INDUSTRIAL UNIONISM

The second dilemma in syndicalist analysis concerned the belief that bureaucratic officialdom was only a tendency rather than an inevitable structural feature of trade union organisation within capitalism. It assumed that a change in the *form* of existing union structures would itself produce an equivalent transformation in their *content*. Amalgamation to form industrial unions was viewed as the chief means to overcome craft sectionalism as well as the conservatism and bureaucracy of union officialdom.[28] Yet while amalgamation and industrial unionism were certainly useful, encouraging existing unions to adopt revolutionary objectives required more than structural change.

The 1913 amalgamation of three railway workers' unions into a single National Union of Railwaymen (NUR) with a 'model' industrial structure[29] (embracing skilled and unskilled, manual workers and clerks, and all those employed by any railway undertaking) did not lead to a fighting union as anticipated.[30] Union officials agreed to amalgamation because competition

26. White (1990: 113).
27. *The Syndicalist*, January 1912.
28. Darlington (2008: 123–4; 2013b: 225–6).
29. Cole (1948a: 337).
30. Bagwell (1963; 1985: 185–200); Howell (1999).

between unions weakened their bargaining power vis-à-vis federated employers' organisation. Also support (however belated) for industrial unionism was a tactical means of diverting membership challenges to their position.

But creating a single railway union had nothing to do with the syndicalist aim of fostering working-class militancy, nor with the aim of overthrowing capitalism. In practice, the supposedly 'non-sectionalist' NUR proved just as willing to compromise and behave 'responsibly' as its sectionalist predecessors, and despite its formally highly democratic structure, the new union was still dominated by its full-time union officials who retained significant centralised, hierarchical and bureaucratic power resources such that membership 'control' was a matter more of form than of substance.[31]

James Connolly, who had championed the sympathetic strike and 'One Big Union' as the 'axe to the root' of capitalism, warned that the type of 'greater unionism' being embraced by union officials would not only destroy rank-and-file spontaneity and the weapons of victory in 1911, but was designed to do just that:

> … the amalgamations and federations are being carried out in the main by officials absolutely destitute of the revolutionary spirit, and that as a consequence the methods of what should be militant organisations having the broadest working-class outlook are conceived and enforced in the temper and spirit of the sectionalism those organisations were meant to destroy.
>
> Into the new bottles of industrial organisation is being poured the old, cold wine of Craft Unionism.[32]

TRIPLE ALLIANCE

The syndicalist notion that union officialdom could be brought to heel through the organisational mechanism of industrial unionism was most graphically tested by the Triple Alliance established between the miners, railway and transport workers' unions in April 1914. The growing support for the establishment of a Triple Alliance led to considerable debate over the proper function of such a body between 1913 and 1914. On the one hand, on the face of it, the Alliance amounted to a significant step towards industrial unionism, and the syndicalists clearly favoured joint action by the Triple Alliance as a means of extending and intensifying workers' struggles that would be capable of inflicting such vast disruption to the daily life of the nation that employers and government would have to concede. Ultimately,

31. Howell (2000: 40).
32. Connolly ([1914] 1974b: 315).

syndicalists hoped it could become a revolutionary weapon to overthrow capitalism via the organisation of a 'general strike'.

On the other hand, most union leaders (notably moderates such as Smillie, Sexton, Thomas and Wilson) saw the Alliance in a quite different light. Officials saw an economic rationale for coordinating action because the mines, docks and railways were so economically interdependent that major disputes in any one of the three industries resulted in layoffs in the other two which depleted unions' funds through having to pay their members unemployment benefit. Therefore, union leaders saw the advantage in developing a common programme of demands and a common timetable for collective action.[33] However, they did not envisage or desire industrial conflict, let alone any general strike that would directly challenge the state.

The text of the scheme establishing the Triple Alliance placed the constituents under no obligation to strike collectively, only to consult one another before proceeding with a major issue, and all other provisions were designed to limit their obligations and safeguard their autonomy.[34] It was grounded in the belief that powerful combined bargaining strength would carry such weight as to be sufficient to force concessions from employers without 'in practice the need for collective strikes [which] would rarely or never arise'. When employers proved intransigent, the mere *threat* of a concerted strike by the Alliance would be enough to cause government intervention, 'more or less as a protagonist of labour'.[35]

Certainly Thomas did not anticipate employing the Triple Alliance in any large-scale action in the immediate future: 'Although … it has been asserted', he said in June 1914, 'that in the course of a few weeks this joint combination will be called upon to paralyse industry, we all make it abundantly clear that this is not the desire or the intention of those responsible for the scheme'.[36] Moreover, many union leaders supported the new venture as a means of reducing the repeated appeals for sympathetic strike action that had resulted in spontaneous 'disjointed' unofficial rank-and-file militancy which was difficult to control.[37] On this basis, the Alliance could be seen as less a 'victory for the syndicalist idea' and 'concession to rank-and-file militancy' but 'a way to control and discipline such militancy'.[38]

---

33. Holton (1973a: 591–2).
34. Phelps Brown (1959: 330).
35. Phillips (1971: 65); Bagwell (1971: 104); Martin (1980: 108).
36. *Railway Review*, 19 June 1914.
37. Smillie, 'The Triple Industrial Alliance', in *The Labour Year Book*, 1915, cited in Arnot (1954: 175).
38. Phillips (1971: 63).

Significantly, the draft constitution of the Alliance preserved the independence of each member union, and gave each the right of veto. It remained firmly in the hands of the national officials who constituted its executive, with joint action requiring a decision of the executive 'of the organisation primarily concerned', submission to the joint body 'for consideration', confirmation from 'the members of the three organisations ... by such methods as the constitution of each organisation provides' and a conference of the three organisations 'to consider and decide the question of taking action'. Since affiliated unions required ballots to sanction a strike, calling a strike of the Triple Alliance in accordance with its rules was likely to be 'a clumsy, prolonged and uncertain undertaking'.[39] Undoubtedly, there were enough safeguards to justify the verdict of the railway union's president, Albert Bellamy, in his address to NUR annual conference in 1914: the alliance 'is neither revolutionary nor Syndicalistic. It is a force which is not intended to be used indiscriminately or frivolously. It is a solidifying movement for mutual co-operation in times of emergency'.[40]

Rivalry between two conflicting approaches to the role of the proposed Triple Alliance proceeded throughout 1913 and 1914, as syndicalist conceptions permeated rank-and-file groups and union officials counter-attacked with their own limited version of the scheme.[41] Before the First World War, it was not a foregone conclusion that officials would succeed in using the Alliance to divert action rather than lead it, and much depended on the level of workers' militancy, the balance of forces inside the unions and ability of rank-and-file activists and members to force the hand of their leaders and/or take the initiative themselves. This point was emphasised by the Unofficial Reform Committee of the South Wales Miners' Federation:

> At the present stage, the Triple Alliance is simply a concentration of the power of the leaders of the various unions involved ... the courage to fight, the wit to devise how to fight, and the wisdom to decide what to fight for – must come from the rank and file itself.[42]

But in practice, a conservative social stratum of full-time officials acting as a brake on membership militancy was a more fundamental obstacle than sectionalism or the problems of union structure which the syndicalists emphasised. Assuming union leadership would automatically be forced,

39. Clegg (1985: 116).
40. Cited in ibid.: 116.
41. Holton (1976: 174).
42. Cited in Woodhouse (1970: 111).

through sheer pressure from below, to become militant or be removed from office, they concentrated their efforts on emphasising the general strike and revolutionary possibilities of the Triple Alliance, with relatively little effort devoted to warning workers of the danger of union leaders attempting to use the Alliance to defuse demands and action from below.[43] Even though the outbreak of war interrupted the new body's chance of being tested, it underlined the difficulties syndicalists faced in attempting to navigate between the twin pitfalls of either dismissing union officialdom out of hand or putting all their faith in them.

RANK-AND-FILE LEADERSHIP

A further dilemma concerned syndicalist antipathy towards leadership. Significantly, union officials' deficiencies were blamed not on poor direction and wrong-headed policies but on the institution of 'leadership' itself. Observing that shopfloor workers tended to become corrupted once they were elected to full-time union office, syndicalists concluded that *all* leadership, whether from official *or* unofficial sources, was bound to stifle the independence and initiative of the rank-and-file. As the *Miners' Next Step* argued:

> Leadership implies power held by the Leader … The possession of power inevitably leads to corruption. All leaders become corrupt, in spite of their own good intentions.[44]

In many respects the syndicalists *did* provide a form of informal leadership to workers, particularly when they urged them to take strike action, often independent of union officials. But paradoxically, as we have seen, in assuming that greater participatory democracy would so radicalise rank-and-file union opinion that effective control could be wrested away from moderate and bureaucratic officials, the syndicalists were primarily committed to militancy being directed into the reconstruction of the unions on a more democratic, class-wide and revolutionary basis, rather than building an *alternative* independent workplace-based rank-and-file organisation and

43. Darlington (2013b: 226). The Triple Alliance was to disastrously fail the test on 'Black Friday', 15 April 1921. In the face of a national lockout of miners as a means of imposing reductions in wages, the leaders of the transport and railway unions declared a national solidarity strike, but then suddenly called it off when the miners refused to enter into discussions with them over the control of the dispute, in the process leaving the miners to suffer an overwhelming defeat that struck a heavy blow on the entire trade union movement.

44. Unofficial Reform Committee (1973: 19).

leadership that might have been able to act as a counter-weight to existing union officials.[45]

Thus, notwithstanding its success in pulling together an embryonic network of militants, the ISEL was characterised by its decentralised, localised and diffuse character, with no definite organisational and leadership structure to speak of beyond Mann and a few of his confidantes. In effect, it existed to propagandise, to spread the ideas of syndicalism, but devoted comparatively few resources to attempting to organise their supporters, and possessed neither a formal membership nor a branch structure. As one leading activist, George Simpson, pointed out: 'It was made up of a small number of loosely organised groups and a large number of individuals scattered all over the country.'[46]

Undoubtedly, activity was widespread, with regular locally based public meetings and educational classes backed up by sales of syndicalist literature and pamphlets; and prominent figures such as Mann, Guy Bowman and Charles Watkins visited a large number of union branches and social groups. However, when major strikes broke out the syndicalists lacked the directive organisation capable of supporting their militants and enabling them to maximise their interventionist potential.

Despite the fact that the ISEL's founding conference on 26 November 1910 took place amidst the South Wales miners' strike, with Noah Ablett in attendance, there was no specific discussion about the strike and taking solidarity action, as opposed to general agreement with overall syndicalist principles.[47] No national event took place whatsoever during 1911 at the zenith of the strike wave, and when two further national conferences were convened in London and Manchester in November 1912, there was no specific discussion of the national miners' and London transport strikes earlier in the year, as opposed to general discussion of the need for direct action, solidarity, amalgamation and the revolutionary general strike.[48]

Likewise, in the 1912 London transport strike there was no real attempt made to win support for solidarity action from provincial ports across the country. In the 1913 Dublin lockout, although the syndicalists (alongside other left groups) publicised the strike and supported fundraising and solidarity meetings, they made no independent attempt to encourage sympathetic industrial action. And while there were different industry-wide Amalgamation Committees linking militants across different workplaces

---

45. Hinton (1973: 275–97); Darlington (2013b: 261–4).

46. *The Syndicalist and Amalgamation News*, January 1913. 'Amalgamation News' was added from this issue.

47. *Industrial Syndicalist*, December 1910.

48. *The Syndicalist*, December 1912.

and employers in industries such as engineering, transport, railway, building and printing, these Committees and the syndicalist-influenced Federation that linked them tended to confine their considerations to concerns with the reform of union structures and campaigns for amalgamation and industrial unionism, as opposed to the strike wave as such.

Ironically, when the ISEL belatedly decided to turn itself into a fully-fledged formal organisation complete with a constitution and branch structure, it led to internecine disputes between groups with differing strategic orientations, culminating in the rapid splintering and disintegration of the broad-based organisation by the end of 1913.[49] Guy Bowman and E.J.B. Allen and a minority ISEL rump switched their allegiance away from the traditional policy of trade union reconstruction towards an essentially IWW position of 'dual unionism', and in developing a cadre-like membership, educated in syndicalist principles, they adopted a highly sectarian approach towards all other labour and socialist movement bodies.

A rival syndicalist body, the Industrial Democracy League and *Solidarity* newspaper was formed by Mann, Jack Tanner and other dissidents from the Amalgamation Committee movement, who were determined to continue the 'old' ISEL strategic orientation, albeit including the subordination of politics to the industrial struggle. In the process, syndicalism lost its effectiveness as a distinct organisational entity, even though ideologically and politically it continued to have significant influence inside the 1914 building workers' strike and sections of the wartime labour movement. Overall, the emphasis on working-class experience and action as the means to overthrow capitalism remained one of syndicalism's defining characteristics (and probably one of the main contributory elements to its wide appeal). But this was accompanied by a relative lack of concern to develop a revolutionary combat organisation, or a coherently formulated and unified body of socialist theory and political strategy.

In sum, although much of the strike activity in the Labour Revolt was sustained by a movement from below in which rank-and-file workers often took the initiative independently of trade union officials, such militancy was insufficiently organised on a national and cross-industry basis. There were no national networks of resistance that could coordinate action from below across the trade union movement and more decisively attempt to overcome the hesitant and often entrenched resistance of the officials. As a result, militant currents were no more unified in organisation or action than the working class as a whole. This meant that the only centralised force in the

49. Holton (1973a: 544–5; 1976: 142–7); *The Syndicalist and Amalgamation News*, February, March/April 1913.

trade union movement were the national union officials who, although small in number, tended to play a highly influential role in restraining action, often despite considerable internal opposition.

In such circumstances it was understandable that many militant activists, whatever their reservations, tended to place their hopes during the Dublin dispute in the official leaders of the TUC (notably left figures like Tillett and Williams), and then in the Triple Alliance to deliver national action. It also meant that even officials like Thomas, Sexton and Wilson continued to exercise a dominating influence and were able to effectively marginalise militants who remained a minority within their respective unions.[50]

The related problem of the separation of *industrial* struggles and *political* action by the both the syndicalist and socialist left within the movement is explored in Chapter 12.

50. Darlington (2016: 519–21).

9
Striking Organisation

As Chapters 3–7 documented, collective mobilisation during the Labour Revolt embraced many different elements. Strike action and mass picketing were used to leverage greater pressure on employers (and also on the government) to force concessions, and in the process, help build union membership and organisation. And there was the belligerent self-confident nature of strike activity in seeking dignity, self-respect and control, with the distinctive role played by young workers. Underpinning such features was the organisation of strike committees and mass meetings, high level of rank-and-file activity, involvement of many women workers, widespread solidarity, and embryonic 'dual power' challenge in certain places in which strike committees with their permit system co-existed with and competed for legitimacy and control with the employers and state. All of these elements form the main focus of this chapter, along with consideration of strike outcomes in terms of material gains and the growth of union membership and development of organisation.

STRIKE ORGANISATION

A crucial role was played throughout the Labour Revolt by thousands of grassroots activists and leaders, including radical left militants, who sought to encourage, organise, spread and build solidarity for strike action. One expression of this was the democratic election and functioning of a myriad of different (often joint union) workplace strike committees that emerged. Sometimes, these were made up of representatives from a variety of different strikebound workplaces and linked up workers employed by numerous employers. Such bodies were responsible for the conduct of the strike, arrangements for picketing, publicity and fundraising, organisation of mass meetings and negotiations with employers. They also played an important role in cultivating solidarity and class identity and in liaising with local and national union officials, as well as attempting to retain grassroots control over the conduct and outcomes of strikes.

Within these bodies new workplace leaders emerged to articulate workers' hopes and possibilities, with Ben Tillett in his *History of the London Transport*

Workers' Strike, 1911 paying homage to rank-and-file initiative, commitment and activism:

> … men who had not thought of the fight and the meaning of life suddenly rousing themselves to the battle and taking part as if to the manner born. These stirring times were all the more significant inasmuch as the workers were bent on organisation. There was military precision about the idea … men formed organisations, elected officers, formulated claims, elected committees … and each of them as serious and as active as if their very world depended on their deliberations.
>
> Wonderful is not the word. The genius of organisation, springing out of hope and confidence, revealed the intuitive powers, the resources of men, an intelligence to form, lead, be led …[1]

Another characteristic was the role of regular mass meetings held in chapels, open spaces, halls and workmen's institutes. For example, during the South Wales miners' strike, mass meetings were attended by thousands of strikers, becoming an integral part of democratising the dispute by providing a forum for open vigorous debate, discussion and collective decision-making which governed the conduct of the dispute. All important questions had to be placed before mass meetings, with virtually every decision the strike committee made (including the decision to use mass picketing to stop 'blackleg' labour and safety officials) was subject to ratification at a mass meeting.[2] Once a decision had been reached, it was then everybody's duty to implement this in a loyal and disciplined manner.

Likewise, in the 1911 London transport workers' strike there were daily mass meetings on Tower Hill with relays of speakers.[3] One observer noted:

> If there is one characteristic that marks an advance made by the recent strike upon all previous labour disputes it is the great part the 'mass meeting' has played. The whole progress of the striker seems to have been indexed by huge orderly meetings … The men's strike has justified itself … They have had a great deal of public sympathy with them.[4]

1. Tillett (1912: 27).
2. Barclay (1978: 28); Evans and Maddox (2010: 52).
3. Tillett (1912: 27).
4. *Hull Daily Mail*, 4 July 1911, cited in Weinberger (1991: 78).

During the 1911 Manchester transport workers' strike, 'the legislative and executive of the unions was rolled into one at mass meetings; men would take decisions themselves, and then act upon them collectively'.[5]

Nonetheless, there were sometimes tensions between different sections of rank-and-file workers, with even the most militant strike committees disagreeing about the conduct of strikes and picketing. And while in some areas links were forged between representatives of different workplace strike committees (such as during the West Midlands metal workers' strikes), as well as nationally (such as during the national transport strikes), there was little direct evidence of links across different industries regionally or nationally. For example, in August 1911 there were effectively simultaneous strikes by railway workers nationally, London and Liverpool transport workers, Manchester railway carriage, transport and other workers, Bristol and Cardiff dockers, Bermondsey women factory workers, Sheffield, Barnsley and Rotherham pit lads and miners, Liverpool Wilson bobbin makers and Leeds apprentice engineers.[6] But these overlapping strikes remained essentially fragmented and isolated from each other, with no organised (either union-sponsored or unofficial rank-and file) attempt to link them together and coordinate a joint assault on employers.

Undoubtedly one of the most remarkable features of the Labour Revolt was the way in which during the transport workers' strikes in Liverpool, Cardiff, Hull, Manchester, Dundee and London, strike committees established systems of 'permits' (which employers were obliged to request) as a means of attempting to control the movement of goods and supplies. In taking over vital elements of power and authority from employers, civic authorities and government began to act as embryonic alternative organs of working-class power. There is no evidence that strike committee members, including even Tom Mann in Liverpool, expressed or proposed anything other than limited industrial objectives, rather than any broader explicit *political* demands or challenge.[7] But while their authority did not herald a 'revolutionary' situation, it was a spectacularly powerful and effective form of workers' power not previously experienced in Britain up to that time.

WOMEN WORKERS

Women workers were neither passive observers nor peripheral to the Labour Revolt, but played an active role within a number of stoppages, with young

5. Ives (1986: 27).
6. Board of Trade (1912: 92–125).
7. Taplin (1986: 100; 2012: 35).

women and girls often the driving force. While the overall number of women workers on strike during 1910–14 was only a fraction of their male counterparts, they participated in numerous strikes both in women-only workplaces and predominately male workplaces. Many strikes took place in workplaces where most, if not all workers, were not union members before the strike and there was no or little prior form of collective organisation, with strike demands often including recognition of the union. However, a number of important large strikes also took place in highly unionised environments, such as the Lancashire 1910 spinners' and 1911–12 weavers' lockouts, and 1912 Dundee jute workers' strike.

Many women strikers appear to have been influenced and emboldened both by the growing industrial militancy in which their predominately male counterparts in the trade unions were involved, as well as by the militant women's suffrage movement in a context in which philosophies based on the notion of militant 'direct action' had become widespread.[8] Women often brought 'specifically female characteristics' to their workplace resistance – spontaneity, lack of restraint, boisterousness and an element of street theatre – which differentiated women's militancy from more formal male trade unionism.[9]

Thus, strikes often displayed a carnival atmosphere very different to the more 'sober and serious' aspect of demonstrations of male workers. They sometimes adopted 'suffrage tactics of propaganda and demonstration'[10] in order to give maximum impact to their actions, with the production of many leaflets, strike songs, banners, postcards, ribbons and badges to publicise their struggles. They participated in huge numbers on local solidarity demonstrations, often marching in their own contingents, and were actively involved in organising picketing and generating financial support and arranging for the collection and distribution of food. And they generated their own organic strike activists and leaders, with women playing a prominent role on many different strike committees in both female and male dominated workplaces – including equal representation alongside their male counterparts in the 1913 Kenrick's and United Hinge Company's West Midlands metal workers' strikes – as well as sometimes forming part of the union negotiating teams with management, as in the 1911 Singer strike.[11]

The overall weakening of traditional respect for 'law and order' and constitutional behaviour that characterised the militancy of both the suffrage

8. Hunt (2014: 49); Cole (1948a: 321).
9. Gordon (1987: 42–4).
10. Thom (1998: 103; 1986: 269).
11. Glasgow Labour History Workshop (1989: 58).

movement and labour struggles of the period was reflected in many women's strikes which were very assertive, using mass picketing to spread the action and stop 'blacklegs'. Women strikers were often involved in attacks on property, confrontations with the police and soldiers, and were amongst those arrested and imprisoned. Occasionally the link between the labour and suffrage revolts was relatively explicit. Thus, at a mass rally in Southwark Park for the Bermondsey women's strikers, platform speaker Charlotte Despard, a leading figure in the suffrage movement who had devoted herself to the strike from the moment it started, was greeted with rapturous cries of 'Good Old Suffragette!'.[12]

From within the suffragette Women's Social and Political Union (WSPU) there were a small minority of critical voices who argued for extending the fight for the vote to include broader social and class issues. The most important theoretical and practical contribution came from Sylvia Pankhurst who became increasingly at odds with the way the WSPU led by her mother and sister (Emmeline and Christabel Pankhurst) had moved away from its labour movement roots and separated feminist and socialist projects.[13] Inspired by studies she conducted of women workers' conditions, including the Bermondsey strike, as well as visits to America in 1911 and 1912 where she met with women strikers and socialists,[14] Sylvia began to move in the direction of challenging both those in the labour and socialist movement who were attempting to ignore questions of women's oppression and the suffragette leadership who insisted that social questions and class were irrelevant to the women's movement.

She persuaded WSPU activists to campaign with her in London's impoverished East End focusing on working-class women in a determined bid to link the struggle for votes for women and the larger struggle for immediate practical social issues – such as pay and working conditions, poverty and housing. A series of large open-air meetings and demonstrations to Parliament were organised, and by the summer of 1913 an East London Federation (ELF) of the WSPU was established, with a network of working-class women drawn into activity, including dockers' wives, like Melvina Walker, who had been involved on the picket line in the 1912 London transport strike.[15] As George Dangerfield commented, Sylvia discovered 'with unerring instinct, the sources of the country's most profound unrest' and 'carried the purple,

12. *Votes for Women*, 25 August 1911.
13. Holmes (2020); Winslow (2021).
14. Connolly (2013: 32–3, 39–44); Holmes (2020: 283–316).
15. Pankhurst (1977: 524); Jackson and Taylor (2014: 81–2).

The Daily Mirror

THE MORNING JOURNAL WITH THE SECOND LARGEST NET SALE

No. 2,432. | Registered at the G.P.O. as a Newspaper. | FRIDAY, AUGUST 11, 1911 | One Halfpenny.

GIANT MASS MEETING OF STRIKERS ADDRESSED BY A WOMAN ON TOWER HILL YESTERDAY.

Thousands of strikers assembled on Tower-hill yesterday and listened with rapt attention to a speech by a woman. It was a very wonderful and impressive sight to watch this great gathering hang upon her every word as she stood above her audience in the centre of a gigantic circle. But she spoke to others besides strikers.

On the fringe of the crowd were scores of men attired in the conventional tweed suit and straw hat, men who are "something in the City," and who had been attracted to the spot by so novel a spectacle. Above, the speaker is seen emphasising a point.—(*Daily Mirror* photograph.)

Figure 9.1 An unknown woman addressing one of the mass meetings of male strikers that were held at Tower Hill during the 1911 London transport strike.

Credit: Mirrorpix.

white and green banner of militant suffrage into the great movement which ... was then surging against the bulwarks of organised Capital'.[16]

Sylvia Pankhurst was on the platform of the *Daily Herald* rally in London's Albert Hall on Saturday 1 November 1913 in support of the imprisoned Jim Larkin and the Dublin workers. This event, which 10,000 people attended and 20,000 were turned away, was one of the high points of the interconnection between the women's suffrage campaign and labour struggles. Speakers also included Connolly, Tillett, Charlotte Despard (Women's Freedom League), Dora Montefiore (BSP socialist-suffragist) and Delia Larkin (secretary of the Irish Women Workers' Union).[17] As Dangerfield reflected, it encapsulated the potential for links between the labour, socialist, suffrage and Irish independence movements:

> ... on the speaker's platform sat, in serried ranks, the united grievances of England. For the first and last time Irish Nationalism, Militant Suffrage, and the Labour Unrest were met together ... its strength was drawn from every factory, every workshop, mine, wharf and slum throughout the length and breadth of England.[18]

Sylvia's participation at this rally proved a step too far for her mother and sister and precipitated a spilt within the Pankhurst's suffragette family that resulted in her and the federation being expelled from the WSPU. In January 1914 the expelled ELF changed its name to the East London Federation of Suffragettes (ELFS) and added red to its suffragette banner colours, symbolising the way it regarded itself as part of the labour movement and the fight for women's rights as part of the working-class struggle for trade unionism and socialism. Using militant tactics, the ELFS continued to increase its influence within working-class communities, building five branches, and in March 1914 launched its *Woman's Dreadnought* newspaper (with Sylvia as editor), which had a weekly print run of 20,000 copies until the outbreak of war,[19] albeit a readership of between 8,000–10,000.[20]

The paper carried interviews with different groups of striking local women factory workers and campaigned in their support. ELFS members spoke at strikers' meetings and strikers attended ELFS meetings.[21] Amidst such activity, the ELFS headquarters was requisitioned for strike meetings and

16. Dangerfield (1997: 176–7).
17. *Daily Herald*, 3 November 1913; Holmes (2020: 370–2); Connelly (2013: 57–8).
18. Dangerfield (1997: 178).
19. Pankhurst (1977: 525).
20. Winslow (2021: 69).
21. *Woman's Dreadnaught*, 25 April, 23 May, 18 July 1914.

'appealed for speakers and help in every sort of way'.[22] Paradoxically it was the great reservoir of working-class women's energy and combativity during the Labour Revolt that had been ignored by the WSPU, which invigorated the suffrage struggle in the East End of London.

Another important development was the formation in September 1911 of the Irish Women's Workers' Union (IWWU), with membership open to all women regardless of their industry or job, albeit in many respects it was closer to a women's section of the ITGWU than an independent union.[23] The union had the active support of leading Irish suffragettes and suffragists, and Delia Larkin (Jim's sister) became the union's general secretary and spoke on suffrage platforms.[24] Although its overall membership was small (despite claiming 1,000 members in 1912, by the summer of 1913 it was down to 600) the women workers who joined – who in the main were very young, often in their early teens – were drawn into the Dublin lockout. When Jim Larkin went to seek support from British workers, Delia effectively took charge of the entire undertaking to feed the ITGWU and IWWU's members and their dependants throughout the six-month dispute. A women's committee of union volunteers, strikers' relatives and the circle of political women in Dublin provided daily breakfasts for 3,000 children, lunches for nursing mothers and the distribution of clothing.[25]

SOLIDARITY

A crucially important characteristic of the Labour Revolt was the remarkable solidarity displayed by rank-and-file workers (trade unionists and non-trade unionists), local communities (including women and children) and labour and socialist organisations, and this contributed enormously to the resilience of the strikers' movement. In order to match the aggressive coordinated power of employers and their federations, it was necessary to overcome sectional divisions among workers and the fragmentation of unions. This need was reflected in the development of new forms of organisation and action, with the formation of the NTWF, NUR and Triple Alliance, as well as Amalgamation Committees within engineering, mining, railway and other industries that advocated industrial-wide forms of union organisation and industrial solidarity. But this need also found expression in a variety of other non-institutional practices and tactics to generate rank-and-file solidarity.

22. Pankhurst (1977: 543).
23. King (1989: 67, 69–70); Moriarty (2006a: 95–6); Jones (1988).
24. Moriarty (2006a: 94–5); Greaves (1982: 64).
25. Moriarty (2006b: 433).

As William Mellor, secretary of Manchester and Salford Trades and Labour Council, outlined in his 1911 Annual Report, the strikes 'ushered in a new era of industrial conflicts. For the first time in England, the "sympathetic strike" was evoked on a large scale and effectively used as a weapon of industrial warfare.'[26] Indeed in many respects it was the 'fundamental strategic innovation of 1910–14',[27] with workers not only refusing to touch 'tainted' goods in solidarity with others in dispute, but sometimes going on strike in support and then raising their own demands. When simultaneous strikes took place, the principle was adopted that each different group would not return to work (despite in some cases having already successfully forced concessions from their employers) until all had obtained satisfactory agreements, as took place during the 1911 transport strikes in Liverpool, Manchester, Cardiff and London.

The extent of the British labour movement's solidarity during the 1913–14 Dublin lockout was vividly expressed in two bouts of rank-and-file unofficial sympathetic strike action by railway workers in different parts of the country, and solidarity action by some dockers in Liverpool and Salford. Meanwhile in Ireland, sympathy action or its threat was applied 'ruthlessly in every Labour dispute',[28] and was central to the success of the ITGWU and the union organisation campaign in Dublin. As Connolly wrote: 'What is the sympathetic strike? It is the recognition by the working class of its essential unity, the manifestation in our daily industrial relations that our brother's fight is our fight, that our sisters' troubles are our troubles, that we are all members one of another.'[29]

Reflecting on the way the sympathetic strike had proved to be 'the greatest weapon against capital' in Britain during 1911, he explained: 'It was its very sporadic nature, its swiftness and unexpectedness, that won. It was ambush, the surprise attack of our industrial army, before which the well-trained battalions of the capitalist crumpled up in panic, against which no precautions were available.'[30]

Undoubtedly for employers and the state, the sympathetic strike threatened to 'revolutionise industrial warfare' by putting a deadly weapon in the hands of workers that could radically alter the balance of forces.[31] As a memorandum to Home Secretary Winston Churchill from George Askwith pointed

26. Manchester and Salford Trades and Labour Council Annual Report, 1911, cited in Frow and Frow (1976: 73).
27. Cronin (1979: 100).
28. *Daily Herald*, 6 December 1913.
29. Connolly (1915: 223).
30. Connolly ([1914] 1974b: 315).
31. O'Connor (2014: 33).

out, 'almost imperceptibly a new force has arisen in trade unionism' in which 'the power of the old leaders has been superseded', with the sympathetic strike on a wide scale becoming prominent and 'the more extensive adoption of the "general strike" policy'.[32]

The periodic suspension of sectional divisions evident within sympathetic strikes produced remarkable occupational unity between different trades. This occurred among seamen, with status-conscious ships' cooks and catering staff allied with manual grades such as seamen and firemen during waterfront militancy. On the railways, there was also evidence of a breakdown of traditional demarcations between skilled drivers and unskilled labourers. Likewise, gender divisions between male and female workers were broken down in a number of disputes, and there was the suspension of religious hostility between Protestants and Catholics in Liverpool during the 1911 general transport strike.

Strikes also often generated considerable levels of support from other workers locally, regionally and even nationally, with regular financial collections in workplaces, trade union branch and trades council meetings and public solidarity rallies and demonstrations, all of which yielded considerable sums and helped to sustain the struggles. An enormous level of solidarity was also generated for individual strikes by the radical left, with a particularly important role played by the *Daily Herald*.

A further vital feature of many strikes was the culture of community support that was generated, with other workers (trade unionists and non-unionists), women and schoolchildren participating in picketing against 'blackleg' labour. When the state reacted with violence, 'this only served to intensify solidarity against what was seen as a hostile force whether represented on the ground by troops or the police',[33] and produced large-scale community confrontations in some places, including Tonypandy, Hull, Liverpool, Manchester, Llanelli, Bristol and Dundee in 1911, Leith in 1912 and Dublin in 1913.

However, there were limitations to solidarity activity during the Labour Revolt. While sympathetic action – whether via a strike or 'blacking' action – was crucial in building the unity and strength of the working-class movement, many union officials viewed such action as an unacceptable breaking of established agreements and conciliation procedures, and insisted on the need to prioritise their *own* members' interests, not the interests of members of *other* unions or the waging of a struggle against the capitalist class as a whole. It was for these reasons that most officials were emphatically opposed to the

32. Askwith Memorandum to Churchill, 'The Present Unrest in the Labour World', 25 June 1911, TNA/CAB/37/107/70; CHAR 12/6/40-49; Churchill (1969: 1265).
33. Haynes (1984: 98).

sympathetic strike advocated by syndicalists and other militants within their ranks and did what they could to stymie unofficial action.

Prompted by regular requests for railway workers to refuse to handle 'tainted goods', the new NUR executive committee issued a circular to members in September 1913. It condemned unauthorised sympathetic action on the railways on the grounds that members should be harnessing their strength towards a united effort for improved conditions, reduced hours and official recognition of the union, rather than engaging in 'sectional and local disputes' which are 'frittering away their power without any real benefit to themselves ... sapping our strength in sham fights'.[34] Likewise, the TUC Parliamentary Committee strained to prevent sympathetic industrial action for the locked-out Dublin workers. And during the 1912 London transport strike NTWF-affiliated officials failed to mobilise effective sympathy action at ports across the country.

Persistent structural divisions within the working class continued to set boundaries to the solidarity of the labour movement, with deeply rooted sectional trade union divisions hampering attempts to win support for amalgamation and industrial unionism, for example, in the building industry. There was also continuing gendered divisions, with the 1913 Midlands metal workers' strikes resulting in a lower pay deal for women workers, and the much-heralded new industrial union, the NUR, rejecting the proposal to call itself the 'National Union of Railway Workers' and decreeing that women (13,000 of whom were employed by railway companies) were to be ineligible for membership.[35]

Meanwhile, there were continuing sectarian and religious rivalries, with the Liverpool transport workers' strike not overcoming the city's well-defined segregated geographical and housing structure, or occupational divisions.[36] And there were the racist overtones of attacks on Chinese businesses during the Cardiff transport strike, and the way in which within a few hours of the Llanelli riots during the railway strike there were riots at Tredegar, Ebbw Vale, Rhymney, Bryn Mawr and Bargoed that displayed strong elements of anti-Semitism and anti-immigrant sentiment.[37]

STRIKE OUTCOMES

Finally, we can make some assessment of the overall outcome of strike activity during the Labour Revolt. Although the Board of Trade kept records of the

---

34. *Railway Review*, 19 September 1913.
35. Wojtczak (2005: 35).
36. Neal (1988: 224–49).
37. Fink (2011: 129); Hopkin (1983: 510).

'results' of strikes in terms of generic headings such as 'in favour of workers', 'in favour of employers' and 'compromised or partially successful', these are perhaps best understood as a measure of what was believed to be happening rather than as an objective index of actual results. This is because the standards against which workers' victories were judged and the extent to which 'compromises' were apportioned to one side or the other could be problematic, based as they were merely on the last claims put forward by the two parties before the strike broke out.

It could be argued that the real issue should be whether workers gained by strikes compared to the situation which would have prevailed if there had been no strike. From this point of view, in dealing with statistical classification of strikes during the period of the Labour Revolt, 'compromises' could generally be judged as being favourable to workers in terms of gains made, both in contexts where strikes were 'offensive' (with demands for advances in workers' position), as well as 'defensive' (opposed to employers' encroachments and/or retaliatory approach to strike threats). The implication is that to obtain an appreciation of workers' achievements in strikes, 'compromises' should be added to workers' victories.[38]

On this basis, we can examine the Board of Trade's categorisation of the statistics for the outcome of strikes across the years 1911–14 (Table 13), which show: in terms of the *number of strikes*: 27 per cent in favour of workers; 44 per cent compromise, 29 per cent in favour of employers; and 9 per cent on employers' terms without negotiation; and in terms of the *number of strikers*: 42 per cent in favour of workers; 44 per cent compromise, 14 per cent in favour of employers; and 3 per cent on employers' terms without negotiation. But if 'compromises' were added to 'workers' victories' as suggested, we would have a 71 per cent success rate in terms of the *number of strikes* and 86 per cent success rate in terms of the *number of strikers*.[39] Even if we acknowledge we cannot take at face value the blunt figures produced by simply adding all 'compromises' to 'workers' victories', we should not entirely discount the way in which at least a half, if not rather more, of strikes that were categorised as 'compromises' by the Board of Trade – in a general context of a Labour Revolt in which many strikes were essentially more offensive than defensive – were more inclined in favour of workers.

Of course, there were undoubtedly a series of very significant workers' defeats during the Labour Revolt, notably the 1910–11 South Wales miners' strike, 1912 London transport strike, 1913 Cornish clay workers' strike, 1913–14 Leeds Corporation strike and Dublin transport workers' lockout,

38. Forchheimer (1948: 301–2); Knowles (1952: 241–2).
39. Knowles (1952: 243).

and 1914 building workers' lockout. Yet overall, not only was there a much higher rate of strike 'success' than the Board of Trade's figures suggested, but the statistics do not capture the way the strike wave generally transformed the balance of class forces in society, paving the way for the many government-driven changes to industrial relations which occurred during and after the First World War.

The most concrete outcome of the strike wave was the enormous stimulus to the growth of trade unionism both as regards numbers and organisation. Significantly, even though the direct initiative for strikes during the Labour Revolt often came from rank-and-file militancy – which by its very nature represented a rebellion against the moderation and conservativism of official union leaders – workers flocked into membership of the unions, no doubt recognising that material gains in terms and conditions of employment could only be secured from collective trade union organisation. But in addition, some respected militant union leaders like Mann, Tillett, Macarthur and Varley, as well as local leaders like Bamber in Liverpool and NSFU secretary R.H. Capner in Manchester, contributed to the process by which workers were inspired and urged to join, with the unofficial momentum that developed in the strike wave forcing other union leaders into more combative positions and to engage in union organising activities as they tried to regain credibility, retain control and expand their membership base.[40] Additionally, there was clearly a wide layer of workplace activists and militants (including syndicalists, socialists and other political radicals) who played a crucial (albeit almost invariably historically unrecorded and ignored) role in recruiting workers and integrating them into existing union structures and new innovative forms of industrial organisation and networks of solidarity. There was a reciprocal relationship between the mass strike mobilisation, leadership dynamics and dramatic union membership growth that took place.

Growth was phenomenal, with a 62 per cent increase in total membership between 1910 and 1914 from 2.5 million to 4.1 million (Table 13) and union density increasing from 14.6 per cent in 1910 to 23 per cent by 1914 (Table 14). On the railways there was a spectacular increase in ASRS membership from 75,153 in 1910 to 116,516 by the end of 1911, and to 132,002 by the end of 1912, 267,611 by the end of 1913 (following the amalgamation into the NUR in that year) and 273,362 by 1914.[41] In the engineering industry, the most successful of all unions in terms of recruitment was the WU, which enrolled primarily semi- and unskilled workers who the ASE ignored. It grew from just 4,500 members in 1910 to 18,000 in 1911, 91,000 by 1913 and

40. Ives (1986: 27).
41. Bagwell (1963: 698).

143,000 by the outbreak of war, with most of the growth coming during the tumultuous strike year of 1913.[42] On the waterfront the membership of the main unions doubled or trebled in size, with the DWRGWU increasing from 20,000 in 1911 to 50,000 by 1912, although this dipped following the defeat of the London transport strike to 37,000 by 1913, and the NUDL increasing from 12,000 in 1911 to 32,000 by 1913.[43]

While the economic recovery and reduction in unemployment provided a favourable background to the expansion of trade union membership, as did the National Insurance Act of 1911 and the Trade Union Act of 1913, it does not explain why it grew so explosively. For that, we have to factor in the new militancy of the workers and the aggressive tactics of unions. As even the moderate Will Thorne, founder and general secretary of the Gas Workers' Union, and Labour MP for West Ham in London, addressing the union's 1912 Biennial Congress remarked: 'it is clear that the organising work put into the movement has been the means of educating the rank-and-file of the wage earners to rebel against the domination of the master classes'.[44]

But crucially the Gasworkers' Union was deeply involved in the wave of strikes during this period, immediately joining the NTWF and playing its part in the London transport strikes of 1911 and 1912 led by the Federation; in 1913 it was the major union in the full-scale strike against the Leeds Corporation, and in 1914 was also involved in the London building industry lockout. Even though many of these strikes were unsuccessful, they did not deter workers from joining the union. On the contrary, union aggressiveness and consequent wage increases achieved in many industries actually attracted new members.[45]

Significantly the reason why the general unions, particularly the National Union of Gas and General Workers (NUGGW) and WU, benefited most was because they were able to bring union organisation into the areas of employment where there were large numbers of unorganised (semi- and unskilled) workers. Even in the Midlands, where the WU achieved notable success in the expanding engineering and metal industries, the NUGGW also benefited, expanding from their secure base in the gas industry into other fields. By the outbreak of war, the union had become one of the five largest in the country, increasing from under 32,000 in 1910 to over 132,000.[46]

---

42. Askwith ([1920] 1974: 355); Hyman (1971: 35–77); Coates and Topham (1994: 384); Clegg (1985: 60).
43. Coates and Topham (1994: 374, 612).
44. Radice and Radice (1974: 65–6).
45. Ibid.: 66.
46. Ibid.: 66–7, 71.

Unlike the 1888–91 strike wave, the years 1910–14 did not see a rapid formation of new unions – in fact, the reverse, for the number of unions actually declined. The strike wave was therefore capitalised on by *existing* unions, with those that had remained on paper since the 'New Unionism' period now revived, and those that had struggled to survive starting to thrive again, with this latter group the most important.[47] There was a combined development in which in some cases workers went on strike *before subsequently joining unions* (as in a number of the women's strikes), and others where union membership growth partly came about *prior to workers taking strike action* and then accelerated during and after the strikes (as with the seamen's and dockers' unions). And, as previously noted, another effect of the strike wave was the stimulus to union organisation, notably the number of important federations and amalgamations. Thus, in 1910 several transport unions set up the Transport Workers' Federation, in 1913 three railway unions combined to form the NUR, and in 1914 an even more advanced step was taken with the formation of the Triple Alliance.

However, despite the extent of workers' militancy and advances in unionisation and organisation, it is necessary to retain some sense of proportion. 'The large majority of British workers did *not* revolt during these turbulent years ... and by 1914 three quarters of them remained outside the ranks of trade unionists.'[48] Female union membership, despite increasing to 427,000 by 1914, still represented only 8 per cent of the female workforce. And sectionalism between unions and work groups and the restraints of union officialdom remained persistent, with neither the NTWF, NUR or Triple Alliance living up to the expectations and possibilities invested in them. Although strike action restored real wages at least to 1906 levels, they remained below the standards of 1900, and even in 1914 'when the poverty line for a man, his wife and three children was set at about 24 shillings a week, nearly a quarter of all the male wage earners in the country were receiving less than 25 shillings a week.'[49] Moreover, women's pay rates remained lower than their male counterparts.

47. Lane (1974: 110).
48. Hyman (1985: 262)
49. Briggs (1961: 51).

10

Countermobilisation and Violence

Even though class struggle during 1910–14 involved workers' collective mobilisation against employers and the state, it also involved significant countermobilisation by these antagonists against the working-class movement, a 'class struggle from above'. This chapter explores the strategies and tactics of both employers and government in the face of the Labour Revolt, as well as the nature and causes of the violence that often resulted from their countermobilisation strikebreaking initiatives.

EMPLOYERS

While invariably decrying the perceived challenge posed by militant trade unionism and strike activity, there were inevitably variations in approach between different employers and their associations as to how resistance should be mounted. Some employers, notably in the shipping and docks industries, determined to maintain their unilateral managerial decision-making prerogative, refused point-blank to countenance any form of trade union recognition and/or collective bargaining that might challenge such authority and control. In the process, they attempted to utilise a battery of coercive strikebreaking tactics to repulse workers' militancy.

By contrast, many employers, in line with the developing trend towards the institutionalisation of industrial relations, implemented an 'incorporative or procedural mode of control over labour',[1] resolving disputes through joint negotiation with union officials (albeit often only belatedly and under pressure) and/or Conciliation and Arbitration Board procedures. As a result, no less than 85 per cent of all strikes between 1911 and 1914 were settled by negotiation, conciliation or arbitration.[2] As the influential Liberal paper *Westminster Gazette* warned:

> The worst feature is, to our thinking, what some short-sighted people appear to think the best. This is the possibility that organised Labour may

1. McIvor (1984: 5).
2. Ministry of Labour, *Eighteenth Abstract of Labour Statistics of the United Kingdom* (Cmd. 2740), 1926, p. 150.

> be ... reduced to impotence by the prolongation of this struggle. Let us be quite sure that the downfall of trade unionism would be a great disaster, since it would merely pave the way for the operation of Syndicalists and other violent agitators whose perpetual themes is that trade unionism is played out.[3]

Hence, some employers believed they could utilise union officialdom to reduce the likelihood and/or extent of militancy and destroy the 'extremist' element within the trade union movement.[4]

However, when confronted by strike action, many employers, irrespective of whether they recognised trade unions or not, often acted in remarkably similar ways in adopting strikebreaking tactics, even if only when established procedures to settle disputes without a stoppage of work had either been exhausted or ignored. Much of this was done on the initiative of individual companies, although powerful multi-employers' organisations to which they were affiliated – whose numbers rocketed from 659 in 1895 to 1,487 by 1914[5] – could also aid these efforts.

An obdurate stance towards strike demands and refusal to compromise was common, even attempting to starve workers into submission by forcing long strikes. Some employers encouraged their workforce to defy strike action by crossing picket lines, many also attempted to import replacement 'blackleg' labour. Policies of victimisation and intimidation, including selective re-employment after strikes, penalised union activists and militants. Lockouts, at a single company or industry-wide, were used by some employers to force through changes in working conditions and wage reductions, invariably in response to threatened strike action opposing changes.[6] Employers also often demanded police protection to prevent strikers mounting effective picket lines, requested the support of troops to reinforce the police, and pressed the government to legislate to restrict strike action and picketing.

Likewise, there were different, but overlapping dimensions to the government and state's countermobilisation to the Labour Revolt, involving both conciliation and coercion.

GOVERNMENT AND STATE

The conservative press and sections of the government and state expressed considerable concerns about the threat posed by the Labour Revolt. Iron-

3. *Westminster Gazette*, 27 March 1912.
4. Pratten (1975: 212–13, 349).
5. Garside and Gospel (1982: 104).
6. McIvor (1984: 19–23, 27–8).

ically, in May 1912 the celebrated novelist and journalist H.G. Wells, a Fabian socialist supportive of MacDonald and Snowden against more radical elements, was commissioned to write a five-part series of articles for the *Daily Mail* entitled 'The Labour Unrest' in which he stated:

> Our country is, I think, in a dangerous state of social disturbance. The discontent of the labouring mass of the community is deep and increasing. It may be that we are in the opening phase of a real and irreparable class war ... The worker is beginning now to strike for unprecedented ends – against the system, against the fundamental conditions of labour ... The old fashioned strike was a method of bargaining, clumsy, and violent perhaps but bargaining still; the new fashioned strike is far less of a haggle, far more of a display of temper ... New and strange urgencies are at work in our midst, forces for which the word 'revolutionary' is only too faithfully appropriate.

Wells' cry was: 'Wake up, gentlemen! ... we have to "pull ourselves together" ... Our class has to set to work and make those other classes more interested and comfortable and contented.'[7] If something was not done to make the condition of the working class more amenable, he warned, there would be a revolution that everyone would regret.

Although the general 'spirit of revolt' that characterised the years leading up to the First World War could not in any real sense be termed 'revolutionary' in the way suggested by the political establishment, and subsequently by Dangerfield and Halévy, there is no doubt that fear of revolutionary *possibilities* sharpened the Liberal government's response to the constant strikes of a newly confident and rebellious working-class movement. Yet the government lacked a strategic industrial relations policy, and had no settled approach for the prevention of strikes or for the regulation of relations between workers and employers. Instead their response to the challenge posed by the Labour Revolt was more or less ad hoc.[8] Ironically Askwith's memoirs contained a scathing critique of the government's alleged apathy and ignorance regarding labour affairs:

> The Members of the Government were strangely outside and ignorant of the labour movements in the country; or of any personal knowledge of the principal labour leaders. The interference of politicians in labour disputes, much as many of them hankered to come in, was deleterious ...[9]

7. Wells (1912).
8. Weinberger (1991: 112–16); Davidson (1978: 572).
9. Askwith ([1920] 1974: 351–2).

However, between June and September 1911, five Cabinet papers on industrial relations were produced which carried such titles as 'The Present Unrest in the Labour World', 'Industrial Unrest' and 'Labour Unrest',[10] reflecting the level and nature of the strike wave sweeping the country. In the process, the government utilised varying approaches to contain workers' militancy.

On the one hand, every effort was made to encourage the settlement of disputes through a process of conciliation via the government-appointed Board of Trade. The Board had already made full use of the powers given to it under the 1896 Conciliation Act to appoint mediators where the contending parties to a dispute were prepared to accept its services, with Askwith emerging as the consummate industrial negotiator achieving compromise settlements in many large disputes, obtaining a return to work and generally attempting to neutralise the mounting scope and social threat of industrial unrest that confronted the government.[11]

At the centre of the Board's approach was the cultivation of amicable relations with 'responsible' trade union officials who could help them contain and limit conflict, as well as the strengthening of moves towards the establishment of Conciliation Boards in different industries. This process was by no means smooth, with Sydney Buxton writing a Cabinet memorandum in August 1911 which bemoaned 'the serious diminution in the control which the leaders of the men used to exercise over their rank and file, with the consequent repudiation of agreements', and declared 'that an effort should be made to maintain a greater control over the position', warning that failure 'may mean the letting loose of forces which would irreparably damage our trade and commerce'.[12]

Nonetheless, Askwith undoubtedly had considerable success as a 'troubleshooter', due in part to his personal patience, tact, ingenuity and ability to concentrate negotiations on the crux of a dispute, but also because many leading union officials relied upon his apparent sympathetic consideration of the causes underlying workers' militancy. Ironically, from the other side of the negotiating table, even Ben Tillett paid homage to Askwith and his team's conduct of meetings during the 1911 London transport workers' strike:

> … it was work, night and day, and the Government officials practically in possession of the disputants … [they] … could not have put in longer or more worrying hours of toil. We were empanelled …

10. Public Record Office [TNA] Handbook No. 4, *List of Cabinet Papers 1880–1914*, HMSO, 1964.
11. Davidson (1974: vii–xiv).
12. Buxton Memorandum to Cabinet, 'Conciliation and the Board of Trade', 9 August 1911, TNA/CAB 37/107/98.

> the greatest danger to the whole fight lay in them; they kept us to the talk, the talk, the Conference, and then another Conference, and then another, the while we might have been rousing the country …
>
> [Askwith] is the most dangerous man in the country. His diplomacy is and will be worse in war.[13]

In 1911, when the strike wave appeared especially menacing, the government established an Industrial Council, composed of leading employers and union officials and chaired by Askwith under the new title of 'Chief Industrial Commissioner', with the aim of encouraging conciliation and arbitration in industrial disputes. But because it had no power to insist on disputes being brought to it nor to enforce its decisions, it was not treated as authoritative and was increasingly disregarded.[14]

Despite its commitment to conciliation, the government was repeatedly forced to directly intervene in industrial relations during the period of the Labour Revolt, and intervene on a scale never previously experienced. The justification given for government intervention was the need to keep public order, maintain essential services and safeguard the economy.[15] In 1911 Buxton observed: 'It is generally recognised now that industrial disputes are not merely the concern of the parties who are immediately involved, and the question is not whether the state should intervene more in trade disputes but what form should their [*sic*] interference take.'[16] That this should be the case was a measure of the growing power of organised labour.[17]

Individual government ministers became prominent in industrial diplomacy, with the Chancellor, Lloyd George, intervening to end the 1911 national railway strike, five ministers involved in trying to settle the 1912 London transport strike, and Churchill, as Home Secretary (for an 18-month period between February 1910 and October 1911), playing a crucial role in overseeing the policing of disputes and military intervention, notably during the South Wales miners' and national transport and railway strikes. Prime Minister Herbert Asquith also personally intervened in the railway strike, holding separate conferences with employers and unions; during the national

13. Tillett (1912: 27, 28–9, 30).
14. Wrigley (1979: 4–6); Davidson (1974: xi); Charles (n.d); Moss (1983); Askwith ([1920] 1974: 178–86).
15. Churchill claimed intervention in the 1911 dock and railway strikes was motivated by responsibility to the public, and the working classes in particular, not by support to either side in the dispute, CHAR 12/12/51.
16. Buxton Memorandum to Cabinet, 'Conciliation and the Board of Trade', 9 August 1911, TNA/CAB 37/107/98.
17. Wrigley (1982: 150).

miners' strike he was forced to take the unprecedented step of bringing in legislation for a minimum wage; and he intervened personally to order a Court of Inquiry to end the Woolwich Arsenal strike.

In April 1912, after the miners' strike, Asquith even set up a special Cabinet Committee on Industrial Unrest with Lloyd George, Lord Haldane (Secretary of State for War), Reginald McKenna (the new Home Secretary), Buxton and others which held several meetings but came to no firm conclusions. Ministerial intervention in the 1912 London transport strike provoked a serious rift between the Prime Minister and a large group of his ministers, with Asquith, frustrated at the way some had tried unsuccessfully to encourage a settlement, gave ministers 'strict orders ... to leave industrial disputes alone and not mix themselves up with them'.[18] His report to King George V on the incident confirmed there was 'considerable diversity of opinion' over how to meet the challenge of the Labour Revolt within the Cabinet.[19]

The question of what the Liberal government should do in the face of further militant strike action was discussed in Buxton's confidential memorandum to the Cabinet circulated on 13 April 1912 entitled 'Industrial Unrest'. It was argued that 'the public, sick of, and suffering from strikes and industrial disputes, would, as a whole, heartily welcome some stringent action to prevent them, or to bring them more speedily to conclusion'. Yet Buxton was unsure how this should be done, acknowledging that compulsory arbitration would be resented and that it would be difficult to use sanctions to enforce decisions; there would be insufficient cells to imprison all strikers; and if strikes were made illegal the men would demand extensive legislation on wages and conditions.[20]

The following day, Askwith issued another Cabinet paper entitled 'Labour Unrest' which investigated various strategic options to end future strikes. First, they could do nothing, but that would mean 'a constant war between the parties, growing bigger until possibly it would reach something like civil war, and even then, matters would remain unsettled'. Second, they could intervene to deal with each difficulty as it arose, but that solution 'ultimately offers no relief from the harassment of industry'. Finally, he suggested, rather than rushing into one of the popular answers such as compulsory arbitration, they should set up a Royal Commission that could look at selected industries and include some labour leaders.[21] Another memorandum to the Cabinet

18. Ibid.: 147–9.

19. Askwith ([1920] 1974: 228); Wrigley (1976: 74–6).

20. Buxton Memorandum to Cabinet, 'Industrial Unrest', 13 April 1912, TNA/CAB 37/110/62; TNA/CAB 37/110/66; LG/C/21/1/10.

21. Askwith Memorandum to Cabinet, 'Labour Unrest', 14 April 1912; TNA/CAB 37/110/63; LG/C/21/1/11.

by Buxton in January 1914, entitled 'Industrial Disputes', deliberated on draft schemes for national industrial agreements along with a conciliation and arbitration procedure in strikes, but recognised that any 'legislative proposals ... would meet with considerable opposition from some labour quarters'.[22]

Ironically, such dissension and equivocation could hardly have been conducive to a 'constructive and determined approach to the labour question'; instead, it encouraged Asquith to postpone the issue whenever possible. Moreover, in the summer of 1911, just as the Liverpool transport strike had brought the question of a serious industrial relations challenge to the forefront of Cabinet debate, ministers' attention was drawn in two other directions – towards the final dramatic phase of the struggle with the House of Lords over the 'People's Budget' and towards the possibility of a European war arising out of the Agadir incident. In fact, the Cabinet, as Askwith conceded: 'remained immersed in major constitutional crises until 1914', and even as war broke out in August 1914, ministers' minds were focused on the drift towards civil war in Ulster. However, an important explanation for the government's uncertain response to the Labour Revolt may owe more to the highly challenging nature of the strike threat and absence of agreed clear-cut solutions than to the mitigating circumstances suggested by the crises-ridden context in which the government operated.[23]

Notwithstanding the way the Liberal government was willing to support the Board of Trade's conciliatory industrial relations initiatives, and its own social welfare policies, in the last resort it repeatedly demonstrated a willingness to turn to the police and army to contain, coerce and repress workers' militancy, particularly when strikes appeared to threaten the economy and the 'rule of law'. Mass ranks of police officers, often buttressed by forces from other areas, notably the Metropolitan Police, were deployed in numerous strikes, not only during large-scale disputes, but also small strikes involving confrontations between pickets and scabs, with the systematic use of violent baton attacks to protect 'blacklegs'. Behind the scenes a strong collaboration developed between the government through Home Secretary Winston Churchill and chief police officers across the country aimed at undermining strike activity. At the same time, the military were utilised in the South Wales, national transport and railway, and Dundee and Leith docks' strikes, as well as kept on standby in the national miners' and London transport strikes. Asquith's assertion to the railway union leaders in 1911 that he would 'employ

22. Buxton Memorandum to Cabinet, 'Industrial Disputes: The Question of Legislation', 23 January 1914, TNA/CAB/37/118/14.
23. Moss (1983: 124–5, 131–2).

all the forces of the Crown'[24] to keep the national network open in the event of a strike graphically expressed the government's willingness to resort to the use of military force in an attempt to overawe and defeat workers' militancy.

The blatant repression sanctioned and utilised by the government and state on picket lines and the streets was also buttressed by the speed and severity of the judiciary's response to the Labour Revolt, with the high-profile political arrests, trials and imprisonment of Tom Mann and others for 'sedition' and Jim Larkin for alleged 'conspiracy', as well as the conviction of hundreds of strikers and their supporters across many different strikes across the country.

SURVEILLANCE

During this period the government deployed the services of the Special Branch of the Criminal Investigation Department (CID) of Scotland Yard, which was part of the Metropolitan Police and used to counter domestic 'subversion'. Originally formed to combat Irish Fenian activists on the British 'mainland', during the years leading up to the First World War it developed into a small, secret counter-subversive agency responsible for day-to-day monitoring of political individuals and groups, answerable to the Home Office.[25] From 1909 to 1913 it doubled the number of its officers from 35 to 70, with the suffragettes a major preoccupation, no doubt because of their physical assaults on Asquith, Churchill and other government ministers and attacks on prominent buildings and sites across the country.[26]

But individuals, notably Tom Mann and other strike leaders seeking to further workers' interests by militant action, were subject to state surveillance during the Labour Revolt.[27] For example, in the 1910–11 South Wales miners' strike there was a sophisticated use of intelligence collection and surveillance by the police and military. First, the War Office sent two Captains specifically to set up an army intelligence department in the strike area, with army officers posted at various centres to analyse reports, rumours and requests

24. Gilbert (1987: 461).

25. Porter (1991): Wilson and Adams (2015); Thomson (1942); Andrew (2010); Allason (1983); Woodman (2018).

26. *The Suffragette*, 6 and 27 February 1914; Porter (1991: 176); Wilson and Adams (2015: 95–109); Atkinson (2018: 322–3).

27. 'Disturbances: Activities of Tom Mann, Agitator', TNA/HO 144/7062/220.603; Report from plainclothes officer to Police Commissioner on Hull strikers, 2 July 1911, TNA/HO 45/10648/210.615/24a; Metropolitan Police report on 'inflammatory speeches' in London, 8 September 1911, TNA/HO 45/10656/212.470/369; Metropolitan Police report on London transport strikers' Hyde Park rally, July 1912, TNA/HO 144/1211/223.877.

for troops.[28] A second strand of the intelligence network was provided by Welsh-speaking CID officers sent from Scotland Yard to assist in collecting information; and these plainclothes officers attended some strike meetings and reported back to General Macready who was in control of both the army and police operations as directed by Churchill as Home Secretary. Third, there was the presence of a 'confidential' Home Office officer in the strike area, J.F. Moylan, whose main function was to provide Churchill with early warning of any serious military confrontation with the strikers. He sent 13 surveillance reports and assessments to the Home Office having toured the disturbed area and attended meetings with both the employers and strikers. The main aspect of this intelligence collection is that it was, compared with earlier industrial disputes, both highly organised and centralised.[29]

Basil Thompson, head of CID in 1913, reflected that from 1911 there had been 'a great wave of industrial unrest'[30] which posed a serious threat: 'During the summer of 1913, in a conversation about [the] Labour unrest, I ... said that unless there were a European War to divert the current, we were heading for something very like revolution.'[31] And in an article entitled 'The Police and the Public', the *Daily Herald* noted the role of the 'political detective' in the surveillance of activists:

> Their business is to obtain information concerning political and industrial movements which are inconvenient to the Government. We have the authority of the Home Secretary that the reporting section attend only Socialist, Syndicalist, and Suffragist meetings. The spy system flourishes.[32]

While Special Branch documents sent to the Cabinet Office and Home Office suggest they contributed to the security of the state,[33] it is difficult to discern any direct or serious impact on the course of strike activity generally.

VIOLENCE

Undoubtedly one of the most important underlying features of the Labour Revolt was the high incidence of violence evident in industrial disputes.

28. General Macready reported to Churchill on the role of his 'excellent' Intelligence Officers in the strike districts who kept their 'finger on the pulse of the belligerents', CHAR 12/6/50-51.
29. Geary (1987: 36–7; 1985: 38–9); Evans (1911: 67–9).
30. Thomson (1942: 262–3).
31. Ibid.: 265.
32. *Daily Herald*, 16 January 1914.
33. Wilson and Adams (2015).

Traditionally, the bargaining power of craft unions lay primarily in their exclusiveness, in the sense that it was derived from a degree of monopoly power over the supply of craftsmen. For many of the unions organising unskilled and semi-skilled workers during the 1910–14 period, on the other hand, bargaining power hinged upon the proportion of the workforce controlled and, as an associated problem, their ability to deter 'blackleg' labour through the use of picketing (peaceful or otherwise) to exclude strikebreakers.

Strikers invariably endeavoured to engage in peaceful dialogue, reasoning and persuasion ('force of argument') with those workers who refused to join strikes and undertook to cross picket lines. Even contemporary hostile press reports concerned with the problem of alleged 'intimidation' frequently let slip that the act of respecting picket lines was often done voluntarily. The culture of respecting picket lines, combined with the wider degree of solidarity generated by strikes, was at least as important in building trade union power as the more dramatic, large-scale confrontations, with other workers sometimes influenced and swayed by the pickets, even if highly reluctantly.

The problem was that circumstances often made this not merely problematic but essentially impossible given the coalition of antagonistic forces that were marshalled against strikers, and there was invariably a hard core of individuals who were immune to reasoned arguments from pickets to join the strikes. This included hundreds of hardcore volunteer strikebreakers in the waterside industries. It meant defence of the picket line became an end in itself that strikers attempted to achieve through sheer collective physical compulsion ('the argument of force').[34]

Chapters 3–7 chronicled the way mass pickets, often involving hundreds and sometimes many thousands of strikers and their supporters, were mounted outside the entrances to strikebound workplaces, so as to make it practically impossible for anyone to get into work, with scabs often threatened, assailed by missiles and physically assaulted. At the same time, frustration with the scale of 'blacklegging' also sometimes led to violence against property and even street rioting. Yet such violence was essentially a direct product of employers' provocative attempts to undermine strike activity either by active encouragement of existing workers to cross picket lines and remain in work and/or by the importation of 'outside' 'free labour'. Significantly, both the 1912 national miners' and 1914 London building workers' strikes generated a much lower incidence of picketing violence or social confrontation on the streets compared with many other strikes, and appears to have been directly linked to limited 'blacklegging', even though the schism between workers and employers remained considerable.

---

34. Darlington (2022).

When strikers faced 'blacklegs', a fundamental cause of violence in many disputes was the way both the police and military repeatedly displayed their primary duty as the defence of employers' property and managerial rights over the employment relationship, unequivocally participating as partisans *against strikers*. Thus, a habitual, immediate stimulus of violence on the picket line was the deployment and intervention of police, with the Metropolitan Police acting as a national backup, their direct role in providing a physical escort for scabs to enter strikebound workplaces, and their denial of strikers' right to exercise 'peaceful persuasion'. Ironically violence regularly occurred not as the result of picketing per se, but because of action by the police to curtail it, notably the way pickets were harassed, arrested and subject to extreme violence for challenging them.[35]

Again and again in disputes, the police responded ferociously to mass picketing with baton-charges and fierce hand-to-hand fighting that resulted in serious casualties. And the presence of thousands of troops, issued with bayonets and ammunition, effectively imposed martial law in strikebound communities. Their conduct in assisting scabs and the employers was widely perceived as being designed 'not so much to suppress disorder as to suppress strikes',[36] an inevitable consequence of which was the fatalities of strikers in Belfast, Dublin, Tonypandy, Liverpool and Llanelli. Yet, notwithstanding repeated protests over violent police and military action against strikers, even from the TUC,[37] there was the absence of any official inquiries into the violence.

Further contributing to the picketing violence in many industrial disputes was the Liberal government's repeated encouragement of strikebreaking initiatives. For example, during the South Wales miners' strike Churchill instructed the commander of police and army forces to ensure that 'intimidation clearly going beyond peaceful persuasion ... should be rigorously prosecuted'.[38] In the seamen's and dockers' strikes, he insisted that it was the duty of the local civic authorities not only to maintain order, but to secure the unloading of perishable cargoes, thereby positively encouraging police and military protection for strikebreaking and to render widespread picketing ineffective.[39] In the national railway strike, the government's direct use of

35. Weinberger (1991: 56, 67).
36. ILP Twentieth Annual Conference Report, Merthyr, 27–28 May 1912, p. 99.
37. Report of Proceedings of the Forty-Fourth Annual Trades Union Congress, Newcastle upon Tyne, 4–9 September 1911, p. 70; Report of Proceedings of the Forty-Fifth Annual Trades Union Congress, Newport, 2–7 September 1912, p. 91; Report of Proceedings of the Forty-Sixth Annual Trades Union Congress, Manchester, 1–6 September 1913, pp. 237–9.
38. Morgan (1987: 160–1).
39. Weinberger (1991:73–4).

troops to protect scabs being employed by the railway companies unequivocally cast the government in the role of strikebreaker.

Ironically, the industrial unrest precipitated a sustained offensive by employers for the repeal of the 1906 Trade Disputes Act's provisions on legal protection for the right to picket, which it was claimed placed unions in a much more powerful position to wage strikes. For example, during the Liverpool general transport strike the city's magistrates frequently complained to the Home Secretary about the ineffectiveness of existing legislation and the need for new measures to deal with the use of 'wholesale intimidation'. A City Report claimed that 'while thousands of workmen desired to work, they were afraid to do so by reason of the present system of intimidation which is carried on under the pretence of peaceful picketing'.[40] The demand for repeal of the law on picketing was supported by the chair of the Liverpool Steamship Owners' Association, who argued that:

> ... such a thing as peaceful picketing is not, and cannot, be practised in the actual progress of a strike ... [Pickets] are out to stop men working ... the power behind the picket by which its orders will be enforced is the violence of the mob, and nothing else – and we have seen over and over again how quickly that violence follows on the slightest disregard of the peaceful persuasion ... We are entitled to the protection of the law against the illegitimate advantages derived from mob violence directed against willing workers.[41]

Such protests were part of a wider campaign by the Conservative Party and the press for proposals which amounted to taking an offensive against the unions. In October 1911 an Employers' Parliamentary Council, supported by 65 other employers' associations, made representations to the Prime Minister, blaming the Trade Disputes Act for the unrest and asking for the Act's repeal, in particular protesting against '"peaceful persuasion" of a mob of unlimited numbers' as 'a form of tyranny so gross and monstrous as to completely [negate] the rights of every law-abiding citizen who declines to subject himself to labour union domination'.[42]

---

40. City of Liverpool, 'Report of the Special Committee of the Justices upon the Need of Legislation on the Subject of INTIMIDATION', 30 August 1911, Liverpool Record Office: 347/MAG/1/1/9, cited in Lyddon and Smith (2007: 222).
41. Liverpool Steamship Owners' Association, 'Picketing and the Protection of Workers', 5 September 1911, Liverpool Record Office: 347/MAG/1/1/9, cited in Lyddon and Smith (2007: 224–6).
42. Cited in Lyddon and Smith (2007: 212); TUC Parliamentary Committee, Tenth Quarterly Report, December 1911, pp. 31–3.

However, the Liberal government resisted this pressure for changes to the Trade Disputes Act and its picketing clause. This was partly because they feared it would threaten their slim parliamentary majority which depended on Labour Party support; and partly because the Cabinet was divided on the best way to contain the industrial militancy given that more repressive measures ran the risk of merely fanning the flames of strike activity, social polarisation and violence; and partly because the Prime Minister felt that even if police powers with regard to intimidation were strengthened, there would remain the problem of obtaining evidence because of the unwillingness of witnesses to come forward. There was a limit to the amount of protection employers could expect for their scab workforce.[43]

Instead, the Home Office urged the police to take much more vigorous action under existing law, with a circular issued under Churchill's direction to provincial police chiefs on 11 August 1911 titled 'Intimidation during Trade Disputes' reiterating that while the 1906 Act allowed peaceful picketing, it did not sanction intimidation or threats of violence for which pickets needed to be prosecuted.[44] This important document, in effect, encouraged the police to extend their own powers, with the process of persuasion to be regarded as evidence of intimidation or coercion if a crowd of pickets was involved.[45] It was Home Office instructions for more aggressive action towards picketing that directly encouraged the arrests, prosecution and conviction of the hundreds of strikers who were fined, and in many cases imprisoned. It both stimulated and provided justification for ongoing police and military violence, with the annual Trades Union Congress of 1913 considering it 'fully entitled to call this Liberal Government a bloody Government'.[46]

Significantly, the use of mass picketing to stop 'blacklegs' and shift the balance of power in disputes in workers' favour, notwithstanding the violence that often occurred provoked by their antagonists' countermobilisation efforts, was often a crucial factor contributing to the difference between success and failure in strikes. Certainly, in many disputes employers' attempts to undermine strike action, either by importing scab labour or by direct encouragement of their existing workforce to cross picket lines, often backed by police and troops, were effectively thwarted by the sheer level of mass picketing, along with the extent of solidarity action by workers not involved

43. Davidson (1978: 591).
44. 'Intimidation during Trades Disputes', Circular to Chief Constables, 11 August 1911, HO 158/15/212.614/57; TNA/CAB 37/107/97, Lyddon and Smith (2007: 216–19).
45. Morgan (1987: 168).
46. Report of Proceedings of the Forty-Sixth Annual Trades Union Congress, Manchester, 1–6 September 1913, pp, 69–70.

in the dispute and local community support that was displayed. Conversely, in some disputes there were important limits to the effectiveness of picketing activity against scabs, contributing to the defeats, notably in the case of the 1912 London transport, and 1913 Leeds Corporation and Leith dockers' strikes and Dublin lockout.

Overall, it seems apparent that the aggressive, and sometimes violent, methods used in the conduct of disputes were viewed, by at least a significant minority of strike participants, as legitimate and necessary if victory was to be achieved. Working-class violence – including physical assaults on scabs (and even sometimes rioting) – could be justified by participants by the way in which it was seen as being directly provoked by the employers' encouragement of scabs and the partisan intervention of police and troops attempting to defeat workers' struggles.

Since the 'New Unionism' period employers had often systematically defeated attempts at strike activity by strikebreaking and victimisation, while the methods of respectability and moderation previously championed by official union and Labour Party leaderships had become associated with failure. In this context, unbridled militancy, sometimes going further than even some radical strike leaders were prepared to countenance, became widely accepted as the only way to counter employers' and state's determined resistance to union organisation. Militant and aggressive forms of strike action, accompanied, if and when necessary, by 'demonstrative violence',[47] ensured that picket lines were scrupulously respected. Attempts to discredit the 1910–14 Labour Revolt with denunciations of 'wholesale intimidation', 'thuggery' and 'mob rule' often reflected class interests and it could be argued that strikers only *dispensed* violence as a form of collective self-defence against the combined force of scabs, employers, police, military, civil authorities and government, and that they themselves were overwhelmingly the *recipient* of intimidation and violence from these combined forces.[48]

---

47. Newsinger (2013a: 8–9).
48. Darlington (2022).

11
Political Radicalisation

In the introductory chapter it was argued that an interpretation of the Labour Revolt as merely the pragmatic pursuit of demands on wages and conditions confined within a form of 'trade union consciousness' ignores its wider aspect and inherent radicalised sentiment and behaviour that was expressed amongst a sizeable layer of workers. This chapter explores the relationship between the industrial struggle and broader political concerns and the extent and limits to which strike activity encouraged a far-reaching political radicalisation. Although this is empirically highly problematic given that systematic evidence on working-class consciousness is effectively non-existent and virtually impossible to measure reliably, it is possible to make a tentative attempt to explore ways in which such political radicalisation manifested itself, as well as the limitations of such a process.

CLASS CONSCIOUSNESS

To begin with, it is clear that workers' struggles were not in themselves revolutionary and strike demands did not consciously aim at the overthrow of the wage system. Collective bargaining was by necessity often conducted around issues on which more limited, albeit tangible, agreements could be made, notably wages and conditions of employment and union organisation and recognition. Yet headline strike demands often masked a variety of other less tangible grievances, including the exercise of managerial control, work intensification and undermining of skill and autonomy, which contributed to a wider dissatisfaction that culminated in strike activity. Underpinning material grievances were more intractable issues related to the desire to retrieve some vestiges of self-respect and dignity, with collective mobilisation often reflecting notions of fairness and injustice rather than mere pragmatic calculation. At no point, therefore, were 'economic interests' straightforward or simply apparent.[1]

1. Gordon (1991: 246).

Moreover, many workers undoubtedly held an elementary form of 'class consciousness'[2] which, despite its uneven, contingent, partial and contradictory nature, was characterised by a tendency to feel affinity to members of their own class, with whom they shared interests and political goals, as well as viewing working-class interests as being divergent, if not diametrically opposed, to the interests of employers and the capitalist class. There were different manifestations of this class consciousness.

On one level, it was evidenced by the unprecedented levels of solidarity displayed, for example, in terms of respect for picket lines, refusal to handle 'tainted' goods, sympathetic strike action, explicit linking of strikes by different groups of workers, refusing to return to work until all sections won satisfactory outcomes, financial donations, public meetings, marches and confrontations with scabs, police and troops. This class solidarity, which involved both workers and trade unionists not directly involved in strike activity themselves, as well as non-wage-earning members of the local community, was the glue that bound together different sections of the working-class movement, and became a powerful tool for organising and defending strikers and their communities.

On another level, the forging of a solidaristic identity with other workers against a common enemy, 'us versus them', led to antagonistic class relations and class conflict which many viewed as a central defining characteristic of capitalist society. Thus, across many strikes there was an explicit recognition and identification of the way in which workers' different grievances and deprivations were firmly rooted in the basic structure of an exploitative capitalist society, with a connection made between their meagre wages and the conspicuous wealth of their employers, and the specific industrial struggles of one group of workers against their employers and the working-class movement against the capitalist class as a whole.

At the same time, while pursuing their immediate goals of increased wages, better working conditions and right to collective union organisation, workers were often confronted not only with intransigent employers and hesitant and sometimes oppositional union officials, but also fierce opposition from state and local civil authorities which invariably politicised their industrial disputes. Repeated and widespread instances of violent police attacks, the use of troops to overpower strikers and the consequent fatalities, the harsh judgements of magistrates and the courts, the government's direct intervention on the side of the employers, and the arrest and imprisonment of many strike activists revealed in sharp relief their class-based partisan role.

2. Meacham (1972: 1343–64; 1977).

Despite claiming to act in a neutral fashion, such forces were widely seen as consistently representing the interests of the employers and broader capitalist class in their defence of 'property rights', with political considerations blatantly affecting their policing, administration of justice and governance. This demonstration of the coercive and repressive side of capitalist liberal democracy had the effect of diminishing the legitimacy it was normally accorded. Thus, Ben Tillett ridiculed the idea that the capitalist state was neutral and Parliament a key channel of redress for workers:

> Parliament is a farce and a sham, the rich man's Duma, the employer's Tammany, the Thieves' Kitchen and the working man's despot … In the 1912 strikes we had to fight Parliament, the forces of the Crown, the judges of the law … We had the press of both parties and the capitalists against us; the police were incensed by the employers and rewarded for every act of violence … Capitalism as a tiger is a tiger; and both are savage and pitiless towards the weak.[3]

Likewise, for Tom Mann's new syndicalist Industrial Democracy League paper, *Solidarity*, 'everywhere and every day the existence of the class struggle in society becomes more vivid and self-evident':

> We are beginning to understand what the class war really means. We have seen how during these industrial disputes, the law, the police, the military, the Church, and the political parties have been brought into operation against the workers. The whole forces of the State are used in the interests of the masters and against the revolting workers.[4]

Meanwhile, many workers became alienated from the Labour Party and parliamentary politics in general as effective channels to redress their material grievances. As Mann explained:

> Those who have been in close touch with the Movement know that in recent years dissatisfaction has been expressed in various quarters at the results so far achieved by our Parliamentarians. Certainly nothing very striking in the way of constructive work could reasonably be expected from the minorities of Socialists and Labour men hitherto elected … Indeed, it is no exaggeration to say that many seem to have constituted themselves apologists for existing Society, showing a degree of studied respect for bourgeois

3. DWRGWU Annual Report, 1912, pp. 5–9, cited in Bullock (1960: 34–5).
4. *Solidarity*, April 1914.

> conditions, and a toleration of bourgeois methods, that destroys the probability of their doing any real work of a revolutionary character.[5]
>
> ... I am not opposed to Parliamentary action. I am only saying – Use the easiest method, rely upon that kind of [trade union] organisation which will enable you to achieve your work in the shortest possible time and in the most efficient fashion.[6]

A crucial political characteristic feature of the Labour Revolt was this polarisation between the constitutional approach of Labour MPs with its commitment to gradualist reform from above, and industrial struggles that could win immediate material improvements through workers' self-initiative, organisation and action from below. As one delegate told the 1912 annual TUC conference: 'Let us be quite clear as to what Syndicalism really is ... a protest against the inaction of the Labour Party.'[7] Even if the ideology of Labourism was by no means destroyed it was nevertheless put under considerable strain, and it was precisely for this reason that the syndicalist movement, which represented both a reaction to and a rejection of the politics of gradualism in favour of militant industrial struggle, could attract widespread support.

Of course, workers' class consciousness during the Labour Revolt was highly contradictory. Even though *objectively* industrial militancy could pose a direct threat to the existing economic, social and political order of Edwardian society, this was not *subjectively* intended or articulated by the majority of workers, for whom piecemeal action was viewed as legitimate within the terms of the political economy of capital. In this respect, the strikes were a revolt against the *effects* of the capitalist system, not at the *causes* of those effects nor the system itself.

Yet there was also a 'sub-culture' inside the working-class movement that contained many elements which questioned and opposed the 'official' norms of society. It was not only that the dichotomy between 'them' and 'us' implied some conception of common class interests that were hostile to those in positions of authority and those exercising control, and the need to act collectively in opposition to advance class (as distinct from merely industrial and trade union) objectives.

It was also that many strikers and their local supporters took it for granted that it was necessary to utilise 'deviant' means to challenge authority, not only

5. *Industrial Syndicalist*, July 1910.
6. Ibid., January 1911.
7. Report of Proceedings of the Forty-Fifth Annual Trades Union Congress, Newport, 2–7 September 1912, p. 274.

extra-parliamentary means of struggle that embraced strike action, but also mass picketing, confrontations with the police and military, and even street rioting and sabotage of property. It involved a 'counter-ideology' to capitalist ideology that embraced a critique of the present social order, even if it was essentially a 'quasi-ideology'[8] – rather than a full-blown radical or revolutionary ideology – with class consciousness co-existing with attitudes that involved a practical, everyday acceptance of the permanence of established institutions and capitalist society.

Within this context there was the emergence of a layer of militant activists and leaders, who played a crucial role in identifying, highlighting and articulating workers' collective forms of interest and identity, attributing the sources of discontent to employers (and potentially the government and capitalist class), and advocating self-assertiveness and militant forms of struggle as legitimate and effective means to seek redress. In this sense, while workers' collective interests were generated by *objective* material conditions underlying their 'every-day' experiences of the underlying exploitative nature of workplace relations and society, the process of building collectivism, solidarity and class-wide forms of consciousness was also *socially constructed*. Activists and leaders, including many whose individual motivations were informed to a greater or lesser degree by broader ideological and political frameworks that embraced notions of exploitation, inequality and class power within capitalist society, helped to form, shape and redefine workers' own definitions of their collective interests in ways which cemented ideas of injustice about their social conditions and promoted solidaristic and militant forms of working-class resistance.[9]

Amongst a smaller, but still sizeable, minority of such activists there was some adherence to a far more coherently developed anti-capitalist and revolutionary ideology. There was a milieu of activists (embracing members and supporters of radical left groups, as well as other non-aligned militants, including those around the *Daily Herald*) who held fairly explicit left-wing views, motivation and commitment, and provided an intensely ideological and political cutting-edge to workers' militancy.

They often explicitly framed issues in terms of a class-based analysis of society, arguing that individual disputes needed to be seen as part of a more general class struggle by the working-class movement. The wholesale revolutionary transformation of society through mass extra-parliamentary working-class action was their objective. For example, the South Wales *Cambrian Strike Manifesto* of 16 June 1911 called on fellow workers 'to put

8. Hyman (1975: 175).
9. Darlington (2006: 485–509; 2018: 621–4).

an end to Capitalistic Despotism and to do battle for the cause of Industrial Freedom',[10] and Mann invariably ended his speeches with calls for workers' control of society.

In the process, the high level of class struggle and political radicalisation became a fertile breeding ground for the sowing of the syndicalist seed. Commentating on the militant workers' struggle in Dublin in 1913, Askwith, acknowledged:

> ... the serious riots in Dublin, although founded on poverty, low wages and bad conditions, included determination to establish the transport workers' union as the 'one big union' in Ireland, and put into practice the doctrines of syndicalism ... The influences ... [for] the overthrow of Capitalism, and revolution against existing authority, were all present.[11]

Obviously, it is important to avoid identifying the sentiments and opinions of the mass of workers with those of the 'avant-garde' of militant activists, because the two were plainly not the same, and yet the fact that militant activists could enjoy considerable influence within the strike wave would appear to reflect not only the deep wellspring of bitterness towards employers and the government, but also the potential correspondence of ideas of working-class collectivism, struggle and solidarity with the experience, needs and aspirations of a significant minority of workers. The growth in support for the radical left in terms of organisational membership and/or readership of their publications, as well as the evident wider appeal of the aspirational dream of a socialist society, was a reflection of such political radicalisation.

By no means did all workers who followed syndicalist-inclined leaders like Mann and Larkin grasp the key tenets of syndicalist theory, or endorse their radical left *objectives* that viewed militant trade unionism as the revolutionary means to overthrow capitalism. Instead, many are likely to have merely subscribed to the *methods* of struggle they advocated ('direct action' and industrial unionism) as the most effective way of improving their immediate conditions.

Nonetheless, even if we cannot speak of any mass *revolutionary* consciousness, it is clear that the bitter and bloody industrial struggles of the period, and influence of left-wing activists, generated a wider political generalisation and sense of class consciousness, in which, as Askwith acknowledged, 'social questions are becoming more and more matters of politics, and are

10. Arnot (1967: 273).
11. Askwith ([1920] 1974: 259).

thus continually coming under political discussion'.[12] The Irish Home Rule crisis, women's suffrage agitation, and the budgetary crisis with the House of Lords all added to the undermining of popular respect for the legitimacy of parliamentary institutions and the broad *zeitgeist* of militant 'direct action', civil disobedience and defiance of employers, government, civil authorities, police and military.

'PROTO-SYNDICALISM'?

Many contemporary prominent observers, including George Askwith, some employers and government ministers, and much of the press, were convinced that a syndicalist 'mood' of revolt and disaffection was widespread inside the working-class movement. And the historian Bob Holton argued that, while the working-class movement contained only a small hard core of avowed activists aligned with syndicalist organisations, there existed a far wider 'proto-syndicalist mentality'. This was evident in the spontaneous, sympathetic and insurgent character of much strike activity, the repudiation of official labour leadership, and violent confrontations on the picket lines and streets with the authorities. Holton pointed to the primary importance of direct action over parliamentary pressure as a means of settling grievances, and to mass support for industrial unionism to oppose employers, assert rank-and-file control over union leaders, and establish workers' control. Although not necessarily expressed in explicit revolutionary commitment, popular support for syndicalism was based upon the uplifting inspiration of fighting collective organisation, with many workers, it was claimed, acting in a 'proto-syndicalist' manner on the basis of a feeling that they could change society through industrial rather than political action.[13]

In other words, Holton's 'proto-syndicalism' was less than *revolutionary* consciousness, but more than *trade union* consciousness. It contained within it the potential to develop into a full-bloodied challenge to the existing social and political order rather than indicating any acceptance of it. In the Irish context, it was known to friends and enemies alike as 'Larkinism', the essence of which was its powerful call for solidarity, refusal to handle 'tainted' goods, indictment of the compromises and betrayals of the trade union leaders, uncompromising anti-capitalism, celebration of militancy and faith in the rank-and-file.[14]

12. Askwith Memorandum to Cabinet, 'The Present Unrest in the Labour World', 25 June 1911, TNA/CAB 37/107/70.
13. Holton (1976: 20, 118–19, 209–10).
14. Newsinger (2002: 5; 2004: 97).

Arguably, the problem with the use of a term such as 'proto-syndicalism' is that (as explored in Chapter 1) a variety of material, ideological and political factors coalesced to provoke what might be more accurately described as the *zeitgeist* of workers' industrial and political militancy of the period. There was a difference between the general movement of industrial militancy and the organised syndicalist or syndicalist-influenced groups that tried to influence it, which is liable to be obscured and confused by the use of a term that renders both as 'syndicalist'.[15] Even though syndicalist activists attempted to provide forms of organisation and guidance to this broader workers' revolt, it was at no stage contained entirely within such a single doctrine (or organisation) and the use of a fairly arbitrary (and partisan) term that suggests otherwise is confusing and misleading.[16]

Unsurprisingly, syndicalist influence, on the one hand, and activities or attitudes that appeared syndicalist, on the other, were often conflated, especially when aspects of its approach – antipathy towards conservative trade union and Labour Party leaders, extra-parliamentary direct action and solidarity, and support for industrial unionism – were advocated by other militants and radical left activists. The fundamental nature and varied forms of workers' militant struggle during the period 1910–14 can be understood and explained without the use of a blanket concept that 'risks containing and codifying diversity'.[17]

Nonetheless, Holton's recognition that syndicalism's appeal was much more widespread than suggested by mere organisational structures and formal membership figures, and was grounded on the distinctive *radicalism* of important minority sections of the working-class movement, he made a valuable contribution to defending syndicalism from those who write it out of working-class experience as an aberration. Although strike militancy and political radicalisation took place largely in workplaces and even industries in which syndicalist activists were not even present, the experience of strike activity against antagonistic employers, magistrates, government, police and military, together with the hostility shown by Labour Party and many leading trade union officials, helped to generate a wider sympathy and interest in syndicalist ideas. Many of the most class-conscious workers knew of the efficacy of syndicalist practice even if they were not fully versed in the theory, and the sheer breadth of working-class struggle reinforced and seemed to confirm syndicalist strategies, tactics and (to some extent) doctrine.[18]

---

15. Peterson (1983: 66); Darlington (2013a: 45–6; 2013b: 155–7); Taplin (1986: 101).
16. Darlington (2013b: 155–7).
17. Howell (2017: 257).
18. Darlington (2013b: 157).

LABOURISM

Clearly there were substantial material and ideological dilemmas limiting translation of the Labour Revolt's radical potential into a wider political movement, including deep sectional divisions based on skill, gender and ethnicity. Moreover, as one account of life in Salford during the period reported, political radicalisation could be contradictory and affect only a minority of workers as a whole:

> Whatever their quarrel with *local* employers, the ultra-patriotic mass remained intensely loyal to the nation and the system as a whole. One week a striking docker might hurl stones at the police and the next, assured of his daily bread, applaud the marching Territorials, or cheer a passing prince to the skies …
>
> One thousand disaffected might cheer the syndicalists and many more strike work, but … [t]he bulk of the unskilled workers, conformist, chauvinistic, went on accepting their lot unchanged.[19]

As even George Dangerfield acknowledged, the disjuncture between the *actions* of workers and their *attitudes* meant that there could be 'distrust of and respect for political democracy … hopelessly intermingled' with 'the Government … simultaneously attacked and defended … by the same people'. While there could be 'unprecedented class hatred' as workers shook 'the very foundations of parliamentary rule', workers 'would have been dismayed at the very mention of the word "revolution"'.[20]

In the two general elections of 1910 the majority of the male working class who participated (on a restricted franchise) cast their votes for either the Liberals or Conservatives, and both parties retained considerable electoral support inside the working-class movement up to 1914 (Table 14). Many Conservative Working Men's Clubs drew on a feeling of deference and respect for those above them, and even Liverpool, with its militancy and religious sectarian divisions, the Conservative Party dominated municipal politics.[21]

In many parts of the country, both the Liberals and Tories were able to adopt varied forms of popular politics aimed specifically at winning over working-class voters, the overall effect of which was to impede the political independence of the organised labour movement. And there remained few signs that the newly formed Labour Party was capable of making signifi-

19. Roberts (1990: 91, 101).
20. Dangerfield ([1935] 1997: 192–3).
21. Waller (1981).

cant parliamentary electoral headway independent of Liberal support. Thus, in the 1910 general election it only fielded 56 candidates, all but 11 of which had Liberal support, and in 14 by-elections in industrial seats between 1911 and 1914 it came bottom of the poll in each case, nowhere taking more than 30 per cent of the vote. It also lost four seats, including three mining districts where it was up against a strong 'Lib-Lab' tradition.

Although the Labour Party aspired to be the political voice of the trade unions, a large minority of trade union members and significant layer of union leaders did not view it as a credible alternative to the Liberals as a means of strengthening labour representation in the House of Commons, with radical ILP socialist candidates deemed 'unsuitable'. Thus, as was noted in Chapter 1, the Miners' Federation did not affiliate until 1908 when it finally brought most of its MPs with it, albeit 45 per cent of the miners who participated in a ballot voted against affiliation.[22] Even if in the period up to 1914 the number of affiliated union members increased rapidly and substantially, very largely reflecting the remarkable growth of trade unionism, it still represented only just over half of the total union membership in these years of rapid overall union advance (Table 13).[23]

While most of the main unions voted to establish political funds under the 1913 Trade Union Act (which reversed the 1909 Osborne judgment that it was illegal for a trade union to contribute to a political party), nearly 40 per cent of the members of the nine largest unions that participated in the ballots opposed their union's funds being used to support ILP candidates. It underlined the far from unanimous hold which Labour had over the loyalty of many individual trade unionists,[24] and in some mining regions like South Wales and the North-East many working-class voters continued to rally to the banner of Liberalism.[25] Thus, there was no direct correlation between the Labour Revolt and parliamentary electoral support for Labour, albeit the party was able to significantly increase its overall share of the vote and expand its representation on local municipal councils.[26]

---

22. Hunt (1981: 333).
23. Clegg (1985: 570).
24. Wrigley (1985: 152).
25. Powell (1996: 113–14).
26. Although Dangerfield's argument that the combined labour, suffrage and Home Rule crises underlined the 'Strange Death of Liberal England' seems broadly justified, the Liberal Party was by no means on the verge of collapse in the pre-war period – it still required the impact of significant political and social change and an internal split between Asquith and Lloyd George during the First World War before the Labour Party was able to supplant them as a parliamentary political party. Likewise, although there were undoubtedly factors encouraging the underlying so-called 'rise of Labour' – such as the (however limited) class politics of its appeal and increasing trade union

Conversely, the level of industrial militancy during 1910–14 was not decided by whether Labour did badly at the polls, but had a rhythm of its own, with workers' self-activity not running to the parliamentary timetable. And the poor Labour vote was not a sign of a lack of working-class confidence, but rather that many workers did not see the party as the means of a wider advance, merely a subsidiary means of extracting Liberal government reforms.[27] The common antipathy, if not hostility, to 'politics' (often conceived of mainly in parliamentary terms) expressed by many union militants and syndicalists during the Labour Revolt was further underlined by the Labour Party leadership's official reaction to the strike wave which, despite occasional criticism of police and military action, was generally not supportive, sometimes hostile, and viewed as highly damaging to the country.

The crucial problem was that the party's strategy – based on the view that gradualist and reformist change was possible through electoral politics that built up Labour representation in Parliament and thus captured government office and control over the state – meant that winning elections (from a much broader constituency than trade unionists or even the working class) necessarily became the primary goal and main form of activity, rather than supporting 'extra-parliamentary' workers' struggles.[28] And with its organisation built on an alliance with leaders of the unions, and with a parliamentary strategy the success of which, for the moment at least, relied upon the co-operation of the Liberals, the Labour Party felt seriously threatened by widespread militancy in the industrial field.

But the aversion of the Labour Party leadership went far deeper than this, with the spectacle of mass industrial struggle challenging the very assumptions about society upon which Labour's political perspective was based. In the face of the contradiction between being an organisation committed to channelling working-class aspirations for change through the institutions of the state, and a strike wave which tended to develop into a battle against the state, and involved the intervention of the police and military to try to prevent or break strikes, the Labour Party leaders took the side of Parliament. For example, Ramsay MacDonald, chairman of the Parliamentary Labour

---

support – the Labour Party's continued relative parliamentary electoral weakness pre-1914 (notwithstanding the vagaries of the Edwardian franchise) reflected the Liberal's ability to retain some working-class support and Labour's inability to pull away from their gravitational pull.

27. Gluckstein (1987: 16–19).

28. The Fabian Society, one of the socialist bodies affiliated to the Labour Party, whose leading figures included Sidney and Beatrice Webb, H.G. Wells, George Bernard Shaw and Ramsay MacDonald, was an influential force in shaping the ILP and Labour Party's reformist doctrine.

Party from early 1911 and a leading ILP figure, wrote a book condemning syndicalism both for its ultimate ends and even more for its methods:

> The Socialist believes in a combination of political and trade union action, the Syndicalist believes in trade union action alone; the Socialist appeals to the whole body of public opinion, the Syndicalist considers the working classes only; the Socialist brings about his changes by legislative moulding, he uses the organic State to transform itself by making such alterations in its own mind and circumstances as must precede all permanent change; the Syndicalist cutting himself off from these organic formative influences, has to fall back upon force, either the passive force of social paralysis, or the active forces of riots, to effect his changes with revolutionary suddenness ...[29]
>
> In fact, Syndicalism is largely a revolt against Socialism. Socialism must be Parliamentary, or it is nothing.[30]

Likewise, Philip Snowden, another ILP leader, wrote another scathing book on syndicalism, setting out to demonstrate the futility of the strike weapon as an instrument of social change, and to dismiss the class struggle as obsolete and futile:[31]

> The old policy of the trade unions was to ... refrain from exasperating the public and the employers by never-ceasing threats of strikes; to exhaust every possible means of conciliation before calling out the men, and then not to do so unless there was a reasonable chance of victory ... The new policy is to enter upon a strike without any effort to obtain a settlement of the grievances by negotiation; to exasperate the employers by every possible means; to indulge in wild and sanguinary language, which makes it impossible for a self-respecting employer to meet such leaders of the men; to never pay any attention to the rather important matter of preparing some means of support during the strike; and to endeavour to cause as much public inconvenience as possible, by involving the services upon which the public needs and depend.[32]

In many respects, the Labour Party, it can be argued, acted as a brake on the Labour Revolt, as becomes apparent by comparing the difference between

29. MacDonald (1912a: 6).
30. Ibid.: 7.
31. Snowden (n.d. c.1913).
32. Cited in Askwith ([1920] 1974: 260).

the leaders of the Labour Party and trade unions, albeit the parliamentary party consisted predominately of union-sponsored MPs and trade union officials, including J.H. Thomas. On the one hand, they both reflected an institutionalised demarcation between 'economics' and 'politics' expressed in the predominant assumption that trade unions should narrowly constrain themselves to the pursuit of the economic struggle in the workplace over wages and conditions, while for political change in society workers should look to the Labour Party to act through the parliamentary process on their behalf. This was an approach that encouraged the belief that the class struggle between capital and labour was a de-politicised, economic and social issue channelled and confined within the framework of capitalist society, and that workers' interests were best served through negotiation and reform through Parliament rather than through the revolutionary transformation of society through workers' own struggles. Thus, the idea the workers might utilise industrial militancy for political ends to challenge the government was completely rejected.

On the other hand, while the interests of the leaders of the trade unions and Labour Party may have coincided in the sense that they were both wary of the Labour Revolt threatening the stability of parliamentary governance and Labour's potential electoral prospects, there was an important difference between them. The union leaders were at 'one remove' from the class struggle, a conservative social layer that mediated between workers and employers when they conflicted with each other to negotiate a settlement, and with no interest in encouraging a level of industrial struggle that could bring down the Liberal government and seriously challenge the employing class. Yet both left- and right-wing union officials came under direct pressure from their rank-and-file members, and therefore had to be prepared to call strikes or support union members who took action in defence of their immediate conditions, and even to utilise left rhetoric, if only in an attempt to reassert their authority inside the unions.

By contrast, the professional politicians that made up the leadership of the Labour Party and its MPs were twice removed from the class struggle, much more insulated from the direct pressures of the working-class movement, and therefore more conservatively committed to the defence of parliamentary democracy and the existing capitalist system.[33] Indeed, the potential valuable role that Labour played in defending the existing order and opposing extra-parliamentary militant direct action from below during the Labour Revolt was underlined by Lloyd George: 'Socialism', he said, meaning the

33. Cliff and Gluckstein (1988: 32–3).

Labour Party, would destroy 'Syndicalism' – 'the best policeman for the Syndicalist is the Socialist'.[34]

Thus, even if the Labour Party did not play much of a direct role in mediating within individual disputes, it did play an important role in attempting to blunt the forward industrial advance and political development of the strike movement, and thereby provide further justification for the union officials' efforts to defuse militant workers' struggles and reassert control over the militants within their unions, a part that was belied by Labour's apparent irrelevance.[35]

It is true that Keir Hardie stood on the side of workers' struggles against employers and the state, and many socialist members of the ILP endorsed the criticisms made in Ben Tillett's 1908 pamphlet, *Is the Parliamentary Party a Failure?*, which argued for greater emphasis on socialist ideas and more strenuous attempts to link the parliamentary party with the working-class movement. Indeed, ILP members offered practical solidarity with those involved in disputes, with some in the forefront of strike action themselves. But despite the ILP's commitment to a 'socialist commonwealth' as an ultimate goal, Labour Party conferences consistently overwhelmingly rejected moves to write such a socialist goal into the party's constitution.

Moreover, like the broader Labour Party, the ILP as an organisation, as well as the bulk of its members, refused to break with their scrupulous commitment to parliamentarism and the fundamental electoral logic that either publicly eschewed the class war or at the very least subordinated it to the political strategy of winning representation in local and national institutions. This meant placing a greater premium on social and political struggles than on industrial struggles and on the locality as the centre of agitational work rather than the workplace.[36]

Even Hardie argued that while strikes were an essential weapon open to workers, they were no substitute for a wider vision of greater political representation, constitutional political action and the implementation of democratic socialism; workers should strive to control the state, not destroy it, and the Labour Party was their predestined instrument:[37]

> The action of the strike can at most only be ameliorative; it can never be revolutionary. That belongs to the sphere of [parliamentary] politics … political action is revolutionary, whereas direct action is but palliative. The

34. House of Commons Debates *(Hansard)*, 19 March 1920, vol. 126, col. 1774.
35. Cliff and Gluckstein (1988: 52).
36. Gordon (1991: 263–5).
37. Holman (2010: 169–70); Morgan (1997: 242–8).

> strike can be used to supplement, but not to supplant political action ... The industrial strike, even when successful settles nothing ... The political strike is the only form of strike which is all gain and no loss.[38]

In sum, the Labour Revolt undoubtedly encouraged the development of political radicalisation, and wider class consciousness, among a sizeable minority of workers. In some respects, workers' propensity to engage in strike action was nurtured by the apparent slowness and ineffectiveness of progress via parliamentary channels, and as it developed the strike wave threw increasing doubt on Labour's parliamentary political project, thereby reinforcing claims that the working class could achieve its goals through direct action on the industrial sphere alone. But the inadequacies of Labour's political project had the effect of blunting the potential political horizons of many workers, a handicap that was not to be overcome by the radical left (Chapter 12).

38. *Socialist Review*, May 1912.

12

Industrial Militancy and the Radical Left

The Labour Revolt provided a favourable opportunity for the radical left to build an alternative leadership to that offered by the trade unions and Labour Party. But by shifting the terms of the debate on the left away from its exclusive concentration on Parliament, and highlighting the severe limitations of the Labour Party's strategy, the 1910–14 strike wave also posed a profound challenge to the radical left's *own* political orientations towards the trade unions and industrial militancy. In assessing the overall dynamics of the strike wave, it is important to assess the role of the radical left. Arguably while it exercised powerful influence amongst a minority of activists inside the working-class movement, played a very important role in supporting many strikes and occasionally assumed leadership roles, the efficacy of the radical left's intervention was also bedevilled by fragmentation, intra-organisational conflicts over strategy and tactics, and its inability to overcome the damaging overarching separation between industrial struggles and political action that handicapped the labour movement generally.

In should be noted that despite organisational fragmentation and variations in political ideology and strategy, there was an absence of rigid divisions between many rank-and-file members of most radical left groups, with the exception of the SLP. Interlocking networks of activists engaged in continuing dialogue with each other, regularly sharing political platforms and exhibiting some fluidity in political ideas. Public meetings organised by the Clarion Scouts and left-wing ILP branches were addressed by speakers drawn from the wide spectrum of political groups and attended by hundreds. Frequent overtures were made by the Social Democratic Party (as the Social Democratic Federation became known after 1908) to the ILP to amalgamate and form a united socialist party, and this willingness to engage in debate created a number of common forums. Likewise, the ISEL, Amalgamation Committees and *Daily Herald* supporters' groups enabled militants and socialists from different political groups to work alongside each other.

All the different organisations emphasised revolutionary propaganda and education as a means of disseminating their ideas and enhancing and developing workers' consciousness. This was achieved through newspapers, journals, pamphlets, educational classes, street soapbox oratory and public meetings. For example, in its educational activities the Plebs League succeeded in introducing workers to basic Marxist concepts about exploitation, surplus value, capital accumulation and class struggle, which was no small achievement in a British labour movement notorious for its aversion to theory.[1] Not only did propaganda reach wide audiences, but its related political activity also involved a much broader constituency than the formal small-scale membership of the different organisations, with often a vibrant local network of radical left propaganda, organisation and activity.[2]

However, there were considerable limitations to the rather abstract nature of this propagandism, notwithstanding variations between different left groupings. It could sometimes mean assuming workers had to be educated into socialism rather than find their own way there through collective struggle, while it often failed to offer practical guidance to trade union activists and militants engaged in the intense strikes of the period.

RELATIONSHIP BETWEEN INDUSTRIAL AND POLITICAL ACTIVITY

A characteristic feature of the radical left was its failure to connect *industrial* struggles with *political* ideas, organisation and leadership, which manifested itself in varying ways between and within the different groups.

British Socialist Party

When Tom Mann returned to England in May 1910 and launched the Industrial Syndicalist Education League, he rejoined the revamped Social Democratic Federation (of which he had been a member between 1885 and 1889) that had become known as the Social Democratic Party in 1908, and which in turn was to be renamed the British Socialist Party in 1911. But when efforts to persuade the SDP's members to repudiate parliamentary tactics in favour of industrial struggle and industrial unionism were rebuffed by the 'old guard' Marxist leaders like H.M. Hyndman, Harry Quelch and H.W. Lee, he resigned after the party's national conference in September 1911:

> I find myself not in agreement with the party on the important matter of Parliamentary action ... I declare in favour of direct industrial organisa-

1. Pitt (1987: 3).
2. Gordon (1991: 262–3).

> tion not as a means, but *THE* means whereby the workers can ultimately overthrow the capitalist system and become the actual controllers of their own industrial and social destiny.[3]

While SDP 'old guard' were committed to revolutionary transformation of society, they conceived of this as a political revolution through Parliament by an elected socialist party that would capture the existing machinery of government as the means to obtain ownership and control of the means of production and distribution and usher in socialism. They argued that, while the failure of the Labour Party to 'make good' caused many workers 'to despair of the political movement, and to declare that political action, so far as the working classes are concerned, is played out', they failed to recognise that the cause of failure was the refusal 'to adopt a policy and programme based upon socialist principles … and not in political action generally as a means at the disposal of the working class'.[4]

By contrast, the SDP leaders insisted, trade unions were merely subsidiary organs for securing limited and temporary gains for workers from within the existing capitalist system, with any concessions that might be gained by strike action far outweighed by the hardship caused to strikers and their families.[5] Despite this stance, once strikes broke out the party was prepared to support them. Thus, in his book *Further Reminiscences*, Hyndman commented:

> Can anything be imagined more foolish, more harmful, in the widest sense of the word, unsocial, than a strike? A number of men … throw down their tools, refuse to go into the factory, declare they will not descend into the mines, decline to work the railway or the ships, and half starve themselves and the persons dependent upon them, in the hope of compelling those who own these various forms of private or company property to give way to their demands. It is a desperate method of fighting …
>
> I have never yet advocated a strike … I have never known what I should call a successful strike.[6]

A similar position was adopted even by Harry Quelch, secretary of the London Trades Council and author of the foreword to Ben Tillett's *History of*

3. *Justice*, 13 May 1911. Mann's membership of the SDP coincided almost exactly with the period during which he edited the eleven monthly issues of *Industrial Syndicalist* which were issued between July 1910 and May 1911.
4. Quelch (1911: 9–10).
5. Ibid.: 7; Kendall (1969: 29); Holton (1973a: 151).
6. Hyndman (1912: 427–8).

the London Transport Workers' Strike, 1911, who explained the party's attitude to the 1912 national miners' strike:

> ... we Socialists have never advocated strikes. We have always maintained that the working class should jealously guard the right and the power to strike ... and we have always given every possible support to any body of workers who have been on strike. But ... had the workers generally used such political power as they have possessed since the last great coal strike in 1893 to capture the political machine, instead of steadily voting their masters into control, the present strike and those of last year would have been absolutely unnecessary. That is the all-important lesson which this series of strikes should have taught the workers – industrial organisation, by all means; industrial action, certainly, in order to defend what you may have, or to win some better conditions – but let your political organisation and political action keep pace with and reflect your industrial organisation and action; for without that the latter must be largely ineffectual and futile.[7]

Likewise, the party's paper *Justice* under Quelch's editorship condemned the syndicalists' advocacy of a general strike as the means to overthrow capitalism and institute workers' control as doomed to failure:

> The strike is not our only weapon. The strike is not our best weapon – not by any means. The vote, properly used, is a far better weapon for obtaining redress of grievances – and is the only way, so far as we can see, by which we can get our masters off our backs. It is as well we should understand and agree on that; as the power of the strike is being unduly magnified just now, and many imagine all things are possible for, say, a 'general strike', forgetting the power in the hands of our lords and governors to enrol special constables to baton their neighbours and to use soldiers to shoot, stab, and whiff with grape-shot, and play the blackleg along with the men in blue. That power rests on the vote, and till that power is wrested from them a general strike, however well organised, would be a murderous failure.[8]

At the same time, instead of throwing themselves wholesale behind rank-and-file workers thrown into battle with their employers, Hyndman argued the party should ally itself with trade union leaders like Ben Tillett and Will Thorne who had 'never advocated a strike in their lives. Their action has invariably been in the direction of moderation.' It was the 'rank and file ...

7. *British Socialist*, 15 March 1912.
8. *Justice*, 2 September 1911.

who were the real organisers and fomenters of strikes', and socialists had to stand alongside the trade union leaders in opposing their misguided militancy.[9]

Ironically the SDF/SDP's 'gradualist Marxism',[10] with its strategic orientation towards a parliamentary transition to socialism, appeared in many respects very similar to the political approach advocated by ILP leaders. And even though many individual trade union members within its ranks were prominent in strikes and organising solidarity activity, the party's overall political approach handicapped its ability to provide practical and coordinated leadership to industrial struggles on a national scale. But as the Labour Revolt reached its zenith in 1911, a growing minority of rank-and-file SDP members began to argue that the party's emphasis on the primacy of political action was inadequate, neglecting the role of strike action in revolutionary strategy. Some leading union activists, including A.A. Purcell from Salford, and A.G. Tufton and Guy Bowman from Walthamstow, had even become 'willing advocates' for syndicalism and members of the ISEL.

Moreover, amidst the growing dissatisfaction with the perceived ineffectualness of Labour Party and ILP leaders amongst the left generally, the formation of a unified British Socialist Party (BSP) – which brought together the SDP with a sizeable number of left-wing ILP branches, Clarion Clubs and local independent Socialist Societies under the banner of 'Socialist Unity' – opened up the possibility of a new approach. Certainly the newly formed organisation had the critical mass to become a serious alternative pole of attraction to political Labourism, and at the same time, under the impact of the Labour Revolt, to reconsider the interplay between political and industrial action as the central means of revolutionary socialist advance. Yet manoeuvring by the SDP leadership meant it rapidly developed into no more than the old SDF/SDP with a new name.

The British Socialist Party's founding conference in May 1912 was held in the wake of the national miners' strike, and discussed what relationship it should have with the industrial organisations of the working class. An executive committee resolution welcomed the growing discontent, but stated: 'The main function of the Socialist Party, however, is the organisation of an independent political party of the working class, aiming at the conquest of political power by that class, as the political expression of the working-class movement, and as a means to its final emancipation'

A minority 'syndicalist' wing, led by executive committee members Leonard Hall, George Simpson (who became northern organiser of the ISEL)

---

9. Hyndman (1912: 158).
10. Campbell (2000: 134).

and Russell Smart, moved an amendment 'to link up the new Party with the new industrial movement ... to declare identity with the industrial revolt, and turn it to socialist aims', with '[i]ndustrial action and political action ... a case of plus not versus'. But Quelch attacked these conceptions, insisting that the main function of the new party was not to organise and conduct industrial operations, but to organise the working class politically, and the amendment was defeated.[11]

Nonetheless, BSP branches and members across London were actively involved in organising meetings, collecting funds and using their local premises to feed the children of the 1912 transport strikers.[12] At the same time, a campaign to popularise syndicalism inside the party was promoted by the ISEL and Mann (following his resignation from the SDP in 1911). A front-page article by Mann and an 'Open Letter to Members of the British Socialist Party' were published in the *The Syndicalist*, noting that many ISEL members were members of the bodies that fused together to constitute the BSP, and calling on the younger, more militant members of the party who supported industrial solidarity and direct action to form an 'Advance Guard' to get rid of the 'Old Guard' leaders.[13]

Internal conflict intensified throughout 1912 between the orthodox 'political socialists' and those rank-and-file BSP members who were sympathetic to the syndicalist emphasis on industrial struggle (but did not entirely reject political activity to achieve change through Parliament). BSP branches were fairly evenly divided in their attitude towards syndicalism.

At one extreme were those who quickly declared support for the majority 'political' wing of the BSP executive committee in denouncing syndicalist perspectives, led by SDP stalwarts like Hyndman and Quelch; in the middle of the spectrum were those branches which took a more neutral position and who invited ISEL speakers, including Mann, Bowman and E.J.B. Allen, to speak to them and explain the syndicalist case; at the other end of the spectrum were those BSP branches which actively supported syndicalism in defiance of the executive committee majority, such as the Birmingham branch under the leadership of Leonard Hall, and the Bristol branch which renamed itself 'Bristol West Syndicalist BSP'. A large section of the BSP was committed to syndicalism with about 25 per cent strongly committed to syndicalism, and another 25 per cent giving it favourable consideration.[14]

11. BSP First Annual Conference Report, Manchester, 25–27 May 1912, pp. 15–16; Kendall (1969: 42–3).
12. *The Socialist Record*, July 1912.
13. *The Syndicalist*, November 1912.
14. Holton (1973a: 470–5).

This syndicalist wing attempted to counteract the party leadership's assaults on their position, with George Simpson pointing out that they were not anti-parliamentarian:

> Industrial and political action must be complementary of each other, for while it is essential to organise the workers into one great industrial organisation, or federation of organisations, it is just as essential that they should be organised into one great revolutionary political party in order that the workers may control the legislative and administrative machinery of this country. Such a party is the British Socialist Party.[15]

Theodore Rothstein advocated a synthesis of political and industrial action, arguing that the strike wave was developing class consciousness: 'It is a revolution in the psychology of the working class' which made it a receptive field for political agitation.

> Never mind that we are a political party and that our object is to fight on behalf of the working class politically; by lending our assistance to the working class in its economic fight ... we shall be helping to widen the area and deepen the contents of the class war and thereby accelerate its transformation into a political movement.[16]

Ben Tillett, following the experience of the defeat of the 1912 London transport strike, wrote an article titled 'Political and Industrial Action' in which he argued trade unionists were 'realising new economic truths' and were 'seeing in trade unionism a wider outlook and greater force than they had hitherto imagined'. He criticised the Parliamentary Labour Party for 'claiming political action can do the work they know to be the work of economic action'. He stated that 'we have no wish to decry political action, but we are trying to glorify economic action', adding that

> the Socialists must make the trade union organisations out and out Socialistic; the organisation of the workers as trade unionists is an economic organisation, and we must use the forces behind the machinery of trade unionism to fight the employer and capitalists. The real fight is an economic one, and not a political one ... we want Revolutionary Socialists to adhere steadfastly to economic facts ... to join in a great movement against capitalism, pledged to the abolition of the wage system.[17]

---

15. *Justice*, 29 June 1912.
16. Ibid., 3 August 1912.
17. Ibid., 21 September 1912.

There was also a significant development in the revolutionary Marxist John Maclean's politics in Scotland. While initially in keeping with the SDF/SDP leadership's pessimism about the role of unions and the value of strikes, his involvement in the 1907 Belfast dock strike, 1910 Neilston textile and 1910–11 South Wales miners' strikes, and 1911 Clydebank Singer strike resulted in a dramatic shift in attitude, as he witnessed the politicising effect of major industrial struggles on workers. Strikes were important in that they revealed the 'true' nature of the capitalist system to workers and provided illustrations of 'the real class war that are more effective than all the theory we might fire at our benighted class from now 'till doomsday. Fighting leads to new facts, thus to our new theory and hence to revolution.'[18] Through subsequent involvement in the national miners' strike, Maclean was drawn even more towards workers' struggles as a crucial weapon in the fight for socialism and recognition of the need to relate to them politically. While continuing to argue for the primacy of politics over industrial struggle, he broke from the party leadership's dismissive attitude towards unions and strikes and their view that socialism could only come through Parliament.[19]

Yet despite such developments, the inevitable split in the BSP eventually took place in the autumn of 1912 when the majority 'political' wing of the executive published a manifesto on 'Political Action and Direct Action' which declared 'that political action is the principal function of the party' and denounced syndicalism as the obsolete 'tactics of the Levellers and Luddites'.[20] *Justice* opened fire on 'the anarchistic Syndicalists who, unable to obtain a foothold in industrial organisations, fasten on to the political movement only to disrupt it'.[21] The BSP was torn apart, with the resignation of the syndicalist-influenced members of the executive committee, and with it, the attempt to break new ground by creating a unified socialist party. The initial enormous boost in the party's membership was replaced by a haemorrhage of members over subsequent months, some of whom gravitated towards the *Daily Herald* League.[22]

At the party's 1913 conference Peter Petroff, a Russian émigré socialist exile, successfully moved a resolution declaring: '... the proper function of the British Socialist Party is to lead the working class in its economic and political struggle', with an instruction to the executive 'to organise the trade union members of the BSP for systematic work and Socialist propaganda

18. Ibid., 24 February 1912.
19. Ripley and McHugh (1989: 52–60); Sherry (2014: 33–7).
20. *Daily Herald*, 31 October 1912.
21. *Justice*, 30 November 1912.
22. Holton (1973a: 469).

inside the trade unions', and calling upon members to strive for the amalgamation and federation of existing sectional unions in each industry.[23]

Another resolution carried stated:

> That the policy of the British Socialist Party towards the so-called purely industrial organisations is not one of mere sympathy and support, but rather of active participation in, both as individual members and as an organisation, the struggles of the trade unions against capitalism, and vigorous support to the growing movement that is surely transforming them from mere reformist wage-raising instruments into revolutionary Socialist unions having for their object the emancipation of the wage earner.[24]

But the leadership's continuing views on industrial organisation and strike action as secondary matters, and dismissive approach to trade unions in the struggle for socialism, impeded the party's ability to capitalise on the mass upsurge of industrial militancy and the widespread antipathy to trade union and Labour Party leaders that existed.

During the Dublin lockout the BSP organised solidarity meetings across the country, but *Justice* condemned Larkin's manifesto appealing for sympathetic action and gave its full support to TUC leaders' attempts to strike a compromise settlement.[25] By contrast, the *Daily Herald* championed unofficial strikes by railwaymen under the headline 'Hurrah for the Rebels', and criticised union leaders who were half-hearted in their support of the Dublin workers. On 6 December 1913 (three days before the special TUC conference) *Justice* published a major article by John Stokes, chair of the London Trades Council, which launched a sustained attack on unofficial action in support of the Dublin workers by 'new inexperienced trade unionists ... against official advice' for 'drag[ging] whole industries into disastrous disputes'. And on 9 December the party came down decisively on the side of trade union officialdom against Larkin.[26]

Socialist Labour Party

Unlike the BSP, the Socialist Labour Party attached enormous importance to workers' struggles at the point of production and declared itself against

23. BSP Second Annual Conference Report, Blackpool, 10–12 May 1913, p, 19.
24. Ibid.
25. Newsinger (2013b: 54).
26. Ibid.: 56, 58.

the existing system of 'capitalist parliamentary democracy'.[27] But while the SLP's partly Marxist and partly syndicalist-inspired attempt to connect revolutionary politics with workplace conflict involved a serious orientation on industry both ideologically and practically, it was also handicapped by severe limitations. It was fervently opposed to existing trade unions on the grounds that, headed by 'class collaborationist' leaders and based on an 'identity of interest between Capital and Labour', they propped up the capitalist order and were impossible to convert to socialism by a 'boring from within' strategy.[28] Yet its alternative 'dual unionist' approach, of attempting to construct completely new, doctrinally pure, revolutionary industrial unions proved to be a sectarian non-starter, apart from some momentary success in the Singer factory.

While the BSP emphasised *political action* to the dismissal of the industrial struggle, the SLP emphasised *industrial struggle* to the relegation of politics. It argued that the need for political differences between workers should be subordinated into the economic need for militant industrial unionism that overcomes sectional and political divisions and brings a new political clarity. As James Connolly (a leading member between 1903 and1907) explained: 'As political parties are the reflex of economic conditions, it follows that industrial unity once established will create the political unity of the working class. Political division is born of industrial division. I feel that we cannot too strongly insist upon this point.'[29]

At the same time, organising through industrial unionism was viewed as performing an ever-higher function of encroaching gradually on the powers of management at the workplace until employers' ownership and prerogatives became mere formalities. In the process:

> ... they who are engaged in building industrial organisations for the practical purposes of today are at the same time preparing the framework for the society of the future ...
>
> Every fresh shop or factory organised under its banner [of industrial unionism] is a fort wrenched from control of the capitalist class and manned with the soldiers of the Revolution ... On the day ... [we] proclaim the Workers' Republic, these shops and factories will be taken charge of by the workers there employed ... the new society will spring into existence ready equipped to perform all the useful functions of its predecessor.[30]

27. *The Socialist*, September 1911.
28. Kendall (1969: 67–9); Macfarlane (1966: 26–7); Challinor (1977: 87–105).
29. Connolly (1974a: 268).
30. Ibid.

In other words, the framework of the future industrial republic could be built up inside the shell of capitalism. Political issues receded into the background: 'All actions of our class at the ballot box are in the nature of mere preliminary skirmishes ... the conquest of political power by the working class waits upon the conquest of economic power and must function through the economic organisation.' From this perspective, what to others seemed merely an industrial struggle appeared differently:

> The power of this idea to transform the dry detail work of trade union organisation into the constructive work of revolutionary socialism, and thus to make of the unimaginative trade unionist a potent factor in the launching of a new system of society cannot be overestimated. It invests the sordid details of the daily incidents of the class struggle with a new and beautiful meaning, and presents them in their true light as skirmishes between the two opposing armies of light and darkness.[31]

The assumption was that if workers organised in industrial unions, then class consciousness would permeate upwards; spontaneous industrial struggle would automatically produce the unity of the working class and in the process transform workers' conceptions in a revolutionary direction. But while collective workers' struggles and industrial unionism *could* potentially show workers the need to unite against not just individual employers but the employing class as a whole, and could begin to break down sectional divisions, such struggles did not *automatically* overcome the ideological and political divisions inside the working class (for example, between competing strategies for reform or revolution), nor did they necessarily clarify the political role of the state (in not only repressing individual strikes but as the ultimate instrument of defence for the capitalist system). The link between industrial militancy and political generalisation still needed to be consciously drawn out and fought for by linking socialist politics with an attempt to provide practical leadership to day-to-day workplace struggles. The SLP's doctrinaire and sectarian approach undermined this process.

Industrial Syndicalist Education League

Compared with the 'political socialists' of both the ILP and BSP, and even to some extent with the SLP's distinct approach, the Industrial Syndicalist Education League had a rather different conception of the dynamics of working-class struggle, albeit with some parallels to the SLP. As we have previously

31. Ibid: 275.

noted, on the basis of a 'boring from within' strategy, Tom Mann repeatedly called for militant trade unionism, solidarity action and the reconstruction of existing unions through their amalgamation into industrial unions on revolutionary lines. To those who were attracted to the syndicalist project of the ISEL, parliamentary democracy and working for reforms through the state were rejected as dead ends.

Instead of the statist conception of socialism introduced *from above*, syndicalists insisted that society's revolutionary transformation necessarily had to come *from below*, the product of workers' own self-activity and self-organisation at the point of production. The road to the liberation of the working class lay through an intensification of the industrial struggle, eventually culminating in a revolutionary general strike that would lead to the overthrow of the capitalist system and its replacement by workers' control of industry and society.[32] The industrial unions would have a double function – as an organ of struggle against the employers on the frontline of the class struggle under the capitalist system and as an organ of economic and industrial administration after its overthrow.

Syndicalist hostility to the perceived conservatism and bureaucracy of trade union and Labour Party leaders encouraged an emphasis on the collective 'direct action' of workers on the *economic* terrain, with the subordination of all political action to the industrial struggle. In some respects, in their dismissal of 'political action' the ISEL were basically rejecting what they saw as the dead end of electoral and parliamentary politics advocated by labour movement leaders. *Industrial Syndicalist* declared:

> Parliamentary Action is secondary in importance to Industrial Action; it is Industrial Action alone that makes Political Action effective; but, with or without Parliamentary Action, industrial solidarity will ensure economic freedom, and therefore the abolition of capitalism and all its accompanying poverty and misery.[33]

This did not preclude some collaboration between syndicalists and members of the BSP, and syndicalists were inescapably 'political' in their commitment to the working-class movement's revolutionary overthrow of the capitalist economic and political system and its replacement by a collectivist society based on workers' control. However, like the SLP, they argued that the solution to all political problems could be found in the workplace

32. *The Syndicalist*, December 1912.
33. *Industrial Syndicalist*, February 1911.

where political differences were subordinated into the economic need for militant and class-wide forms of industrial unionism. A.G. Tufton explained:

> Politics, like religion, was a matter for the persons themselves; and it was of no concern to the workers whether other workers were Liberals or Conservatives. All that was necessary for workers was to understand the solidarity of their class.[34]

This subordination of ideological and political questions meant that during the 1911 Liverpool transport strike political and religious sectarianism between Catholic and Protestant workers was not explicitly challenged. As Tom Mann argued, it was necessary to concentrate on trade unionism and industrial struggle on purely non-political lines: 'We must ... avoid dealing with religion and politic[s] as we did during the industrial campaign.'[35] But while the strike clearly demonstrated the power of a mass united action, and the possibility of undermining existing sectarian divisions to some extent, the unwillingness to confront religious and political issues was counterproductive in a city like Liverpool, where trade union leaders were not politically neutral, the issue of a proposed Home Rule Bill could not be skated over, and there was a layer of hostile working-class organisations for whom the question of Ireland was absolutely central. It effectively kowtowed to existing prejudice and left Liverpool politics unhindered in the hands of 'Tory Democracy', the Irish Nationalists and right-wing Labour Party and trade union leaders for lack of a political alternative.[36]

Another consequence of focusing attention virtually exclusively on the point of production and industrial struggles of workers, with the subordination of wider political issues, was the dismissive stance adopted towards the women's campaign for the franchise. In December 1913 *The Syndicalist and Amalgamation News*, under Guy Bowman's helm, bemoaned the way the 'magnificent heroism' of the suffrage campaign should be thrown away on 'so worthless a cause' since when women won the vote they would find it of no more use to them than it was 'to us men', accomplishing 'nothing' towards the overthrow of capitalism and the wage system.[37]

At the same time, notwithstanding its rejection in principle of the politics of conciliation and reformism propagated by trade union and Labour Party leaders, syndicalism's primary emphasis on the *industrial* unionism and

34. Ibid., December 1910.
35. *Transport Worker*, November 1911.
36. Smith (1984: 40–2).
37. *The Syndicalist and Amalgamation News*, December 1913.

struggle meant that in practice it effectively failed to provide a consistent revolutionary *political* and *organisational* alternative. As already mentioned, as an essentially educational and propagandist body the ISEL did not really develop a distinct centralised, national combat organisation or leadership that was capable of practically intervening in the strike wave (beyond merely as a loose network of individual supporters).

One which was capable of forging a link between union militants and political activists across the various groups to act as a solidarity network for disputes, offering an analysis of the tactics adopted within individual strikes and advocating proposals for the best way to win, attempting to link up different struggles into a national class-wide movement against employers and government, encouraging and coordinating workplace-based rank-and-file organisation and leadership both within/across unions. One which could both pressure and mobilise action independently of officialdom where that became necessary, fighting to raise the general level of political consciousness and action of those they influenced, linking the immediate aspirations of workers to the central political aim of the need to overthrow the system as a whole, and providing a revolutionary political and organisational alternative to the trade union and Labour Party leaders.[38]

Summation

While the radical left (in a context of the rising confidence, strength and power of the strike movement and widespread political generalisation) made significant headway during the period of 1910–14, its influence was circumscribed by its tendency to *reflect* rather than *overcome* traditional divisions between politics and economics inside the working-class movement. The syndicalists' preoccupation with the industrial struggle to the subordination, if not outright dismissal, of broader political questions, meant in practice it represented the mirror image of the BSP's (and ILP and Labour Party's) primary focus on socialist propaganda and political organisation and action. Some individual figures within the radical left groups did explicitly grapple with the tactical pathway by which the two could be fused, but such viewpoints did not become the predominant stance.

38. A related limitation of syndicalism's dismissal of political action was that it did not explicitly address the problem of how a revolutionary general strike to establish workers' control would overcome the state's monopoly of armed force in defence of the capitalist economic and social order. It also did not consider the question of the conquest of political power, the need for a political revolution as well as an economic one. Darlington (2013b: 247–60).

This meant the most militant and class-conscious workers, whose practical experience had driven them to challenge trade union officialdom and political Labourism, were left without an effective political body that crystalised its left-wing *ideas* into forms of revolutionary *organisation* and *leadership* that could intervene in industrial struggles and provide practical direction to the strike movement and develop the process of political radicalisation amongst workers.

The independent *Daily Herald*'s role was highly significant in routinely supporting strikes and attacking labour movement leaders who opposed them, as well as embracing and promoting a wide range of social and political causes (including Irish Home Rule and female suffrage). But while it brought together 'rebel' supporters from the different left groups as well as many who were unaffiliated (embracing syndicalists, independent socialists, supporters of Guild socialists and radical Christian socialists), the paper lacked a unified revolutionary ideological and political stance and well-developed organisational means to generalise and provide leadership to workers' struggles.

As a consequence, the leadership vacuum was filled by default by trade union and Labour Party leaders, whose conciliatory and parliamentary reformist strategy of working within the system and accommodating to it ultimately predominated, notwithstanding considerable challenge.

PART IV

Aftermath

13

Dénouement, Sequel and Political Legacy

Events during the 'Edwardian Age' took place against a background of growing international tension. By the early part of 1914 the labour movement became increasingly aware that war might not be far over the horizon. The Liberal government, already facing the contentious issues of Irish Home Rule and women's suffrage, feared that the already high level of strike action would be exacerbated by a fresh wave of mass workers' struggles. But on 4 August, with what George Dangerfield termed the 'providential intervention of a world war',[1] such challenges suddenly appeared to be completely overturned by the jingoism and patriotic frenzy that gripped the country as 750,000 workers enlisted into the armed forces in the first eight weeks and a further million in the next eight months.

Like other European labour and socialist parties affiliated to the Second International, the Labour Party had pledged itself to an internationalist position of resisting, by all possible means, any outbreak of war which could lead to the workers of different countries killing each other, and if war should nonetheless break out, to utilise the economic and political crisis created to 'rouse the populace and to hasten the fall of capitalist domination'. But once the Liberal government declared Britain to be at war, the majority of the Parliamentary Labour Party adopted a policy of full support for the war effort, encouraging trade unionists to pull together in the 'national interest'.

At the same time, virtually every trade union executive declared an embargo on all current and pending pay claims, and committed themselves to an 'Industrial Truce' and suspension of all strikes for the duration of the war. The TUC's Parliamentary Committee encouraged enlistment and published a joint manifesto with the Labour Party claiming a German victory would mean 'the death of democracy'.[2] With miners, engineering workers, shipbuilding workers and other rushing en masse to the recruiting stations,

1. Dangerfield ([1935] 1977: 69).
2. Pratten (1975: 317).

the labour movement leaders 'had caught the war mood. They did not care to argue.'[3]

Within this changed context, there was an immediate collapse in the level of strike action as employers and workers agreed to submerge their differences and work together to resolve conflicts. Askwith recalled: 'Disputes melted away as fast as the hours of the day, and often the night, gave time for the hearing of difficulties' as he travelled up and down the county to bring about settlements.[4] While on 4 August there were 100 strikes in existence, by the end of the month this had fallen to only 20, and whereas during the first seven months of 1914, 308,000 workers had taken strike action, in the last five months of the year it was a mere 18,000 (Table 5). According to the official *History of the Ministry of Munitions*, the first six months of the conflict saw 'a time of peace in the labour world such as had never existed before'.[5] Keir Hardie, one of the few Labour leaders to oppose the war, was shouted down when he tried to speak at a meeting in Aberdare on 6 August. *The Times* celebrated the way:

> The class war of Socialism and the international peace movement associated with it have evaporated into words and are in the process of collapsing altogether ...
>
> The spectacle we are witnessing furnishes convincing proof that the tie of nationality is still incomparably stronger than that of class ... With one accord employers and employed have called a truce to the stubborn and widespread conflicts which were being waged in continuance of the industrial warfare that has signalled the last four years.[6]

While it came as no surprise that moderate trade union leaders like J.H. Thomas of the railwaymen and Herbert Smith of the miners became 'recruiting sergeants' for the war effort, even leaders like Ben Tillett and 'Captain' Tupper of the seamen's union toured the country pouring out atrocity stories against the Germans and encouraging enlistment.[7]

However, the war did not completely sweep away all pre-war conflicts of interest between workers and employers. Although nationalist enthusiasm was by far the most powerful impulse initially amongst the mass of workers, such patriotic fervour co-existed with continuing hostility to employers, not

3. Cole (1948b: 21).
4. Askwith [1920] (1974: 358).
5. Cited in Waites (1987: 186).
6. *The Times*, 7 and 10 August 1914.
7. Tupper (1938: 105–6); Lawson (1948: 128); Fuller (1933); Schneer (1982).

least over the deterioration of shopfloor conditions of employment. And after only one or two years of war, with inflation growing steadily and reducing real wages, widescale profiteering by employers, and war weariness at the sheer extent of casualties on the front, there was an increase in the strength of class consciousness and willingness of different sections of workers to engage in industrial struggle.

Remarkably, during 1917 and 1918, strike activity reached roughly half the levels of the 1910–14 Labour Revolt, but in extraordinary wartime conditions during which not only were labour movement leaders pledged to industrial peace, but strike action was illegal in many industries. Such industrial militancy was in defiance of both trade union officials and the state, and often led by small but active groupings of anti-war radical left trade union activists, many of whom had cut their teeth during the pre-war Labour Revolt and who, although initially isolated amidst the patriotic fervour gripping the country, were gradually able to exert significant influence.

The ILP refused to support the war, instead issuing a manifesto signed by Hardie, MacDonald, Snowden and James Maxton that declared 'Long Live International Socialism', albeit the party's anti-war position was essentially pacifist and focused on individual resistance rather than a collective defence of terms and conditions of employment. Inside the BSP fervent arguments for a massive increase in the British defence budget to defeat Germany's threat to British interests had been advanced by Hyndman since 1909, and from August 1914 Hyndman and the majority on the party's executive supported the war effort. But this stance had met strong opposition from Theodore Rothstein, John MacLean and growing numbers of members, eventually leading to the removal of Hyndman from the leadership and a radical shift in policy towards an anti-war position of international working-class solidarity.[8]

From the outset the tiny SLP also took a firm stance of working-class internationalism and propagandised for turning the capitalist war into a socialist revolution.[9] Sylvia Pankhurst, unlike those suffragettes who followed her mother and sister's jingoist support for the war and abandonment of the suffrage campaign, continued to campaign for votes for women and speak out against the war on pacifist and socialist platforms.[10] And most syndicalist activists, despite their organisational disintegration, opposed the 'capitalist' and 'imperialist' war,[11] although Mann concentrated on demands for the

8. Crick (1994: 25); Klugmann (1968: 16).
9. Challinor (1977: 125–6).
10. Connelly (2013: 69–72); Holmes (2020: 429).
11. White (1991: 191–3).

defence of workers' conditions and did not agitate to stop the war or join the active anti-war opposition.[12]

The most important and growing arena of strike activity occurred in the engineering industry arising from the enormous rapid changes due to the war, with strikes led by shop stewards on Clydeside in February 1915, Sheffield in November 1916 and an England-wide strike by 200,000 engineers in May 1917, as well as a threatened national strike against the government's introduction of military conscription of engineers in January 1918. Emerging during the wartime struggles, a Clyde Workers' Committee that brought together shop stewards' representatives from numerous workplaces provided a model for other Workers' Committees in engineering centres across the country and from which a powerful national Shop Stewards' and Workers' Committee Movement developed that was committed to the revolutionary goals of workers' control of production and the abolition of capitalism, led by a number of members of the SLP, BSP, ISEL and engineering Amalgamation Committee Movement, and influenced by syndicalist ideas.[13] Significantly, their leadership role of rank-and-file militancy led the SLP to abandon its previous attachment to 'dual unionism' and the BSP to focus on supporting workers' industrial struggles.

But although they rejected the pro-war policies of the trade union and Labour Party leadership, the shop stewards' leaders did not offer an alternative policy of their own. Unlike the Russian Bolsheviks, they refused to agitate *politically* against the war on the shopfloor, albeit from a minority position. Instead, they argued the issue was beyond Workers' Committees' bounds and that they should limit themselves to concerns over wages and conditions. They felt that maximum unity to win militant action on immediate industrial issues was more important than the broader, more hotly disputed political questions of the war which threatened to puncture such unity, and they remained satisfied to act merely as delegated representatives of industrial discontent.

This approach was highlighted in sharp relief by the publication of J.T. Murphy's pamphlet *The Workers' Committee*, the chief theoretical statement to emerge from the National Administrative Council of the shop stewards' movement, which sold 150,000 copies.[14] Despite being written in 1917, the pamphlet did not mention the war and the political issues it raised. Instead, it reduced the immense economic and political problems that lay behind the growth of the Workers' Committees to the level of industrial organisa-

12. Tsuzuki (1991: 178); Kirk (2017: 237–42).
13. Gallacher and Campbell ([1919] 1972); Pribicevic (1959); Hinton (1973).
14. Murphy ([1917] 1972).

tion. Even those shop stewards' leaders who were members of the Socialist Labour Party and British Socialist Party acted no differently. While Murphy, Arthur MacManus and others were opposed to the war, they made no attempt to propagate their views amongst the rank-and-file in the factories (many of whom were, initially at least, pro-war) for fear of losing support, and remained content to merely defend workers against the threats to their organisation brought about by the effects of the war.[15]

Yet in many respects every issue that workers faced during the period 1914–18, and every industrial dispute over wages and conditions of work, were inherently profoundly political, since they all arose directly as a result of the government's determination to win outright victory in the war. As a consequence, the extreme political circumstances of the war, and the abject failure of the trade union and Labour Party leaders to defend workers in the face of attacks by employers and the state, opened possibilities for a *class*-wide agitation for militant trade unionism that fused immediate economic issues with a political challenge to the war. In the event, relying simply on the industrial struggle had the effect of handing the political initiative to the 'patriotic' reformist labour movement leadership, isolating the movement to the engineering industry and limiting its overall potential.[16]

With the end of the war there was a renewed strike wave that dwarfed the 1910–14 period (Table 1), with a large-scale Glasgow engineering strike and a national railway strike in 1919, national miners' strike in 1920, Metropolitan Police strikes in 1918 and 1919, and army munities in 1918 and 1919[17] But crucially experience from the wartime engineering struggles and development of a national shop stewards' movement, as well as immediate post-war struggles, encouraged a reconsideration of socialist strategy, tactics and organisation which led to a marked advance on the pre-war radical left's trade union and political theory and practice in three important ways.[18] First, the shop stewards' leaders developed the theory of independent rank-and-file organisation that could operate both *within* and *outside* official union structures to counteract full-time officials' influence. Based on the experience of the workshop committees of shop stewards that represented all workers (irrespective of craft, grade or trade union affiliation) and linked to local Workers' Committees (with aspirations to extend from engineering to the rest of industry), there was the conception of an all-encompassing class organisa-

15. Gluckstein (1985: 71); Darlington (1998: 42–3).
16. Gluckstein (1985: 59–89); Cliff and Gluckstein (1986: 63–9); Darlington (2013b: 242–3).
17. Rosenberg (1987); MacAskill (2019).
18. Hinton (1973: 275–337); Gluckstein (1985: 59–89); Darlington (1998: 30–58).

tion on a national scale that would be capable of mobilising and organising militant sections of the rank-and-file to take strike action independently of union officials where that became necessary through lack of support. Unlike the strategy of pre-war syndicalism – which had either sought to replace existing unions with entirely new revolutionary ones, or reconstruct them via amalgamation into new industrial unions – there was the fusion of both these elements into a novel synthesis that advocated a rank-and-file movement which walked on two legs, *official* and *unofficial*.

Second, after the 1917 Bolshevik Revolution in Russia, the shop stewards' and radical left leaders increasingly called for the revolutionary overthrow of capitalism, and saw the Workers' Committees as embryonic soviets or workers' councils on the Russian model that could become the economic and political nucleus of a future workers' state. While the development of this idea of soviet power owed a great deal to the Russian Revolution, it was also influenced by their practical British experience. This identification of the soviet as the agency of working-class power and socialism marked a decisive break with both pre-war syndicalist and 'political socialist' (ILP and BSP) notions that political change would occur either through (reconstructed) trade unions or Parliament.

Third, there was the tentative discovery of the need for a new relationship between the radical left and the working-class movement. No one at the time grasped the Bolshevik doctrine of a revolutionary vanguard party that aimed to overcome the unevenness of organisation and fragmentation of political consciousness by systematically intervening in rank-and-file workers' struggles and seeking to generalise each particular battle between capital and labour with the class struggle to overthrow capitalist state power. But the shop stewards' leaders and the radical left generally in Britain were not alone in this; it was part of the limitation of the bulk of the pre-1917 revolutionary left.

Even so, the wartime struggles had forced many within the British radical left to reconsider the separation between socialist politics and industrial militancy, pointing towards a new sort of revolutionary practice that explicitly attempted to link the two, with the need to develop a new type of leadership and organisation. Undoubtedly the Bolshevik Revolution and subsequent role of the Third (Communist) International (formed in Moscow in March 1919 by the leaders of the Russian Communist Party with the specific aim of establishing Communist Parties across the world and encouraging workers' revolutions) acted as crucial catalysts to cause these elements to fuse together and to complete the process with the formation in 1920 of the Communist Party of Great Britain (CPGB). This 'party of a new type' brought together members from the BSP, a 'Communist Unity Group' within the SLP, National Shop Stewards' and Workers' Committees Movement, South Wales Socialist

Society (originating from members of the Plebs League and Unofficial Reform Committee who had established a Rhondda Socialist Society, which in 1919 became the South Wales Socialist Society), Guild Communist Group, and left-wing members of the ILP and *Daily Herald* Leagues. Some of the leading militants of the pre-war and wartime struggles immediately joined up, including Tom Mann, Jack Tanner, J.T. Murphy, Tom Bell, William Paul, Arthur MacManus and Willie Gallacher.[19] But notwithstanding its external stimulus, the genesis and training ground of such a political development had undoubtedly been forged domestically, and not only through the experience of the wartime and immediate post-war struggles but also by the preceding 1910–14 Labour Revolt.

To conclude, it is true that the Labour Revolt was by no means unique by comparison with other countries internationally during the period 1910–14, with many countries, including Italy, Spain, America, Australia and Russia, racked with strikes and civil unrest.[20] And by comparison with other historical strike waves in Britain, even though the Labour Revolt reached much higher levels of strike activity than in 1888–91 it was considerably lower than during 1919–21 when Britain saw an even more heightened phase of strikes and class confrontation. Caused largely by the unprecedented and dramatic unbottling of years of frustration built up during the war and the dashed hopes and expectations after the end of the war, as well as the ripple effect of the Russian revolution internationally, 1919 appeared to be 'closer to a workers' revolution than ever before or since'.[21] However, the pre-war Labour Revolt, despite the absence of such a similar exceptional context, extended over a much longer period than similar strike waves in other countries at the same time and other British strikes waves before and immediately afterwards. It also had some very distinctive militant features that were not replicated, or at least not quite in the same intense and wide-ranging fashion, which remain of considerable relevance for contemporary union activists and socialists.

19. For varying political reasons, including opposition to the new party's embrace of Communist International directives that it should seek affiliation to the Labour Party and participate in parliamentary elections for propaganda purposes, 'official' leaders of the SLP, John MacLean, Sylvia Pankhurst and others refused to join.

20. Darlington (2013b: 78–80); Brown (2006: 56–7, 59); Whitson (2013: 29); Boll (1985).

21. Rosenberg (1987: 7).

Biographical Profiles

Ablett, Noah (1883–1935)
Attended Ruskin College, 1907–08; one of the editors of *Plebs* and founders of the Central Labour College, 1909; key figure in the South Wales miners' strike, 1910–11; attended ISEL founding conference, 1910; one of the authors of *The Miners' New Step*, 1912; elected to the Executive Committee of the South Wales Miners' Federation, 1911; activist in Industrial Democracy League, 1913–14.

Allen, E.J.B. (1884–1945)
Gas worker, a former member of the SDF, founder member of SLP, secretary of British Advocates of Industrial Unionism branches; led breakaway in 1908 and founder member of Industrialist League; author of *Revolutionary Unionism*, 1909; became assistant general secretary of the ISEL and 'dual unionist' advocate.

Askwith, George Ranken (1861–1942)
Board of Trade Assistant Secretary, 1907–08; Controller-General of Labour Department, 1909–11; Chief Industrial Commissioner from 1911; intervened in numerous strikes, including transport workers' strike, 1911, Lancashire cotton, miners' and London docks' strikes, 1912, Black Country metal/engineering and Dublin lockout, 1913; and London building workers' and Woolwich Arsenal strikes, 1914; wrote a number of memorandums to the Cabinet on the Labour Revolt.

Asquith, H.H. [Herbert Henry] (1852–1928)
Liberal MP from 1886; Liberal government Home Secretary, 1892–05; Chancellor of the Exchequer, December 1905–April 1908; Prime Minister from 1908; opposed to giving women the vote; intervened to introduce Minimum Wage Bill to end national miners' strike, 1911.

Bell, Tom (1882–1944)
Scottish iron moulder; joined the SDF in 1903, then founder member of SLP in Glasgow and propagandist for industrial unionism; member of the Singer's branch of the IWGB involved in the 1911 strike, before being victimised and sacked.

Bower, Fred (1871–1942)
Liverpool-based member of Operative Stonemasons Union; close friend of Larkin; attended ISEL founding conference, 1910; wrote 'Open Letter to British Soldiers' for the *Irish Worker*, 1911; Industrial Democracy League activist, 1913–14.

Bowman, Guy (unknown c.1897–unknown)
Leading anarcho-syndicalist; visited Paris with Tom Mann to study the CGT; general secretary of the ISEL; editor of *The Syndicalist* from 1912; imprisoned with Mann for 'incitement to mutiny', 1912; abandoned the traditional ISEL policy of trade union reconstruction in favour of 'dual unionism', 1913–14.

Buxton, Sydney (1853–1934)
Liberal MP for Poplar, 1886–1914; Postmaster General, 1905–10; President of Board of Trade, 1910–14; wrote a number of memorandums to the Cabinet on the Labour Revolt.

Churchill, Winston Spencer (1874–1965)
MP from 1900; President of Board of Trade: April 1908–February 1910; Liberal government Home Secretary, February 1910–October 1911; First Lord of the Admiralty from 1911; dispatched troops to intervene in South Wales miners' strike, 1910, and seamen's and dockers' strikes, Liverpool general transport strike and national railway strike, 1911.

Clynes, John Robert (1869–1949)
Textile worker; organiser for National Union of Gasworkers and General Labourers, 1891; MP, North-East Manchester Labour MP from 1906; vice-chairman of Labour Party, 1910; President of (renamed) National Union of Gas and General Workers from 1912.

Connolly, James (1870–1916)
Born in Ireland, lived in Edinburgh, member of the SDF, helped to found SLP; organiser for the ITGWU in Belfast, deputy to Larkin within the union nationally; central figure in Dublin lockout, 1913–14; head of Irish Citizen Army.

Cook, A.J. (Arthur James) (1883–1931)
South Wales miners' leader, member of the ILP, attended the Central Labour College, member of Unofficial Reform Committee; activist in Industrial Democracy League and *Daily Herald* League, 1913–14.

Despard, Charlotte (1844–1939)
SDF member from 1895; member of WSPU (1906–07) and imprisoned twice; broke away from the suffragettes in 1907 to co-found the Women's Freedom League, but remained a convinced socialist and republican.

Gosling, Henry (1861–1930)
Secretary of Amalgamated Society of Watermen and Lightermen from 1893; elected to London County Council, 1904; President of NTWF from 1910; prominent leader in 1911 and 1912 London transport strikes; member of TUC Parliamentary Committee from 1908.

Hall, Leonard (1886–unknown)
Early member of SDF before moving to ILP; founder member of BSP and elected to Provisional Executive Committee at 1911 Unity Conference; elected to BSP Executive in 1912; gravitated towards syndicalism and broke with BSP, later joining the SLP.

Hardie, James Keir (1856–1915)
Secretary, Scottish Miners' Federation, 1886; chairman, Scottish Labour Party, 1888; West Ham South independent labour MP, 1892–05; helped establish the ILP, 1893; re-elected to Parliament for Merthyr Tydfil from 1900; chairman, ILP, 1893–1900; 1913; Parliamentary Labour Party leader, 1906–08; feminist and anti-imperialist.

Henderson, Arthur (1863–1935)
Glasgow-born, moved to Newcastle aged 12; Friendly Society of Iron Founders organiser, 1892–1902, national organiser, 1902–11, and President of (renamed) National Union of Foundry Workers from 1911; Barnard Castle Labour MP from 1903; treasurer of Labour Representation Committee, 1903; member of Executive Committee of Labour Party, 1904–11; chairman of Parliamentary Labour Party; leader of Labour Party, 1908–10, and secretary from 1911.

Hicks, George (1879–1954)
Hampshire-born bricklayer; founding member of Socialist Party of Great Britain, 1904, resigned same year and rejoined 1908–10; national organiser of Operative Bricklayers' Society from 1912; linked with ISEL and its successor the Industrial Democracy League; leading figure in London building workers' lockout, 1914.

Hyndman, Henry (1842–1921)
Founder and leader of the Democratic Federation from 1881, later named SDF; authoritarian and inflexible leadership led to splits in the party in 1903–04; after initial revolutionary enthusiasm of 1880s adopted an essentially parliamentary stance; his views on trade unionism and strikes increasingly challenged after the SDF merged into the BSP in 1911.

Lansbury, George (1859–1941)
Liberal Party member; left to join the SDF from 1889, becoming political secretary in 1897; joined ILP around 1903; supporter of women's suffrage and syndicalism, edited *Daily Herald* from 1913; Bow and Bromley Labour MP, 1910–12.

Larkin, Delia (1878–1949)
Liverpool-born secretary of Irish Women Workers' Union, a women's section of the ITGWU; contributor to 'Women Workers' Column' in the ITGWU's *Irish Worker*; women's suffrage supporter; organiser of food and clothing relief for strikers and their families during the 1913–14 Dublin lockout, with a women's committee of volunteers.

Larkin, James (1874–1947)
Liverpool-born docker; organiser, National Union of Dock Labourers, 1906–08; led Belfast dock strike, 1907, and Dublin carters' strike, 1908; suspended from NUDL, and founded and became general secretary, ITGWU from December 1908; editor of *The Irish Worker*; helped form the Irish Labour Party, 1912; elected to Dublin Corporation, 1912; Dublin lockout leader, 1913–14, with 'Fiery Cross' campaign for solidarity action by the British labour movement.

Lee, H.W. [Henry] (1865–1932)
Secretary of SDF from 1885 and BSP until 1913; became editor of *Justice* in 1913; loyal Hyndman supporter.

Lloyd George, David (1863–1945)
Liberal MP from 1890; President of Board of Trade from December 1905–April 1908; Liberal government Chancellor of Exchequer from 1908; introduced Finance Bill ('People's Budget), 1909; Parliament Act, 1911; intervened to end national railway strike, 1911.

Macarthur, Mary (1880–1921)
President of the Scottish National District Council of the National Union of Shop Assistants and secretary from 1902; general secretary, Women's Trade

Union League, 1903; founder and President of NFWW from 1906, and general secretary from 1908; ILP National Administrative Council member, 1909–12; organiser around the 1910 chain-makers' and 1911 Bermondsey's women's strikes.

MacDonald, James Ramsay (1886–1937)
Scottish-born; joined ILP, 1894; secretary of Labour Representation Committee, 1900–12; secretary of London Trades Council executive from 1896–1913; Leicester Labour MP from 1906; chairman of the Parliamentary Labour Party, 1911–14; author of *Syndicalism: A Critical Examination*, 1912.

MacLean, John (1879–1923)
Graduate of Glasgow University; primary schoolteacher; joined the SDF in 1902 and became its principal speaker in Glasgow; initially orthodox to SDF, he became estranged from party leadership and advocated the link between industrial militancy and socialist politics.

Mann, Tom (1856–1941)
Engineering apprentice; SDF organiser; one of the leaders of 1899 London dock strike; President of DWRGLU, 1889–91; general secretary of ILP, 1893–95; founder of Workers' Union, 1898; toured Australasia 1901–10 and returned a syndicalist; formed the ISEL, edited *Industrial Syndicalist*; rejoined the SD[P], but resigned in 1911; organiser for NSFU and NTWF; chairman of 1911 Liverpool transport strike committee, and activist around many strikes; imprisoned for 'incitement to mutiny', 1912; speaking tours of America, August–December 1913, and South Africa, March–July 1914.

McManus, Arthur (1889–1927)
Leading member of SLP; employed at the Singer factory on Clydebank and involved in 1911 strike as an active member of his shop committee; became secretary of the Glasgow SLP branch in 1913 and editor of *The Socialist*.

Montefiore, Dora (1851–1933)
Joined the SDF in 1890s; executive member in 1903–04 and 1908–09; worked closely with Sylvia Pankhurst in London organising campaign; left the WSPU but remained prominent advocate of full adult suffrage and close to Sylvia Pankhurst; left the BSP at the end of 1912; involved in 'Kiddies Scheme' to send Dublin locked-out workers' children to stay with sympathetic families in Britain, 1913.

Murphy, J.T. [Jack Thomas] (1888–1965)
Sheffield engineering shop steward at the Vicars plant; 'syndicalist socialist' activist in local engineering Amalgamation Committee and *Daily Herald* League secretary; later joined SLP and became chief theoretician of the wartime National Shop Stewards' and Workers' Committee Movement; author of *The Workers' Committee*, 1917.

Pankhurst, E. Sylvia (1882–1960)
Younger daughter of Emmeline Pankhurst; founder member of WSPU, 1903; leading campaigner, writer, artist and agitator for the suffragettes, and organiser of its East London Federation, 1913; expelled from the WSPU, 1914, but continued with a refashioned and named East London Federation of the Suffragettes; editor of *Workers' Dreadnought*; made two speaking tours across America, January–April 1911 and January–April 1912.

Purcell, A.A. [Albert Arthur] (1872–1935)
Secretary, Amalgamated Society of French Polishers, 1898–1910; organiser, National Amalgamated Furnishing Trades Association from 1910; member of both SDF and ILP, elected as ILP member to Salford Borough Council, 1907–12; chaired founding ISEL conference, 1910; Executive Committee member of Manchester and Salford Trades Council from 1910; influential activist in 1911 Manchester transport and railway workers' strikes.

Quelch, Harry (1886–1954)
Joined the Democratic Federation (forerunner of the SDF) and two years later elected to its executive; heavily involved in the 1889 London dock strike; elected several times as chair of the London Trades Council; journalist and editor of *Justice*, 1886–1913; loyal supporter of Hyndman.

Rees, Noah (unknown)
Secretary of the 1910 South Wales Cambrian Combine strike committee and leading figure in 1912 national miners' strike; one of the authors of *The Miners' Next Step*, 1912; elected to the Executive Committee of the SWMF, 1911.

Sexton, James (1856–1938)
Liverpool docker; general secretary, National Union of Dock Labourers from 1893; supporter of NTWF; member of TUC Parliamentary Committee from 1900 and chairman 1904–05; member of Liverpool transport workers' strike committee, 1911; Labour Party Executive Committee member, 1902–04.

Snowden, Philip (1864–1937)
Yorkshire-born; Liberal Party member; joined the ILP and became chairman, 1903–06; leading ILP propagandist and economic expert; Blackburn Labour MP from 1906; author of *Syndicalism and Socialism*, 1913.

Sorgue, Madame [Antoinette Cauvin] (1864–1924)
French anarcho-syndicalist orator and journalist; travelled widely across Southern Europe supporting many strikes; described by the public prosecutor in Milan as 'the most dangerous woman in Europe'; addressed striking South Wales miners in 1910, Hull dockers in 1911 and Leith dockers in 1913.

Tanner, Jack (1889–1965)
Leading London engineering activist; member of SDF; moved towards anarchism and became active ISEL member, 1910; joined Industrial Democracy League, 1913, and contributor to its paper *Solidarity* as well as the French CGT's *La Vie Ouvriere*.

Thomas, J.H. [James Henry] (1874–1949)
Executive member, Amalgamated Society of Railway Servants, 1903; President, 1904; and National Organiser, 1906–11; Derby Labour MP from 1910; prominent leader in 1911 national railway strike; assistant general secretary, National Union of Railwaymen from 1913; denounced sympathetic strikes by railway workers for locked-out Dublin workers, 1913.

Thorne, Will (1857–1946)
Helped found the National Union of Gas Workers' and General Labourers and its general secretary from 1889; member of the TUC Parliamentary Committee from 1894; West Ham Labour MP from 1906.

Tillett, Ben (1860–1943)
Bristol-born; formed Tea Operatives and General Labourers' Union, 1887; on the London docks, 1887, one of the leaders of 1889 London docks' strike and became general secretary of the renamed DWRGLU; secretary of TUC Parliamentary Committee, 1892–05; founder member of ILP and Labour Party; joined SDF in 1908 and member of its (and BSP) executive; helped form the NTWF, 1910; prominent leader of London transport workers' strikes, 1911 and 1912; helped set up the *Daily Herald*; syndicalist sympathiser, but denounced Larkin at December TUC special congress.

Tupper, 'Captain' Edward (1872–1942)
Employed by Havelock Wilson as local NSFU organiser in Cardiff; prominent leader of 1911 seamen's and waterside workers' strikes in the city; part

swashbuckling militant and unscrupulous adventurer and part collaborator with the shipping bosses; no evidence of ever having been a 'Captain'.

Varley, Julia (1881–1952)
Branch secretary of Bradford Weavers' and Textile Workers' Union; joined the WSPU (serving two spells of imprisonment) and NFWW; first woman member of the Birmingham Trades Council executive, 1909; appointed women's officer for the Workers' Union, 1912; involved in organising women in a number of strikes, including Cradley Heath chain-makers, 1910, Black Country metal workers, 1913, and mobilised women in support of striking Cornish clay workers, 1913.

Watkins, Charles (1875–unknown)
Chesterfield/Sheffield-based railwaymen, attended Ruskin, 1907; founder of Plebs League and active in the Central Labour College movement; prominent activist in national railway strike, 1911; edited and published *The Syndicalist Railwayman* from September 1911; played leading role in campaign for union amalgamation leading to the foundation of the National Union of Railwaymen in early 1913.

Williams, Robert (1881–1936)
Welsh-born; President of National Amalgamated Labourers' Union, unknown–1912; elected first secretary of the NTWF from 1912; Swansea Labour Party councillor 1910–12; supported Larkin's 'Fiery Cross' campaign for solidarity action for locked-out Dublin workers.

Wills, Jack (1887–1933)
London-based building worker, member of the SDF/BSP until resigning to become prominent ISEL member; Mayor of Bermondsey; treasurer of Central Labour College and executive member of National Council of Labour Colleges; secretary of Amalgamation Committees' Federation, 1912; Operative Bricklayers Society activist in London building workers' lockout, and founder and secretary of new 'dual union' BWIU, 1914.

Wilson, Havelock (1858–1929)
Secretary, National Amalgamated Sailors and Firemen's Union, 1889–1903, and President from 1894; TUC Parliamentary Committee, 1889–98; Middlesbrough Independent labour MP, 1892–95, but allied with the Liberal Party and fiercely critical of the Labour Party; elected Middlesbrough Liberal MP, 1906–10; leader of seamen's strike, 1911.

Tables

Table 1 Annual average strike figures, 1895–1921

Year(s)	*Number of strikes*	*Workers involved*	*Working days lost*
1895–99	793	172 000	7 524 000
1900–10	529	240 000	4 576 000
1911–13	1074	1 034 000	20 908 000
1914–18	844	632 000	5 292 000
1919–21	1241	2 108 000	49 053 000

Source: Hyman (1989: 28); Haynes (1984: 89).

Table 2 Indicators of strike activity, 1910–14

Year	*Number of strikes*	*Workers directly involved*	*Workers indirectly involved*	*Total number of workers involved*	*Working days lost*
1910	531	385 000	130 000	515 165	9 895 000
1911	903	831 000	131 000	961 980	10 320 000
1912	857	1 233 000	230 000	1 463 000	40 915 000
1913	1497	516 000	173 000	689 000	11 631 000
1914 (Jan–July)	848	308 000	115 000	423 000	9 964 000
1914 (Aug–Dec)	151	18 000	6 000	25 000	*147 000*
1914 (total)	999	327 000	121 000	448 000	10 000 000

Note: Figures for the 'United Kingdom' which at the time included Ireland.

Source: Board of Trade (1914: 63; *Labour Gazette*, October 1915, p. 355 and July 1925, p. 230; Lyddon (2012: 244). It should be noted some individual figures differ slightly with those provided in Cole (1953: 302); Kendall (1975: 370); Clegg (1985: 568); Cronin (1998: 83); Wrigley (2002: 42).

Table 3 Number of strikes by industry group, 1910–14

Year	Mining and quarrying	Textiles	Metals, engineering and shipbuilding	Transport	Building	Clothing	Other	Total
1910	224	90	97	19	17	40	44	531
1911	179	133	255	99	27	46	164	903
1912	155	136	234	73	58	68	133	857
1913	192	243	392	123	198	75	273	1496
1914	176	97	232	53	177	50	187	972

Source: Lyddon (2012: 244).

Table 4 Number of strikers (directly and indirectly) involved in strikes by industry groups, 1910–14 (thousands)

Year	Mining and quarrying	Textiles	Metals, engineering and shipbuilding	Transport	Building	Clothing	Other	Total
1910	297	132	55	20	1	4	5	514
1911	141	221	94	449	3	10	45	963
1912	1107	56	83	155	6	31	25	1463
1913	214	94	153	86	40	15	67	669
1914	273	22	51	13	38	7	43	447

Source: Lyddon (2012: 245).

Table 5 Number of working days lost in strikes by industry group, 1910–14 (thousands)

Year	Mining and quarrying	Textiles	Metals, engineering and shipbuilding	Transport	Building	Clothing	Other	Total
1910	5524	918	3147	71	35	59	141	9895
1911	4101	1434	1322	2730	75	94	563	10 319
1912	31 594	3698	1369	2985	107	601	560	40 914
1913*	1656	2028	2988	1245	824	174	1016	9931
1914	3777	765	1308	87	3184	79	678	9878

Note: * The impact of the Dublin lockout (1,700,000 working days in 1913) is not included in the figures for any industry group but is included in the total for 1913. Another 200,000 days were lost in this dispute in 1914 but these are omitted from the 1914 total in the table as the industrial breakdown only exists (retrospectively) for Great Britain and (what became) Northern Ireland.

Source: Lyddon (2012: 245).

Table 6 Reasons given for striking – by number of *strikes*

Year	*Wage increases*	*Wage cuts*	*Other wage questions*	*Length of working day*	*Employment of particular person(s)*	*Working conditions, discipline, etc.*	*Trade union status*	*Sympathy or other causes*	*Total*
1910	103	37	162	22	80	75	41	11	531
1911	374	41	161	31	140	66	79	11	903
1912	321	49	169	27	149	50	70	22	857
1913	776	36	170	49	236	73	133	24	1497
1914	425	47	131	28	180	56	82	23	972

Note: Figures for 1914 include strikes between August and December.

Source: Cronin (1979: 212, table B.3).

Table 7 Reasons given for striking – *by* number of *strikers involved*

Year	*Wage increases*	*Wage cuts*	*Other wage questions*	*Length of working day*	*Employment of particular person(s)*	*Working conditions, discipline, etc.*	*Trade union status*	*Sympathy or other causes*	*Total*
1910	20 748	7154	48 572	9 ,927	114 793	62 207	32 777	6907	38 085
1911	333 647	16 280	33 288	13 161	32 639	68 009	327 588	6492	831 104
1912	114 606	7 967	897 847	8 961	34 985	42 068	120 924	5658	1 233 016
1913	239 874	16 356	26 916	13 688	53 714	20 159	120 470	24 860	516 037
1914	61 000	106 000	34 000	11 000	31 000	14 000	50 000	19 000	326 000

Note: Figures for 1914 include strikes between August and December.

Source: Cronin (1979: 215–16, table B.4).

Table 8 Outcome of strikes, 1910–14 – by number of *strikes*

Year	*Workers' victories*	*Compromises or partial workers' victories*	*Employers' victories*	*Unknown*
1910	135	199	194	1
1911	227	389	287	–
1912	235	362	260	–
1913	428	687	382	–
1914	240	407	325	–

Source: Board of Trade (1914: 52–3); Cronin (1979: 220, table B.5).

Table 9 Outcome of strikes, 1910–14 – by number of *strikers involved*

Year	*Workers' victories*	*Compromises or partial workers' victories*	*Employers' victories*	*Unknown*
1910	63 000	267 000	52 000	2000
1911	55 000	699 000	77 000	*
1912	918 000	136 000	177 000	2000
1913	162 000	245 000	109 000	–
1914	64 000	213 000	49 000	–

Note: * = less than 500 strikers.
Source: Board of Trade (1914: 52–3); Cronin (1979: 222, table B.6).

Table 10 Strike outcomes, 1911–14

1911–14	*(1) In favour of workers (%)*	*(2) Compromise (%)*	*(3) In favour of employers (%)*	*On employers' terms without negotiation – included in (3) (%)*
Number of strikes	27	44	29	9
Number of strikers	42	44	14	3

Source: Knowles (1952: 243).

Table 11 Proportion of workforce engaged in strike activity, 1910–14

Year	*No. of workers on strike*[a]	*Total union member -ship*	*Union members on strike (%)*	*Total work-force*	*Total workforce on strike (%)*	*Total manual workforce*	*Total manual workforce on strike (%)*	*Total workforce employed in industries involved in strikes (%)*
1910	385 000	2 565 000	15.01	17 596 000	2.19	12 763 588	3.02	4.9
1911	831 000	3 139 000	26.47	17 726 000	4.68	12 884 000	6.45	9.0
1912	1 233 000	3 416 000	36.09	17 841 000	6.91	12 941 304	9.53	13.4
1913	516 000	4 135 000	12.48	17 920 000	2.88	12 998 608	3.97	5.6
1914	326	4 145 000	7.86	17 998	1.81	13 055 187	2.50	4.0
	3 291 000[b]							

Notes:
[a] Workers directly involved (excluding those indirectly involved, such as workers laid off); to ensure consistently the figure for 1914 includes workers on strike from August to December, totalling 18,000.
[b] This total figure is inflated because it includes those workers, notably the miners and transport workers, who took strike action more than once during the 1910–14 period – an adjusted figure for the total number of (different) workers who took strike action would be about 2.58 million.

Source: Bain and Elsheikh (1976: 134, table E1); Routh (1980: 6, 34); Board of Trade (1914: xiii); *Labour Gazette*, October 1915.

Table 12 Trade union membership and density, 1900–14

Year	*Male* Membership	Density (%)	*Female* Membership	Density (%)	*Total* Membership	Density (%)	TUC affiliated membership	Potential union membership
1900	1 869 000	16.7	154 000	3.2	2 022 000	12.7	1 200 000	15 957 000
1904	1 802 000	15.5	165 000	3.3	1 967 000	11.9	1 541 000	16 599 000
1906	1 999 000	16.8	211 000	4.2	2 210 000	13.1	1 700 000	16 932 000
1908	2 230 000	18.5	255 000	4.9	2 485 000	14.4	1 705 000	17 262 000
1910	2 287 000	18.6	278 000	5.3	2 565 000	14.6	1 662 133	17 596 000
1911	2 804 000	22.6	335 000	6.3	3 139 000	17.7	2 001 633	17 762 000
1912	3 027 000	24.3	390 000	7.2	3 416 000	19.1	2 232 446	17 841 000
1913	3 702 000	29.6	433 000	8.0	4 135 000	23.1	–	17 920 000
1914	3 708 000	29.5	437 000	8.0	4 145 000	23.0	2 682 357	17 998 000

Note: The figures include the whole of Ireland. Figures were not made available for 1913 owing to the cancellation of the 1914 TUC conference.

Source: For trade union membership: Halsey (1972: 123); Bain and Price (1980: 37); Cronin (1984: 241). For TUC-affiliated membership: Pelling (1987: 262). For potential trade union membership: Bain and Elsheikh (1976: 134).

Table 13 Labour Party membership, 1900–14

Year	*Trade union affiliated membership*	*Total membership*
1900	353 070	375 931
1904	900 000	900 000
1906	855 270	998 338
1908	1 127 035	1 158 565
1910	1 394 402	1 430 539
1911	1 501 783	1 539 092
1912	1 858 178	1 895 498
1913	–	–
1914	1 572 391	1 612 147

Note: Arising from the Osborne judgment, no membership figures were compiled for 1913.

Source: Cole (1948b: 480); Pelling (1978: 175); Knowles (1952: 321).

Table 14 Labour Party's share of the vote, 1900–14

Year	*Seats contested*	*Votes*	*% of vote*	*Number of MPs elected*
1900	15	62 698	1.3	2
1906	50	329 748	5.9	29
1910 (Jan)	78	505 657	7.6	40
1910 (Dec)	56	371 802	7.1	42

Source: Laybourne (2001: 174).

Table 15 Independent Labour Party and radical left branches/membership, 1900–14

Year	*ILP*	*SDF/SDP*	*BSP*	*SLP*
1900		96 (9000)		
1903				(80)
1907		186/200 (6000)		
1908		232 (10 000–12 000)		
1909	887 (22 000)	NA (17 000)		
1910		235 (NA)		20 (300)
1911	796	189 (10 000–12 000)		25
1912	745 (28 000)		343 (40 000)	28
1913	713		NA (15 313)	NA
1914	672		NA (13 755)	15 (300)

Note: The first figure provided is for number of branches, with membership figures provided in parentheses.

Source: Kendall (1969: 311–12, 314); Dowse (1966); Challinor (1977); Crick (1994); BSP Conference Reports, 1912, p. 4; 1913, p. 40; 1914, pp. 36, 39; Report of the Thirteenth Annual Conference of the Labour Party, London, 29–31 January 1913, p. 12.

Bibliography

ARCHIVAL SOURCES

British Newspaper Archive: www.britishnewspaperarchive.co.uk
CHAR: Chartwell Papers, Churchill Archives Centre, Cambridge
Hansard: *Parliamentary Debates in the House of Commons*, London
LG: Lloyd George Papers, Parliamentary Archives, Houses of Parliament, London
LHASC: Labour History Archive and Study Centre, People's History Museum, Manchester
MRC: Modern Records Centre, University Warwick
TNA/CAB: National Archives, Records of the Cabinet Office, Kew TNA/HO: The National Archives, Home Office, Kew
WCML: Working Class Movement Library, Salford

NEWSPAPERS AND PERIODICALS

Bradford Daily Argus
Bridport News
British Socialist – British Socialist Party (journal)
Clarion – independent/Robert Blatchford
Common Cause – National Union of Women's Suffrage Societies
Cornish Guardian
Daily Chronicle
Daily Citizen (Labour Party and TUC)
Daily Dispatch
Daily Express
Daily Herald (January–April 1911; April 1912–September 1914)
Daily Mail
Daily Mirror
Daily News
Daily Telegraph and Daily Witness
Docker's Record (DWRGWU)
Draper's Record
Dublin Evening Herald
Dundee Advertiser
Dundee Courier
English Review
Forward – Scottish Independent Labour Party
Freeman's Journal (Dublin)

Glasgow Herald
Hull Daily Mail
Hull Daily News
Industrial Syndicalist (July 1910–May 1911) – Industrial Syndicalist Education League
Irish Worker – Irish Transport and General Workers' Union
Justice – SDF; and British Socialist Party from 1911
Labour Leader – Independent Labour Party
Liverpool Courier
Liverpool Daily Post and Mercury
Manchester Evening News
Manchester Guardian
Monthly Journal and Report – Amalgamated Society of Engineers
Morning Post
Northern Daily Telegraph
Plebs Magazine – Plebs League and Central Labour College
Railway Gazette
Railway News
Railway Review – Amalgamated Society of Railway Servants/National Union of Railwaymen
Reynold's News
Rhondda Socialist – Independent Labour Party
Salford Reporter
School Government Chronicle
Scotsman
Seaman – NSFU
Sheffield Daily Telegraph
Sheffield Evening Telegraph
Socialist – Socialist Labour Party
Socialist Record – British Socialist Party (internal bulletin)
Socialist Review – Independent Labour Party (journal)
Solidarity – Industrial Democracy League (September 1913–April 1914)
South Wales Daily News
South Wales Press
South Wales Worker – Rhondda socialist paper
Spectator
Suffragette – Women's Social and Political Union (from 1912)
Syndicalist – Industrial Syndicalist Education League (January 1912–December 1912)
Syndicalist and Amalgamation News (January 1913–August 1914) – Industrial Syndicalist Education League
Syndicalist Railwayman – ISEL (September 1911–December 1911)
The Times
Transport Worker – Merseyside Transport Workers' Federation (August 1911–March 1912)

Vote – Women's Freedom League
Votes for Women – Women's Social and Political Union (1903–1912) and then Emmeline and Fred Pethick-Lawrence (1912)
Western Mail
Westminster Gazette
Wolverhampton Express and Star
Woman Worker – National Federation of Women Workers
Woman's Dreadnought – East London Federation of the Suffragettes (from March 1914)
Yorkshire Post

CONFERENCE REPORTS

BSP First Annual Conference Report, Manchester, 25–27 May 1912.
BSP Second Annual Conference Report, Blackpool, 10–12 May 1913.
BSP Third Annual Conference Report, London, 12–13 April 1914.
DWRGWU Annual Report, 1911.
DWRGWU Annual Report, 1912.
ILP Twentieth Annual Conference Report, Merthyr, 27–28 May 1912.
NFWW Fifth Annual Report, 1912.
Official Report of the Socialist Unity Conference, Salford, 30 September–1 October 1911, British Socialist Party (Provisional Executive Committee).
Report and Decisions of ASRS Special Meeting in Liverpool, 15 August 1911, and Ordinary Meeting, London 11–15 September 1911.
Report and Decisions of the Joint Conference of the Executive Committees of the ASRS, ASLEF, GRWU and UPSS, Liverpool, 15–16 August 1911, and London, 17–24 August 1911.
Report of Proceedings of the Forty-Fourth Annual Trades Uunion Congress, Newcastle upon Tyne, 4–9 September, 1911.
Report of Proceedings of the Forty-Fifth Annual Trades Union Congress, Newport, 2–7 September 1912.
Report of Proceedings of the Forty-Sixth Annual Trades Union Congress, Manchester, 1–6 September 1913.
Report of the Thirteenth Annual Conference of the Labour Party, London, 29–31 January 1913.
TUC Parliamentary Committee, Tenth Quarterly Report, December 1911.
TUC Parliamentary Committee Report, 18 November 1913.
TUC Parliamentary Committee Report of Special Conference Held at the Memorial Hall, 9 December 1913.

OTHER CONTEMPORARY MATERIAL

Allen, E.J.B. (1909) *Revolutionary Unionism!*, London: The Industrialist League.
ASE Monthly Journal and Report, June 1913.

Board of Trade, *Labour Gazette*, December 1907; February 1908; July 1910; August 1910; January 1911; February 1912; August 1914; monthly issues 1913; January 1915; July 1925; October 1915.

Board of Trade (1910) *Report on Collective Agreements between Employers and Workpeople in the United Kingdom*, Cd 5366.

—— (1912) *Report on Strikes and Lock-outs and on Conciliation and Arbitration Boards in the United Kingdom in 1911*, Cd 6472.

—— (1913a) *Report on Strikes and Lock-outs and on Conciliation and Arbitration Boards in the United Kingdom in 1912*, Cd 7089.

—— (1913b) *Sixteenth Abstract of Labour Statistics of the United Kingdom*, Cd 7131.

—— (1914) *Report on Strikes and Lock-outs and on Conciliation and Arbitration Boards in the United Kingdom in 1913*, Cd 7658.

—— (1915) *Seventeenth Abstract of Labour Statistics of the United Kingdom*, Cd 7733.

Bowman, G. (1913) *Syndicalism: Its Basis, Methods and Ultimate Aims*, London: ISEL.

'Certain Disturbances at Rotherhithe on June 11th 1912, and Complaints against the Conduct of the Police in Connection Therewith', *Parliamentary Papers 1912–13* vol. xlvii (Cd 6367).

Colliery Strike Disturbances in South Wales: Correspondence and Report, November 1910, Parliamentary Papers, Cd 5568, HMSO, 1911.

Cole, G.D.H. and R. Page Arnot (1917) *Trade Unionism on the Railways: Its History and Problems*, London: Fabian Research Department.

Commission of Enquiry into Industrial Unrest, No. 7 Division (1917) Report of the Commissioners for Wales, including Monmouthshire, London: HMSO, 1917 (Cd 8668).

Connolly, J. (1915) *The Re-conquest of Ireland*, Dublin: Maunsel Roberts.

—— (1974a) 'Socialism Made Easy', in *James Connolly: Selected Political Writings*, New York: Grove Press: 243–85.

—— (1974b [1914]) 'Old Wine in New Bottles', in *James Connolly: Selected Political Writings*, New York: Grove Press: 312–18.

Ellis Barker, J. (September 1911) 'The Labour Revolt and Its Meaning', *Nineteenth Century and After*.

Employment of Military during Railway Strike: Correspondence between Home Office and Local Authorities, London: HMSO, 1911.

Evans, D. (1911) *Labour Strife in the South Wales Coalfield 1910–1911*, London: Educational Publishing.

Gallacher, W. and J.R. Campbell (1972 [1919]) *Direct Action: An Outline of Workshop and Social Organisation*, London: Pluto Press.

Great Britain, Parliament, *Parliamentary Papers* (Commons), 1915, Cd 7733.

House of Common Debates (Hansard), 10 August 1911; 16 August 1911; 22 August 1911; 19 March 1920.

MacDonald, J.R. (1912a) *Syndicalism: A Critical Examination*, London: Constable and Co.
—— (1912b) *Labour Party's Policy*, London: ILP.
—— (1912c) *The Labour Unrest: Its Causes, Effects and Remedies*, London: Labour Party.
Manchester and Salford Trades and Labour Council Annual Report, 1911.
Mann, T. (1913a) *From Single Tax to Syndicalism*, London: Guy Bowman.
—— (1913b) *The Labourers' Minimum: A Demand for 25s a Week*, Manchester [Publisher unknown].
Ministry of Labour, *Eighteenth Abstract of Labour Statistics of the United Kingdom* (Cmd. 2740), 1926.
Murphy, J. (1972 [1917]) *The Workers' Committee: An Outline of Its Principles and Structure*, London: Pluto Press.
Public Record Office [TNA] Handbook No. 4, *List of Cabinet Papers 1880–1914*, HMSO, 1964.
Quelch, H. (1911) *Social Democracy and Industrial Organisation*, London: Twentieth Century Press.
Report into the Housing Conditions of the Working Classes in the City of Dublin, Parliamentary Papers, Cd 7273, 1914, vol. xix.
Report of the Royal Commission on the Railway Conciliation and Arbitration Scheme 1907, Cd 5922, 1911.
Snowden, P. (n.d. c.1913) *Socialism and Syndicalism*, London: Collins.
Tillett, B. (1912) *History of the London Transport Workers' Strike, 1911*, London: National Transport Workers' Federation.
Unofficial Reform Committee (1973 [1912]) *The Miners' Next Step: Being a Suggested Scheme for the Reorganisation of the Federation, Unofficial Reform Committee*, London: Pluto Press.
Wells, H.G. (1912) *The Labour Unrest* (Reprinted from the *Daily Mail* 13–20 May 1912), London: Associated Newspapers.
Wilson, J.H. (1913) *The Dublin Dispute: A Statement of the Seamen's Case*, London: National Sailors' and Firemen's Union.

AUTOBIOGRAPHIES

Addison, P. (1992) *Churchill on the Home Front, 1900–1955*, London: Cape.
—— (2007) *Winston Churchill*, Oxford: Oxford University Press.
Bell, T. (1941) *Pioneering Days*, London: Lawrence and Wishart.
Blatchford, R. (1931) *My Eighty Years*, London: Cassell and Company.
Bower, F. (1936) *Rolling Stonemason: An Autobiography*, London: Jonathan Cape.
Braddock, J and B. (1963) *The Braddocks*, London: Macdonald.
Edwards, W.J. (1956) *From the Valley I Came*, London: Angus and Robertson.
Gosling, H. (1927) *Up and Down Stream*, London: Methuen.
Haywood, B (1929) *Bill Haywood's Book: The Autobiography of William D. Haywood*, New York: International Publishers.

Hyndman, H.M. (1912) *Further Reminiscences*, London: Macmillan.
Kearley, H.E. Hudson Devenport Lord: Viscount Devonport (1935) *The Travelled Road: Some Memories of a Busy Life*, Rochester, NY.
Lansbury, G. (1925) *The Miracle of Fleet Street: The Story of the Daily Herald*, London: Victoria House.
Lloyd George, D. (1938) *War Memoirs of David Lloyd George: Vol. 1*, London: Odhams Press.
Macready, N. (1924) *Annals of an Active Life: Vol. 1*, New York: Doran.
Mann, T. (1923) *Tom Mann's Memoirs*, London: Labour Publishing Company.
Montefiore, D.B. (1927) *From a Victorian to a Modern: An Autobiography*, London: E. Archer.
Pankhurst, S. (1977) *The Suffragette Movement: An Intimate Account of Persons and Ideals*, London: Virago.
Rocker, R. (2005) *The London Years*, Chico, CA: AK Press.
Sexton, J. (1936) *Sir James Sexton, Agitator*, London: Faber and Faber.
Thomas, J.H. (1937) *My Story*, London: Hutchinson.
Thomson, B. (1942) *Queer People*, London: Hodder and Stoughton.
Tillett, B. (1931) *Memories and Reflections*, London: John Long.
Tupper, E. (1938) *Seamen's Torch: The Life Story of Captain Edward Tupper: National Union of Seam*en, London: Hutchinson.

BIOGRAPHIES

Connolly, K. (2013) *Sylvia Pankhurst: Suffragette, Socialist and Scourge of Empire*, London: Pluto Press.
—— (2019) *A Suffragette in America: Reflections on Prisoners, Pickets and Political Change*, London: Pluto Press.
Darlington, R. (1998) *The Political Trajectory of J.T. Murphy*, Liverpool: Liverpool University Press.
Davies, P. (1987) *A. J. Cook*, Manchester: Manchester University Press.
Fuller, B. (1933) *The Life Story of the Rt. Hon J.H. Thomas*, London: Stanley Paul.
Gordon, A. (2010) 'Charles Watkins: Syndicalist Railwayman', *Socialist History*, 37: 1–13.
Groves, R. (1975) *The Strange Case of Victor Grayson*, London: Pluto Press.
Hamilton, M.A. (1925) *Mary Macarthur: A Biographical Sketch*, London: Leonard Parsons.
Heath, A. (2013) *The Life of George Ranken Askwith, 1861–1942*, London: Pickering and Chatto.
Holman, B. (2010) *Keir Hardie: Labour's Greatest Hero?* Oxford: Lion Books.
Holmes, R. (2020) *Sylvia Pankhurst: Natural Born Rebel*, London: Bloomsbury.
Hunt, C. (2019) *Righting the Wrong: Mary Macarthur 1880–1921: The Working Woman's Champion*, Birmingham: West Midlands History.
Jenkins, R. (1978) *Asquith*, London: Collins.

Kirk, N. (2017) *Transnational Radicalism and the Connected Lives of Tom Mann and Robert Samuel Ross*, Liverpool: Liverpool University Press.

Larkin, E. (1968) *James Larkin: Irish Labour Leader 1876–1947*, London: New English Library.

Lawson, J. (1948) *The Man in the Cap: The Life of Herbert Smith*, London: Methuen.

Masterman, L.B.L. (1939) *C.F.G. Masterman: A Biography*, London: Nicholson and Watson.

Milton, N. (1978) *John MacLean: In the Rapids of Revolution*, London: Allison and Busby.

Morgan, K.O. (1997) *Keir Hardie: Radical and Socialist*, London: Phoenix Giant.

Nevin, D. (2006) *James Larkin: Lion of the Fold*, Dublin: Gill and Macmillan.

O'Connor, E. (2015) *Big Jim Larkin: Hero or Wrecker?* Dublin: University College Dublin Press.

Postgate, R.W. (1951) *The Life of George Lansbury*, London: Longmans, Green and Co.

Radice, E.A. and G.H. Radice (1974) *Will Thorne: Constructive Militant*, London: Allen and Unwin.

Rees, J. (2017) 'Mary Hardie Bamber 1874–1938', *North West Labour History Journal*, 42: 41–6.

Ripley B.J. and J. McHugh (1989) *John Maclean*, Manchester: Manchester University Press.

Roberts, A. (2018) *Churchill: Walking with Destiny*, London: Allen Lane.

Schneer, J. (1982) *Ben Tillett: Portrait of a Labour Leader*, Beckenham: Croom Helm.

Sheldon, M. (2013) *Young Titan: The Making of Winston Churchill*, London: Simon and Schuster.

Sherry, D. (2014) *John Maclean: Red Clydesider*, London: Bookmarks.

Taylor, H. (2021) *Victor Grayson: In Search of Britain's Lost Revolutionary*, London: Pluto Press.

Torr, D. (1956) *Tom Mann and His Times: Vol.1: 1856–1890*, London: Lawrence and Wishart.

Tsuzuki, C. (1991) *Tom Mann, 1856–1941: The Challenges of Labour*, Oxford: Clarendon Press.

White, J. (1991) *Tom Mann*, Manchester: Manchester University Press.

Winslow, B. (2021) *Sylvia Pankhurst: Sexual Politics and Political Activism*, London: Verso.

Wrigley, C. (1976) *David Lloyd George and the British Labour Movement*, Hassocks: Harvester Press.

THESES AND DISSERTATIONS

Charles, R.C. (n.d.) 'National Consultation and Co-operation between Trade Unions and Employers in Britain 1911–1939', D.Phil, University of Oxford.

Grant, L.M. (1987) 'Women and the Sexual Division of Labour: Liverpool 1890–1939', PhD thesis, Liverpool University.

Hebert, R. (1975) 'Syndicalism and Industrial Strife 1910–1912: The Significance of the Cambrian Combine Strike, Liverpool General Transport Strike and London Dock Strikes as Barometers for a Better Understanding of the "Labour Unrest 1910–1912" in the British Isles', PhD, University of Maryland.

Holton, B. (1973a) 'Syndicalism and Its Impact in Britain with Particular Reference to Merseyside 1900–14', D.Phil, University of Sussex.

Ives, M. (1986) 'Understanding the Workers' Revolt of 1911 with Special Reference to the Transport Strikes in Manchester and Salford', BA Thesis, University of Manchester.

Moss, C.P. (1983) 'Industrial Co-partnership, Labour Unrest and the Last Liberal Government', MA dissertation, School of Graduate Studies, McMaster University.

Physick, R. (1998) 'An Analysis of the Great Strikes, the Role Played by Rank-and-File Committees on Tyneside and Merseyside', MA dissertation, University of Newcastle.

Pratten, J.D. (1975) 'The Reaction to Working Class Unrest, 1911–1914', PhD, University of Sheffield.

Smith, J. (1980) 'Commonsense Thought and Working-Class Consciousness: Some Aspects of the Glasgow and Liverpool Labour Movements in the Early Years of the Twentieth Century', PhD, University of Edinburgh.

Woodhouse, M.G. (1970) 'Rank and File Movements amongst the Miners of South Wales 1910–26, unpublished D.Phil, University of Oxford.

BOOKS, ARTICLES AND OTHER SECONDARY SOURCES

Adams, R. (1991) *Protests by Pupils: Empowerment, Schooling and the State*, Basingstoke: Falmer Press.

Aikin, K.W.W. (1972) *The Last Years of Liberal England 1900–1914*, London: Collins.

Alcock, G.W. (1922) *Fifty Years of Railway Trade Unionism*, London: Co-operative Printing Society.

Allason, R. (1983) *The Branch: History of the Metropolitan Special Branch: 1883–1983*, Seeker and Warberg.

Andrew, C. (2010) *The Defence of the Realm: The Authorised History of MI5*, London.

Arnot, R.P. (1954) *The Miners: Years of Struggle from 1910 Onwards*, London: Allen and Unwin.

—— (1967) *The South Wales Miners: A History of the South Wales Miners' Federation 1898–1914*, London: Allen and Unwin.

Askwith, Lord (1974 [1920]) *Industrial Problems and Disputes*, Brighton: Harvester Press.

Atkinson, Diane (2018) *Rise up Women! The Remarkable Lives of the Suffragettes*, London: Bloomsbury.

Bagwell, P.S. (1963) *The Railwaymen: The History of the National Union of Railwaymen*, London: Allen and Unwin.

—— (1971) 'The Triple Industrial Alliance, 1913–1922', in A. Briggs and J. Saville (eds), *Essays in Labour History 1886–1923: Vol. 2*, London: Macmillan: 96–128.

—— (1985) 'The New Unionism in Britain: The Railway Industry', in W.J. Mommsen and H-G. Huseng (eds), *The Development of Trade Unionism in Great Britain and Germany, 1880–1914*, London: Allen and Unwin: 185–200.

Bain, G., R. Bacon and J. Pimlott (1972) 'The Labour Force', in A.H. Halsey (ed.), *Trends in British Society since 1900: A Guide to the Changing Social Structure of Britain*, London: Palgrave Macmillan: 97–128.

Bain, G.S. and F. Elsheikh (1976) *Union Growth and the Business Cycle: An Econometric Analysis*, Oxford: Blackwell.

Bain, G.S. and R. Price (1980) *Profiles of Union Growth: A Comparative Statistical Portrayal of Eight Countries*, Oxford: Oxford University Press.

Baker, W. (2010) 'Explaining the Outbreak and Dynamics of the 1911 School Strike Wave in Britain', *Reflecting Education*, 6(1): 25–38.

Balfour, C. (1970) 'Captain Tupper and the 1911 Seamen's Strike in Cardiff', *Transactions of the Glamorgan History Society*, 14: 62–80.

Bantman, C. (2014) 'The Franco-British Syndicalist Connection and the Great Labour Unrest, 1880s–1914', *Labour History Review*, 79(1): 83–96.

Barclay, M. (1978) '"The Slaves of the Lamp" – the Aberdare Miners' Strike 1910', *Llafur*, 2(3): 24–42.

Barnsby, G.J. (1989) *Birmingham Working People: A History of the Labour Movement in Birmingham 1650–1914*, Wolverhampton: Integrated Publishing Services.

Barnsley, T. (2010) *Breaking Their Chains: Mary Macarthur and the Chainmakers' Strike of 1910*, London: Bookmarks.

Baxter, K. and W. Kenefick (2011) 'Labour Politics and the Dundee Working Class, c1895–1936', in J. Tomlinson and C.A. Whatley (eds), *Jute No More: Transforming Dundee*, Dundee: Dundee University Press: 191–219.

Blaxland, G. (1964) *J. H. Thomas: A Life for Unity*, London: Fredrick Muller.

Boll, F. (1985) 'International Strike Waves: A Critical Assessment', in W.J. Mommsen and H.G. Husung (eds), *The Development of Trade Unionism in Great Britain and Germany, 1880–1914*, London: Allen and Unwin: 78–99.

Boston, S. (1980) *Women Workers and the Trade Union Movement*, London: Davis-Poynter.

Boyd, A. (1972) *The Rise of the Irish Trade Unions 1729–1970*, County Kerry: Anvil Books.

Briggs, A. (1961) *Social Thought and Strike Action*, London: Longman.

Broder, J. (1980) 'Patterns of Disenchantment: The Position of the Liberal and Labour Party: 1910–1914', Senior Honours Thesis, Department of History, Oberlin College.

Broodbank, J.G. (1921) *History of the Port of London: Vol. 2*, London: Daniel O'Connor.

Brooker, K. (1979) *The Hull Strikes of 1911*, Hull: East Yorkshire Local History Series, 35.

Brown, G. (1974) 'Introduction', in G. Brown (ed.), *The Industrial Syndicalist*, Nottingham: Spokesman: 5–29.

—— ed. (1975) 'Introduction', in G. Brown (ed.), *The Syndicalist 1912–14*, Nottingham: Spokesman: vii–ix.

Brown, K.B. (2006) 'The Strikes of 1911–1913: Their International Significance', in D. Nevin (ed.), *Jim Larkin: Lion of the Fold*, Dublin: Gill and Macmillan: 56–63.

Bullock, A. (1960) *The Life and Times of Ernest Bevin: Vol. 1; Trade Union Leader 1881–1940*, London: Heinemann.

Burgess, K. (1975) *Origins of British Industrial Relations*, London: Croom Helm.

—— (1980) *The Challenge of Labour: Shaping British Society 1850–1930*, London: Croom Helm.

—— (1989) 'The Political Economy of British Engineering Workers during the First World War', in L. Hamison and C. Tilly (eds), *Strikes, Wars and Revolutions in an International Perspective*, Cambridge University Press: 289–320.

Callaghan, J. (2012) 'The Edwardian Crisis: The Survival of Liberal England and the Rise of a Labour Identity', *Historical Studies in Industrial Relations*, 33: 1–23.

Campbell, A. (2000) *The Scottish Miners, 1874–1939*, Aldershot: Ashgate.

Carr, F.W. (1978) 'Engineering Workers and the Rise of Labour in Coventry 1914–1939', PhD, University of Warwick, September.

Challinor, R. (1977) *The Origins of British Bolshevism*, London: Croom Helms.

Charlesworth, A.D. Gilbert, A. Randall, H. Southall and C. Wrigley (1996) *An Atlas of Industrial Protest in Britain 1750–1990*, Houndmills: Macmillan.

Charlton, J. (1999) *'It Just Went Like Tinder': The Mass Movement and New Unionism in Britain 1889*, London: Redwords.

Chinn, C. (2006) *Poverty amidst Prosperity: The Urban Poor in England, 1834–1914*, Lancaster: Manchester University Press.

Church. R. (1987) 'Edwardian Labour Unrest and Coalfield Militancy, 1890–1914', *The Historical Journal*, 30(4): 841–57.

Churchill, R.S. (1969) *Winston S. Churchill: Volume 11: Companion Part 2 1907–1911*, London: Heinemann.

Clegg, H.A. (1985) *A History of British Trade Unions since 1889: Vol. 2: 1911–1933*, Oxford: Clarendon Press.

Clegg, H.A., A. Fox and A.F. Thompson (1964) *A History of British Trade Unions since 1889: Vol. 1: 1889–1910*, Oxford: Oxford University Press.

Cliff, T. and D. Gluckstein (1986) *Marxism and Trade Union Struggle: The General Strike 1926*, London: Bookmarks.

—— (1988) *The Labour Party: A Marxist History*, London: Bookmarks.

Coates, K. and T. Topham (1994) *The Making of the Labour Movement: The Formation of the Transport and General Workers Union 1870–1922*, Nottingham: Spokesman.

Cohen, S. (2006) *Ramparts of Resistance: Why Workers Lost Their Power and How to Get It Back*, London: Pluto Press.

Cole, G.D.H. (1946) *British Working-Class Politics 1832–1914*, London: Routledge.

—— (1948a) *A Short History of the British Working-Class Movement, 1789–1947*, London: Allen and Unwin.

—— (1948b) *A History of the Labour Party from 1914*, London: Routledge.

—— (1953) *An Introduction to Trade Unionism*, London: Allen and Unwin.

—— (1973) *The World of Labour: A Discussion of the Present and Future of Trade Unionism*, London: Harvester Press.

Costley, N. (2013) *The 1913 China Clay Strike*, South West TUC.

Cowan, K. (2013) '"The Children Have Such Freedom, I Might Say, Such Possession of the Streets": The Children of Dublin 1913', in F. Devine (ed.), *A Capital in Conflict: Dublin City and the 1913 Lockout*, Dublin: Dublin City Council: 129–44.

Crick, M. (1994) *The History of the Social Democratic Federation*, Keele: Ryburn Publishing.

Cronin, J.E. (1979) *Industrial Conflict in Modern Britain*, London: Croom Helm.

—— (1982a) 'Strikes 1870–1914', in C. Wrigley (ed.), *A History of British Industrial Relations 1875–1914*, Brighton: Harvester Press: 74–98.

—— (1984) *Labour and Society in Britain 1918–1979*, London: Batsford.

—— (1998) 'Strikes and Power in Britain, 1870–1920', in L. H. Haimson and C. Tilly (eds), *Strikes, Wars, Revolutions in an International Perspective*, Cambridge: Cambridge University Press: 79–100.

Crowley, D.W. (1952) 'The Origins of the Revolt of the British Labour Movement from Liberalism, 1875–1906', PhD dissertation, University of London.

Cunningham, S. and M. Lavalette (2016) *Schools out! The Hidden History of School Student Strikes*, London: Bookmarks.

Dalton, I. and M. Dominguez (2013) *The Battle of Leeds and Other Episodes in Workers' Struggles in West Yorkshire*, London: Socialist Publications.

Dalton, R.D. (2000) 'Labour and the Municipality: Labour Politics in Leeds 1900–1914', PhD, University of Huddersfield.

Dangerfield, G. (1997 [1935]) *The Strange Death of Liberal England 1910–1914*, London: Serif.

Darlington, R. (2006) 'The Agitator "Theory" of Strikes Re-evaluated', *Labor History*, 47(4): 485–509.

—— (2008) 'British Syndicalism and Trade Union Officialdom', *Historical Studies in Industrial Relations*, 25/26: 103–40.

—— (2013a) 'Syndicalism and Strikes, Leadership and Influence: Britain, Ireland, France, Italy, Spain, and the United States', *International Labor and Working-Class History*, 83: 37–53.

—— (2013b) *Radical Unionism: The Rise and Fall of Revolutionary Syndicalism*, New York: Haymarket.

—— (2014a) 'Strike Waves, Union Growth, Bureaucracy and the Rank-and-File/ Bureaucracy Interplay: Britain 1889–1890, 1910–1913 and 1919–1920', *Labor History*, 55(1): 1–20.

—— (2014b) 'The Role of Trade Unions in Building Resistance: Theoretical, Historical and Comparative Perspectives', in M. Atzeni (ed.), *Workers and Labour in Globalised Capitalism*, Houndmills: Palgrave Macmillan: 111–38.

—— (2016) 'British Labour Movement Solidarity in the 1913–14 Dublin Lockout', *Labor History*, 57(4): 504–25.

—— (2018) 'The Leadership Component of Kelly's Mobilisation Theory: Contribution, Tensions, Limitations and Further Development', *Economic and Industrial Democracy*, 39(4): 617–38.

—— (2020) 'The Pre-First World War Women's Suffrage Revolt and Labour Unrest: Never the Twain Shall Meet?' *Labor History*, 61(5–6): 466–85.

—— (2022) 'Strikers versus Scabs: Violence in the 1910–1914 British Labour Revolt', *Labor History*, 63(3): 332–52.

Davidson, R. (1974) 'Introduction', in Lord Askwith, *Industrial Problems and Disputes* [1912], Harvester Press, Brighton: vii–xiv.

—— (1978) 'The Board of Trade and Industrial Relations 1896–1914', *The Historical Journal*, 21(3): 571–91.

—— (1985) *Whitehall and the Labour Problem in Late Victorian and Edwardian Britain: A Study in Official Statistics and Social Control*, London: Croom Helm.

Davies, S. (2012) '"Crisis? What Crisis?": The National Rail Strike of 1911 and the State Response', *Historical Studies in Industrial Relations*, 33: 97–125.

Davies, S. and R. Noon (2014) 'The Rank-and-File in the 1911 Liverpool General Transport Strike', *Labour History Review*, 79(1): 55–81.

de la Mare, U. (2008) 'Necessity and Rage: The Factory Women's Strikes in Bermondsey, 1911', *History Workshop Journal*, 61(1): 62–80.

Devine, F. (2012) 'The Irish Transport and General Workers' Union and the Labour Unrest in Ireland, 1911', *Historical Studies in Industrial Relations*, 33: 169–88.

Dowse, R. (1966) *Left in the Centre: The Independent Labour Party, 1893–1940*, London: Longman.

Drake, B. (1984) *Women in Trade Unions*, London: Virago.

Drucker, J.M. (1980) 'One Big Union? Structural Change in Building Trade Unionism', PhD, University of Warwick.

Edgerton, D. (2018) *The Rise and Fall of the British Nation: A Twentieth-Century History*, London: Allen Lane.

Edwards, G. (1922) *From Crow-Scaring to Westminster: An Autobiography*, London: Labour Publishing Company.

Edwards, J. (1988) *Remembrance of a Riot: The Story of the Llanelli Railways Strike Riots of 1911*, Swansea: Graham Harcourt.

Edwards, N. (1938) *History of the South Wales Miners' Federation*, London: Lawrence and Wishart.

Evans, G. and D. Maddox (2010) *The Tonypandy Riots 1910–1911*, Plymouth: University of Plymouth Press.

Evans, N. (1988) '"A Tidal Wave of Impatience": The Cardiff General Strike of 1911', in G.H. Jenkins and J. Beverley-Smith (eds), *Politics and Society in Wales, 1840–1922*, Cardiff: University of Wales Press: 135–59.

Fink, L. (2011) *Sweatshops at Sea: Merchant Seamen in the World's First Globalised Industry from 1812 to the Present*, Chapel Hill, NC: University of North Carolina Press.

Fishman, W.J. (2004) *East End Jewish Radicals 1875–1914*, London: Five Leaves Publication.

Foot, P. (2005) *The Vote: How It Was Won and How It Was Undermined*, London: Viking.

Forchheimer, K. (1948) 'Some International Aspects of the Strike Movement', *Bulletin of the Oxford University Institute of Statistics*, 10(9): 281–304.

Frow, E. and R. Frow (1976) *To Make That Future – Now! A History of the Manchester and Salford Trades Council*, Manchester: E.J. Mortens.

—— (1990) *The General Strike in Salford in 1911*, Salford: Working Class Movement Library.

Garside, W.R. and H.F. Gospel (1982) 'Employers and Managers: Their Organisational Structure and Changing Industrial Strategies', in C. Wrigley (ed.), *A History of British Industrial Relations 1875–1914*, Brighton: Harvester Press: 99–115.

Geary, R. (1985) *Policing Industrial Disputes:1893 to 1985*, London: Methuen.

—— (1987) 'Tonypandy and Llanelli Revisited', *Llafur*, 4(4): 34–45.

Gilbert, B.B. (1987) *David Lloyd George: A Political Life*, London: B.T. Batsford.

Glasgow Labour History Workshop (1989) *The Singer Strike, Clydebank 1911*, Glasgow: Clydebank District Library.

—— (1996a) 'The Labour Unrest in West Scotland, 1910–1914', in W. Kenefick and A. McIvor (eds), *Roots of Red Clydeside 1910–1914?: Labour Unrest and Industrial Relations in West Scotland*, Edinburgh: John Donald: 18–40.

—— (1996b) 'A Clash of Work Regimes: "Americanisation" and the Strike at the Singer Sewing Machine Company, 1911', in W. Kenefick and A. McIvor (eds), *Roots of Red Clydeside 1910–1914?: Labour Unrest and Industrial Relations in West Scotland*, Edinburgh: John Donald: 193–213.

Gluckstein, D. (1985) *The Western Soviets*, London: Bookmarks.

—— (1987) 'Class Struggle and the Labour Vote', *Socialist Review*, June: 16–19.

Gordon, E. (1987) 'Women, Work and Collective Action: Dundee Jute Workers 1870–1906', *Journal of Social History*, 21(1): 42–4.

—— (1991) *Women and the Labour Movement in Scotland 1850–1914*, Oxford: Clarendon Press.

Gore, V. (1982) 'Rank-and-File Dissent', in C. Wrigley (ed.), *A History of British Industrial Relations 1875–1914*, Brighton: Harvester Press: 47–73.

Gorman, J. (1980) *To Build Jerusalem*, London: Scorpion.
Gray, J. (1985) *City in Revolt: Jim Larkin and the Belfast Dock Strike of 1907*, Belfast: Blackstaff Press.
Greaves, C.D. (1982) *The Irish Transport and Transport General Workers' Union: The Formative Years, 1909–1923*, London: Gill and Macmillan.
Griffiths, R. (2009) *Killing No Murder: South Wales and the Great Railway Strike of 1911*, Croydon: Manifesto Press.
—— (2012) *Cardiff Cigar Workers and the 'Feminine Strike' of 1911*, Our History pamphlet no. 4, London: Communist Party.
Groves, R. (1949) *Sharpen the Sickle! The History of the Farm Workers Union*, London: Porcupine Press.
Guarita, C. (2015) *Clarence Austin: The Photographer and the Bridport Wildcat Women*, Bridport: Just Press.
Halévy, E. (1961) *A History of the English People, Vol. 2: 1905–1915*, London: Ernest Benn.
—— (1999) *Edwardian England: A Splendid Illusion*, London: Folio Society.
Halsey, A.H. (ed.) (1972) *Trends in British Society since 1900*, London: Macmillan.
Hattersley, R. (2012) *The Edwardians*, London: Abacus.
Haynes, M. (1984) 'The British Working Class in Revolt: 1910–1914', *International Socialism*, 2(22): 87–116.
Heffer, S. (2017) *The Age of Decadence: Britain 1880 to 1914*, London: Random House Books.
Herberg, W. (1943) 'Bureaucracy and Democracy in Labour Unions', *Antioch Review*, 3: 405–17.
Hikins, H.R. (1961) 'The Liverpool General Transport Strike, 1911', *Transactions of the Historic Society of Lancashire and Cheshire*, 113: 169–95.
Hinton, J. (1973) *The First Shop Stewards Movement*, London: Allen and Unwin.
—— (1982) 'The Rise of a Mass Labour Movement: Growth and Limits', in C. Wrigley (ed.), A *History of British Industrial Relations 1875–1914*, Brighton: Harvester Press: 20–46.
—— (1983) *Labour and Socialism: A History of the Working-Class Movement 1867–1974*, Brighton: Wheatsheaf.
Hobsbawm, E. (1968) Review of H. Pelling, 'Popular Politics and Society in Late Victorian Britain', *Bulletin of the Society for the Study of Labour History*, 18: 49–54.
Holton, B. (1973b) 'Syndicalism and Labour on Merseyside 1906–14', in H.R. Hikins (ed.), *Building the Union: Studies on the Growth of the Workers' Movement: Merseyside 1756–1967*, Liverpool: Toulouse Press: 121–50.
—— (1974) 'Daily Herald v. Daily Citizen, 1912–15: The Struggle for a Labour Daily in Relation to the "Labour Unrest"', *International Review of Social History*, 19(3): 347–76.
—— (1976) *British Syndicalism 1900–1914*, London: Pluto Press.
—— (1985) 'Revolutionary Syndicalism and the British Labour Movement', in W.J. Mommsen and H. Husung (eds), *The Development of Trade Unionism in Great Britain and Germany, 1880–1914*, London: Allen and Unwin: 266–82.

Hopkin, D. (1983) 'The Llanelli Riots 1911', *Welsh History Review*, 11(4): 488–515.

—— (1989) 'The Great Unrest in Wales 1910–1913: Questions of Evidence', in D.R. Hopkin and G.S. Kealey (eds), *Class, Community and the Labour Movement: Wales and Canada 1850–1913*, Aberystwyth: *Llafur*/Canadian Committee on Labour History: 249–75.

Howell, C. (2005) *Trade Unions and the State: The Construction of Industrial Relations Institutions in Britain, 1890–2000*, Princeton, NJ: Princeton University Press.

Howell, D. (1991) 'Railway Safety and Labour Unrest: The Aisgill Disaster of 1913', in C. Wrigley and J. Sheppard (eds), *On the Move: Essays in Labour and Transport History Presented to Philip Bagwell*, London: Hambledon Press: 123–54.

—— (1999) *Respectable Radicals: Studies in the Politics of Railway Trade Unionism*, Aldershot: Ashgate.

—— (2000) 'Taking Syndicalism Seriously', *Socialist History*, 16: 27–48.

—— (2012) 'The Contribution of Direct Action to Gradualism: The Railway Strike of 1911', *Historical Studies in Industrial Relations*, 33: 61–96.

—— (2017) Book Review of E. O'Connor, 'Big Jim Larkin', *Historical Studies in Industrial Relations*, 38: 255–70.

Humphries, S. (1981) *Hooligans or Rebels? An Oral History of Working-Class Childhood and Youth, 1889–1939*, Oxford: Blackwell.

Hunt, C. (2011) 'The Fragility of the Union: The Work of the National Federation of Women Workers in the Regions of Britain, 1906–1914', in M. Davies (ed.), *Class and Gender in British Labour History: Renewing the Debate (or Starting It?)*, Pontypool: Merlin Press: 171–89.

—— (2013) 'Binding Women Together in Friendship and Unity? Mary Macarthur and *The Woman Worker*, September 1907 to May 1908', *Media History*, 19(2): 139–52.

—— (2014) *The National Federation of Women Workers, 1906–1921*, Houndmills: Palgrave Macmillan.

Hunt, E.H. (1981) *British Labour History 1815–1914*, London: Weidenfeld and Nicholson.

Hyman, R. (1971) *The Workers' Union*, Oxford: Oxford University Press.

—— (1975) *Industrial Relations: A Marxist Introduction*, London: Macmillan.

—— (1985) 'Mass Organisation and Militancy in Britain: Contrasts and Continuities', in W.J. Mommsen and H-G. Husung (eds), *The Development of Trade Unionism in Great Britain and Germany, 1880–1914*, London: Allen and Unwin: 250–65.

—— (1989) *Strikes* (fourth edition), London: Macmillan.

Jackson, S. and R. Taylor (2014) *East London Suffragettes*, Stroud: The History Press.

Jeffery, S. (2018) *The Village in Revolt: The Story of the Longest Strike in History*, Bungay: Higdon Press.

Jones, M. (1988) *These Obstreperous Lassies: A History of the IWWU*, Dublin: Gill and Macmillan.

Kelly, J. (1988) *Trade Unions and Socialist Politics*, London: Verso.

Kendall, W. (1969) *The Revolutionary Movement in Britain 1900–22*, London: Weidenfeld and Nicholson.

—— (1975) *The Labour Movement in Europe*, London: Allen Lane.

Kenefick, W. (1996) 'A Struggle for Control: The Importance of the Great Unrest at Glasgow Harbour, 1911 to 1912', in W. Kenefick and A. McIvor (eds), *Roots of Red Clydeside 1910–1914: Labour Unrest and Industrial Relations in West Scotland*, Edinburgh: John Donald: 129–52.

—— (2000) *'Rebellious and Contrary': The Glasgow Dockers, 1853–1932*, East Linton: Tuckwell Press.

—— (2007) *Red Scotland: The Rise and Fall of the Radical Left, c. 1872 to 1932*, Edinburgh: Edinburgh University Press.

—— (2012) 'An Effervescence of Youth: Female Textile Workers' Strike Activity in Dundee, 1911–1912', *Historical Studies in Industrial Relations*, 33: 189–221.

—— (2015) 'Locality, Regionality and Gender: Revisiting Industrial Protest among Women Workers in Scotland 1910–13', *Journal of Irish and Scottish Studies*, 8(2): 34–58.

Kershen, A.J. (1995) *Uniting the Tailors: Trade Unionism amongst the Tailors of London and Leeds 1870–1939*, London: Routledge.

King, C. (1989). 'A Separate Economic Class?', Book Review: 'These Obstreperous Lassies: A History of the Irish Women's Workers' Union', *Saothar*, 14: 67–70.

Kirk, N. (1994) *Labour and Society in Britain and the USA: Vol. 2: Challenge and Accommodation, 1850–1939*, Aldershot: Scolar Press.

Klugmann, J. (1968) *History of the Communist Party of Great Britain: Vol. 1*, London: Lawrence and Wishart.

Knowles, K.G.J.C. (1952) *Strikes: A Study in Industrial Conflict*, Oxford: Basil Blackwell.

Knox, W. (1984) '"Down with Lloyd George": The Apprentices' Strikes of 1912', *Scottish Labour History Society Journal*, 19: 22–36.

Knox, W. and H. Corr (1996) '"Striking Women": Cotton Workers and Industrial Unrest, c1907–1914', in W. Kenefick and A. McIvor (eds), *Roots of Red Clydeside 1910–1914: Labour Unrest and Industrial Relations in West Scotland*, Edinburgh: John Donald: 107–28.

Labour Market Trends, Office for National Statistics, January 1996.

Lane, T. (1974) *The Union Makes Us Strong: The British Working Class, Its Politics and Trade Unionism*, London: Arrow Books.

Laybourn, K. (1994) 'The Failure of Socialist Unity in Britain, c.1893–1914', *Transactions of the Royal Historical Society*, Sixth Series (4): 153–75.

—— (1997a) *A History of British Trade Unionism c1770–1990*, Stroud: Sutton Publishing.

—— (1997b) *The Rise of Socialism in Britain c1881–1951*, Stroud: Sutton Publishing.

—— (2001) *A Century of Labour: A History of the Labour Party*, Stroud: Sutton Publishing.

Lewenhak, S. (1977) *Women and Trade Unions: An Outline History of Women in the British Trade Union Movement*, London: Ernest Benn.

Lovell, J. (1969) *Stevedores and Dockers: A Study of Trade Unionism in the Port of London, 1870–1914*, London: Macmillan.

Lyddon, D. (2012) 'Postscript: The Labour Unrest in Great Britain and Ireland, 1910–1914: Still Uncharted Territory?', *Historical Studies in Industrial Relations*, 33: 241–65.

Lyddon, D. and P. Smith (2007) 'The Home Office Circular on Picketing (1911) and Reports on Picketing and Intimidation in Liverpool (1911)', *Historical Studies in Industrial Relations*, 23/24: 209–32.

MacAskill, K. (2019) *Glasgow 1919: The Rise of Red Clydeside*, Glasgow: Biteback Publishing.

Macfarlane, L.J. (1966) *The British Communist Party: Its Origins and Development until 1929*, London: Macgibbon and Kee.

Macintyre, S. (1986) *A Proletarian Science: Marxism in Britain 1917–1933*, London: Lawrence and Wishart.

Mahon, J. (1976) *Harry Pollitt: A Biography*, London: Lawrence and Wishart.

Marsh, A. and V. Ryan (1989) *The Seamen: A History of the National Union of Seamen*, Oxford: Malthouse Press.

Marson, D. (1973) *Children's Strikes in 1911*, History Workshop Pamphlets, no. 9, Oxford: Ruskin College.

Martin, R.M. (1980) *TUC: The Growth of a Pressure Group 1868–1976*, Oxford: Clarendon Press.

Mates, L. (2016) *The Great Labour Unrest: Rank-and-File Movements and Political Change in the Durham Coalfield*, Manchester: Manchester University Press.

McIvor, A.J. (1984) 'Employers' Organisation and Strikebreaking in Britain, 1880–1914', *International Review of Social History*, 29(1): 1–33.

Meacham, S. (1972) '"The Sense of an Impending Clash": English Working Class Unrest before the First World War', *The American Historical Review*, 77(5): 1343–64.

—— (1977) *A Life Apart: The English Working Class 1890–1914*, London: Thames and Hudson.

Meers, F. (2014) *Suffragettes: How Britain's Women Fought and Died for the Right to Vote*, Stroud: Amberley Publishing.

Middlemas, K. (1979) *Politics in Industrial Society: The Experience of the British System since 1911*, London: André Deutsch.

Mogridge, B. (1961) 'Militancy and Inter-Union Rivalries in British Shipping, 1911–1929', *International Review of Social History*, 6(3): 375–412.

Mor-O'Brien, A. (1994) 'Churchill and the Tonypandy Riots', *Welsh History Review*, 17(1): 67–99.

—— (n.d [2019]) *Charlie Stanton and the Block Strike in Aberdare 1910*, independently published: Amazon Fulfilment.

Moran, B. (1978) '1913, Jim Larkin and the British Labour Movement', *Saothar*, 4: 35–49.

Morgan, J. (1987) *Conflict and Order: The Police and Labour Disputes in England and Wales 1900–1939*, Oxford: Clarendon Press.

Moriatory, T. (2006a) 'Larkin and the Women's Movement', in D. Nevin (ed.), *Jim Larkin: Lion of the Fold*, Dublin: Gill and McMillan: 93–101.

—— (2006b) 'Delia Larkin: Relative Obscurity', in D. Nevin (ed.), *Jim Larkin: Lion of the Fold*, Dublin: Gill and McMillan: 428–38.

Mutch, A. (1982/3) 'Lancashire's "Revolt of the Field": The Ormskirk Farmworkers' Strike of 1913', *North West Labour History Society Journal*, 8: 56–67.

Neal, F. (1988) *Sectarian Violence: The Liverpool Experience 1819–1914*, Liverpool: Liverpool University Press.

Newsinger, J. (2002) 'Irish Labour in a Time of Revolution', *Socialist History*, 22: 1–31.

—— (2004) *Rebel City: Larkin, Connolly and the Dublin Labour Movement*, London: The Merlin Press.

—— (2013a) *Jim Larkin and the Great Dublin Lockout of 1913*, London: Bookmarks.

—— (2013b) '"The Duty of Social Democrats in this Labour Unrest': *Justice*, the British Socialist Party and the Dublin Lockout', *Saothar*, 38: 51–60.

—— (2015) *Them and Us: Fighting the Class War 1910–1939*, London: Bookmarks.

Nurse, P. (2001) *Devils Let Loose: The Story of the Lincoln Riots, 1911*, Grantham: Barny Books.

O'Brien, M. (2012) 'The Liverpool Transport Strike of 1911: "Overcomings", Transformations and the "New Mentalities" of the Liverpool Working Class', *Historical Studies in Industrial Relations*, 33: 39–60.

O'Connor, E. (1992) *A Labour History of Ireland 1824–1960*, Dublin: Gill and Macmillan.

—— (2005) 'What Caused the 1913 Lockout? Industrial Relations in Ireland, 1907–13', *Historical Studies in Industrial Relations*, 19: 101–21.

—— (2014) 'Old Wine in New Bottles? Syndicalism and "Fakirism" in the Great Labour Unrest, 1911–1914', *Labour History Review*, 79(1): 19–36.

O'Day, A. (1979) 'Introduction', in A. O'Day (ed.), *The Edwardian Age: Conflict and Stability 1900–1914*, London: Macmillan: 1–12.

Orage, A.R. (1914) *National Guilds*, London: Macmillan.

Outram, Q. (2008) 'Early British Strike Statistics', *Historical Studies in Industrial Relations*, 25/26: 177–96.

Pelling, H. (1968) *Popular Politics and Society in Late Victorian Britain*, London: Macmillan: 147–64.

—— (1978) *A Short History of the Labour Party* (sixth edition), London: Macmillan.

—— (1987) *A History of British Trade Unionism*, London: Penguin.

Peterson, L. (1983) 'The One Big Union in International Perspective: Revolutionary Industrial Unionism, 1900–1925', in J.E. Cronin and C. Sirianni (eds), *Work, Community and Power: The Experience of Labor in Europe and America, 1900–1925*, Philadelphia, PA: Temple University Press: 49–87.

Phelps Brown, E.H. (1959) *The Growth of British Industrial Relations: A Study from the Standpoint of 1906–14*, London: Macmillan.

—— (1983) *The Origins of Trade Union Power*, Oxford: Clarenden Press.

Phillips, G.A. (1971) 'The Triple Industrial Alliance in 1914', *The Economic History Review*, 24(1): 55–67.

Pitt, B. (1987) 'Syndicalism in South Wales: The Origins of *The Miners' Next Step*', www.whatnextjournal.org.uk/Pages/History/Nextstep.html (accessed 11 October 2022).

Pollard, S. (1963) *The Development of the British Economy, 1914–1950*, London: Edward Arnold.

Porter, B. (1991) *The Origins of the Vigilant State: The London Metropolitan Police Special Branch Before the First World War*, Rochester, NY: Boydell and Brewer.

Postgate, R.W. (1923) *The Builders History*, London: The National Federation of Building Trade Operatives.

Powell, D. (1996) *The Edwardian Crisis: Britain, 1901–1914*, Houndmills: Macmillan.

Powell, L.H. (1950) *The Shipping Federation: A History of the First Sixty Years, 1890–1950*, London: Shipping Federation.

Pribicevic, B. (1959) *The Shop Stewards' Movement and Workers' Control 1910–1922*, Oxford: Blackwell.

Price, R. (1980) *Masters, Unions and Men: Work Control in Building and the Rise of Labour 1830–1914*, Cambridge: Cambridge University Press.

—— (1986) *Labour in British Society: An Interpretative History*, London: Croom Helm.

Prochaska, A. (ed.) (1982) *History of the General Federation of Trade Unions, 1899–1980*, London: Allen and Unwin.

Pugh, M. (2002) *The Making of Modern British Politics 1867–1945*, Oxford: Blackwell.

Rabbetts, T. (2019) 'We Want Our Rights', *Dorset Life*, January.

Rawlinson, G. and A. Robinson (1996) 'The United Turkey Red Strike, December 1911', in W. Kenefick and A. McIvor (eds), *Roots of Red Clydeside 1910–1914?: Labour Unrest and Industrial Relations in West Scotland*, Edinburgh: John Donald: 175–92.

Read, D. (ed.) (1982) *Edwardian England*, London: Croom Helm with the Historical Association.

Redman, L. (2013) 'State Intervention in Industrial Disputes in the Age of New Liberalism: The London Docks Strikes of 1911–12', *Historical Studies in Industrial Relations*, 34: 29–48.

Rees, J. (2020) '"The Time Is Now Rotten Ripe to Strike": The 1912 Garston Bobbin Workers' Dispute', *North West Labour History Journal*, 45: 45–52.

Richardson, M. (2008) '"Murphyism in Oxfordshire" – the Bliss Tweed Mill Strike, 1913-14: Causes, Conduct and Consequences', *Historical Studies in Industrial Relations*, 25/26: 79–102.

—— (2013) *Bliss Tweed Mill Strike, 1913–14*, Bristol: Bristol Radical History Group.

Riddell, F. (2018) 'Can We Call the Suffragettes Terrorists? Absolutely', *BBC History Magazine*, May: 66–7.

Roberts, R. (1990) *The Classic Slum: Salford Life in the First Quarter of the Century*, London: Penguin.

Rose, J. (2001) *The Intellectual Life of the British Working Classes*, New Haven, CT: Yale University Press.

Rosenberg, C. (1987) *1919: Britain on the Brink of Revolution*, London: Bookmarks.

Routh, G. (1980) *Occupations and Pay in Great Britain, 1906–79*, London: Palgrave Macmillan.

Rubenstein, D. (1991) 'Trade Unions, Politicians and Public Opinion 1906–1914'. in B. Pimlott and C. Cook (eds)., *Trade Unions in British Politics: The First 250 Years*, London: Longman: 48–68.

Ryan, W.P. (1913) *The Labour Revolt and Larkinism*, London: Daily Herald.

Saluppo, A. (2019) 'Strikebreaking and Anti-Unionism on the Waterfront: The Shipping Federation, 1890–1914', *European History Quarterly*, 49(4): 570–96.

Saville, J. (1967) 'Trade Unions and Free Labour: The Background to the Taff Vale Decision', in A. Briggs and J. Saville (eds), *Essays in Labour History*, London: Macmillan: 317–50.

—— (1996) 'The Trades Disputes Act of 1906', *Historical Studies in Industrial Relations*, 1: 11–45.

Skidelsky, R. (2014) *Britain since 1900: A Success Story*? London: Vintage Books.

Sloane, N. (2018) *The Women in the Room: Labour's Forgotten History*, London: I.B. Tauris.

Smith, C. (1971) 'The Years of Revolt', *International Socialism*, 48: 18–22.

Smith, D. (1988) 'From Riots to Revolt: Tonypandy and the Miners' Next Step', in T. Herbert and G.E. Jones (eds), *Wales 1880–1914*, Cardiff: University of Wales: 107–37.

Smith, J. (1984) 'Labour Tradition in Glasgow and Liverpool', *History Workshop Journal*, 17.

—— (1991) 'Taking the Leadership of the Labour Movement: The ILP in Glasgow, 1906–1914', in A. McKinlay and R.J. Morris (eds), *The ILP on Clydeside: 1893–1932: From Foundation to Disintegration*, Manchester: Manchester University Press: 56–82.

Smyth, J. (1996) '"From Industrial Unrest to Industrial Debacle?" The Labour Left and Industrial Militancy, 1910–1914', in W. Kenefick and A. McIvor (eds), *Roots of Red Clydeside 1910–1914?: Labour Unrest and Industrial Relations in West Scotland*, Edinburgh: John Donald: 240–58.

Smyth, J.J. (2000) *Labour in Glasgow 1896–1936: Socialism, Suffragism, Sectarianism*, Scottish Historical Review Monograph no. 11, East Linton: Tuckwell Press.

Soldon, N.C. (1978) *Women in British Trade Unions 1874–1976*, Bristol: Gill and Macmillan.

Staples, C.L. and W.G. Staples (1990) '"A Strike of Girls": Gender and Class in the British Metal Trades, 1913'. *Journal of Historical Sociology*, 12(2): 158–80.

Sweeney, J. (1980) 'The Dublin Lockout, 1913: The Response of British Labour', *Saother*, 6: 104–8.

Tanner, F. (2014) *British Socialism in the Early 1900s*, Socialist History Occasional Publication, 35.

Taplin, E. (1986) *The Dockers' Union: A Study of the National Union of Dock Labourers, 1889–1922*, Leicester: Leicester University Press.

—— (1994) *Near to Revolution: The Liverpool General Transport Strike of 1911*, Liverpool: Bluecoat Press.

—— (2012) 'The Liverpool General Transport Strike, 1911', *Historical Studies in Industrial Relations*, 33: 25–38.

Thom, D. (1986) 'The Bundle of Sticks: Women, Trade Unionists and Collective Organisation', in A.V. John (ed.), *Equal Opportunities: Women's Employment in England 1800–1918*, Oxford: Blackwell: 261–89.

—— (1998) *Nice Girls and Rude Girls: Women Workers in World War 1*, London: I.B. Tauris.

Tressell, R. (1973 [1914]) *The Ragged Trousered Philanthropists*, Frogmore: Panther.

Tuckett, A. (1967) *The Scottish Carter: The History of the Scottish Horse and Motormen's Association 1899–1964*, London: Allen and Unwin.

Waites, B. (1987) *A Class Society at War: England 1914–1918*, Leamington Spa: Berg.

Waller, P.J. (1981) *Democracy and Sectarianism: A Political and Social History of Liverpool 1868–1939*, Liverpool: Liverpool University Press.

Webb, B. and S. Webb (1920) *The History of Trade Unionism, 1666–1920*, London: Longman.

Weinberger, B. (1991) *Keeping the Peace? Policing Strikes in Britain 1906–1926*, Oxford: Berg.

White, J.L. (1978) *The Limits of Trade Union Militancy: The Lancashire Textile Workers, 1910–1914*, Westport, CT: Greenwood Press.

White, J. (1982) '1910–1914 Reconsidered', in J.E. Cronin and J. Schneer (eds), *Social Conflict and the Political Order in Modern Britain*, London: Croom Helm: 73–95.

—— (1990) 'Syndicalism in a Mature Industrial Setting: The Case of Britain', in M. van der Linden and W. Thorpe (eds), *Revolutionary Syndicalism: An International Perspective*, Aldershot: Scolar Press: 101–18.

Whitson, C. (2013) 'The 1913 Dublin Lockout and the British and International Labour Movements', in F. Devine (ed.), *A Capital in Conflict: Dublin City and the 1913 Lockout*, Dublin City Council: 27–56.

Williams, J.E. (1962) *The Derbyshire Miners*, London: Allen and Unwin.

—— (1971) 'The Leeds Corporation Strike in 1913', in A. Briggs and J. Saville (eds), *Essays in Labour History 1886–1923: Vol. 2*, London: Macmillan: 70–95.

Wilson, M.V. (2008) 'The 1911 Waterfront Strikes in Glasgow: Trade Unions and Rank-and-File Militancy in the Labour Unrest of 1910–1914', *International Review of Social History*, 53(2): 261–92.

Wilson, R. and I. Adams (2015) *Special Branch: A History: 1883-2006*, Hull: Biteback Publishing.

Wojtczak, H. (2005) *Railwaywomen: Exploitation, Betrayal and Triumph in the Workplace*, Hastings: Hastings Press.

Woodhouse, M.G. (1995) 'Marxism and Stalinism in Britain, 1920–26', in B. Pearce and M. Woodhouse (eds), *A History of Communism in Britain*, London: Bookmarks: 7–110.

Woodman, C. (2018) *Spycops in Context: A Brief History of Political Policing in Britain*, Centre for Crime and Justice Studies.

Wrigley, C. (1979) *The Government and Industrial Relations in Britain, 1910–1921*, Loughborough: Loughborough University.

—— (1982) 'The Government and Industrial Relations', in C. Wrigley (ed.), A *History of British Industrial Relations 1875–1914*, Brighton: Harvester Press: 135–58.

—— (1985) 'Labour and the Trade Unions', in K.D. Brown (ed.), *The First Labour Party 1906–1914*, London: Croom Helm: 129–51.

—— (2002) *British Trade Unions since 1933*, Cambridge: Cambridge University Press.

—— (2004) 'Churchill and the Trade Unions', in D. Cannadine and R. Quinault (eds), *Winston Churchill in the Twenty-First Century*, Cambridge University Press: 47–67.

Yeates, P. (2000) *Lockout: Dublin 1913*, Dublin: Gill and Macmillan.

Zoll (1976) *Der Doppelcharakter der Gewerkschafen*, Frankfurt: Suhrkamp.

Index

ill refers to an illustration; *n* to a note